A History of Mortgage Banking in the West

A HISTORY OF MORTGAGE BANKING IN THE WEST

Financing America's Dreams

E. Michael Rosser

Diane M. Sanders

UNIVERSITY PRESS OF COLORADO
Boulder

© 2017 by University Press of Colorado

Published by University Press of Colorado
5589 Arapahoe Avenue, Suite 206C
Boulder, Colorado 80303

 The University Press of Colorado is a proud member of
Association of University Presses.

The University Press of Colorado is a cooperative publishing enterprise supported, in part,
by Adams State University, Colorado State University, Fort Lewis College, Metropolitan State
University of Denver, Regis University, University of Colorado, University of Northern Colorado,
Utah State University, and Western State Colorado University.

∞ This paper meets the requirements of the ANSI/NISO Z39.48–1992 (Permanence of Paper).

ISBN: 978-1-60732-622-9 (cloth)
ISBN: 978-1-60732-851-3 (paperback)
ISBN: 978-1-60732-623-6 (ebook)

Library of Congress Cataloging-in-Publication Data

Names: Rosser, E. Michael, author. | Sanders, Diane M., author.
Title: A history of mortgage banking in the West : financing America's dreams / E. Michael
    Rosser, Diane M. Sanders.
Description: Boulder : University Press of Colorado, [2017] | Includes bibliographical references
    and index.
Identifiers: LCCN 2017028692| ISBN 9781607326229 (cloth) | ISBN 9781607326236 (ebook) |
    ISBN 9781607328513 (pbk)
Subjects: LCSH: Mortgage banks—West (U.S.)—History. | Mortgage banks—Colorado—History.
    | Mortgage banks—Law and legislation—United States—History.
Classification: LCC HG2040.5.U6 R67 2017 | DDC 332.3/20978—dc23
LC record available at https://lccn.loc.gov/2017028692

Cover images © chippix/Shutterstock.com (top); © Bronwyn Photo/Shutterstock.com (bottom)

For Anne and Keren; for Herman Sanders, who never stopped believing in me; and for the men and women of the mortgage banking industry who go to work every day to help fulfill America's dreams.

It's important to remember that the founders of [the] MBA were leaders in the farm mortgage field and were owner proprietors of their businesses. They were principles with a stake in their communities. Their success or failure depended upon the exercise of sound judgment in their efforts to bring the distant investor and local borrowers together, to the end that the ownership of real property might rebound to the benefit of all parties concerned.

—*Frederick Champ*
Utah Mortgage Loan Company
Mortgage Bankers Association, 1942

Contents

Acknowledgments

This book would not have been written with its current depth and detail without tremendous assistance from the archivists and librarians at three valued institutions: the Western History Collection at the Denver Public Library, the Stephen H. Hart Library and Research Center at History Colorado in Denver, and the University Libraries at the University of Denver. In particular, Professor Chris Brown, research librarian, and Katie Rosier were especially helpful in tracking down obscure sources and photographs. Their patience and persistence are gratefully appreciated.

I want to express my gratitude to the late Dr. Harry Rosenberg and Dr. James Hansen, emeritus professors of history at Colorado State University, longtime friends and mentors who encouraged me to pursue the study of history and hence this adventure. And to Dr. John E. Roberts Jr., Professor of History at Lincoln Land Community College. Diane and I must also give credit to Dr. Jared Orsi of Colorado State University, without whose support, guidance, and skillful critiques of earlier drafts this book would not have graduated from a wishful dream to a published work. Thank you.

We also thank those individuals in the real estate development and mortgage banking industries who carved out time from their schedules to share their knowledge and experiences with us. They include Terry Jones, Al Morrison, Rodger Hara, Chuck Perry, Charles Rhyne, Janet Hewitt, and many others. The list is simply too long to allow us to include everyone. Each of these individuals provided insights and details that otherwise would have been lost.

We also feel compelled to acknowledge the following individuals for their lifelong contributions to the mortgage industry: Edwin M. Rosser, MAI; Fred E. Kirk, Esq.; William A. Wildhack, CMB; Aksel Nielsen; Everett C. Spelman Sr., MAI; Robert G. Boucher, CMB; Herbert Tasker, CMB; James Nelson, CMB, CRE; Thomas Cronin, CMB; William Cumberland, Esq.; Leslie Hall; Dr. Lyle Grambling; Dr. Preston Martin; Robert Ferguson, CMB; Kate Armstrong, CMB; Julie Piepho, CMB; Scott Burgh; Hillary Escajeda, Esq.; W. Randolph Leathers; Dr. Mark Reidy; and David Stevens.

Thanks also to Jeff May and his colleagues for providing office space and supplies to help in this endeavor and to Sandy Heth and Karen Goetz, both respected colleagues for several decades.

For a nonacademic practitioner and until now an unpublished historian, the prospect of a peer review of your manuscript can be a bit nerve-wracking. As it turned out our fears were unwarranted. Dr. Kenneth Snowden and Dr. Ronnie Phillips, along with several industry practitioners, were extraordinarily helpful with their comments and observations. In each case we studied their advice. We found some of the suggestions, while insightful, to be beyond the scope of our book. But most others were incorporated and enhanced the final product immensely. We thank all of our reviewers for their time and careful critiques of our manuscript.

Not to be overlooked, our editors at the University Press of Colorado, Laura Furney and Cheryl Carnahan, have earned our unconditional appreciation. Their attention to detail proved invaluable. Thank you.

Without question, this work would not have found its way into print without the collaboration and support of the Public Lands History Center at Colorado State University. Professor Mark Fiege's keen interest, guidance, and suggestions widened the scope of our work and in the process helped us to add invaluable context to the story. Professors Ruth Alexander and Janet Ore, in addition to Jared Orsi, also improved the quality of our manuscript through their precisely worded inquiries and thoughtful advice. And Maren Bzdek, bless her heart, diligently but unsuccessfully attempted to keep us on task and on schedule. Our gratitude to you is boundless.

However, this personal memoir and industry history could not have been written without the talented skills of Diane Sanders. Her contribution went far beyond that of a skilled writer. In many cases she completely rewrote sections of my drafts and rearranged the content to bring the narrative to life. She often made me explain concepts and processes in extremely elementary terms so that she could then present material in language that non-industry readers could understand. While chapter 1 is almost entirely her work, she also conducted additional research that added depth and context to every other chapter. I am grateful for the immeasurable contributions she has made to this manuscript. It is not an exaggeration to name Diane as a coauthor.

We also want to extend a special thanks to our families. To Keren Rosser, whose patience and encouragement were critical and unflinching in support of this publication and for my career. She is a wonderful humanitarian and a caring physician. To Kevin Rosser and Wil Rosser for their encouragement as well as their editorial and legal advice. And to Craig Peterson who quietly supported our pursuit.

Acronyms / Abbreviations

ACORN	Association of Community Organizations for Reform Now
AIG	American International Group United Guaranty
ARM	adjustable-rate mortgage
AU	automated underwriting
CDH	Colorado Division of Housing
CEO	chief executive officer
CFO	chief financial officer
CFPB	Consumer Financial Protection Bureau
CHFA	Colorado Housing and Finance Authority
CMB	Certified Mortgage Banker
CMBA	Colorado Mortgage Bankers Association
CMIC	Colorado Mortgage and Investment Company of London
CMLA	Colorado Mortgage Lenders Association
CRA	Community Reinvestment Act
DBR	Denver Board of Realtors
DMBA	Denver Mortgage Bankers Association

DOE   Department of Energy (US)
DORA   Department of Regulatory Agencies (Colorado)
DURA   Denver Urban Renewal Authority
e.g.   for example (used only in parentheses)
FDIC   Federal Deposit Insurance Corporation
FHA   Federal Housing Administration
FHFA   Federal Housing Finance Agency
FHLB   Federal Home Loan Bank
FIRREA   Financial Institutions Reform, Recovery, and Enforcement
             Act
FLA   Federal Farm Loan Act
FMBA   Farm Mortgage Bankers Association
FNMA   Federal National Mortgage Association (Fannie Mae)
Freddie Mac Federal Home Loan Mortgage Corporation
FSLIC   Federal Savings and Loan Insurance Corporation
FTC   Federal Trade Commission
GAO   Government Accountability Office
GNMA   Government National Mortgage Association
GSE   government-sponsored enterprise
HECM   Home Equity Conversion Mortgage
HERA   Housing and Economic Recovery Act
HFA   housing finance agency
HHFA   Housing and Home Finance Agency
HOLC   Home Owners Loan Corporation
HUD   Department of Housing and Urban Development (US)
i.e.   that is (used only in parentheses)
IRS   Internal Revenue Service
LUC   Colorado Land Use Commission
MBA   Mortgage Bankers Association
NAR   National Association of Realtors
NMA   National Mortgage Association
OFHEO   Office of Federal Housing Enterprise Oversight
PERA   Colorado Public Employees Retirement Association
PMI   PMI Mortgage Insurance Company
PUD   planned unit development (capped when part of the name
             of the act)

REIT	real estate investment trust
RFC	Reconstruction Finance Corporation
RIHA	Research Institute for Housing America
RTC	Resolution Trust Corporation
RTD	Regional Transportation District
S&P	Standard and Poor's
SIC	Service Investment Company
SRO	single-room occupancy
TARP	Troubled Asset Relief Program
TOD	transit-oriented development
ULI	Urban Land Institute
US	United States (used as an adjective)
VA	Veterans Administration
WKH	Wheeler Kelly and Hagny Investment Company
YMBC	Young Mortgage Bankers Committee

Preface

In 2004, I began planning for my retirement from a long career in the real estate finance industry. At that time I had been working in the national accounts division of American International Group United Guaranty (AIG) for over ten years, providing products and services to mortgage lenders. Soon after joining the firm I added a new project to my bucket list, one I knew would have to wait until retirement. For some time I had been pondering the idea of writing a history of the mortgage banking industry that would include an explanation of the role mortgage bankers play in the economy, beginning with their contribution to the opening of the West. When I joined the firm in 1994 and began giving this book more serious thought, AIG was the world's largest insurance company. No one could have anticipated then that it would later become one of the casualties of the Great Recession of 2008.

Certainly, my view of the mortgage crisis is somewhat jaded. My disclaimer is that my viewpoint is that of someone on the inside looking out. It is influenced by nearly fifty years of experience and training in the mortgage banking industry. My anger and sadness about the mortgage crisis stem from the fact that I, like many others, relied on the predictive models of "experts" instead of trusting my own judgment. In a groupthink culture, dissent carries a certain element of risk, particularly if respected members of the industry and affiliated institutions are all drinking the same Kool-Aid.

The collapse of the US real estate market beginning in 2006 and the subsequent Great Recession impacted every American, some more than others. Though an oversimplification, the problems began within the mortgage finance industry and its systematic loosening of creditworthiness requirements beginning in the 1990s. The strategy enabled many families who otherwise could not have afforded to purchase a home to achieve that ubiquitous American dream. But it also resulted in the approval of riskier and riskier loans, as well as greatly inflated real estate values. When the mortgage finance industry imploded, for reasons explained later, the repercussions spread throughout the entire economy, causing job losses and widespread home foreclosures. It was a painful experience for everyone involved.

The goals of this book are to explain the reasons behind that economic disaster and also the important contributions the mortgage banking industry has made to the American public and the nation's economy. To understand its collapse, one needs to understand the development and goals of the mortgage banking industry since its inception. Therefore, we discuss the formation and development of the industry beginning with the micro-financing of farms in the Midwest during the decades after the Civil War. We explain the industry's importance to the settlement of the West and its growth over the succeeding 150 years, as well as its involvement in the Great Recession. In doing so, we draw on examples from Kansas and Colorado, the states the principal author knows best. Whenever possible, we include stories from my lifelong mortgage banking career. As a result, this book is a combination of history and personal memoir. It is the story of my life, but it is also part of everyone's life story because we all live in some type of residence, whether a single-family or multi-family home, an apartment, or a houseboat. We attend schools, shop in stores, and work in all manner of buildings. Mortgage bankers arranged for the financing for most of these structures that we use every day, regardless of whether we as individuals own them.

To assist readers' understanding, we begin with a brief overview of the mortgage banking industry. First, mortgage banking is now a multi-trillion dollar industry. Yet the role of the mortgage banker is not well understood.

Often, the terms *mortgage banking* and *mortgage banker* are confused with commercial banking or investment banking. A mortgage banker is an individual or firm that originates, sells, and services mortgage loans for individuals and institutional investors. Typically, the mortgage banker retains the servicing rights on loans that have been sold. That means the mortgage banker will collect the payments from the borrower and forward those funds to the investor. He or she will also maintain a separate account to pay for insurance on the property and real estate taxes. The mortgage banker handles all communications with the borrower on behalf of the investor, including collecting delinquent payments and initiating foreclosure and disposing of the property if necessary.[1]

The mortgage banker cultivates a correspondent or contractual relationship with the investor. A mortgage loan correspondent represents the investor and performs the function of acquiring real estate and mortgage assets to meet the investor's ever-changing portfolio needs. Correspondent/investor relationships form the core of a mortgage banking company and are its most valuable assets. Operating in an ethical and lawful manner, the mortgage banker provides sound, prudent investments that adhere strictly to the investor's risk and credit standards. By definition, a good loan for the investor is a good loan for the borrower. This book examines such relationships over time and illustrates how they have worked to strengthen communities, serve borrowers, and build a nation.

A mortgage banking firm (mortgage bank) does not collect deposits or offer financial services such as credit cards or automobile loans. Historically, mortgage banking firms have included an insurance agency and a property management department along with a real estate brokerage business. Many large banks, community banks, savings and loans, and credit unions operate a mortgage banking function within their institutions. Any lender who sells and services mortgage loans operates a mortgage banking function.[2]

Since its birth in the 1850s, the industry has served as a bridge to distribute capital. Except for a brief respite during the Civil War, the mortgage banking industry grew and prospered as migration prompted by the building of railroads increased and more lands for settlement became available following

---

1   Albert Santi and James Newell, *Encyclopedia of Mortgage and Real Estate Finance* (Washington, DC: Real Estate Finance Press, 1997), 247.

2   Ibid.

passage of the Homestead and Pacific Railway Acts in 1862. Mortgage bankers created a conduit for investors to provide funds to farmers and livestock raisers as they moved west through Minnesota, Iowa, Kansas, and Colorado. Not to be overlooked, urban lending experienced its first major boost by providing capital to rebuild Chicago after the Great Fire in 1871 destroyed much of the city.

Mortgage bankers financed the transition from subsistence to commercial agriculture. When the Industrial Revolution triggered the growth of cities, mortgage bankers were on the scene to provide the capital to build the nation's urban centers. When veterans returned from World War II, mortgage bankers financed the homes, apartments and shopping centers of suburbia to meet the needs of the growing nation. In each case, mortgage bankers provided the necessary capital.

Every mortgage contains varying elements of risk for both the investor and the buyer, and it is up to the mortgage banker to accurately assess those risks. First is the credit risk based on the borrower's past, present, and future ability to meet all of his or her financial obligations. Second are the elements of real estate risk related to the value of the property: the property's location and the probability of the property maintaining or increasing its value over the life of the mortgage. Appraisal students learn three approaches for estimating the value of real estate—the income approach, the cost approach, and the market approach. But the experienced mortgage loan officer often employs a fourth method. While on the site the officer will look at the property and its surroundings and ask, "If I make the loan, can I sell this property for what I have invested in it?" The final risk element includes the loan elements of interest rate, term length, payment plan, and loan-to-value ratio. For instance, if the interest rate is too low, the investor supplying the funds will not make enough profit to justify making the loan; if it is too high, fewer borrowers will be able to qualify for the loan. In either case, if a loan is not made, the investor must search for another investment opportunity, and the potential buyer is forced to abandon his or her quest for home ownership or wait until lower, more affordable interest rates return.

Relative to the property, three characteristics are considered in the process of evaluating the property. First is the ratio of the loan amount to the valuation of the property. Higher loan amounts mean the borrower has less equity or cash investment in the property. Therefore, he has less to lose if he defaults on the loan. Second is the ratio of the mortgage term to the estimated remaining economic life of the property, and last is the ratio of the monthly mortgage payment to the rental value. The purchaser of a rental property wants the rental income to be sufficient to pay for the mortgage and, it is hoped, all related costs.

With regard to the borrower, risk is reduced when a lower loan-to-value ratio and lower debt-to-income ratio combine with a borrower whose past performance has earned him or her a high credit rating. All of these risk characteristics are studied during the loan approval process. Yet family circumstances and economic changes, namely job loss, are out of the lender's control after the transaction closes. So the credit, real estate, and economic risks dictate the performance of mortgage portfolios.[3] We will tell the story of how this played out in Kansas and Colorado from 1862 to 2014.

In this story we illustrate the complexities of real estate capital on the evaluation of risk and reward. We outline the conflicts between the need of the investor for a return of the capital invested as well as a profit and the changing conditions of the investment marketplace. The investor must be prepared to take the long-term interest rate risk of a fifteen-, twenty-, or thirty-year mortgage. In addition, the investor must have confidence in the correspondent's judgment regarding the borrower's ability to repay the loan. The borrower's possible default in a poor real estate market is also part of the interest rate calculation. The higher the risk, the higher the interest rate. But the fact remains that future events and factors such as loss of employment, illness, or death can defeat the best judgment.

Surprisingly, the process of making a real estate loan has changed very little over time. On a narrow scale, the local mortgage banker and his or her investor apply guidelines, analyze the characteristics of the borrower and the property, and ask if they match up with the investor's portfolio needs. On a broader scale, associated legal and regulatory issues must be understood, and they demand compliance. Aspects of both macro- and regional economics also figure significantly in the decision to invest, particularly in commercial mortgages. Ignoring environmental factors can contribute to substantial financial losses and damage to reputations. Consistent and properly

3   Federal Housing Administration, *FHA Underwriting Manual, Sections 332–334, Revised Underwriting Analysis under Title II, Section 203 of the National Housing Act, National Housing Agency* (Washington, DC: Federal Housing Administration, January 1947), 202–5.

administered zoning and land-use laws also contribute to a property's or an area's long-term value and economic sustainability.

All of these factors weighed together make a successful mortgage loan. We hope to track the evolution of the industry, the role of government and government-sponsored enterprises, and the financial engineering that is responsible for preserving the thirty-year fixed-rate mortgage to which American homeowners have become accustomed. We close with a discussion of the recent Great Recession and the principal author's perspective on its causes.

I, Mike Rosser, represent the third generation of mortgage bankers in my family. My father's career began in Kansas with the Wheeler Kelly and Hagny Investment Company (WKH), a firm that served as a mortgage loan correspondent for the Prudential Insurance Company of America (Prudential). He joined Prudential during the Great Depression and stayed with the company until 1950. During those years he worked in Kansas City, Kansas, Denver, Colorado, and Houston, Texas. When he left Prudential, he moved our family back to Denver and joined another firm.

Other members of my family had been involved in mortgage financing before my father. My great-uncle Edwin A. Rosser, a Civil War veteran and prisoner of war held at the confederate camp at Andersonville in Georgia, conducted a small mortgage and title practice within his law firm in Coffeyville, Kansas. And my maternal grandfather, Will Ratliff, operated a small mortgage agency from an office above his general store in Ogden, Kansas. Recognized as a successful businessman, farmer, and civic leader, he was also a major stockholder and executive of the State Bank of Ogden.

My professional career started in August 1965 at the mortgage banking firm Kassler and Company in Denver. However, my exposure to the industry began two decades earlier when, at age seven, I joined my father while he conducted appraisal and construction loan inspections. I realize now that what began as simple Saturday morning outings with my father developed into a fundamental course in mortgage underwriting. Driving throughout Houston and later Denver, he pointed out various features, explaining which aspects differentiated outstanding properties from average or poor ones. He taught me the importance of inspecting not just the individual property in question but also the immediate neighborhood, the subdivision, and the community as a whole. My father explained that parks, recreation areas, and open space were critical components of every community and neighborhood.

When combined with good schools and good public services, they formed the foundation of good mortgages. I learned the importance of good land-use laws, including adequate zoning and code enforcement. He taught me to look for overall functionality, the aesthetics of the design, and the use of quality building materials. Peppered throughout were explanations of the concepts of economic and functional obsolescence.

These are the things I learned from my father. Little did I know at the time that the seeds for a lifelong fascination with mortgage financing had been sown. Those Saturday outings, which continued until my father's sudden death in 1957, enabled me to develop the ability to recognize and understand what made a quality development. Hindsight now allows me to recall particular projects from thirty, forty, even fifty years ago and remember the judgments I made when I first saw them. Some assessments were correct, some were not, but cumulatively they fostered in me a strong preservation and conservation ethic, as well as an appreciation for the enduring quality of sound real estate development.

Admittedly, subjective judgment comes into play when determining whether a real estate development has enduring quality. The Oxford Hotel in Denver is an excellent example of both good original development and preservation. When built it was constructed of the best-quality materials and excellent design. The recent remodel has maintained many of its best features while being upgraded to meet current tastes, demands, and uses.

An example of enduring, quality real estate development that informed my early years is the J. C. Nichols Country Club Plaza in Kansas City, Missouri. I remember going there with my parents on numerous occasions during the short time we lived in Kansas City. We returned periodically, and in 2005 my cousins and I came together for a weekend reunion at the Plaza. The layout, the design, the amount of activity, and its adaptation to modern retailing demonstrated the foresight of the Nichols Company. It had developed and overseen a project that could adapt and change without destroying the Plaza's original functional and architectural integrity. Upon reflection, my commitment to preservation and proper land use really took root during those brief years of in which I lived in Kansas City.

Now back to my professional life. The timing for launching my career in Denver in 1965 could not have been worse. Not long after I joined Kassler and Company, one of the area's major employers, the Martin Company, began laying off a substantial number of its workers. As the ripple effect spread throughout the real estate industry, I, too, became a casualty of the economic distress. I was devastated. Fortunately, I found another job opportunity that enabled me to gain hands-on experience in real estate management. I learned that to understand real estate economics and markets, a person needs to experience firsthand the workings of real estate asset management.

In 1969, I restarted my mortgage banking career at Service Investment Company (SIC), a small mortgage banking firm. My first position with the company was as a loan officer with the builder division. I also handled the processing of developers' subdivision applications for FHA and VA approvals. Later, I oversaw the selling of loans to the secondary market.

While with SIC I took advantage of the company's informal training program for junior members and attended the Mortgage Bankers Association's School of Mortgage Banking at Northwestern University. Adding a graduate degree in urban and regional planning from the University of Northern Colorado to my earlier BS in social science with an emphasis in history and government from Colorado State University provided me with a well-rounded education that further enhanced my career growth.

In 1974, market conditions and the spike in interest rates adversely affected SIC, by then renamed United Mortgage Company, and resulted in major changes for me. The company's economic troubles led me to secure a one-year position as a junior staff member and policy analyst for the Colorado Land Use Commission (LUC). I spent most of the year on a variety of projects, including the Beaver Creek Ski Area permit application to the US Forest Service. I also handled inquiries about the 1974 Colorado Land Use Act, which dealt with matters surrounding the state's highway interchanges, airports, and mining activities. I also attended meetings about the Rocky Flats Nuclear Weapons Plant and its potential as an environmental hazard. I did not realize for several years the potential impact Rocky Flats could have had on the mortgage banking, real estate, and home building industries.

In 1975, when my commitment to the LUC ended, I joined the PMI Mortgage Insurance Company (PMI) as a regional manager for the states of Colorado and Wyoming, later adding Utah and New Mexico to my territory. The highlight of my ten years at PMI was the development and rollout of the PMI Mortgage Corporation, the first modern mortgage conduit. A mortgage conduit assembles loans from multiple lenders, thus creating a pool of loans.

The conduit then issues and may distribute a series of securities to investors in long-term debt instruments. PMI Mortgage Corporation also operated as a master servicer for a $50 million thirty-year fixed-rate mortgage-backed security placed with the Colorado Public Employees Retirement Association pension fund. These were but a few of the projects I oversaw and consider major accomplishments during my tenure at PMI that enhanced my professional development and my career.

Following my ten years with PMI, I spent three wonderful, productive years at Moore Mortgage Company. The Moore family of companies included one of Denver's leading mortgage banking firms, an insurance agency, and one of the region's dominant real estate brokerage companies. I was part of the mortgage banking company charged with establishing a division to purchase loans from other mortgage banking firms affiliated with real estate brokerage companies in twelve major markets across the country. We would then sort, package, and resell the loans in the secondary market.

While I was at Moore Mortgage, Robert G. Boucher, president and CEO of First Denver Mortgage, recruited me to join the Mortgage Bankers Association (MBA) Board of Governors. Boucher was aware of my activities in the industry in Colorado and also knew that I had chaired the Young Mortgage Bankers Committee of the MBA in 1978. His support and friendship opened doors for me to serve on a number of committees and attain various leadership positions over the next thirty-five-plus years. My long participation in the MBA provided unparalleled opportunities to study the inside of the industry and to expand my career opportunities. Earning my Master Certified Mortgage Banker (CMB) designation in 1988 was a watershed event. The professional designation is a significant achievement within the industry.

When I joined United Guaranty, a subsidiary of AIG, in 1991, being a CMB provided me with access to senior management positions involving the firm's customers that otherwise might not have been readily attainable. My work in the national accounts division required me to manage the company's relationships with some of the twenty largest mortgage banking firms in the country. I was tasked with a risk management function as well as the sale of mortgage insurance products and services. As a result, I gained unique insight into the operation of the industry and was privy to the business strategies of the mortgage banking firms with which we conducted business. I stayed with AIG until my retirement in 2013.

Over the course of my fifty-plus-year career in real estate finance, I have not only witnessed but actively participated in the financing and development of urban, suburban, and rural real estate. Yet, it is my work with the MBA that garners my deepest pride. I consider reorganizing the makeup of the CMB designation and elevating the standards of professional education to be my greatest industry achievements. Having been a faculty member at the School of Mortgage Banking since 1984, I considered industry education and training to be of major importance and a way for me to give back to the industry. Consequently, I led a task force in the effort to modernize the CMB designation, taking it beyond mere knowledge to include more hands-on training applications, thus making it more relevant to today's industry professionals.

From inside these institutions both large and small that have provided the necessary capital to finance real estate and worked to establish housing finance policy, I have watched Americans develop an almost obsessive desire to own and build equity in real estate for their personal security. This is nothing new. America has embraced this love affair with land and real estate throughout its history; the obsession has simply grown more intense. But over the span of my career the actions and demands of government, the public, and the industry have created a philosophical conflict between individualism and collective action, free markets and government-sponsored enterprises. These conflicts form the basis of a never-ending national dialogue.

Over the span of my career, I had heard numerous stories and oral traditions about the business but had never seen a definitive history. The stories and legends I had heard spoke of the origin of mortgage banking in farm lending in the Midwest. I had read about the Great Depression's causes and impacts on property owners. I knew about the formation of the FHA in 1934 and the establishment of the Federal National Mortgage Association (FNMA), known as Fannie Mae, in 1938. I had the special privilege of serving on the Fannie Mae regional advisory board and attending Fannie Mae's 50th birthday celebration in Washington, DC. All of my personal recollections, combined with the stories I had heard, prompted me to begin a memoir to tell the story of mortgage bankers and how they enabled the development of the United States and the American West.

As 2013 drew to a close, so did my forty-four years of formal participation in the MBA. On October 30, 2013, I left the 100th Annual Convention of the MBA of America held in Washington, DC, and put that part of my life in the rearview mirror. It seemed fitting that I said goodbye by attending the convention that celebrated the ssociation's 100th year in existence. As I look back over those many years of my career, I feel enormously blessed at my great good fortune; for the colleagues, friends, and mentors who have supported and guided me and for a father who planted the seed of a career that has enriched my life. It was a great ride!

The time had finally arrived to put on paper the history of an industry that has contributed so much to American prosperity and to a sense of well-being for homeowners across the nation.

Part I

WESTWARD EXPANSION AND EARLY
MORTGAGE BANKING DEVELOPMENT

1

Westward Ho!

EXPANSION

Prior to the conclusion of the Revolutionary War, there was little need for mortgage bankers. Colonial governments often granted land to farmers, and tradesmen typically started businesses with the tools they brought with them from England or Europe. If funds were needed to establish a business or expand a farm, individuals typically borrowed from a relative or a wealthy community member. Over the next century, land acquisition became more complicated as the nation moved west.

Victory over the British had resulted in much more than political independence for the fledgling United States. Victory also moved the western border of the new nation far beyond the original thirteen colonies. The 1783 Treaty of Paris demanded that Britain cede the trans-Appalachian West, all of the land between the Appalachian Mountains and the Mississippi River, to the United States. Americans were able to leave the crowded cities along the eastern seaboard to establish new towns and businesses in the interior. More important, the land was perfect for agriculture, the economic foundation of

DOI: 10.5876/9781607326236.c001

the country. Some farmers in the East vacated their marginal farms to move across the mountains. And many second sons, denied land inheritance by the legal tradition of primogeniture, took advantage of the opportunity to establish their own farms, especially in the fertile region of what became the Northwest Territory, or Old Northwest—the lands north of the Ohio River.

To facilitate expansion and settlement, under the powers granted by the Articles of Confederation, the Continental Congress passed the Land Ordinance of 1785, which ordered the survey and division of the land into a uniform grid system. The system enabled verifiable legal descriptions for each plot of land, minimizing land ownership disputes and laying a foundation for mortgage lending. Once surveyed, the federal government sold the land, thus generating revenue to govern the newly established nation. Even though the Native Americans who had lived in trans-Appalachia for centuries contested American expansion, by the early 1800s the region was bustling with American immigrants.[1]

A few years later, in 1803, the purchase of what was then called Louisiana, virtually all of the land from the Mississippi to the Rocky Mountains, nearly doubled the size of the country. In the eyes of President Thomas Jefferson and his supporters, possession of this enormous tract of land assured the fledgling country that it would not succumb to overpopulation and economic stagnation. However, not until several events occurred during the late 1840s did a surge of settlement spread westward. The first was the ratification of a treaty with Great Britain in 1846 that gave sole possession of Oregon Country to the United States.[2] Suddenly, the nation's northern tier extended from the Atlantic to the Pacific. Two years later, the military victory over Mexico in the Mexican-American War moved the border to include most of what is now known as the American Southwest and California. When combined with Texas, annexed by the United States in 1845, and the Oregon Country to the north, the nation became truly continental in scope.

But the discovery of gold in California in late 1848 was what really spawned the movement of large numbers of immigrants to the West. Following the

---

1   Elliot West, "American Frontier," in *The Oxford History of the American West*, ed. Clyde A. Milner II, Carol A. O'Connor, and Martha A. Sandweiss (New York: Oxford University Press, 1994), 124–27, 130–32.

2   Oregon Country included what would later become the states of Washington, Oregon, Idaho, and parts of Montana and Wyoming.

California Gold Rush, additional discoveries of gold and silver induced others to seek their fortunes in Nevada, Colorado, and other areas of the West. On the heels of the miners came entrepreneurs who developed towns and cities such as Denver that supported the miners, providing them with desperately needed supplies and various services, from blacksmiths to laundries. As the towns and cities of the West developed, farmers from the East and from Europe began to arrive, ready to claim and cultivate lands made available through the Homestead Act passed by the US Congress in 1862. Settlement of the West exploded during the second half of the nineteenth century.

Yet the federal government did not possess clear title to much of the land the farmers wanted. Native American peoples still controlled some of the best agricultural lands. The government would have to negotiate treaties with numerous tribes and in many cases force them onto reservations located on less desirable lands. An example is the Osage Nation's claim on a large segment of southeastern Kansas. On September 29, 1865, government officials finalized negotiations with tribal representatives to acquire their "surplus lands," allowing official surveys to proceed. But the treaty stipulated that the bulk of the land was to be sold and therefore was not available for homesteading. Government surveys were crucial to providing land titles based on accurate legal descriptions, a necessary component for granting and selling property and for mortgage lending.[3]

Congress envisioned the Homestead Act and its legislative partners, the Pacific Railway Act and the Morrill Act passed and enacted in 1862, as tools to expand America's capitalist agrarian economy. Through the Homestead Act, the federal government gave 160 acres of land at no cost to individuals who agreed to live on and develop the land for productive use for a period of five years. At the end of the five-year term they would receive title to the land. Settlers could also exercise the option to purchase the land outright at a discounted rate of only $1.25 per acre after just six months of occupancy. Like the Land Ordinance of 1785, the Homestead Act was designed to draw

---

3   An appraisal conducted by A. G. Bowes and Company in 1952 concluded that the actual market value of the land on September 29, 1865, would have been $1,740,000 and that, as a result of increased demand causing rises in land prices, had the land been subdivided and sold "on the most advantageous terms" as required by the treaty, it would have garnered $3,493,000 at true market value if sold between 1865 and 1870 (Watson Bowes, *Appraisal of Lands Covered by the "Treaty with the Osage, 1865"* [October 1952, appraisal cover letter, A. G. Bowes and Sons, MSS01087, File 202, History Colorado, Denver]).

the poor, the unemployed, and the children of farmers in the East to the trans-Mississippi West, transforming them into prosperous, independent farmers—the ideal of a republican society.

The Pacific Railway Act attempted to achieve two goals—first, to establish a transcontinental railway system to connect the East and West Coasts and second, to provide rail service to the newly established farm communities in the West so they could readily transport their produce to distant markets across the nation and the globe. The federal government subsidized the railroads by granting them title to up to ten acres of land for every mile of track they laid. Later amendments increased that amount to forty acres. Congress anticipated that the railroad companies would sell the granted lands, all located adjacent to the tracks, to prospective farmers. The funds raised would help finance railroad construction while providing those same farmers with ready access to the railroad networks that would transport their goods to market and bring manufactured goods to them while at the same time enabling mortgage bankers to invest in new farming and ranching communities.[4]

The third component, the Morrill Act, granted public lands to individual states for the express purpose of raising funds to finance the establishment of higher education institutions that would develop agricultural and mechanical/engineering curriculums in addition to other sciences and traditional liberal arts programs. Known as land-grant colleges, they specialized in research to advance agricultural practices in an effort to increase the productivity and profitability of America's farmers. In combination, these three statutes created a framework to develop a robust and prosperous agriculturally based economy in the West, at least in theory.

One of the crucial factors the crafters of the Homestead Act failed to consider was the arid climate that engulfed much of the West. The farming knowledge and methods most settlers brought with them were adapted to the humid climate east of the Mississippi River. Efforts to apply that expertise to the arid West without supplemental irrigation proved disastrous. Without irrigation, 160 acres of land was insufficient to generate enough food for subsistence, let alone a profit. As a result, almost half of all farms established under the act failed and were abandoned before the end of the five-year

---

4   Richard White, *It's Your Misfortune and None of My Own: A New History of the American West* (Norman: University of Oklahoma Press, 1991), 145–46.

Weld County, Colorado, farm and irrigation ditch. Irrigation was critical to the success of agriculture in the West. Understanding its importance led a number of investors, including the Colorado Mortgage and Investment Company of London, to pursue irrigation projects in what are now Boulder, Denver, Larimer, and Weld Counties. Courtesy, Denver Public Library.

occupancy requirement, the farmers never having secured title to the land. In addition, the Homestead Act failed to address the needs and practices of cattle and sheep ranching. Ranchers typically did not cultivate the land as required by the law and needed much more than the allotted 160 acres of land to support a viable, productive herd.

Mining also lured men to Colorado. In 1858, about ten years after the California Gold Rush, major silver and gold strikes drew thousands to the mountains of Nevada and Colorado. Some, such as Horace Tabor, amassed a considerable fortune. Tabor parlayed some of his mining profits into other commercial and real estate investments with mortgage financing funded by Northwestern Mutual and other investors. Before losing most of his fortune in the silver crash of 1893 and the ensuing recession that crippled Colorado's

William Henry Jackson photograph of the Windsor Hotel, ca. 1880–90. The hotel was demolished as part of urban renewal in the 1970s. Courtesy, Denver Public Library, Western History Collection.

economy, Tabor's real estate holdings included Denver's iconic Windsor Hotel and the Tabor Grand Opera House.[5] He ultimately lost the opera house. In addition, Northwestern foreclosed on his Tabor Block building, the last of his real estate holdings.

Until large-scale industrial mining replaced small-scale prospectors, most mining financing was provided by men like Horace Tabor who grubstaked individual prospectors. Grubstaking meant that someone like Tabor provided prospectors with picks, shovels, shaker tables, and other equipment as well as food supplies in exchange for a percentage ownership. If the mine came in big, everyone, including the grubstaker, could become extremely wealthy, as

5   Betty Moynihan, *Augusta Tabor: A Pioneering Woman* (Evergreen, CO: Cordillera, 1988), 12, 36–37, 51–72; Augusta G. Tabor, "$800,000 Worth of Gold Dust," in *So Much to Be Done: Women Settlers on the Mining and Ranching Frontier*, ed. Ruth Moynihan, Susan Armitage, and Christine Dichamp (Lincoln: University of Nebraska Press, 1998), 146. The Denver branch of the Kansas City Federal Reserve now occupies the site at Sixteenth and Curtis Streets where the Tabor Grand Opera House once stood (David Ballast, *The Denver Chronicle: From a Golden Past to a Mile-High Future* [Houston: Gulf, 1995], 45).

happened with several of Tabor's investments. Meanwhile, mortgage bankers only participated indirectly in mining. They facilitated the financing of railroads; the agricultural needs of farming, ranching, and irrigation; housing, and the building of mining towns such as Leadville and Cripple Creek.

CURRENCY AND ECONOMIC WOES: 1870S–1893

Large investment companies as well as private investors in the East provided mortgage loans that aided the development of the West. In addition, especially from the 1870s forward, foreign companies, many from Great Britain, invested heavily in American agriculture, equities, and mortgage securities. These investors all relied on the expertise of local representatives, correspondents, to assess the reliability of each loan applicant and his or her ability to repay the debt. Some investment companies, such as the Colorado Mortgage and Investment Company of London (CMIC) and its subsidiaries, also became involved in urban real estate development and irrigation projects that distributed water to cities and farms. However, investment in everything from industry to individual farms was interrupted several times before the turn of the century—once in the period 1884–85, again during the early 1890s, and culminating with the Panic of 1893.

The crisis of 1884–85 and the Panic of 1893 resulted from the US commitment to bimetallism. However, motivated by the discovery of large gold deposits in California and Australia, during the 1850s the leading commercial countries of Europe, led by France, began converting from silver to gold as their primary currency. By the 1870s all of the leading European nations and Great Britain had completed the transfer to gold and were selling their silver on the open market. The resultant worldwide devaluation of silver created havoc for the American economy and its currency. The growing output of silver mines in the American West, which the federal government began subsidizing as a result of the Bland-Allison Act in 1878, exacerbated the problem.[6]

The financial crisis of 1884–85 began with an expanding economic slowdown in 1883. Individuals curtailed unnecessary spending. Decreasing revenues prompted banks to hoard their more valuable gold and pay customs revenues to the Treasury with silver. At the same time, the Treasury was still

---

6   William Jett Lauck, *The Causes of the Panic of 1893* (Boston: Houghton, Mifflin, 1907), 16–19.

spending a large portion of its gold reserves to purchase the Bland-Allison Act's mandated monthly allotment of silver. By early 1884 the burden of the silver purchases combined with the government's other financial obligations to cause a perilous reduction in the Treasury's gold supply while generating an oversupply of silver. Knowledge of the situation caused many people, especially investors, to anticipate that the government would soon be unable to continue making gold payments. The resulting unease regarding the American government's currency stability prompted many foreign investors to cease investing in the United States, which drastically curtailed the availability of mortgage credit. Investors also sold their existing holdings in America for payment in gold, further reducing the gold reserves. Only when the government took measures to induce banks to resume payments to the Treasury with gold to stabilize the silver/gold currency distribution did the crisis pass. Had the United States joined Europe and Great Britain in converting to the gold standard during the previous decades, the currency crisis would have been averted altogether.[7]

The international Panic of 1890 can largely be attributed to the collapse of Argentina's economy and government in July of that year. Speculative investment in that country by European banks and other investors, especially from Great Britain and Germany during the previous decade, resulted in extreme economic distress when Argentina failed. To cover the losses incurred in Argentina, British investors began selling US railroad stocks, bonds, and other securities. Still nervous about American currency, they demanded payment in gold. A significant decline of foreign investment in western mortgages, particularly farm mortgages, accompanied the selloff. Investors also failed to renew farm loans, even for borrowers who had maintained their payments. As a result, there was a substantial decrease in the credit market and an increase in foreclosures. Thus the strong economic growth enjoyed on both sides of the Atlantic from 1886 until 1890 ended abruptly with a severe economic contraction.[8]

Yet as Britain and Europe experienced a gradual, steady recovery beginning in 1891, the American economy stagnated. Concern regarding the stability of US currency remained. When Congress passed the Sherman Silver

---

7   Ibid., 21–23.

8   Ibid., 63–65, 73–75.

Purchase Act in July 1890, apprehension grew. The new law more than doubled the Treasury's silver purchase requirement. Foreign and domestic investors continued to divest themselves of American holdings, demanding payment in gold, and they sought investment opportunities elsewhere. By mid-1893 the US economy found itself in a virtually identical situation to the one in 1885.

Exacerbated by British investors' sell-off of their US investments, especially railroad stocks, and their refusal to renew short-term mortgage loans, American institutions and individuals alike hoarded their gold and curtailed spending. Once again, payments to the Treasury were made with silver certificates while the Treasury had to make its silver purchases with gold. Any remaining confidence in the government's ability to maintain the gold standard of payments evaporated, and the Panic of 1893 gained momentum.[9] Not until Congress repealed the Sherman Silver Purchase Act later that year and embraced the gold standard for the currency did the fear subside, and the crisis waned.

In short, continued uncertainty about the stability of American currency led to the US economic problems between 1878 and 1893. The withdrawal of investors from the marketplace caused a severe decline of available credit for western farmers and businesses. Droughts during the period compounded the problem by decreasing agricultural production, resulting in a severe reduction of farm income that led to a monumental escalation of foreclosures, which in turn negatively impacted investors' willingness to fund farm mortgages. The repeal of the Silver Purchase Act restored confidence in American currency but proved devastating to the silver mining industry, until then a major contributor to the economy of Colorado and other areas of the West. Consequently, recovery in Colorado continued at a slower pace than in most of the country as investors maintained a very conservative approach to western mortgages, especially farm mortgages, through the end of the century.

BUT WHAT ABOUT WATER?

With the currency challenges all but resolved, the federal government turned its attention once again to the water concerns of western farmers. The Desert

---

9   Ibid., 111–22.

Land Act of 1894, better known as the Carey Act, marked the government's first real attempt to support western agriculture by addressing the region's lack of water. Under the act, the Federal Land Office could cede up to 1 million acres to each western state that developed approved reclamation projects. It amounted to a land subsidy much like the one granted to the railroads under the Pacific Railway Act. Proceeds from the sale of the lands would offset, at least partially, the costs of the development of the irrigation projects. Developers would recoup their investments through the sale of water to the farmers the projects serviced, and the states would benefit from the collection of additional taxes. But few states took full advantage of the law. Most of the available lands were too far away from viable water sources. The best lands had already been homesteaded, and the costs of sizable irrigation projects were substantial; finding investors proved difficult. Wyoming and Idaho have the most Carey Act projects. It is estimated that 60 percent of all land irrigated by Carey Act projects is in Idaho.[10]

Finally, the Newlands Reclamation Act of 1902 ushered in a new era of federal government involvement in the West.[11] The act marked the beginning of a decidedly proactive, hands-on approach to development in the region. Under the leadership of President Theodore Roosevelt, the government recognized that the scale of irrigation projects necessary for the region's success was simply too great for private business or even local and state governments to finance.[12] Reservoirs created by massive dams on western rivers constructed by the newly created Bureau of Reclamation opened vast new areas for agricultural and urban development, and mortgage bankers understood the potential for exponential market growth.

In 1909, Congress aided the West again by approving the Enlarged Homestead Act, which doubled the size of land grants per homestead to 320 acres. Further

---

10   "August 18, 1894: Carey Act Signed," *This Day in Water History*, accessed May 21, 2015, https://thisdayinwaterhistory.wordpress.com/2015/08/18/august-18-1894-carey-act-signed-2/; Phil Roberts, "Chapter 13: Water and Irrigation," *New History of Wyoming*, accessed April 15, 2015, http://www.uwyo.edu/robertshistory/New_History_of_Wyoming_chapter_13_water.htm.

11   Carl Abbott, "The Federal Presence," in *The Oxford History of the American West*, ed. Clyde A. Milner II, Carol A. O'Connor, and Martha A. Sandweiss (New York: Oxford University Press, 1994), 471.

12   William Cronon, "Landscapes of Abundance and Scarcity," in *The Oxford History of the American West*, ed. Clyde A. Milner II, Carol A. O'Connor, and Martha A. Sandweiss (New York: Oxford University Press, 1994), 618.

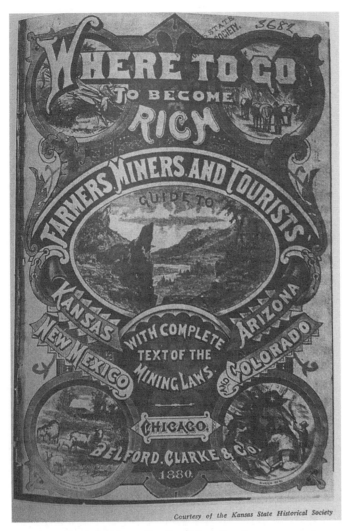

Courtesy of the Kansas State Historical Society

*Sample marketing brochures distributed by railroads to promote reloca-
tion in the West during the late 1800s.*

recognizing the aridity of the West, the government encouraged more settlement in 1916 when it passed the Stock Raising Homestead Act, which offered
640-acre tracts of rangeland to ranchers.[13] Both facets of agriculture, farming

---

13 Abbott, "Federal Presence," 472.

and ranching, expanded into new areas from 1900 to 1920, but it was the urban centers that experienced a major population explosion in the decades that followed. Mortgage bankers stepped up to the challenge of serving that ever-expanding urban market and the increasing desire for homeownership.

RAILROADS—PROVIDING MORE THAN JUST TRANSPORTATION

Railroad companies were also heavily involved in the development of the West. Aside from providing transportation, they produced much of the marketing that promoted the different regions for settlement. The Kansas Pacific, a.k.a. the Union Pacific Central Division, as well as others sponsored vigorous advertising campaigns to stimulate immigration and land sales. These promotional pieces advertised the improved quality of life gained by living on the prairie, away from the congestion of the East, while also telling of the modern amenities to be found in Kansas cities. An 1890 promotional brochure circulated by the Union Pacific Railroad Company described the features of the state's capital, Topeka—"the handsome public library building . . . excellent system of electric street railways . . . well paved [streets] and the city is provided with water-works, gas-works, and electric lights."[14] These marketing pamphlets and brochures spoke of the farming potential provided by rich soils and adequate rainfall. And they lured dedicated, hardworking individuals with the promise of a chance for real independence and a fresh start on the wide-open prairie. Railroad companies sold large acreages of land in Kansas and Colorado to domestic and foreign investors who then divided them into smaller parcels and resold them to people migrating to the West.

Promotional material provided by the railroads as well as individual towns and businesses proved critical to attracting both borrowers and investors. Mortgage bankers also provided information about local education, cultural institutions, civic organizations, and, most important, churches. Since the 1850s, Kansas has been a state of diverse religious convictions. Lawrence, Topeka, and Manhattan had unwavering abolitionist sentiments backed by strong Protestant communities. Ogden, St. Mary's, and Atchison developed vibrant European Catholic communities. Ogden, like many communities, also had a small but vibrant Jewish community, including the city's German

---

14 Union Pacific Passenger Department, "The Resources and Attractions of Kansas for the Home Seeker, Capitalist and Tourist" (Battle Creek, MI: Wm. G. Gage and Son, 1890), 13.

Jewish brewmaster. Everywhere along the railroads, American and European immigrants answered the call to settle the prairie.

But the Union Pacific and other western railroads had another reason to lure people westward. They had received substantial financial incentives—the most important of which were land grants—through the Pacific Railway Act of 1862 and its amendments that followed to build their lines. As the railroads pushed west, they needed to capitalize on those incentives as quickly as possible to repay the federal government and other investors. That meant selling their real estate and developing customers for their freight and passenger businesses. If they could sell their land to entrepreneurs such as Jabez Bunting Watkins in Kansas and Colorado developers, including James Duff of the Colorado Mortgage and Investment Company of London and Colorado governor Benjamin H. Eaton (1885–87), so much the better. But in the absence of institutional investors, selling land to small farmers throughout the West and carrying back the financing also made economic sense because doing so enabled the railroads to earn a steady rate of return while creating customers who needed to ship their commodities. In many cases the railroad companies also financed town lots and invested their own capital to build depots, shops, and yards. All of these activities created an economic stimulus for the towns that developed along the right-of-way.

As authorized by the Pacific Railway Act, alternate sections, each comprising 640 acres for a distance of twenty miles on each side of the right-of-way, were granted to the railroad companies. To sell those lands, the railroads demanded many of the same requirements of buyers as the government did of those claiming land under the Homestead Act. An 1880 brochure issued by the Union Pacific provided guidelines for prospective buyers in Nebraska. Eligible buyers had to be at least twenty-one years old and be US citizens or persons of foreign birth who had agreed to become citizens. Each could be granted up to a quarter of a section, which equaled 160 acres. Applications had to be made at the nearest US Land Office.[15]

These lands were divided into three principal categories. First and probably the most recognizable were farmlands. In general, those lands were located principally in Kansas, Colorado, and the Grand Valley of Nebraska. Grazing lands, which constituted the second category, were particularly prevalent

---

15 Union Pacific Railroad Company, Land Department, "Cheap Homes: Nebraska Farms Land Guide" (Lincoln, NE: Union Pacific Railroad Company, 1880), unnumbered.

in the states of Wyoming, Colorado, and Utah. Third were those considered wastelands, found across the various states and territories of the West. They earned the designation as wastelands because they held no potential for either agriculture or grazing. Ironically, some of those wastelands, particularly in Colorado and Wyoming, housed large reservoirs of coal deposits.[16]

The railroads advertised aggressively to fill in the empty prairie along the rights-of-way. A promotional brochure published by the Central Branch of the Union Pacific Railroad in 1879 claimed that "Every Man Can Own His Home." The brochure advised the purchaser on what to look for when purchasing land and set forth many of the same conditions that appeared in the Farm Mortgage Bankers handbook. The purchaser was advised to study the fertility of the land and the climate, as well as proximity to the railroad and to the best markets. In Kansas, the Union Pacific advertised that the available lands were 100 miles to 250 miles closer to viable markets than those offered by other land-grant railroad companies. The company claimed its land prices were the lowest of those of any company, ranging from three dollars to six dollars per acre. It also advertised 100 improved farms. Furthermore, all lands could be purchased with long-term credit.[17]

The railroad companies financed the purchase of these properties in much the same way as did farm mortgage bankers, and, as stated above, they applied many of the requirements demanded by the Homestead Act. Land was sold on the condition of the purchaser occupying and improving the tract for at least five years. To encumber the land with a mortgage, homesteaders only had to produce a receipt verifying that they had paid the minimum application and survey fees. Interest rates for such loans could be as low as 6 percent. At the end of the mortgage term, typically five to ten years, the buyer had to prove, essentially with the testimony of two witnesses, that he had complied with the law in regard to occupying and improving the land. Title to the land became as simple as obtaining a patent from the railroad company land office following receipt of the full final payment.[18]

The Union Pacific Railroad offered and advertised the availability of its Kansas landholdings for purchase on much the same terms as those advertised

---

16 Ibid.

17 W. F. Downs, "Farms and Homes in Kansas" (Atchison, KS: Central Branch of the Union Pacific Railroad Company Land Office, 1879), unnumbered.

18 Union Pacific Railroad, *Cheap Homes*, unnumbered.

in Nebraska. It offered liberal discounts to buyers who made cash purchases. The company also financed purchases over five- to seven-year terms that demanded interest-only payments to be made semiannually. The interest rate for such loans was 10 percent. The Union Pacific also offered buyers the option to make one or two principal installment payments at the end of each semiannual (July) or annual (January) period. The company required a cash down payment of twenty dollars for most of its financing plans. Special terms were offered to military veterans.[19] Such favorable financing terms broadened the buyer pool while developing potential customers who would ship their commodities on the railroad. At the same time, providing carry-back financing generated a market rate of return to the railroad with minimal risk. Thus the Pacific Railway Act provided a vehicle whereby public lands became private holdings and further stimulated both settlement of the West and expansion of the mortgage banking industry by inviting hardworking individuals to act on their dream of owning their own farm.

19 Downs, *Farms and Homes*, unnumbered.

2

Overview of Banks and Mortgage Banking in the United States

As a nation, the American people have endured a fractured and contentious relationship with banks and banking for over 250 years. From the days when Alexander Hamilton founded the First Bank of the United States in 1791 to the financial crisis of 2008 and its aftermath, the role of banks and other financial intermediaries has been and continues to be complicated and misunderstood. However, for our purposes it is important to understand and appreciate the history of the banking industry since the end of the Civil War because of the limitations placed on different types of banks, especially national banks, to allow them to participate in the real estate mortgage sector.

The term *bank* is often misused and misunderstood by the media and the public in general. In total, five types of banks conduct business in the United States. The public is most familiar with commercial banks, the institutions where most consumers and businesses deposit their funds, obtain credit cards, and borrow money to purchase everything from cars and trucks to houses. Thrift institutions such as federal savings banks, savings banks, and savings and loan associations are also depository institutions and closely

DOI: 10.5876/9781607326236.c002

resemble commercial banks. Historically, these institutions have made mortgage loans predominantly on homes, small apartment complexes, and some
student housing.

Distinct from commercial banks and thrift institutions that take in customers' deposits are three other types of banks: investment banks, merchant banks,
and mortgage banks. Investment banks assist individuals and corporations in
raising the capital necessary to start a new firm or to finance the operation
and expansion of existing firms. They also provide a broad menu of advisory
services to their customers. Investment banks do not offer checking or savings
accounts or issue credit cards. Instead, they make markets by offering trading desks for customers to access for the purchase of financial investments,
and they underwrite the sale and trading of stocks, bonds, and other financial
instruments. Other financial intermediaries that use the term *bank*, such as
merchant banks, are institutions that invest in the stock of privately owned
companies. Industrial banks virtually disappeared following the recession in
the 1980s. Now found in only a few states, they may take some deposits but
are limited in scope as to the types of consumer loans they can offer.

The 1864 National Banking Act established the office of the Comptroller
of the Currency, which charters and regulates national banks. But because of
the many restrictions placed on the new national banks, especially regarding
real estate investment, few state banks rushed to convert to national charters.
An unintended consequence was an explosion in the chartering and development of new state banks. As a result, a dual state and national banking
system emerged that still exists. Today, individuals who want to start a bank
can opt for a national charter or a state charter. In addition, an application for
a bank charter must be approved for insurance on its accounts by the Federal
Deposit Insurance Corporation. Membership in the Federal Reserve System
is mandatory for all national banks. Although membership is optional for
state-chartered banks, virtually all of them are also members of the Federal
Reserve System.[1]

Many economists believe this dual banking system stimulated competition and innovation between state-chartered and national banks. Regulations
imposed by the National Banking Act effectively forbid nationally chartered
banks to make mortgage loans, thereby granting state-chartered banks

---

1   Kenneth Spong, *Banking Regulation: Its Purposes, Implementation and Effects*, 5th ed. (Kansas City:
     Division of Bank Supervision and Structure, Federal Reserve Bank of Kansas City, 2000), 16.

greater authority for making real estate loans and thus allowing them to fill the gap and control much of the mortgage finance segment of the market.[2] And state-chartered trust companies had even greater powers than either state or national banks for direct investment in real estate and real estate mortgages. However, one advantage of a national charter was its prestige, which made the purchase of stock in a national bank more attractive.

Typically, state-chartered banks had more local investors than did national banks. For example, the officers and directors of the State Bank of Ogden Kansas were members of the community, like my grandfather Will Ratliff. They put their own capital at risk, whereas nonresidents owned about one third of the stock of all national banks in the Rocky Mountain states in 1889.[3] By 1913, when the Federal Reserve Act was passed, state banks were twice as numerous as national banks because the former required less capital investment and were allowed greater participation in mortgage lending.

The authors of the 1864 National Banking Act imposed the real estate restrictions to keep banks from carrying a concentration of long-term loans that could not be liquidated to meet depositor needs. The limitations also aided in controlling the credit and interest rate risks inherent in real estate loans. A loan term longer than five years could pose a serious threat to the safety and soundness of the bank if its cost of funds rose above the interest rate earned on the mortgage portfolio. That asset-liability mismatch, caused when the interest rate paid on depositors' accounts exceeds the rate earned by the bank's loan portfolio, contributed to the failure of the savings and loan industry in the late 1980s and continues to be problematic today.[4]

The limited real estate powers of national banks created a huge vacuum in agricultural financing in the late nineteenth century. The gap in the credit markets presented an opening for the development of the modern mortgage banking industry. Mortgage bankers originated, closed, funded, and delivered farm mortgages for investors in the United States, the United Kingdom, and Germany. During the period 1864 to 1912, some national banks circumvented the law by establishing outside loan offices or establishing their

---

2   Ronnie J. Phillips, *The Chicago Plan and New Deal Banking Reform* (Armonk, NY: M. E. Sharpe, 1995), 15.

3   Benjamin Klebaner, *Commercial Banking in the United States: A History* (Hinsdale, IL: Dryden, 1974), 58.

4   Spong, *Banking Regulation*, 67–68.

own mortgage and trust companies to compete for farm mortgages. In the absence of an affiliate, an outside mortgage company would pay a fee to the bank for the referral of farm loans, which, in turn, were sold to long-term investors.

State-chartered banks, devoted to serving their communities and agricultural interests, began to emerge in Kansas in the 1880s. In the absence of federal deposit insurance, state-chartered banks in Kansas subscribed to a privately sponsored deposit guarantee fund. According to an advertisement for the State Bank of Ogden, the insurance fund had a capitalization of $500,000. Responding to the needs of borrowers in the farming community, many states, such as Kansas, allowed their state-chartered banks to make longer-term loans than did national banks. However, many well-run banks, including the State Bank of Ogden, that provided such loans failed, in part because of their concentration of assets in their local communities and their minimal capitalization. Aggravated by the closure of banks, the agricultural community, led in many states by the Farmers' Alliance and the Populist movement, still continued to voice dissatisfaction regarding the availability and terms of credit; it advocated for the creation of a government-sponsored enterprise to provide credit on more favorable terms.[5]

The thrift industry is composed of building and loan associations, savings banks, savings and loan associations, and fraternal, neighborhood, and ethnic societies. The Philadelphia Savings Fund Society, founded in 1816, became the first savings bank in the United States. The first savings and loan, the Oxford Provident Building Association, established in 1831 in suburban Philadelphia,[6] operated independent of state regulation until 1860. By 1900 every state had passed some form of thrift regulation. Virtually the entire thrift industry restricted its lending activities to making home mortgages. Because of their charters, savings and loans received preferential tax treatment while building their reserves. Also, Regulation Q of the Federal Reserve Act allowed savings and loans to pay a higher return on savings deposits, giving them a distinct advantage over commercial banks in encouraging home ownership.

Savings banks, located mostly in the East, were restricted to purchasing municipal bonds and originating long-term mortgages that required large

5   Klebaner, *Commercial Banking*, 68–70.

6   David L. Mason, *From Buildings and Loans to Bail-Outs: A History of the American Savings and Loan Industry, 1831–1995* (Cambridge: Cambridge University Press, 2004), 17–18.

down payments. They were also limited to lending only in the state where they were chartered and were not able to purchase mortgages outside of their lending territory, usually about a 100-mile radius. The creation of the Federal Home Loan Bank System in 1932 and of the Federal Savings and Loan Insurance Corporation in 1934, which insured the deposits of both state- and federally chartered savings and loans, motivated the nationalization of the savings bank industry as individual institutions were required to join the Federal Home Loan Bank System. However, the 1980s savings and loan crisis virtually assured that they were no longer the primary specialists in the home mortgage lending industry because of the mismatch between the interest they were paying on current deposits and what they were receiving in interest on their mortgage portfolios. By 2014 there was no discernible difference to the consumer between commercial banks and savings and loans.

Mortgage bankers are, by the nature of their business, entrepreneurs who put their own capital at risk. Until passage of the Dodd-Frank Wall Street Reform and Consumer Protection Act (usually referred to as Dodd-Frank) in 2010, mortgage bankers were not regulated at the federal level. Over time, they have been licensed by a variety of state agencies, including state banking commissions, divisions of savings and loans, and the departments of commerce and real estate. In more modern times, residential mortgage bankers have been subject to a number of laws and regulations enforced by the Department of Housing and Urban Development (HUD), the Federal Trade Commission (FTC), and the Federal Reserve. Business practices have also been regulated by various government-sponsored enterprises (GSEs), including Fannie Mae, the Federal Home Loan Mortgage Corporation (Freddie Mac), the Federal Housing Administration (FHA), and the Loan Guarantee Division of the Veterans Administration (VA). Mortgage bankers' business practices are also regulated by various non-banking state agencies involved in consumer protection, such as the states' attorneys general.

EARLY DEVELOPMENT AND OPERATIONS OF MORTGAGE BANKING

Following the conclusion of the Civil War, westward expansion surged forward on the heels of the profusion of railroad development. The need for capital grew at a corresponding rate. Mortgage banking institutions filled the credit gap for foreign and domestic investors that could not be met by existing institutions that were either prohibited from making long-term loans on real estate or were too small to do so. Mortgage bankers responded by deploying the necessary long-term funds to expand industrial agriculture in the United States and Canada.

Thrifty and shrewd Scottish businessmen from Edinburgh and Dundee played a significant role in the development of the American West. They funneled surplus funds through English limited liability companies and investment companies based primarily in London. Most of those funds found their way into profitable investments in American agricultural enterprises. These sophisticated, savvy investors possessed the patience to withstand the ups and downs of economic cycles.[7]

Just as the United States established itself as the dominant world power from the early twentieth century to the present, Great Britain held that position during the nineteenth century. Noted western historian W. Turrentine Jackson explains that Britain required much less capital investment to industrialize than what was needed for resource-rich underdeveloped nations such as the United States.[8] Consequently, investment opportunities abounded in the United States during the closing decades of the nineteenth century compared with those in Great Britain. In addition, the US legal system, based on the sanctity of contracts and a corruption-free judiciary, provided certainty of title, thereby welcoming foreign investment in real estate development and mortgage loans.

As described in chapter 1, passage of the nation's land disposition and settlement laws and policies created a favorable environment for investment. The framework provided certainty of land ownership and a verifiable chain of title. Just as important, the survey system allowed for an accurate legal description of the land purchased and mortgaged. The United States developed the "lien system" of pledging real estate as security for a loan as well as reasonably consistent procedures for foreclosure in the event of a default, both of which added to the security of mortgage investors.[9]

---

7   W. Turrentine Jackson, *The Enterprising Scot: Investors in the American West after 1873* (New York: Routledge, 2000), viii.

8   Ibid.

9   Andra Ghent, *Research Institute for Housing America Special Report: The Historical Origins of America's Mortgage Law* (Washington, DC: Research Institute for Housing America, 2012), 15.

A number of foreign investment companies and trusts operated in the United States, particularly in the West. One such company was the Scottish American Mortgage Company. Founded in 1873, the company became fully capitalized in 1876 with the addition of new investors from Great Britain and the United States. Directors in both Edinburgh and America, along with a US advisory board, reviewed each application based on the recommendation of the local agent. Following an extensive approval process, the first mortgage loans, based on a 30 percent loan-to-value ratio and yielding 9 percent to investors for five- to seven-year terms, were closed and delivered in October 1874. Although it was a time-consuming process, it provided increased comfort and security for the investors. In 1879, as competition increased in Iowa and Minnesota, the company began investing in Kansas and Missouri through the mortgage banking firm Underwood and Clark of Kansas City.[10]

Competition escalated throughout the 1870s as Scottish companies searched for higher yields on their mortgages. Initially, they concentrated their investment activity in the upper Midwest states Minnesota and Iowa and, like the Scottish American Mortgage Company, later expanded into Kansas. Many of the firms operating in the Midwest had established themselves much earlier with investments along the Pacific Coast of California, Oregon, and Washington immediately following the discovery of gold in that region in 1848. These companies found success in the growing and prosperous agricultural landscapes of Washington and Oregon.

To make good investment decisions, foreign institutions needed a distribution system. That system relied on the financial intermediary we call mortgage banking. Farm mortgage bankers began to appear in the late 1850s. By the end of the Civil War their position as financial intermediaries was well established, and farm mortgage bankers practiced many of the same methods and principles as do today's mortgage bankers.

The organization and functions of mortgage banking houses have changed very little over time. Typically, the company structure consisted of a home office staff located in the eastern state where the company was licensed. It included individuals responsible for managing the origination and closing of loans. Generally, a staff lawyer reviewed the title evidence and prepared the mortgage documents. The typical mortgage company had a branch office

---

10 Jackson, *Enterprising Scot*, 15–19.

or retained a number of independent loan agents or brokers in its western territories. In addition, the company hired a team of traveling supervisors to manage the agency's relationship with others and to assure the quality and integrity of the loans delivered to the company. The traveling supervisor monitored not only the individual agents but also the overall quality of the real estate markets in locations where they invested. Supervisors also oversaw actions that arose as a result of loan defaults and foreclosures.

The home office also employed one or more individuals whose sole responsibility was to place the company's loans with investors. Through the years this critical role has remained of utmost importance. The individual in this position verifies that the correct loan rate and term are delivered to the investor as agreed, that all funds are properly accounted for, and that the credit analysis meets the terms of the agreement in the contract with the investor.

During the early years of farm mortgage banking, many loans were delivered on an individual basis by the branch office or the field agent and were processed by the mortgage banking firm before submission to the investor for final underwriting and approval. During the 1880s it became evident that this system was too cumbersome and inefficient. While some investors, such as insurance companies, continued to underwrite and purchase loans on an individual basis, many preferred to buy a mortgage debenture or "covered bond" with a number of agreements, warrants, and guarantees. A "covered bond" or debenture is a financial instrument created from mortgage loans or other debt obligations backed by a pool of loans. "Covered bonds typically carry a 2–10-year maturity rate and enjoy relatively high credit ratings, depending on the quality of the pool of loans ('covered pool') backing the bond. Covered bonds are often attractive to investors looking for high-quality instruments that offer attractive yields. They provide an efficient, lower-cost way for lenders to expand their business rather than issuing unsecured debt instruments."[11] These early mortgage-backed securities proved to be an attractive investment for individuals and institutions that lacked the internal structure to manage large flows of mortgage paper. When approached conservatively, the farm loan business model of incorporating a large number of small loans with low loan-to-value ratios worked well.

---

11   Investopedia, "Covered Bond," accessed May 11, 2014, http://www.investopedia.com/terms/c/coveredbond.asp.

Also in the 1880s, mortgage guarantee insurance companies began to develop in New York. These companies guaranteed the title to the property as well as the creditworthiness and performance of the borrower. Many of them survived until the Great Depression, when the real estate industry collapsed and many of these companies failed. Certainly, there were flaws in the development of third-party guarantees, but they have lasted into the second decade of the twenty-first century. Nevertheless, the lessons learned from the early mortgage banking and mortgage guarantee insurance companies provided the basis for the formation of the Home Owners Loan Corporation (HOLC) in 1933 and the FHA in 1934.

Today, the core of the mortgage banking business remains entrepreneurial. Mortgage banking firms must meet certain financial and legal requirements and adhere to prescribed industry standards of conduct. The key to the success of today's mortgage banker remains what it has been since the 1850s—to develop and retain the trust and confidence of the investor; the mortgage banker's moral character must be beyond reproach. The investor relies on a knowledgeable individual to provide informed and critical opinions on the economic and business conditions in his or her locality. Relationships based on trust and confidence remain the essential ingredient for the individual's or the firm's long-term success.

Kingman Nott Robins has professed that the farm mortgage banker of this period "must be a real banker, not a mere money lender, using business judgment, taking a sympathetic and cooperative interest in the affairs of his patrons, and strong enough to say 'no' when the collateral security tempts a violation of the principle, and bold enough to say 'yes' when the collateral security may be less inviting, but when the moral and economic hazard deserve assistance. The ideal banker is, if anything, rarer than the ideal farmer, but laws cannot do much to increase his breed."[12]

The farm mortgage banker's function was to work with a managing director or the investor's representative to make loans on real estate. The mortgage banker managed the loan portfolio through the initial application process to closing and then serviced the loan until curtailment or payoff. This

---

12 Kingman Nott Robins, *The Farm Mortgage Handbook: A Book of Facts Regarding the Methods by Which the Farmers of the United States and Canada Are Financed, Especially Intended for Investors Seeking Information Regarding Investments in Farm Mortgages* (Garden City, NY: Doubleday, Page, 1916), 13.

obligation required inspecting the property annually in addition to collecting the interest payment, either annually or semiannually.[13] Other responsibilities included verifying that the borrower maintained the proper level of insurance on the property and paid the local property tax.

Two overriding principles of underwriting mortgage loans apply as much today as they did in the 1870s. The first is to determine the borrower's ability to repay. That is, does the borrower have the character, capital, and capacity to meet his or her financial obligations, even if stressed? Second, is the value of the security ample for the investor to recapture what is owed to the institution in the event of foreclosure? In other words, can you sell it for what you have in it?

When evaluating the borrower, the farm mortgage banker would have followed the same process that is done today: completing a detailed loan application. First, determination of the purpose of the loan and how the funds would be used is critically important. Second, the borrower's financial condition needed to be assessed; this is known as the capacity criteria. Character and capital (cash on hand) were and continue to be critical ingredients. The farm mortgage banker was charged with determining how the individual measured up. In the days before credit reports, mortgage bankers surveyed local merchants to determine if the borrower paid his bills on time. In rural America at that time, the most likely merchants or individuals to be interviewed for that purpose were the owner of the general store, the proprietor of the seed and feed store, and the local county treasurer. Often, confidential references would be obtained from the borrower's banker and pastor, as well as a local judge or sheriff. Capital played a role in determining whether the borrower had established a pattern of savings by living within his means. In small-town rural America, an individual's reputation meant everything. A borrower would never enter into a loan agreement if there was any foreseen chance that he might not be able to fulfill his obligation to repay the loan; there was no such thing as allowing debt forgiveness to create a moral hazard.

One story I heard, attributed to a Depression-era mortgage banker, claims that the automobile contributed to the downfall of the industry. In the early

---

13   Investors structured almost all loans to include one payment of the entire principal amount at the end of the term of the loan, called a balloon payment. Until then, the borrower only made periodic annual or semiannual interest payments.

days, the farm mortgage banker traveled by horse and buggy to inspect his properties. While doing so, he spoke with all the farmers and ranchers in a given community. Neighborhood gossip provided information identifying which farmers might be becoming overextended, enabling the banker to more closely monitor potentially problematic loans. The arrival of the automobile eliminated old-fashioned personal interactions with the community at large, limiting the banker's inspections to his specific properties and thus eliminating the early warning system. No doubt, the overextension of credit was instrumental in my grandfather's decision to sell his interest in the State Bank of Ogden.

Assessing the value of the real estate to be used as security for the mortgage and the quality of the borrower's farm management abilities comprised the mortgage banker's third task. Three "references" would attest to the ability of the farmer and the value of the real estate. Even loans for amounts equaling only 30 percent to 40 percent of the value of the real estate offered as collateral still required an informed valuation opinion.

Robins's *Farm Mortgage Handbook* included these basics of underwriting guidelines for information to be included in the appraisals of farm loans in Iowa, Kansas, and Colorado:

1. Soils: a soil must be "capable of producing the staple crops in such quantity and with such expenditure for labor and preparation as will enable those cultivating it to compete on an equality with farmers in other sections" (164).

2. Climate: "adaptability to the cultivation of diversified crops . . . [with] sufficient uniformity of conditions . . . to minimize crop failures, [and] freedom from violent or destructive storms and floods"; adequate rainfall "to mature the staple crops and to furnish fodder for livestock, or that a deficiency must be supplied by a sure and adequate system of irrigation" (167–68).

3. Crops: "a diversified number of great staple crops—cotton, corn, the small grains and fodder crops . . . [for] supporting livestock." One-crop farming was deemed unsatisfactory (174).

4. Population: an "intelligent, industrious, economical, and progressive population" (177) is necessary to supply an adequate workforce to support agriculture.

5. Other factors included "a constant sustained demand for farmlands" (163),
   "open and fair laws and government and governmental services" (194–96),
   and "proximity to markets and transportation" (193–94). It was not considered prudent for an investor to make a loan on a property farther than
   twenty miles away from the railroad.

Even with solid underwriting, excellent servicing, and professional management, problems still occurred. Market unpredictability resulting in frequent panics, recessions, and depressions could and did cause a rash of foreclosures. Life issues such as unexpected illnesses and deaths created financial
hazards for borrowers. Failure to understand the environmental conditions of
the West, such as the droughts that led to the dust storms of the 1930s, posed a
risk to mortgage portfolios. Poorly thought-out public policy remedies, such
as foreclosure moratoriums and debt forgiveness, often created burdens on
lenders as well as borrowers. All of these objective and subjective factors
combined to challenge the intellectual and financial resources of mortgage
bankers as they sought to help Americans achieve homeownership. However,
it was the challenges of acquiring credit that farmers faced, especially in the
West and the South, that spawned the greatest changes in mortgage banking.

J. B. WATKINS LAND MORTGAGE COMPANY: AN EXEMPLAR

As many as several hundred companies were formed to channel private
American, British, and Scottish investments into rural credits and urban real
estate during the last three decades of the nineteenth century and the early
years of the twentieth century. Their involvement began in Illinois, providing
much of the funding to rebuild Chicago after the historic 1871 fire. These
investors then expanded into the farm loan sector; spreading across the
Midwest, they lent money in Minnesota, Iowa, and eventually Kansas. Most
of these companies reached their peak in the 1870s and 1880s. One such company was the J. B. Watkins Land Mortgage Company. But among Watkins's
biggest competitors were the railroad companies. Not only did they have
land to sell; they also had the resources to finance mortgage loans.

The J. B. Watkins Land Mortgage Company of Lawrence, Kansas, originally
J. B. Watkins and Company, became the largest and most prominent company in the region during this era. The company grew to dominance through

J. B. Watkins, founder of J. B. Watkins Land Mortgage Company of Lawrence, Kansas. Courtesy, Kansas State Historical Society, Topeka.

the origination and distribution of rural credits to investors in the United States and abroad.[14] An 1869 graduate of the University of Michigan Law School, Jabez Bunting Watkins began his career practicing law in Champaign, Illinois. His mortgage empire developed out of his early activities of collecting loans and acting as an agent for at least one insurance company.[15]

Having laid the foundation for his company in Illinois, Watkins moved to Lawrence, Kansas, in 1873. The explosion in railroad construction supported

14   Allan G. Bogue, "The Land Mortgage Company in the Early Plains States," *Agricultural History* 25, no. 1 (1951): 22.

15   Allan G. Bogue, *Money at Interest: The Farm Mortgage on the Middle Border* (Lincoln: University of Nebraska Press, 1955), 79–82.

westward expansion, making Kansas the perfect place to start a new mortgage business. Lawrence offered more lucrative mortgage loan interest rates
and fewer competitors. Many academic papers have studied the disparities
in interregional lending practices, especially in regard to interest rates. The
differences have been largely explained by the varying appetites for risk
attached to the unknown characteristics of newly settled areas. Within the
proven regions of Illinois and Iowa, the farm mortgage market was already
well-established and underwriting factors such as soil quality, climate, and
the proximity to markets were well-known. The unknowns of unsettled eastern Kansas justified investors' demand for higher interest rates. In addition,
Lawrence occupied an ideal location between the banking center of Kansas
City and the seat of government in Topeka. Lawrence's favorable mortgage
market and location combined with ready access to rail transportation and
reliable telegraph service to make the town of 7,000 an ideal community for
Watkins to establish his business.

Like the railroad companies, Watkins and the broader mortgage banking
industry also engaged in boosterism, the long established tradition of "selling"
their local community and state and their expertise to investors. Watkins utilized many of the same promotional marketing techniques employed by the
railroads to establish and grow his business in Lawrence. His practices have
come down in one form or another to the present day. Investors considered
the unemployment rate, the mix of industry and government employment,
taxation levels, and laws governing business operations and foreclosure procedures. They assessed the quality of education in the community, including
access to higher education; the availability of recreational opportunities; and
the variety of cultural institutions. Mortgage investors continue to incorporate these factors into their decision models when evaluating real estate
markets in which to lend.

One of Watkins's selling tactics included inviting investors to visit Kansas
to tour the farms and see for themselves the quality of his loans. According to
Allan G. Bogue, Watkins and other mortgage bankers of the time needed to
convince investors not only "that the farm mortgage was a superior investment
but also that Bloody Kansas and the Great American Desert were a myth."[16] A
century later, mortgage bankers in Colorado also found themselves needing

---

16 Ibid., 84.

to clarify their state's image and potential. Many people who had never visited Colorado thought of Denver as a city in the mountains blanketed by snow 365 days a year. They could not envision a bustling city on the open plains east of the Front Range warmed by Chinook winds. Separated by 100 years, both groups worked diligently to present 1870s Kansas and 1970s Colorado as rich, prosperous states populated by healthy, honest, hardworking people who took pride in their property and their community.

The practices used today in managing the back-room operations of the mortgage banker are the same ones used by Watkins's company and many others in the 1870s. While the credit decisions involved in loan closing and funding utilize the same architecture today, the custodial responsibility and function are also the same. Watkins's company packaged the note (the written evidence of debt), mortgage, deed of trust or bond (documents placing the property as security for money borrowed), title (legal description of the property verifying ownership and any other obligations against the property), and property information (information necessary for hazard insurance and documentation of real estate taxes) for delivery to the investor. Many individuals have correctly made the analogy that this process is a manufacturing function. In other words, each of these component documents must be assembled into one package for delivery to the investor; today's mortgage banking companies call this process *shipping*. Watkins often held on to groups of loans using his own funds or short-term borrowings until he sold them in a lot to an investor. Today, this action of holding on to groups of loans in lots is known as *warehousing*.

Watkins's services continued after loan approval and funding. As a loan servicer, he collected the scheduled payments and forwarded them to the investors. In addition, he ensured that the borrowers paid their taxes and maintained both insurance coverage and the property. Failure of the borrower to make the scheduled interest payments, to pay the taxes or maintain insurance, or to maintain the property (called the wasting clause) could trigger a foreclosure upon thirty days' notice.[17] Watkins's service package to the investor also included providing a detailed report with the results of annual inspections of the properties. He instituted a practice of guaranteeing timely payment of principal and interest or the repurchase of any loan in default and in doing so

---

17 Bogue, *Money at Interest*, 84.

assured investors of the return of their principal investment and interest. This practice worked well as long as real estate appreciated in value and farm prices rose or at least remained stable. However, this same practice caused Watkins's company to fail during the economic crises of the early 1890s.

Initially, Watkins operated his mortgage and real estate business as a sole proprietor. As he began to issue guaranteed debentures both at home and abroad and also began purchasing large tracts of land, he recognized the need to incorporate. So in 1883 the J. B. Watkins Land Mortgage Company incorporated in Colorado, even though it continued to maintain its operational headquarters in Lawrence. Colorado was one of the few states at the time that did not demand personal liability of stockholders. The law stipulated that financial liability be limited only to the value of stock or share ownership. Watkins capitalized the new corporation at $750,000 with 52,000 acres of land obtained through foreclosure, plus an additional $100,000 in liquidity.[18]

As the Watkins Company grew its business during the 1870s and into the 1880s, it opened offices in Dallas and other cities. From its home base in Lawrence, Watkins fed his investors' appetite for farm mortgages. To do so, his network expanded as far away as the Dakota Territory, and he began to move farther west along the Arkansas Valley and into other areas of western Kansas and eastern Colorado.

Notwithstanding the fact that Watkins had incorporated in Colorado, he did not open an office in the state until the spring of 1884. However, the Greeley office experienced a short life, closing in 1885. A more hazardous farming environment existed west of the 98th meridian, the semiarid region that stretched west of central Kansas. One great myth of late-nineteenth-century agriculture was that rain would follow the plow. As extended droughts demonstrated, rain did not follow the plow. Unfamiliarity with dryland farming along with more favorable cattle ranching opportunities in other areas may have caused Watkins to withdraw from Colorado. Undoubtedly, he and his investors did not possess sufficient knowledge of the necessary water storage and irrigation technologies, which in future decades would transform western Kansas and eastern Colorado into a highly productive agricultural landscape.

Generally speaking, by the 1870s and 1880s, guidelines for prudent lending principles existed, which the Watkins Company undoubtedly followed. Yet

---

18 Ibid., 126.

however well vetted the farmer, his land, and the community might have been, unpredictable factors could result in default. Extended droughts and insect infestations could cause crop failures, destroying a farmer's entire annual income. If such conditions persisted for several years, foreclosure was inevitable. Irrational exuberance and land speculation could also spell disaster; drought and speculation combined to contribute to the failure of the Watkins Company.

When Robins wrote his *Farm Mortgage Handbook* in 1916, it was clear that many of the risks involved in farm mortgage banking had been identified and some hard lessons had already been learned. Understanding the soil, suitability of crops, climate, and water were well understood by then. Information on the borrower's character and ability to repay was readily available. Proximity to transportation to move crops and livestock was critical. However, the environmental risks of hail, tornados, floods, droughts, grasshoppers, and locusts were unpredictable, as was the volatility of global commodity prices. One hazard that existed then and continues today is the ability to promptly recognize fraud and deceit on the part of borrowers and loan agents.

Whether in the field of farm mortgage banking during the 1880s or urban lending in the twenty-first century, the risks associated with mortgage lending are abundant; investors who assume those risks certainly need to understand and have confidence in whoever manages the assets. To its credit, the Watkins Company was a well-managed organization. The company put prudent policies and procedures in place and implemented the proper controls to make sure it was able to secure the soundest possible mortgage assets for its investors and the purchasers of its securities. Watkins was careful in searching out borrowers who were creditworthy. He recruited agents who were well-known in their communities, with good references and reputations. These were individuals with experience in the legal, banking, or real estate professions.

In the beginning, these agents were only allowed to take applications; the rest of the processing, underwriting, closing, and sale of the mortgage to the investor was handled at Watkins's corporate headquarters in Lawrence. Watkins insisted that to maintain the goodwill of the farming community, agents be prohibited from charging exorbitant fees. His agents were tutored and supervised by the company's traveling superintendents and inspectors.

The instruction of the agents can best be described as Agriculture 101. They were taught to examine and evaluate the size of the operation and to understand the differences between upland and bottomland, fenced versus unfenced, and cultivated versus uncultivated land. They stressed that the use of the land, whether for crops, orchards, livestock feeding and grazing, or timber, was equally important to the appraisal process. Just as important as the land itself, agents learned that the borrower's marital status and reputation in the community were also considerations when making the credit decision. The axiom of the company was that "he [Watkins] would loan only to responsible borrowers with ample security and unquestionable title."[19]

The issues of ample security and questionable title are the Achilles heel of the mortgage industry. Watkins had changed his views over time regarding lending to borrowers who would not receive their final patent for the land. Fraudulent transfers were as common on the frontier as they are today. Examinations of titles were typically done by abstractors or lawyers who would provide the Watkins Company with an abstract or summary of all ownership rights. Included in the abstracts would be a record of previous transfers of ownership, the release of prior mortgages, and the status of the current mortgage or lien. The abstractor or lawyer would render an opinion regarding whether the title was clear and merchantable. It was important for the company to know that its mortgage was in a first position and secured the loan with the first right to recover the asset in the event of foreclosure. Because of the growing volume and increasingly complex nature of real estate transactions, in 1876 the title insurance industry originated in Philadelphia. The purpose was to provide assurances and protection to purchasers of real estate or real estate securities against loss from forgeries, easements or rights-of-way, air and subsurface rights, and future interests.[20]

During this period, title insurance was underwritten by local companies and, later, trust companies depending on the state. After World War II, many of the state and local companies consolidated into large national underwriters of title insurance and distributed their products through local agents commonly called title companies. Many of these companies provided

---

19 Allan G. Bogue, "The Administrative and Policy Problems of the J. B. Watkins Land Mortgage Company, 1873–1894," *Bulletin of the Business Historical Society* 27, no. 1 (1953): 33–34.

20 American Land Title Association, *Title Insurance: A Comprehensive Overview* (Washington, DC: American Land Title Association, n.d.), 2–4.

information, closing and settlement services, and escrow services to the real estate and mortgage lending community. They were and are a vital part of the entire real estate industry. Those that were in the title business spun off their mortgage lending operations.

The issue of fraud remains an enormous problem for the industry and for policymakers. Multiple laws, regulations, and policing efforts have been instituted to prevent fraud. Notwithstanding all the due diligence, including character references and community reputation, fraud and misrepresentation are common yet extremely difficult to determine. Industry estimates of the existence of fraud in both prime and subprime mortgage loans that went into foreclosure during the Great Recession were substantial.

If ample security is part of the Achilles heel in determining the value of real estate, it is because the appraisal process has always been open to great misunderstanding. An appraisal is an opinion of value based on the market, income generated by a property, or cost of the property secured by the mortgage. It is a snapshot of a given market, on a given day, at a given time in the property's history. In Watkins's time, an appraisal was essentially the opinion of one or more informed professionals in the community. In frontier times the opinion on values or an appraisal in an area could be wrong, and problems might not be recognized until the property went into default. The weakness in the appraisal process at that time could have arisen because of fraudulent transfers, incompetence, incomplete market data, or a changing land-use pattern. Even in the twenty-first century, with the sophisticated statistical analytical tools developed by the industry, irrational exuberance and speculation cause problems in determining an opinion of value.

All of these issues in one way or another came to a head with the Watkins Company in 1880. The company had grown, and in spite of its controls, problems began to surface. The company began to do business in counties west of the 98th meridian. Most of these areas were settled in the 1870s when speculation ran rampant and issues concerning the validity of titles were questionable. An issue that plagued the industry in the 1880s and still exists today is unbridled optimism. The myth that real estate will always appreciate in value was as strong then as it was in 2008. The company hired an agent in Kingman, Kansas, named R. G. McClain, a former deputy sheriff with solid references from respected members of the community. However, many of the loans he originated contained forged documents. Loans were obtained for nonexistent borrowers and individuals living on unsettled government land. Miles Dart, the Watkins Company's superintendent, was able to get deputized in Kingman, and he arrested McClain.[21] With inflated appraisals and weak credits, the final blow came with the droughts of 1879 and 1880. Borrowers and agents worked to get generous loans to tide them over, loans that most could not afford. Compounding the problem were speculators who lost their equity and gave their land back to the Watkins Company, an action known today as *strategic default*.[22]

In the case of the Watkins Company, despite of all of its hard work and commitment to best practices, many of these problems were almost unavoidable. For a highly principled businessman, this was a hard lesson and a heavy burden for Watkins and his company. The risks and problems of lending, even by the most capable and cautious managers, could not avoid the inevitable cycle of risk and reward in conjunction with the weakness of human nature. While they understood the risk:reward equation, it is likely that Watkins's management team was unaware of or did not understand the environmental risks and drought cycles that plagued the Plains states. Such was the case again in 1887 when drought hit western Kansas and put the company in the unenviable position of taking back large tracts of land. The environmental consequences of the drought were not enough to spawn a cycle of foreclosures, but they did reveal a pattern of fraud in western Kansas. Suspicion grew that many of the homesteaders had not proved up their titles at the General Land Office, and these irregularities could cause those titles to be canceled. If that had happened, the land would likely have reverted back to the General Land Office, the mortgage extinguished, and the principal lost to either the company or its investor. But Watkins had an agreement with his investors assuring them against loss of principal, so there is no doubt that the company suffered significant losses.[23]

Things began spiraling out of control for the Watkins Company in 1889 and 1890. With the droughts recurring in western Kansas, foreclosures began to mount. The Watson Company had arranged lines of credit with eastern and Kansas City–based banks. These lines of credit were used to support the guarantees the company had made to investors and bondholders that they would not suffer any loss because the company would buy out defaulted loans and

---

21 Bogue, "Administrative and Policy Problems," 37–38.

22 Ibid., 39.

23 Ibid., 50–51.

pay investors the principal. By 1894 the company owned 250,000 acres of land, and Watson had assumed title to another 100,000 acres. The central factor in the failure of the J. B. Watkins Land Mortgage Company was its inability to understand the risks, mostly environmental, of its expanded territory. That lack of understanding coupled with insufficient cash reserves made it impossible for the company to convert the land into ready cash to meet its obligations. Watkins held on to the land and attempted to sell it for the highest possible price. But the banks had withdrawn their lines of credit, and as prices declined in the region, it was impossible to realize enough cash to meet his obligations.[24]

The company went into receivership in April 1894 and was never able to resume active business. Total liquidation was not completed until 1928. Bogue argued that "if Watkins' good faith was doubted by some investors in the 1890s, he was seemingly to vindicate himself during the liquidation, putting up additional property as security for the company's obligations . . . Finally, seven years after his [Watkins's] death, the liquidation was complete. The principal owed to debenture holders had been paid off with substantial amounts of interest. Of the major creditors only the stockholders received nothing for their claims."[25]

The hard lessons of the Watkins Company include (1) the realization that constant vigilance is required over the actions of even the most trusted employees and agents, (2) recognition of the risks inherent in the real estate lending process, and (3) an understanding of the economic and environmental issues that exist in the lending territory.

Overly ambitious speculation during the 1880s followed by droughts at the end of the decade and into the early 1890s led to the failure of the Watkins Company. Because of its guarantee to its investors to make good on all loans, the company took control of approximately 40,000 acres of farmland through foreclosure. This story of irrational speculation and a false belief in unlimited market expansion repeated itself on a national scale in 2005 and developed into an overly inflated real estate "bubble." But in that case, neither droughts nor plagues shared the blame; greed, reliance on technology, and the removal of experience and judgment from the equation resulted in the subsequent real estate market collapse and the Great Recession of 2008.

---

24 Ibid., 54.
25 Ibid., 56–57.

3

Mortgage Banking in Early Colorado

Until 1858, Colorado had been largely bypassed except for a few trading posts built to serve trappers. During the California Gold Rush, most migrants traveled across the Oregon Trail through Wyoming and on to the Pacific Coast. The Santa Fe Trail entered Colorado along the Arkansas River but turned abruptly south-southwest at Bent's Fort, dropping into New Mexico over Raton Pass. In 1858 the discovery of gold in Cherry Creek, near the future site of Denver, initiated the rush to the Rockies. Just three years later, in 1861, Congress created Colorado Territory out of the western counties of Kansas. In spite of the need for gold to support the Civil War effort and the influx of miners to the area, investment in Colorado progressed slowly until the conclusion of the war. However, a few visionaries saw the great potential of the future state and began laying the groundwork to build Colorado Territory.

Rapid growth during the 1870s and into the 1880s helped American investments become quite lucrative for British investors, particularly in Colorado. For decades, devastating fires were commonplace in urban centers around the country. In response to a fire that gutted much of Denver in 1863, the city

DOI: 10.5876/9781607326236.c003

adopted building codes that outlawed fire-prone building materials, thereby protecting real estate investments. Those codes made loans on Denver properties particularly attractive to out-of-state mortgage investors.

In addition, an excess supply of capital and a shortage of investment opportunities in Britain during these decades added to the attractiveness of US investments. The British and Scots held over 1,000 small loans in Indiana, Minnesota, Iowa, Dakota, and Kansas. Average loans ranged in value from $300 to $600 and were placed at 7 percent to 8 percent interest. By today's standards, these loans would fall under the category of micro-finance and were the harbinger of greater investments in the years to come.[1] British investors also sought out US government bonds yielding 7.5 percent compared with other foreign government bonds yielding only 4.4 percent. The performance of US railroad bonds also surpassed that of those elsewhere in the world.[2]

THE COLORADO MORTGAGE AND INVESTMENT COMPANY OF LONDON AND STATE BOOSTERISM

On February 24, 1877, the Colorado Mortgage and Investment Company of London (CMIC) registered in London as a joint-stock company under the British Incorporation Acts of 1862 and 1867. A joint-stock company is a business entity in which different amounts of stakes or shares can be bought and owned by shareholders; it closely resembles today's corporations and limited liability companies. According to the company's first prospectus statement, CMIC's primary purpose was to invest or lend money on real estate or on the first mortgage bonds of railways and municipalities in Colorado. The company was also empowered to invest up to one fourth of its subscribed capital in land and in developing properties it owned. Justifying the expansion into Colorado, the company's 1877 prospectus hailed the state's great potential for agriculture and stock raising, the opportunities for investing in land at favorable terms, and its mineral wealth, especially its extensive deposits of high-quality coal.[3] British

---

1   Jackson, *Enterprising Scot*, 36.

2   Ibid., 35.

3   Colorado Mortgage and Investment Company of London, *Reports of the General Meetings of the Colorado Mortgage and Investment Company of London, Limited; the Denver Mansions Company, Limited; and the Platte Land Company, Limited*, vols. 1–11 (London: Colorado Mortgage and Investment Company of London, 1877), 4–5.

investors in particular understood the importance of coal to the Industrial Revolution—the fuel for steam engines to power railroads and factories, to produce heat and electricity.[4] Without navigable rivers, Colorado would have to rely on railroads to transport all agricultural goods out of the state and to receive the finished goods that would line store shelves. Investment in land, agriculture, and railroads created a very promising business plan.

As a final lure to new investors the document also stated, "The climate is so healthful that Colorado has of recent years been recommended by physicians of the eastern states for persons in delicate health."[5] This and similar statements surely contributed to the immigration of many individuals suffering from tuberculosis and other respiratory diseases and spawned the building of sanitariums to treat the unfortunate. Lawrence Phipps, a former partner of Andrew Carnegie, was among the tuberculosis patients who sought treatment in Denver. He went on to represent Colorado in the US Senate from 1919 until 1931 and sponsored the construction and operation of Denver's Agnes Memorial Sanitarium for the Treatment of Pulmonary Tuberculosis. The Army Air Corp later acquired the sanitarium site for a training base and renamed the property Lowry Field, later known as Lowry Air Force Base. Following its official closing in 1994, Lowry has become one of Denver's most desirable in-fill neighborhoods with shopping, a community college campus, and recreational amenities, to say nothing of its Wings over the Rockies Air and Space Museum.

Sponsored by people of faith, the sanitariums of yesteryear exist today as some of the region's premier hospitals. The Sisters of Charity of Leavenworth, Kansas, founded St. Joseph Hospital in 1873—perhaps the oldest hospital in Denver. Another early healthcare facility in the city was St. Luke's Hospital, opened by the Episcopal Church in 1881. Initially built and funded by Denver's Jewish community, the nondenominational National Jewish Hospital for Consumptives (tuberculosis patients) received its first patient on December 10, 1899. Known today as National Jewish Health, it

---

4   Thomas G. Andrews, *Killing for Coal: America's Deadliest Labor War* (Cambridge, MA: Harvard University Press, 2008), 25–26.

5   Colorado Mortgage and Investment Company of London, *Prospectus Statement* (London: Colorado Mortgage and Investment Company of London, ca. 1877), 2.

enjoys a worldwide reputation for treating patients with respiratory diseases. Many others, including today's Swedish and Lutheran Hospitals, were founded under similar circumstances.

Most of these facilities were financed by charitable contributions; however, as the region grew, many institutions received financing from private contributors. Later, mortgage bankers such as Wheeler Kelly and Hagny Investment Company provided bond financing for the building of hospitals in Kansas. Similar financing methods were obtained by mortgage bankers in Colorado. Aksel Nielsen and Robert G. Boucher of the Mortgage Investment Company served on the board of Presbyterian Hospital. Boucher was on the board that negotiated the merger of Presbyterian and St. Luke's Hospitals and the sale to Health One in 1992.[6] Proceeds from the sale formed the Colorado Trust Foundation, which supports a wide variety of health initiatives across Colorado.

Although not directly involved, the contributions of investment capitalists such as CMIC to the region's early development created a catalyst for these charitable organizations to serve the citizens of Colorado. The mortgage banking industry's interest in hospitals led it to continue to use programs such as the Federal Housing Administration (FHA) and Ginnie Mae as financing tools. The industry urged the Colorado legislature to create the Colorado Health Facilities Authority in 1977 to provide a means for public and nonprofit healthcare facilities to access tax-exempt financing.[7] Fred Kirk of United Mortgage Company served on the board and Morris McDonald, a former chief operating officer of United Mortgage, acted as financial adviser to the authority.

JAMES DUFF, COLORADO'S FIRST MORTGAGE BANKER

The CMIC clearly performed all the functions of a mortgage banker, as stated in its initial prospectus. However, it also performed in much the same manner as today's investment banking/private equity firms and real estate investment trusts. The company acted not only as a first mortgage lender but also as a direct owner and developer of real estate. Furthermore, the company

---

6   Historical information for the hospitals was acquired from their websites. See the bibliography.

7   Colorado Health Facilities Authority, "Overview," accessed July 27, 2015, http://www.cohfa
    .org/overview.html.

empowered its general manager in Colorado, James Duff, with broad discretionary powers to make investments on CMIC's behalf.

Duff arrived in Denver from Forfarshire, Scotland, to serve as the company's first manager in 1877. Sophisticated, cautious, and formal in bearing, he had made an earlier trip to Denver before accepting the position with the British investment group.[8] Upon returning to Denver to assume his new position, Duff found that the landscape had changed and many more opportunities existed than he had originally imagined.

By today's definition, Duff should certainly be recognized as Colorado's first mortgage banker. While taking advantage of the investment value of prudently underwritten farm mortgages, he executed a more diversified business model than most other mortgage investment managers. He broadened the company's investments to include railroads, canals, and urban real estate. Duff's skill set included the ability to analyze railroad companies and their investments. Through him, on behalf of its British investors, the company indirectly financed the Denver and Rio Grande Railroad Company by purchasing its bonds. One of CMIC's subsidiaries, the Denver Mansions Company, undertook the development of the Windsor Hotel and the Barclay Block office building on Larimer Street that housed the CMIC offices as well as the Colorado legislature until completion of the capital building. The Platte Land Company and the Larimer and Weld Irrigation Company were just two of several CMIC affiliates responsible for rural land and water projects in northern Colorado. The company entrusted Duff with assessing the potential profitability of each of these investments and, if approved by the board of directors, with the oversight of every endeavor undertaken during his time in Colorado.

Duff also reached out to other investment companies to partner with CMIC on select projects. The Dundee Land Investment Company, founded in 1878, declined an offer to join the CMIC in financing a Platte Land Company project. The plan included the purchase of 300,000 acres of land in northern Colorado from the Kansas Pacific and Denver Pacific Railroads, construction of a canal system to irrigate the land, and finally the sale of farmlands served by the system. Declining the offer meant the Dundee Land Investment Company passed up the opportunity to invest in some of the most productive

---

8   Jane E. Norris and Lee G. Norris, *Written in Water: The Life of Benjamin Harrison Eaton* (Athens: Swallow/Ohio University Press, 1990), 125.

farmland in America.[9] The Dundee Company may have decided that the risk level associated with the project was too high, or it may have decided that there was no need to expand into Colorado when it was enjoying continued success in the Pacific Northwest.

Contemporaries described Duff as an energetic and enterprising man who quickly earned the respect and friendship of many in the Denver business community. In his obituary published on April 19, 1900, the *Denver Republican* quoted Duff's friend Hugh Butler, who described Duff as a man who thought more about Denver's interests than anyone else of his time. Duff imagined Denver as a great city in need of the same high-quality amenities found in other great cities around the world.

A true visionary, Duff ignored the naysayers who claimed his plans for the Windsor Hotel were overly ambitious, that it was too big and could not turn a profit. A Denver Mansions Company project, the Windsor opened in 1880 as the city's first luxury hotel. Duff reportedly paid $100,000 for the hotel's site, which included nine city lots. He spent an additional $350,000 to build the hotel. Duff was committed to building a first-class facility with modern conveniences of hot and cold running water, elevators, and an adequate sewage system.

Upon its completion, Duff turned the management of the hotel over to the Colorado firm Tabor, Bush, and Hall. Horace Tabor, Colorado's Silver King, had amassed a fortune from his mines in Leadville. That wealth allowed him to invest in equally lucrative real estate ventures. Tabor and his partners spent an additional $200,000 to get the Windsor in running order, a risky venture for a city with a population of just 36,000 in 1880. Over the years, guests included four presidents and numerous celebrities. One of Denver's many urban legends tells of a tunnel beneath Eighteenth Street that connected the hotel to the Barclay Block. Guests utilized the tunnel to move unseen between the Windsor and the spa and steam baths housed in the Barclay Block building. In the late 1950s, documentation provided by the Public Service Company and the Mountain States Telephone Company validated the presence of this and several other tunnels beneath Denver's streets.[10]

Duff ignored similar pessimistic prophecies about the Barclay Block office building; after completion, it housed the offices of CMIC and other

---

9   Jackson, *Enterprising Scot*, 30–32.

10   Louisa W. Arps, *Slices of Denver* (Denver: Sage Books, 1959), 142–43.

businesses as well as the Colorado legislature for over a decade until construction of the Capitol Building reached completion. His optimistic vision about the future of Denver never faded.

Duff was also a visionary about the potential of Colorado agriculture. It appeared obvious to him at the time that for Colorado and the City of Denver to prosper, the economy needed a strong agricultural component. For that to develop, water had to be delivered to more land. His involvement in financing irrigation projects in Arapahoe, Weld, and Larimer Counties proved instrumental in the success of the region's farms.[11] He found good fortune and a strong partner in Benjamin H. Eaton, who later became Colorado's fourth governor. Eaton held contracts to purchase land adjacent to the Denver Pacific Railroad in Larimer and Weld Counties. The two men saw the possibility of immense profits from the sale of irrigated farmland. In 1879 they joined forces on construction of the Larimer and Weld Canal, also known as the Eaton Ditch, which diverted water from the Cache la Poudre River. When completed, it was the largest and longest irrigation canal in the state.[12]

The following year, CMIC created another subsidiary, Northern Colorado Irrigation, which built the less successful High Line Canal project designed to transfer water from the South Platte River to nearby farmlands and dairies. As conceived by Duff and Eaton and designed by Edwin Neddleton and Elwood Mead,[13] water for the canal was diverted by a rock dam into a tunnel and flume in the South Platte River Canyon.[14] The canal transported water through the foothills and along the crest of the South Platte River basin, which houses metropolitan Denver. After traveling seventy-three miles, it completes its run in Adams County near Denver International Airport.

Even though the canal had the capability to distribute water to a large area, two elements conspired to limit the High Line's success. First, the Prior Appropriation Doctrine in the state's constitution allowed for water usage based on time of appropriation. Those holding older rights to the water were

---

11 The City of Denver and Denver County were originally part of Arapahoe County. Denver County was created in 1905 by carving out a portion of Arapahoe County.

12 Norris and Norris, *Written in Water*, 140–46.

13 Professor Elwood Mead, a water and civil engineer, created the nation's first civil engineering and irrigation course at the Colorado State Agricultural College, now known as Colorado State University, in Fort Collins.

14 Norris and Norris, *Written in Water*, 140.

The High Line Canal, Denver, 1938. Courtesy, History Colorado, Denver.

allowed their entire allotment before holders of newer rights could use any water. Second, winter snowpack fed the canal. During years of low snowfall, very little water flowed into the canal. By midsummer, the water level in the canal could be measured in inches, too little to irrigate crops. On the back of a 1938 photo of the canal, a commentator and wandering photographer lamented the passing of the High Line Canal and its return to its desert roots.

However, Mead and Neddleton's engineering marvel has survived into the twenty-first century. When water levels allow, the High Line Canal still provides water to over thirty customers of the Denver Water Board, including the historic Fairmount Cemetery. Today, the High Line runs through seven political jurisdictions, provides a wide range of recreational resources, and proudly carries the distinction of a National Heritage Trail. While many projects of the CMIC and the Denver Mansions Company have been razed and replaced, the High Line Canal remains as physical evidence of James Duff's lasting legacy.

The water in the canal was instrumental in the development of the Crestmoor, Hilltop, and Montclair neighborhoods on the east side of Denver. One of the attractions of these neighborhoods was their parks and

The original Denver Club building, which opened in 1889, sits in the foreground of the Denver landscape near the turn of the century. Courtesy, History Colorado, Denver.

parkways, which would not have been possible without the High Line. Today, walkers, runners, cyclists, and others enjoy the trails that line many stretches of the canal, and its vegetation provides habitat for an abundance of birds and other wildlife.

A true mortgage banker, Duff was one of many individuals who became major civic leaders; their legacies are evidenced in the success and accomplishments of Colorado's major institutions, as well as many residential and commercial developments found throughout the state. As a charter member of the Denver Club, Duff was instrumental in the construction of the club's original building at Seventeenth and Glenarm Streets. A beautiful red sandstone building, the structure was demolished in the 1950s. The new Denver Club Building, a twenty-plus-story office building constructed by John Murchison, an oil man from Texas, now occupies the site. To induce the club to sell the property, Murchison gave it a ninety-nine-year lease for the two top floors of the building, which command a majestic view of the Front Range and the Rocky Mountains looming in the background.

Duff's visionary community involvement and the broad scope of his investments on behalf of CMIC helped establish Denver as the financial center of the Rocky Mountain region, a position the city maintains over a century later.

OTHER INVESTORS AND THEIR HISTORIC DENVER PROPERTIES

Second only to his friend James Duff, Henry R. Wolcott became one of Colorado's most prominent and influential mortgage bankers, importing vast amounts of capital. After arriving in the state in 1869, he quickly became involved in mining, holding management positions at several smelters—including the Argo Smelter—before becoming treasurer of the Colorado Smelting and Mining Company. His mining expertise led to his serving as vice president of the Colorado Fuel and Iron Company owned by the Rockefeller family, which owned and operated numerous coal mines across the state. By the mid-1870s he also sat on the board of directors of the Equitable Life Assurance Society of the United States (Equitable) and represented the company as agent for its Colorado investments. He also spent a decade as vice president of the First National Bank of Denver. Those positions solidified his connections with the New York financial community and enabled him work with David H. Moffat to obtain the necessary financing for the construction of two of Denver's iconic buildings, the Boston Building and the Equitable Building. Construction of the Equitable Building at Seventeenth and Stout Streets required an investment by the company of $1.5 million. The building still stands and remains the cornerstone of Denver's Seventeenth Street financial district.[15]

Wolcott's civic involvement included joining James Duff in founding the Denver Club; he became its first president. Wolcott also became involved in state politics, representing Gilpin County in the state senate at the same time his brother Edward was representing Clear Creek County. Wolcott's many endeavors made him instrumental in the development of Denver real estate and Colorado's economy during the closing decades of the nineteenth century into the early years of the twentieth century.

David H. Moffat was another of the earliest and most important contributors to the development of Colorado. In financial circles, Moffat was almost a mirror image of Wolcott. Both held pivotal positions with the First National Bank of Denver (First National), which served as the bank for CMIC and

---

15   Lyle W. Dorsett and Michael McCarthy, *The Queen City: A History of Denver*, 2nd ed. (Boulder: Pruett, 1986), 71–75.

The Equitable Building, ca. 1900, has changed very little over its 120-year history. Courtesy, Denver Public Library.

continued to be the principal bank for the mortgage banking industry in Colorado through the 1990s. Like Wolcott, Moffat also served as a director of the Equitable Life Assurance Company. As a major stockholder of Equitable, he almost certainly joined Wolcott in obtaining mortgage financing from the company for multiple Denver-area developments and in the company's decision to not only open an office in Denver but also to build the impressive Equitable Building. A few years after its completion, Moffat followed other distinguished local businesses by relocating First National Bank to the Equitable Building.[16]

Moffat's collaboration with others in addition to Wolcott contributed greatly to the growth of Colorado. He joined forces with former territorial governor John Evans in spearheading the construction of a rail line in 1869 that connected Denver to the Union Pacific Railroad by way of Cheyenne, Wyoming. He also partnered with Jerome B. Chaffee,[17] investing in and assum-

---

16   Kathleen Barlow, "Spirits and Scandals on 17th and Stout Streets," Center for Colorado and the West at Auraria Library, accessed February 5, 2015, https://coloradowest.auraria.edu/content/equitable-building.

17   Chaffee became one of the first US senators to represent Colorado after it achieved statehood; he served from November 1876 until March 3, 1879.

ing oversight responsibilities for over 100 gold, silver, and coal mines across the state.[18] Moffat's excellent stewardship of First National as its cashier, a position he assumed in 1867, led to his succeeding Chaffee, the bank's first president, in 1880; he held the position for nearly thirty years. Under Moffat's guidance, the bank selectively invested in mining, railroads, real estate, and other ventures—enabling the bank and its investors to weather the financial crisis of 1893 and the silver crash that crippled Colorado's economy.

Many East Coast investors joined CMIC and the others in their rush to invest in Colorado during the last quarter of the nineteenth century. Denver proved an especially attractive market. Andrew Morrison's 1890 regional economic report estimated that in 1888 the industry imported $19 million in mortgage activity. The report favorably compared Denver real estate with real estate in Kansas City, Minneapolis, and St. Paul. The real estate firm of John M. Berkey, established in 1870, brought a significant amount of eastern capital to Denver. The oldest active real estate firm in the state at the time of the 1890 report, its investors provided $400,000 for development of the Boston Block at Seventeenth and Champa Streets.[19] For many years the building headquartered the city's most influential investment banker and stockbroker, Boettcher and Company. Today, much of the Boston Block has been converted into loft apartments, a transformation financed by the Colorado Housing and Finance Authority. The beautiful Mining Exchange Building, financed and built by Equitable in 1891 at Fifteenth and Arapahoe Streets, was razed during the Skyline Urban Renewal Project of the 1960s and 1970s. The sandstone and granite landmark of the mining heritage was replaced by the Brooks Towers Buildings, also financed by Equitable.

The legacies of numerous investment companies and individuals can be found throughout Denver. They have survived the economic stresses of depressions, wars, and urban renewal. Many are included on the National Register of Historic Places. Among them, Morrison's report discusses the Chamberlain Observatory in Observatory Park, now owned by the University of Denver. Financed by the Chamberlain Investment Company,

---

18 *Colorado Business Hall of Fame: David H. Moffat*, Junior Achievement–Rocky Mountain Inc. and the Denver Metro Chamber of Commerce, accessed September 14, 2014, http://www.coloradobusinesshalloffame.org/david-h-moffat.html.

19 Andrew Morrison, ed., *The City of Denver and State of Colorado* (St. Louis: Geo. Engelhardt, 1890), 52.

at the time it was "the highest station of its kind on earth."[20] Eastern capital financed both the Masonic Temple, built in 1889 for $250,000, and the Kittredge Building, built in 1891 for $200,000. Trinity United Methodist Church, at the corner of Eighteenth Street and Broadway, cost $250,000 to construct in 1888. Each of these buildings demonstrates a belief in the permanence and potential of Denver and Colorado that engulfed investors during the closing decades of the nineteenth century.

However, only Henry Cordes Brown's beliefs matched the vision of James Duff. Brown arrived in Denver in 1860 and almost immediately began purchasing property. Over the years he accumulated a vast fortune by selling his real estate investments as they appreciated in value. His stalwart faith in Colorado prompted him to donate to the state the land on which the State Capitol building now stands. But his legacy is best demonstrated by the iconic Brown Palace Hotel. Begun in 1888, the same year Trinity United Methodist Church held its first services, Brown invested $1.6 million constructing the luxury hotel, which took four years to complete. He spent another $400,000 in furnishings, bringing the total cost to $2 million, an astronomical sum for the time. Brown would be pleased to know that his hotel continues to maintain its reputation as one of Denver's most prestigious luxury hotels and that it, too, is included on the National Register of Historic Places.[21]

The year 1888 was significant for another reason. Not only were several historic buildings either completed or under construction in Denver and the city achieved a record dollar volume in mortgage investment, but 1888 marked the founding of the Denver Real Estate Exchange. Eventually evolving into the Denver Board of Realtors (DBR), the organization functioned "for the purpose of regulating sales, exchanges and loans, and other real estate transactions."[22] Twenty years later its national counterpart, the National Association of Real Estate Exchanges, opened its doors. It adopted its current name, the National Association of Realtors (NAR), in 1974. Since its inception, the organization has contributed immensely to the development of the real estate and

---

20 Morrison, *City of Denver*, 40.
21 "An Exceptional Heritage among Denver Luxury Hotels," the Brown Palace Hotel and Spa, accessed February 8, 2015, http://www.brownpalace.com/About-the-Brown/From-the-Archive.
22 Dorsett and McCarthy, *Queen City*, 69–75.

mortgage lending industries. In 1913 it adopted a Code of Ethics.[23] During the 1930s the National Association of Real Estate Boards established the American Institute of Real Estate Appraisers and the Institute of Real Estate Management to provide industry education and respond to the problems created by the Crash of 1929 and the subsequent Great Depression. Evolving out of the real estate and mortgage lending industries of the nineteenth century, both the DBR and the NAR continue to provide member support and training in state-of-the-art practices for all facets of the real estate industry.

---

23 National Association of Realtors, *Realtors® Celebrate 100 Years of Professionalism in Real Estate,* November 7, 2013, accessed May 5, 2014, http://www.realtor.org/news-releases/2013/11 /realtors-celebrate-100-years-of-professionalism-in-real-estate.

Part II

MORTGAGE BANKING IN A
MODERN FINANCIAL NETWORK

4

Thrifts, Trusts, and Title Companies as Participants in the Mortgage Market

THE THRIFT INDUSTRY

While the roots of the American mortgage banking industry lie in agricultural lending, individuals and ethnic and social organizations funded most residential mortgage loans after the Civil War up until the savings and loan crisis in the late 1980s. To a large extent, these mutual organizations emulated similar institutions founded in Great Britain during the eighteenth century as part of the self-help movement. Homeownership and thrift were seen as ways to improve the lives of working-class men and women and to alleviate the social ills brought about by the Industrial Revolution. Another outgrowth of the social reform movement was the creation of the mutual savings bank in 1804.[1]

Colonial America did not need a home mortgage finance system. Land was cheap, if not free, and building materials were readily available. During the first Industrial Revolution in the early nineteenth century, however, the

---

1   Mason, *Buildings and Loans*, 12–15.

DOI: 10.5876/9781607326236.c004

need for housing for the expanding populations of cities like New York and Philadelphia outstripped the ability of private sources to meet the demand.[2]

Responding to the need, in 1816 the Philadelphia Savings Fund Society—the first US mutual savings bank—was founded. The society became the largest of these thrift organizations in the country and lasted into the 1990s. Other early mutual savings organizations include Emigrant Savings Bank, founded in 1850 in New York, and the Harlem Savings Bank, now known as Apple Savings Bank, which followed in 1863. These organizations supplied large sums of mortgage capital in their communities in the East by gathering and investing the savings of their members, many of whom were working-class laborers. Later, when northeastern states became capital-surplus areas, they also became large purchasers of mortgages in the West when changes to their charters and regulations allowed them to invest out of state. The structure of the mutual savings bank as a cooperative institution served as a blueprint for the formation of the nation's building and loan societies, savings and loan associations, and other thrift entities in that all of these organizations are owned by their depositors.

Colorado's building societies began to emerge in the 1880s. Two of the earliest were the Denver Home and Savings Association and the Capital Building and Loan Association. The depositors owned both of these mutual associations. These organizations became major lenders in working-class neighborhoods, such as the communities developed along South Broadway in Denver. Two classes of membership existed in these early building societies: depositing members and borrowing members. Shareholders owned the assets on a pro rata share basis. Furthermore, a weekly payment of twenty-five cents per share of stock owned was required from depositing members; dividends were distributed semiannually. Loans, based on the available accumulated deposits, were issued only to borrowing members. All loans required review and approval by the societies' trustees.

Colorado's most revered building and loan association had its roots in the ethnic communities of Central City and Denver. In April 1885 three building societies—the Albion, Cambrian, and Caledonian—composed of English, Welsh, and Scottish members, met and agreed to form the Cooperative Building and Loan Association. A significant contributor to the association's

---

2 Ibid., 20.

early success was its relationship with employees of the Argo Smelter and other workers in the north Denver neighborhood. Argo Smelter had an employee payroll withholding savings plan designed to help workers purchase a home.[3] David Seerie received the first loan from the association for $1,000 at 9 percent interest. Typically, the association funded loans for borrowers like Seerie in amounts up to 60 percent of the value of the property.

In 1934, two years after the founding of the Federal Home Loan Bank System, the Colorado Building and Loan Association received Denver's first federal savings and loan charter, triggering a name change to First Federal Savings and Loan Association of Denver. The organization survived panics, the Great Depression, multiple wars, and the collapse of the savings and loan industry in 1988–89. Only three presidents led First Federal: its founder, Joseph Collier; his son; and later his grandson, Malcolm "Bud" Collier. The company's lending strategy focused on the origination of mortgages for traditional one- to four-family residential properties, limited multi-family residences, and a small number of commercial real estate loans within its market areas. First Federal's officers and directors frequently spent their Saturdays participating in neighborhood events and festivals. The development of close relationships with its borrowers and active participation in community events across its market combined with conservative underwriting standards to create an effective risk management tool for the company. The institution retained its management, even though it changed names and operating status twice before being sold to Commercial Federal Savings and Loan in 1998.[4] Commercial Federal has since been sold to the California-based and French-owned Bank of the West.

By the 1950s, many of the ethnic societies had disappeared. One that remained active into the 1970s served Denver's Slovenian community. Like First Federal, it was located on West Thirty-Eighth Avenue. The organization provided small first and second mortgages to its members. Denver also had an African American thrift, Equity Savings, located for many years in the North Park Hill neighborhood. Credit unions are similar in structure,

---

3   L. B. Reed, *The First Hundred Years: A History of Federal Savings Bank and Its People since Its Organization on April 25, 1885* (Lakewood, CO: First Federal Savings Bank, 1985), 3.

4   In 1983, the change from a savings and loan association to a federal savings bank resulted in the adoption of First Federal Savings Bank of Colorado as the company's name. In 1995 it was renamed First Federal Bank of Colorado.

but until recent years they were not major mortgage lenders because of their limited size. One exception was Pueblo's Mount Carmel Credit Union, a significant lender that provided mortgages for steelworkers employed by Colorado Fuel and Iron.

In 1966, while Denver was experiencing a minor foreclosure crisis result-ing from cutbacks at the Martin Company—a national leader in aerospace, cement, aggregates, electronics, and chemicals industries—the first round of disintermediation occurred. Disintermediation happens when funds from one financial instrument, attracted by a higher rate of interest or other more favorable terms, flow to another financial instrument. When the rate on US three-month treasury notes rose above 4 percent, funds began to move from insured accounts to US treasuries.[5] This event was considered a major disrup-tion in 1966. Even though the Denver housing economy took additional time to recover, this move in the market would pale in comparison to the levels of disintermediation created by the high rates of inflation that resulted in mortgage rates as high as 17 percent during the 1980s.

This asset liability mismatch problem lasted through the end of the 1980s and became a major contributing factor in the collapse of the savings and loan industry. Despite various reforms to mitigate the effect of the US Treasury as a competitor to local banks and savings and loans, the die was cast. The Treasury's 1968 decision to issue thirty-year bonds caused the desta-bilization of the asset base. The unintended consequence was the destruc-tion of the value of the savings and loans' portfolios; bonds were considered a better investment, so depositors moved their funds from thrifts to invest in thirty-year bonds. Consequently, between 1986 and 1995, almost a third of all thrifts failed.[6]

TRUST COMPANY ACTIVITIES

There has been little examination of the role trust companies played in the real estate finance industry. During the 1890s, trust companies emerged as a finan-cial intermediary in US capital markets. Trust companies took on multiple

---

5   Richard K. Green and Susan M. Wachter, "The American Mortgage in Historical and Interna-tional Context," *Journal of Economic Perspectives* 19, no. 4 (2005): 97–100.

6   Timothy Curry and Lynn Shibut, "The Cost of the Savings and Loan Crisis," *FDIC Banking Review* 13, no. 2 (2000).

roles. They served as banks, insurance underwriters, mortgage bankers, bond underwriters, and document custodians in addition to functioning as developers and managers of real estate. Their unique position resulted from the restrictions on real estate lending placed on national banks by the National Banking Act of 1864. In combination with the National Banking Act of 1863, the primary goals of the acts were to establish a system of national banks and a national currency.[7] But the 1864 act also severely limited the activities of national banks regarding real estate transactions and the holding of mortgages. Later, as regulations began to change and evolve, banks continued to possess very limited real estate powers and in fact were unable to match short-term, volatile deposit liabilities with long-term fixed-rate mortgage assets. For the most part, these trust companies and state-chartered banking institutions catered almost exclusively to a wealthier clientele.[8]

Controversy surrounding the role of trust companies stretches back almost to when they entered the market in the 1890s. According to economic historian Larry Neal, once trust companies gained the authority to receive deposits and invest in securities on behalf of their clientele, they began to move away from their traditional lines of business—life insurance, fire insurance, safety deposits, and title insurance. Neal cited Alfred B. Noise's argument that the expansion of trust company activities occurred because the number of national banks, while increasing, was still insufficient to handle the rapidly expanding volume of trade. Noise also commented on the fact that trust companies paid interest on their clients' deposits while banks did not.[9]

Additional concern about trust companies arose because many felt their reserves were insufficient to withstand an economic recession. However, during this period, many of the larger money center–based trust companies had a stronger capital structure than did some national banks.[10] But even with the creation of new financial instruments such as commercial paper

---

7   Edward Flaherty, "National Banking Acts of 1863 and 1864," in *American History: From Revolution to Reconstruction and Beyond,* accessed May 9, 2014, http://www.let.rug.nl/usa/essays/general/a-brief-history-of-central-banking/national-banking-acts-of-1863-and-1864.php.

8   Larry Neal, "Trust Companies and Financial Innovation, 1897–1914," *Business History Review* 45, no. 1 (1971): 35–36.

9   Ibid., 38.

10 Money centers are locations in cities such as New York, Boston, and London, where major investment companies, banking institutions, and corporations are headquartered or maintain offices. Wall Street is the money center of New York.

(short-term loans of thirty–ninety days) to meet the credit needs of a grow-ing economy, some trust companies failed during the Panic of 1907 while others adapted their business practices and survived.[11] Chicago Title and Trust Company was one of the companies that elected to remain in the title insurance business, continuing as one of the nation's leading title insurance companies until the merger mania of the early 2000s. In the 1970s, Chicago Title purchased Kansas City Title and Trust, the company responsible for the US Supreme Court decision that validated the constitutionality of gov-ernment-sponsored enterprises. However, one company that does continue today began as the Wheeler Kelly and Hagny Company (WKH).

WHEELER KELLY AND HAGNY INVESTMENT COMPANY

In 1894, Howard Wheeler founded the WKH in Wichita, Kansas. Established only twenty-one years earlier, Wichita already had a reputation as a cattle and railroad town. Against that background, the company soon became one of the leading firms in Kansas, specializing in mortgage financing, real estate, and insurance. Wheeler based his company's success on excellent customer service and the relationships he built with clients based on trust. The com-pany's first customer wanted to secure a $500 first mortgage, but WKH did not have enough money to fund the loan. Determined to satisfy his clients' needs, Wheeler quickly solicited several potential private investors. He found one individual who agreed to purchase the loan, and the transaction closed the following day. Satisfying his clients' needs was tantamount to Wheeler's success then and continues to be an integral component of the company's business plan today.

WKH participated fully in Wichita's economic development. As the com-pany grew over the years, a number of prominent community members invested in it. Because Wheeler had been chosen by so many citizens of Wichita as their trustee to advise them on an array of financial matters and there was an attendant demand for trust services, the company reorganized as Wheeler Kelly and Hagny Investment Company. Having survived the Great Depression, two world wars, and the Korean conflict, the company liq-uidated its trust business in 1953 to focus on its real estate and mortgage facets.

---

11   Neal, "Trust Companies," 39–40.

Building THE HILLCREST HOMES IN WICHITA BROUGHT FORTH A WHEELER KELLY HAGNY BOND ISSUE OF $600,000. THE SECURITY WAS SO AMPLE THAT UPON COMPLETION OF THE BUILDING, THE ENTIRE ISSUE WAS CALLED AND THE LOAN PLACED WITH THE PRUDENTIAL INSURANCE COMPANY OF AMERICA, ONE OF OUR INVESTMENT CLIENTS. INVESTORS IN THE BONDS RECEIVED PAR AND ACCRUED INTEREST, PLUS A PREMIUM OF ONE PER CENT.

Wheeler Kelly and Hagny's professionally produced brochures demonstrated the scope of the company's business, generating confidence among its clients regarding the company's capabilities and the scope of its projects. Courtesy, Wichita [KS] Historical Society.

Eventually, the company sold its mortgage banking division to Boatman's Bank, and it was later purchased by Bank of America.

The continuing theme is the role mortgage bankers played in the economic and cultural expansion of their communities. Not only did they import investment capital, but many, much like James Duff in Colorado, became significant community leaders. Wheeler contributed his energy and leadership skills to the founding of the Wichita Chamber of Commerce. As a mortgage banker committed to economic development, he also spearheaded the building of the municipal airport and helped bring four aircraft companies—Cessna, Beech, Boeing, and Stearman—to Wichita.

Typical of trust and investment companies at that time, WKH issued bonds in various denominations to multiple investors to finance numerous structures in the city, including the Union National Bank Building. These mortgage bonds also funded construction of the Criterion Theater in Oklahoma City. The company established a correspondent relationship with the Prudential Life Insurance Company of America (Prudential). Through WKH, Prudential placed a $600,000 loan on the Hillcrest Homes apartment project, a ten-story development in downtown Wichita. As with many institutions of its kind, the trust and confidence WKH cultivated with its investors enabled it to finance a wide variety of projects. The company arranged for the financing of Wesley Hospital in addition to many Catholic hospitals and parochial schools. One such project was St. Mary's Hospital in Winfield, Kansas, operated by the Sisters of Saint Joseph. The company's home mortgage division also financed a number of Wichita's finest neighborhoods before the advent of Fannie Mae, Freddie Mac, or the Federal Housing Administration (FHA). Earning the trust and confidence of investors allowed companies such as WKH to grow.

The Great Depression of the 1930s created havoc in the industry. Notwithstanding the low loan-to-value ratios of many mortgages on farms, commercial properties, and homes, even borrowers with proven capital, character, and capacity were forced into foreclosure. Investors realigned their relationships with their mortgage correspondents. Investors such as Prudential sought out individuals from among their correspondents, including employees of WKH such as my father, who possessed the knowledge necessary to manage real estate—to negotiate workout terms, loan modifications, and deferred payment plans to protect the investors' interest while still aiding the borrower.

COLORADO TRUST COMPANIES

From the 1880s into the twentieth century, Colorado, like Kansas, benefited from a number of vibrant trust companies. During the 1880s and 1890s a number of such organizations operated in Denver. Little detail is known about these companies, but they performed many of the same functions as WKH. One of the more prominent Denver firms, the Equitable Loan and Trust Company, acted as a receiver, guardian, trustee, and executor as well as an asset/property manager for its clients. The firm received deposits and made loans. However, it was Equitable's chief business of making first mortgage loans that contributed significantly to improving Denver real estate. The firm claimed a unique advantage over both local and eastern investors because its mortgages had a principal note and interest coupons similar to a corporate or municipal bond. The investor would "clip the coupon" and deposit it with the trust company to be converted to cash.

Many of the city's early leaders were involved directly or indirectly with other enterprises in the region. They participated in developing financial institutions, transportation companies, water companies, cultural and civic institutions, and real estate. H. B. Chamberlain served as president of both Equitable and the Chamberlain Investment Company, a loan agent for eastern investors. Best remembered for his donation of the Chamberlain Observatory to the University of Denver, Chamberlain also became involved with the Denver Chamber of Commerce and the Denver Real Estate Exchange.[12]

By 1890, Denver had emerged as the financial center of the Rocky Mountain West. With the Mining Exchange, six national banks, and one state bank already in existence, the Denver Real Estate Exchange found its footing in 1888 along with four building societies and several trust companies. Investment capital was finding a welcome home in the state. Money was coming into Colorado on a scale that matched its awe-inspiring mountains.

In Colorado as well as Kansas, many banks acted as agents for mortgage investors. In addition, most real estate firms also performed as mortgage agents. Morrison's 1890 report listed twenty-five such firms.[13] Many of these banks and business firms had officers and directors who engaged in the same or other business activities with affiliated enterprises. The Anthony, Landon, and Curry Abstract Company, founded in 1867, provides another example of these interlocking relationships.

As the name implies, the Anthony, Landon, and Curry Abstract Company performed all of the above duties in addition to offering the services of a

---

12 Morrison, *City of Denver*, 39.

13 Ibid.

mortgage banker. In 1952, the separation of its title and mortgage divisions resulted in the creation of the Mortgage Investment Company of Denver; the Landon Abstract Company survived into the 1970s as the Title Guaranty Company. The Mortgage Investment Company became an industry leader for many decades and produced three national presidents of the Mortgage Bankers Association (MBA). It was sold to the First National Bank Corporation in the late 1960s.

An abstract company performed a critical role in real estate transactions. Typically, an attorney or licensed abstractor searched title histories in the office of the county clerk and recorder. That person provided a "title opinion," an abstract or summary report of the chain of title, thereby giving a legal opinion and advice to the principles of the transaction regarding any break in the chain of title or other imperfections. For example, an imperfection might be the failure to record a deed transferring a property to a new owner. The abstractor listed all of the mortgages recorded against a property and, if those mortgages had been paid off, verified that a "release" had been properly documented and that the seller was giving a good and merchantable title.[14]

The terms *title company* and *abstract company* are essentially synonymous. The term *title company* came into use when abstractors became agents for the title insurance underwriters who provided insurance against any defect or oversight in the search process. Generally speaking, real estate attorneys handled the closing of real estate transactions and the title insurance protected both the new owner and the lender. Today, title companies not only write title insurance but also provide a menu of closing and settlement services to the parties in real estate transactions.

Other trust companies such as the DC Burns Realty and Trust Company also survived into the late twentieth century. A major mortgage banker, developer, and builder in Denver, DC Burns Realty and Trust Company is best remembered for the Burns Better-Built Bungalows developments in southwest Denver and Aurora. These compact, two-bedroom homes had steeply pitched roofs covered with asphalt shingles. The exteriors were clad with clapboard siding, and a small concrete slab served as the front porch. Built on concrete slabs, the basic model did not include a basement, garage, or attic. In addition to the bedrooms, the homes provided owners with a combination living-dining room, a kitchen with a small storage room/pantry, and one bathroom. It was the perfect starter home for veterans and other families in the early 1950s.[15]

Franklin L. Burns built the DC Burns Realty and Trust Company into a major force in home building, real estate, and mortgage banking in Denver. His uncle, Daniel C. Burns, established the company in the 1890s. Following his uncle's death in 1939, Franklin became executive vice president and succeeded to the presidency in 1942. Over its history the company developed and built a total of 13,000 multi-family, single-family, and commercial projects at an estimated value of $129 million[16] in Colorado and surrounding states.[17]

Part of the company's long history and dedication to housing for low- and moderate-income families began in the 1920s. The idea started with a savings plan held by the company's trust department in which the home buyer would agree to make regular weekly or monthly payments into a "home purchase plan savings account" dedicated to the purchase of a home. When the prospective home buyer had accumulated an amount equal to 10 percent of the purchase price for the down payment, Burns would finance the balance of the purchase. The company created this program almost ten years before the FHA came into existence, with more generous terms than those that would be allowed by the FHA.[18]

DC Burns built its first speculative house in 1939 as the Great Depression wound to a close. Consisting of only 228 square feet, the cozy house contained just two-and-a-half rooms. Burns's small-house concept targeted the lower-end market and entry-level homeowners with limited incomes. The house sold for $1,250. A later larger version, the "Handyman House," expanded into four-and-a-half room house or bungalow that came partially finished. Meeting FHA minimum property standards and quality were key components of the organization's success.[19]

---

15 Nancy Muenker, *Franklin L. Burns: Master Builder of Denver*, Builders Series (Denver: University of Denver, 1997), 9–11.

16 The date of valuation was not given. It could have been as of the publication date in 1997 or earlier.

17 Muenker, *Franklin L. Burns*, 4–5.

18 Ibid., 7.

19 Ibid., 6.

To meet the needs of returning veterans after World War II, the company developed the Burns Brentwood subdivision in southwest Denver. A buyer could use his or her G.I. Bill benefits to purchase a Burns home with a loan that required no down payment and only a small amount of cash for closing costs. Best of all, the loan structure provided low, affordable monthly payments. The company also developed and implemented a package mortgage program that included all of the home's appliances, including a Bendix washing machine. Burns stood at the forefront in the development of such progressive mortgage loan programs. Later, the company developed a home warranty and service program for its buyers.[20]

The company's commercial developments include the Brentwood Shopping Center, a perfect compliment to its adjacent residential neighborhood. It also reserved a site across the street from the shopping center where Lincoln High School now stands. In addition to its single-family residential and commercial projects, the company built 500 multi-family units, including the Burns Montclair Apartment complex and military housing at Fitzsimmons Army Hospital and Lowry Air Force Base.[21]

After the 1980s the company focused its attention on commercial properties, including its signature property, the Hampton House Apartments. Renamed The Burnsley, the property operated as a boutique hotel until its sale in 2012, after which it converted back to high-end, upscale apartments. Another part of the company's focus on commercial development involved construction of an office building at Eighth Avenue and Grant Street. Controversy surrounded the project because it resulted in the 1972 demolition of the historic Moffat Mansion, home to the pioneer railroad, mining, and banking family of David H. Moffat.

One positive outcome of the demise of the Moffat Mansion was a greater awareness of the need for historic preservation and the establishment of Historic Denver, Inc. The organization has been pivotal in the rescue and restoration of many of Denver's iconic structures, including the Paramount Theater.

Whether working with insurance companies, trust companies, or real estate developers, mortgage bankers have been instrumental in the growth of communities large and small in Colorado and elsewhere. They are

---

20 Ibid., 7.
21 Ibid., 6, 10, 13.

responsible for bringing in the investment capital for the construction of the buildings that house the places where we work and conduct business, the medical facilities we turn to for our healthcare, and the homes in which we live. Without mortgage bankers, only the extremely wealthy would be able to achieve the dream of homeownership.

5

Mortgage Bankers, Insurance Companies, Real Estate Companies, and the Correspondent System

As trust companies lost much of their influence within the industry and real estate companies began their ascendancy as the originators and servicers of mortgages, the stronger, more diversified real estate firms began to cement their relationships with life insurance companies. The mortgage divisions of real estate companies provided a broad array of services and expertise to insurance companies. The most important functions were as mortgage loan correspondents, appraisal services, real estate sales, and property management. For their part, the insurance companies provided a steady flow of capital to fund real estate development and the mortgages of countless homeowners.

Insurance companies are regulated by the state government in which the company is domiciled. Over the years, New York has maintained a reputation as a strict regulator. Until the 1890s, it prohibited resident companies from making investments outside the state except within a limited distance of New York City. Conversely, early on Connecticut and Wisconsin enacted very liberal investment regulations. Therefore, the majority of Connecticut-based insurance companies, as well as Northwestern Mutual Life Insurance

DOI: 10.5876/9781607326236.c005

Company of Wisconsin (Northwestern), had been funding mortgage loans in the Midwest and the West for decades. By 1898 other states relaxed their regulations, at which point the Connecticut- and Wisconsin-based companies found themselves competing against some aggressive newcomers. By 1910 they, too, had developed strong correspondent relationships and were poised to take advantage of the evolving farm mortgage market and the burgeoning urban market. A few insurance companies—the Equitable Life Assurance Society of New York (Equitable), Northwestern, Connecticut General, and Prudential Life—were particularly prominent in financing real estate markets in Colorado during this period.

NORTHWESTERN MUTUAL LIFE INSURANCE COMPANY

Probably the largest insurance company to invest in Colorado mortgages beginning in the 1880s was Northwestern Mutual Life Insurance Company. In 1890 the company's total loan portfolio nationwide amounted to $27 million. It also claimed direct ownership of $1.25 million in real estate. The Hayden and Dickinson Company, one of the twenty-five real estate companies described in Morrison's 1890 report on Denver and Colorado, acted as Northwestern's Colorado loan agent and mortgage correspondent.[1]

In 1861, Northwestern made its first loans of $500 to $700 on several lots in downtown Milwaukee. The total size of its portfolio at year's end was $2,200 at an average interest rate of 10 percent. In 1863, the Wisconsin legislature relaxed its restrictions, allowing management to make loans outside Wisconsin. No doubt the Wisconsin Insurance Department had seen Northwestern's success in real estate lending within the state and had confidence in the company's conservative and prudent management.[2] Northwestern moved ahead cautiously, making its first out-of-state loan in Indianapolis for $5,000. In 1865 it became licensed to sell insurance in Kansas and opened a sales office in Colorado the following year. By the end of 1868, Northwestern maintained a mortgage portfolio in excess of $1.5 million; urban real estate made up the majority of its loans.[3]

---

1   Morrison, *City of Denver*, 44.

2   Harold Williamson and Orange A. Smalley, *Northwestern Mutual Life: A Century of Trusteeship* (Evanston, IL: Northwestern University Press, 1957), 31.

3   Ibid., 45.

In 1874, Northwestern held $74,300 in outstanding loans in Colorado. By 1881, that number had grown to nearly $130,000, a considerable sum for the time. About 52 percent of the loans were secured by urban properties; the balance were farm loans.[4]

Northwestern's management continued to see real estate as an attractive investment opportunity. As those opportunities grew, the company developed more formal policies and procedures to assure that the loans it underwrote were prudent investments. The company adopted the same loan processing method described earlier. Loan requests were submitted on forms provided by the company. Using the same process as the one employed by farm mortgage bankers, an appraisal including a valuation opinion by two responsible parties, as well as character and credit references on the borrower, were required. Typical mortgage loan parameters included terms of two to five years with interest collected semiannually. Loans rarely, if ever, exceeded 50 percent of the value of the property.[5] Yet it soon became obvious to the company's management that allowing the life insurance sales force to originate loans created a serious conflict of interest; loans could be made contingent on the purchase of life insurance.

In 1872, Northwestern experienced its first foreclosure in Kansas. Within eight years the special asset category (real estate taken back through foreclosure) exceeded $1.5 million. Headline risk or bad publicity was as much a problem for investors in the 1870s as it is today. The company had employed prudent underwriting standards, but foreclosures inevitably appeared. The company's management recognized this problem and clearly understood the principle that your first loss is your best loss, an understanding that proved valuable in the future.[6]

As a consequence, Northwestern formed a special asset department to manage and liquidate defaulting mortgages.[7] Their long history of managing credit quality in loan portfolios coupled with an understanding of the principles of managing different categories of real estate differently firmly established Northwestern and other life insurance companies as the primary long-term providers of real estate capital. The knowledge and experience

---

4   Ibid., 78.
5   Ibid., 44–47.
6   Ibid., 74.
7   Ibid., 77–78.

gained by insurance companies over time enabled these firms to withstand the economic challenges of wars and depressions, thereby benefiting not just their policyholders but the nation's economy as well.

During the 1890s, the risk of agricultural lending increased. The general volatility of farmland prices and the operational risk of each borrower, combined with the difficulty of anticipating "acts of God," caused many companies to reduce their farm loan lending in the West. Consequently, some investors who elected to stay in farm mortgage lending demanded compensation proportionate to the increased risk. This risk evaluation created interregional disparity in interest rates, length of terms, and underwriting guidelines. These interregional disparities combined with global economic conditions to create discontent across the prairie and mountain states. That discontent led to some popular uprisings by the Farmers' Alliances and members of the Populist movement that contributed to the later creation of the farm loan system.[8]

Northwestern was among the first companies to build a formal correspondent system, yet for many years the company successfully managed and supervised an informal network of loan agents in its new territories. During the period 1877–78, the company began formalizing a method to acquire mortgage investments using a system of loan agents in its territories. The company's president, Henry Palmer, recognized the need for special expertise and began searching throughout the company's current lending territories for individuals of integrity and experience to serve as loan agents. These individuals became salaried company employees; they were not paid commissions on the loans they generated.

Palmer required loan agents to have experience in real estate valuation and appraisal. Above all else, they had to have the necessary skills and knowledge to accurately estimate a property's value so they could make a secure loan and be in compliance with insurance regulations. Having an experienced, knowledgeable appraiser on staff was critical for both the insurance company and the integrity of the correspondent. Palmer also demanded that his agents possess a thorough understanding of the real estate laws in the area where they conducted business, as these laws vary from state to state. However, possession of the requisite skills did not mean that agents operated

---

8   Ibid., 78.

independently; they were closely monitored, and managers received regular reports on their activities.

By 1907 Northwestern had expanded its lending operations to twenty-three states, including Colorado. In fact, during those years Colorado was the only mountain state in which the company conducted business.[9] Northwestern financed the seven-story Ernest and Cranmer Block in Denver, completed in 1891. Its design applied Richardsonian influences to a classically inspired tripartite structure. The two lower floors, constructed of rusticated red sandstone, formed the base. The five floors that rose above to create the middle section stood apart from the base because of their brown brick facade. The columns of windows in this middle section were capped by arches and separated by pilasters to accentuate the building's height. A horizontal band of windows and a bracketed cornice topped the impressive building.[10]

Northwestern held the mortgage for another historic Denver building, the Tabor Block at the corner of Sixteenth and Larimer Streets. The company had no other option than to foreclose on it when its owner, Colorado's Silver King Horace Tabor, met financial ruin in the economic crash of 1893. Tabor was so overextended that he had taken out both a second and a third mortgage on the property.

From the 1870s until today, Northwestern has maintained a strong presence as a direct lender and equity investor. Even after the company downsized its correspondent network and became a direct lender in the 1960s, many mortgage banking companies were able to refer or broker commercial mortgages and real estate projects to Northwestern for funding. This has certainly been the case in Denver.

An interesting trend exhibited in the 1970s was a partnership between certain "credit borrowers" and large insurance companies. Companies such as Northwestern, the Hartford, and the Principal provided large packages of very sophisticated long-term real estate financing for prime, high-quality corporate entities. However, earlier, in the 1930s Prudential had negotiated a long-term "credit deal" with Safeway stores across Colorado. Located in trade areas and neighborhoods across the state, the 1930s Art Deco–influenced

9   Ibid., 80–81.

10   William G.M. Stone, *The Colorado Hand-book: Denver and Its Outings: A Guide for Tourists and Book of General Information, with Some Bits of Early History* (Denver: Barkhausen and Lester, Printers, 1892), 46–47.

buildings were designed for Safeway with great functionality; many survive to this day in other capacities.

OTHER INSURANCE COMPANY AND MORTGAGE BANKER COLLABORATIONS

The 1890s were watershed years for the industry. Mortgage lending benefited from the many lessons learned about the risks and techniques of responsible lending practices through previous economic panics and depressions. The emerging correspondent system proved to be the needed survival safety net for the stronger, prudent mortgage bankers. Local correspondents with the intellectual resources and abilities to deal with borrowers in financial difficulty, as well as the ability to manage and liquidate foreclosed urban and farm properties, proved cost-effective and valuable resources. The life insurance industry recognized the benefit of this relationship and for the most part supported and maintained its correspondents whenever possible.

In 1911 the young Henry Van Schaack founded Van Schaack and Company in Denver. By 1923 it had full-service real estate brokerage, property management, insurance, and mortgage banking departments. For a long time the company maintained offices in the Equitable Building before moving into its own building on Seventeenth Street in 1949. The company cultivated significant relationships within the Denver business community. With its full menu of real estate services, the firm became the logical correspondent for a number of insurance companies, including Prudential and New York Life Insurance Company (New York Life).[11]

Denver's first open mall shopping center, Cherry Creek, opened in the 1950s. Initially financed by Van Schaack, New York Life provided the permanent loan. The $14 million project featured Bauers Restaurant and was anchored at the west end by the Denver Dry Goods Company and at the east end by a Miller Supermarket. As with many other projects of the time, the quality of the architecture and its layout have stood the test of time. Cherry Creek remains the region's most prestigious retail complex.

In 1958 Henry Van Schaack became chairman of the board of the company, and Thomas B. Knowles took over as president. After moving to Denver,

---

11   Thomas J. Noel, *Denver: Rocky Mountain Gold* (Tulsa, OK: Continental Heritage, 1980), 242.

The Cherry Creek Shopping Center transformed former wheat fields and other open space into the region's first major suburban retail complex in the 1950s. The photo shows the plaza with the Denver Dry Goods Company store at the far end. Courtesy, Denver Public Library.

Knowles, a Harvard graduate, emerged as a major force in real estate and civic affairs. He served on the board of the Colorado Military Academy. The school had moved from Evans Avenue, near the University of Denver, to Wellborn Farm near Hampden Avenue on Pierce Street, and it had fallen on hard times. Knowles, Thomas Howard, and Frances Newton set out to recruit a new headmaster and change the school from a military academy to a traditional boys' college preparatory school.[12]

Part of the school's financial difficulties centered on the construction of a classroom building and the rehabilitation of a number of antiquated surplus barracks into living quarters and classrooms. Knowles, Howard, and Newton began an aggressive fundraising campaign to save the school and update the

12 Ibid., 242–43; E. Michael Rosser, interview with Charles "Chuck" Froleicher, Denver, CO, 2011.

The Knowles Building of Colorado Academy, Denver, ca. 1961. Courtesy, Colorado Academy.

facilities. To recruit new students, it was important to build a new classroom building and replace the barracks. As evidence of its strong relationship with the Van Schaack Company and the company's reputation as a major correspondent, in 1960 Connecticut General Life Insurance Company made a sizable $350,000 twenty-year loan to construct a new classroom building. Given the underwriting requirements of companies like Connecticut General, loans such as this were outside its normal investment portfolio parameters. The loan was obviously made based on the long-term relationship with, reputation of, and confidence the firm had in Knowles and his real estate and mortgage banking firm.[13]

Because Van Schaack represented several of the major life insurance companies, his company became deeply involved with a number of urban initiatives in the 1970s and 1980s. It worked with a consortium of Denver banks that financed Dana Crawford and her investors in the preservation of the 1400 block of Larimer Street, known as Larimer Square. This pioneering effort to preserve one of Denver's oldest neighborhoods was unique among many similar projects because its initial success provided the incentive for

---

13   E. Michael Rosser, interview with Charles "Chuck" Froleicher, Denver, CO, 2011.

New York Life to provide a $2 million permanent mortgage loan in 1973 that assured the long-term viability of Larimer Square.[14] Industry observers have noted that although other institutions made similar mortgage investments in other cities, this was one of only a few loans of this type that did not enter into foreclosure.

The development of Larimer Square provided a springboard for the restoration and redevelopment of other buildings in the surrounding neighborhood. The implementation of new zoning ordinances, building codes, and tax incentives, combined with local, state, and federal programs, further encouraged preservation and redevelopment. The city enacted B–7, a new historic preservation zoning classification that laid the essential groundwork for the preservation of lower downtown. B–7 gave institutional investors the confidence to invest in these projects without fearing that they would be adversely impacted by otherwise inconsistent and nonconforming land-use changes that previously could have resulted in diminished values. In passing the new zoning classification, Denver's administration acted as a catalyst to preserve a neighborhood that might have been replaced by a freeway. Denver's historic roots might have been lost forever. Instead, the actions of many individuals and organizations coalesced to save the architectural, historical, and economic treasures that remain a part of the city's urban fabric.

OTHER INFLUENTIAL MORTGAGE BANKERS

The Colored American Loan and Realty Company of Denver facilitated many mortgages for Denver's African American community. Established in 1901 with offices in the city's Five Points neighborhood, it also funded loans for properties in Colorado's most noteworthy independent black settlement, Dearfield. Other individuals, including several single women, opted to homestead farmlands surrounding the town instead of purchasing the land.[15] Oliver Toussaint (O. T.) Jackson founded the community in 1910 after purchasing 480 acres of land east of Greeley in Weld County. The Colorado State Board of Immigration supported Jackson's development—which was promoted as

---

14 Thomas J. Noel, *Denver's Larimer Street. Main Street, Skid Row, and Urban Renaissance* (Denver: Historic Denver, Inc., 1981), 39.

15 Sue Armitage, Theresa Banfield, and Sarah Jacobus, "Black Women and Their Communities in Colorado," *Frontiers: A Journal of Women Studies* 2, no. 2 (Summer 1977): 49.

a valley resort—as did several current and former state officials for whom Jackson had worked.

The town was laid out with lots for businesses and residences, as well as larger five- to ten-acre blocks. Town lots were offered for sale beginning at $25, with larger tracts selling for $250 or more depending on their location in relation to the town center. At its height in 1921, Dearfield boasted a population of almost 500 residents, and it had a city well and telephone service, a church, and businesses including a general store and gas station, at least one restaurant, a boardinghouse, a cement block factory, and a blacksmith shop. When combined with the output of the local farms, the town's appraised value exceeded $1 million.[16] Agricultural production on the farms surrounding Dearfield reached $500,000 per year before the Great Depression, but ongoing drought resulted in its decline.[17] In the decades since, Dearfield has become a ghost town, but the Black American West History Museum in Five Points has undertaken the task of preserving the town site and its remaining buildings. Dearfield was added to the National Register of Historic Places in 1995. It is also a Colorado Registered Historic Landmark.

Al Morrison, a Denver native and vice president of First Denver Mortgage Company beginning in the 1970s, took a keen interest in preserving the city's historic structures. Formerly the Mortgage Investment Company, First Denver Mortgage served as the mortgage lending arm of Title Guaranty Company, whose roots date back to the 1860s as the Landon Abstract Company. One of the projects Morrison and First Denver Mortgage undertook with developer William Saslow was the transformation of an old building at Eighteenth and Market Streets into the Market Street Mall.

Saslow had relocated to Denver from the East Coast in 1971, bringing his architectural and community development expertise. He immediately recognized the potential of the nondescript yet structurally sound building. The building's initial restoration and rehabilitation was completed in 1974.[18] First Denver Mortgage financed the project and placed the loan with the Denver

<hr>

16   Bob Brunswig and George H. Junne Jr., *The Story of Dearfield, Colorado*, accessed July 24, 2014, http://www.unco.edu/cce/docs/Dearfield_Talk_CAS_4_2011.pdf.

17   Greeley Municipal Museum, "Building the Town of Dearfield" (Greeley: Colored American Loan and Realty Company, 1917).

18   Bill Hemingway, "Rebirth of Lower Downtown," *Empire Magazine of the Denver Post* (July 12, 1981): 15.

John Thams builidng and entrance to the Elephant Corral, ca. 1900. Courtesy, Denver Public Library.

Public Schools Pension Fund.[19] A 1979 addition expanded the Market Street Mall to 28,000 square feet. At the time it housed a variety of businesses, including "art galleries, travel agencies, and an interior-design studio [as well as] the Germinal Stage theater."[20]

At about the same time, Morrison and his First Denver Mortgage colleagues financed the restoration of Denver's oldest and one of its most important historic sites, the Elephant Corral. The Elephant Corral is believed to be the site of the original 1857 St. Charles Town Company claim. Charles Nichols, credited with naming the company, registered the first cabin on this site in 1858. Less than a year later, Gen. William Larimer jumped Nichols's claim and renamed the settlement Denver, in honor of Kansas territorial governor James W. Denver.[21] Colorado was part of the western section of Kansas Territory until incorporated as a separate territory in 1861.

19 E. Michael Rosser, interview with Al Morrison, Denver, CO, 2012.

20 Hemingway, "Rebirth of Lower Downtown," 14.

21 Ibid., 15.

There seems to be great confusion about the source of the name Elephant Corral. Like a caravanserai alongside Asia's Silk Road, the property served as a stopping-off place for those traveling to the newly discovered Colorado goldfields. The Elephant Corral provided ample room to water and feed livestock while the Denver House, a log structure that replaced the site's original cabin, offered lodging accommodations and a saloon. In addition to its role as a stagecoach stop, the enterprise became Denver's first post office when the Leavenworth and Pikes Peak Express Company "arrived on May 7, 1959 [actually 1859], carrying mail from the East."[22] A new two-story brick structure, corrals, and a sales arena were built after Denver's historic fire in 1863. It was at this time that the moniker "Elephant Corral" was first attached to the property. Common wisdom dictates that the name arose because the size of the generous open space allowed a stagecoach drawn by a team of horses to turn around. The formal addition of the corrals and the sales arena made the Elephant Corral "Denver's first stockyards and cattle auction house."[23] As such, it owns the claim as the original ancestor of today's National Western Stock Show.

Through Morrison's efforts, John and Natasha Querard purchased the property and completed a major renovation in 1980. While upgrading it to house 150,000 square feet of modern office space, they retained the original red brick walls and many of the other architectural features of this great Denver landmark. Morrison also assisted with facilitating the preservation of the property by obtaining permanent financing from the Metropolitan Life Insurance Company.

The Elephant Corral provides a particularly unique case study. Not only is it special because of the historic nature of the site, dating back to 1857, but it also demonstrates the continuing commitment to preserve the region's heritage. Granted, the owner, mortgage banker, and investor enabled the project to happen, but the community's conscience and commitment to the preservation of its western pioneer legacy provided additional motivation. Tracking the ownership record and events associated with various properties helps tell not only their history but the history of the community as well.

---

22 Ibid.
23 Ibid.

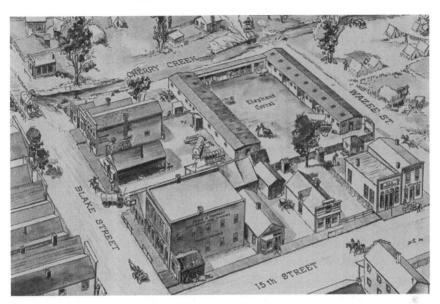

Illustrated map of early Denver with the Elephant Corral, ca.1870. Courtesy, Denver Public Library.

The Title Guaranty Company together with the Landon Abstract Company published an advertising brochure that was reprinted as a series in the *Denver Post* explaining the purpose and importance of title insurance by relating the story of the city's creation. It told the legend of how Denver got its name from a group of claim jumpers. According to the advertisement, the organizers of the St. Charles Town Company were the first to claim the land on the north side of Cherry Creek across from Auraria for a town site, and they constructed the first rudimentary cabin on the site during the summer of 1858. The group then decided to return to Kansas for the winter. However, before they reached Kansas, Charles Nichols, a member of the St. Charles Town Company, was sent back to build additional improvements on the site to perfect the company's claim.[24]

The brochure went on to tell that upon his return, Nichols found that the claim had been jumped by General William Larimer. Larimer and his group

---

24 Title Guaranty Company, "17 Flags Flew over Colorado" and other segments from promotional information (Denver: Title Guaranty and Landon Abstract Companies, ca. 1950), Steven H. Hart Library and Research Center, History Colorado, Denver.

had begun platting the land and laying out the streets for their newly established Denver City Town Company. When Nichols protested, Larimer and his associates warned Nichols that if he continued to push his claim he would be the guest of honor at a "necktie party," a favorite event in early Denver. Valuing his life over ownership of the town site, Nichols acquiesced. In an effort to assure its claim, the Denver City Town Company cleverly named its city after the territorial governor of Kansas, James W. Denver. Governor Denver visited the city only once in the 1880s.[25]

The Title Guaranty brochure also claims that these early town companies possessed dubious title to the land they were developing. In reality, they were merely squatters on Indian lands. The Cheyenne and Arapahoe peoples occupied much of Kansas and eastern Colorado. As with the Osage people in eastern Kansas, the federal government recognized the tenure in common land ownership of the Cheyenne and Arapahoe. According to the Treaty with the Arapaho and Cheyenne (1861), also known as the Treaty of Fort Wise, these two tribes ceded most of the land "owned, possessed, or claimed by them" to the United States. The tribes retained only a comparatively small parcel in the southeastern corner of the Colorado.[26] Congress then enacted a law for the relief of the citizens of Denver that established congressional land grants confirming and making good the plats and ownership records of the town organizations. The issues with native lands would come up again in the late 1940s and 1950s with the establishment of the Indian Lands Claims Commission.

The issues surrounding the validity of land titles in the Pikes Peak region, along with those in Kansas and other states, explain the close relationship between real estate finance institutions and the abstract and title companies. The obligation of the title and abstract companies is to provide clear evidence of the ownership of the property to be sold and secured by a mortgage. But the buyer and lender must also be aware of and understand other rights to the property, such as leases, easements, encroachments, and rights of way. All of these can impact the value of the property and the ability of the lender to foreclose in the case of default.

---

25 Ibid.

26 "Treaty with the Osage, 1865," *Indian Affairs: Law and Treaties*, vol. II: *Treaties* (Washington, DC: Government Printing Office, 1904), 807, accessed March 11, 2014, http://digital.library.okstate.edu/kappler/vol2/treaties/osa0878.htm.

President Dwight Eisenhower (left) and Aksel Nielsen showing off their not very impressive catch during one of the president's vacation trips to the ranch in Fraser, Colorado, owned by Nielsen and Carl Norgren.

Similar to Van Schaack, the Mortgage Investment Company, founded and chaired by Aksel Nielsen, had a stable of large institutional investors such as Metropolitan Life; like other firms at the time, it also had a number of private individuals looking for more attractive yields than those provided by bonds or stocks. Not widely known is the fact that Nielsen's good friend, President Dwight Eisenhower, was an investor in many of the company's construction loans for properties in the Bear Valley and Broomfield Heights neighborhoods. My friends and colleagues at the company related numerous stories about the Eisenhower-Nielsen relationship. They admitted that they would go to Nielsen's secretary to learn when he was scheduled to be out of the office. They knew that Nielsen conducted construction loan inspections on a regular basis, especially of those properties in which Eisenhower had invested; but some of the company's officers would secretly inspect the construction progress a day or two before Nielsen's visits to assure that all was in order and on schedule.

In 1968, First National Bank of Denver acquired the Mortgage Investment Company from Nielsen and changed its name to First Denver Mortgage Company (First Denver). First Denver gained a national reputation by providing apartment developers with the full complement of Federal Housing Administration (FHA) project loan types. Many of these loans were aimed at creating affordable housing for low- and moderate-income families. Because of the complexity of FHA's multi-family programs, only a company of considerable size that had the requisite expertise and capital to generate enough loan volume could make a reasonable profit. First Denver had the resources, and its second president, Robert G. Boucher, provided the necessary commitment and leadership. In 1972 United Mortgage Company sent me to school to learn about the FHA multi-family programs so it could develop a department to enter that business. I recommended, and management agreed, that First Denver had such a sizable presence in the market that we could not compete, and the initiative was abandoned.

First Denver Mortgage aligned with a variety of investors to finance a multitude of other new construction and redevelopment projects using a battery of FHA programs. One of its most enduring projects is Sakura Square, located in Denver's Skyline Urban Renewal area. First Denver Mortgage financed it, the Volunteers of America Apartments, and a number of other projects using the FHA 236 multi-family program, an interest rate subsidy program. It converted others to the FHA 221 program, which allowed for Section 8 housing vouchers. More important, these properties, along with Aurora Presbyterian Hospital, which was financed with the FHA 242 healthcare financing program, were marketed to institutional investors using Government National Mortgage Association (Ginnie Mae) guaranteed mortgage–backed securities. This process proved to be a major breakthrough in providing affordable financing.[27]

At roughly the same time, in the late 1960s and early 1970s, life insurance companies began to differentiate themselves from other members of the industry as investment policies began to reflect the size and scope of their operations. I watched as the large national firms gained dominance over local and regional companies, and investment requirements became more stratified and segmented.

---

27 For a list of the most commonly used FHA insurance programs, see appendix A.

Given the diversity of property types and the geographic distribution of the correspondents who remained the principal sources of business, life insurance companies adapted, becoming more selective. Some preferred commercial office buildings; others favored hotels, apartment and condominium projects, or other investment types. Interestingly, Prudential intensely disliked making loans on hotels. No doubt the decision not to participate in the hospitality market resulted from the company's experience during the Depression. Not even the opportunity to invest in the luxurious, star-studded Shamrock Hotel in Houston, Texas, passed muster at Prudential, even though the hotel site stood less than a mile from the company's regional headquarters.

A case study presented to a class I attended at the School of Mortgage Banking provided by the Hartford Insurance Company demonstrated what can happen when a potential environmental hazard is not addressed. The case involved the development of a K-mart store in Charlotte, North Carolina, in the 1970s, which the Hartford financed through a credit deal. Apparently, when evaluating the proposed building and its site plan, neither the developer nor the investor noticed a ditch that ran through the property and its potential to cause serious damage. A week before the grand opening, while the store was being stocked with merchandise, a sudden thunderstorm caused the ditch to overflow, flooding the store. To salvage its investment, Hartford paid for the mitigation of the ditch and repairs to the building so the store could open, albeit behind schedule, a year later.

Many companies such as Pacific Life of Newport Beach, California, invested heavily in luxury apartments. Life insurance companies were the best mortgage holders because they possessed huge capital resources and were patient investors, qualities they continue to maintain today. Sometimes they used their capital and expertise to salvage potentially disastrous projects. Park Mayfair in Denver presents a classic example. Originated by a local mortgage banking firm, Pacific Life approved the loan and construction commenced. In the late 1960s, when Park Mayfair was under construction, I lived within a block of the property. When the building was three stories out of the ground, Denver began to experience earthquakes. At the time, earthquakes were unheard of in Denver.[28]

---

28 A geology professor at the Colorado School of Mines determined that the US Army and its contractor at the Rocky Mount Arsenal were pumping toxic petroleum-based waste down deep wells lubricating the natural fissures in the rocks, which led to the earthquakes.

Many cynical observers thought Pacific Life might walk away from the project. However, as a California-based company, it understood how to make loans in earthquake-prone areas. The three stories were torn down, and the foundation was reengineered to withstand earthquakes. Although delayed, the project was completed and remains one of Denver's premier condominium residences. Shortly after this episode I had the good fortune to learn the details of the story from a respected colleague, Everett Spelman Jr. He was vice president of Western Securities Company and was responsible for originating the loan for Pacific Life.[29]

But the forty-two-story Brooks Towers apartment complex stands as the largest and most remarkable of the early 1970s urban investment initiatives. Located on the site of the old Mining Exchange Building at Fifteenth and Curtis Streets, when completed in 1968, not only were the towers the tallest buildings in the city, but they were also the tallest apartment buildings between Chicago and San Francisco.

The project was championed by Elwood Brooks, hence the name Brooks Towers. A Kansas banker, Brooks relocated to Denver in 1943 after accepting the presidency of Denver's Central Bank and Trust (Central). Under his leadership, Central grew into the fourth-largest bank in the city and was an important departure from the well-established Seventeenth Street silk stocking institutions of Denver's old monied families. It became the working person's bank. Located near the streetcar loop, it was convenient for the working person to deposit his or her Friday paycheck on the way home from work. In addition, the bank financed a number of homes for its customers in the area and was for a time one of the top mortgage servicers among commercial banks in the nation. Unusual for its time but complimentary to its customer base, Central Bank and Trust, like First Denver Mortgage Company, Van Schaack, and Service Investment Company, was a big lender that utilized FHA and VA loan programs.

At the urging of Brooks, the company's senior vice president, Armand "Ozzie" Asborno, spearheaded the development of Brooks Towers. Asborno represented Central Bank and Trust as it assembled four additional investors—Security Life and Accident, Western Farm Bureau Life, National Farm Bureau Life, and Western American Life—to finance the purchase of the land

---

29 John Waldach of Pacific Life confirmed this information in an email to Mike Rosser on May 2, 2017.

from the Denver Urban Renewal Authority. Then three other banks joined Central to finance construction of the complex that contained 537 apartment units. Thomas Murphy, senior manager of Equitable Life Assurance Company's Denver office, secured the permanent mortgage financing for his company. Years later the complex was converted to condominiums as an FHA-approved project.[30]

Garrett Bromfield Company was another company with deep roots in Denver; its activities mirrored those of DC Burns Realty and Trust Company. It offered an array of financial services and became involved in many significant development projects throughout the city. Van Holt Garrett and Donald Bromfield founded the company in 1929. Bromfield headed the company's stock brokerage and insurance functions while Garrett managed the real estate, mortgage, and property management activities.

A native of Augusta, Georgia, Garrett attended Georgia Tech and then entered the cotton brokerage business. When his wife, a Denver native, contracted tuberculosis, they returned to Denver for her treatment. During the train ride to Colorado he made the acquaintance of J. C. Nichols, developer of the Kansas City Country Club District and the Country Club Plaza Shopping Center and retail district. This fortuitous meeting resulted in Nichols being instrumental not only in shaping a career and a company but also in influencing the development of another city through Garrett.[31]

Garrett's real estate career followed the same early path as that of Henry Van Schaack, as a rent collector and property manager. A warm and gracious southern gentleman, Garrett's knowledge of real estate brokerage, appraisal, and development as well as mortgage banking gained him a national reputation. In 1945, while serving as president of the National Association of Real Estate Boards, now the National Association of Realtors, he strongly supported the removal of commercial rent controls and revocation of the wartime order that banned all ordinary construction. A cavalry officer and veteran of World War I, Garrett advocated for the VA loan guarantee program.[32]

---

30 Warren Lowe, "Brooks Towers," *Rocky Mountain News*, June 12, 1966, 1.

31 Bakemeier, Alice M. *Crestmoor Park Heritage: A History and Guide to a Denver Neighborhood.* Denver: Heritage, 2005.

32 Ibid.; "Van Holt Garrett, President of the National Association of REALTORS—1945" (Chicago: National Association of Realtors, 1980), accessed May 5, 2017, https://www.nar.realtor/bios/van-holt-garrett.

Country Club Plaza, Kansas City, Missouri.

Garrett served for a time on Denver's Zoning Board of Adjustment. His experiences there, combined with his earlier encounter with Nichols, influenced the Garrett Bromfield Company's projects. In addition to the inclusion of parks and open space, the firm's undertakings were known for classic architecture, elegant streetscapes, and protective covenants that prohibited purchase by African Americans and all other racial groups.[33] The company's first major development was Belcaro Park in 1931. In 1936 it began to develop old Crestmoor, located on Sixth Avenue Parkway. A decade later, in an effort to meet the needs of returning World War II veterans, it built the Chaffee Park neighborhood and shopping center in North Denver at Forty-Eighth and Pecos. All of Garrett Bromfield's neighborhoods have an enduring quality. Insurance companies and other institutional mortgage investors seek out the well-considered land-use design and architectural integrity of its developments.

Because of their start-to-finish control of projects, Garrett Bromfield and other full-service development companies garnered the trust and confidence

33 Bakemeier, 17, 20–21; Belcaro Park Homeowners Association, "Covenants: Declaration and Agreement, Article 11," March 19, 1946.

Single-family home in Chaffee Park, Denver, 2014. Courtesy of the authors.

of insurance companies. These firms put the land under the builder; they loaned the builder the funds to purchase the land in addition to providing construction loans. The companies' mortgage divisions then assumed responsibility for the marketing and sales of the new homes and for providing the mortgage loans for buyers.

Smaller life insurance companies such as Equitable of Iowa and Omaha-based Woodmen of the World sought conventional loans in Denver's Crestmoor Park and other Garrett Bromfield–developed neighborhoods. They particularly appreciated the firm's strong influence over not only the architectural design of the homes but also the long-term architectural controls, which gave investors great comfort that the property and the neighborhood would be maintained over the life of the loan. The trust and confidence inherent in the partnership between the developer and the insurance company resulted in many fine projects.[34]

34 E. Michael Rosser, telephone interview with Bruce Bowler (former vice president of Garrett Broomfield), May 7, 2017.

In 1924, Denver attorney Walter Black, George Kellogg, and Ray Bushey, plus a group of investors, founded another Denver mortgage banking firm, the Service Investment Company (SIC). Like many companies of that era, SIC provided private capital to finance homes for individuals and families. Early in the 1930s the company recognized the value of becoming an approved FHA lender. Management quickly adopted many of the new programs, which enabled SIC to make significant inroads into the homebuilders' community that emerged in Denver following World War II. When the VA launched the G.I. loan program, SIC participated, helping returning veterans finance homes offered by the company's stable of builders. The company also became an early Fannie Mae–approved lender.

Service Investment Company's thorough understanding of the approval process for subdivisions and architectural plans utilized by the FHA and the VA proved invaluable. The company guided its builders through that process, enabling the development of many new neighborhoods. Providing the financing for Woodcrest Townhomes, the first FHA- and Fannie Mae–approved townhouse project in Colorado, stands as one of the firm's major accomplishments.

SIC also provided a source of funding for many startup builders; several grew to be national-scale production builders. One such builder was Witkin Homes, founded by Lou and Jack Witkin. A later partner, Philip Winn, went on to serve as the commissioner of the FHA. In the early 1970s the company built Aurora's Village East and Jefferson County's Westlake subdivisions. Its houses ranged in price from around $25,999 to $36,000. After developing into a substantial regional company, it was purchased by US Home Corporation, now known as Lennar Homes.

Fred E. Kirk became SIC's president in 1961. A lawyer and World War II B24 pilot, Kirk had a reputation for honesty, integrity, and dedication to the law. His word was his bond. Even when later events became difficult or costly, he could be counted on. He was also known for his skill, knowledge, and ability to negotiate complex real estate transactions. In one case Kirk negotiated a transaction between a landowner and three of Colorado's largest home builders. The parcel being sold was south of Arapahoe Road and Holly Street in what is now known as the city of Centennial. The package included acquisition and development financing, construction financing, and permanent loans to the eventual homeowners.

Unlike most other comparable firms, SIC instituted a training program in the 1960s that allowed new junior members of the firm to attend and participate in the weekly executive committee breakfast for a month. Trainees, including myself, were exposed to the inner workings of a mortgage banking firm, from loan origination to loan processing and closing. Instruction also included the processes of loan servicing, an understanding of the legal framework of mortgage banking, and development of the skills necessary for investor relations and secondary marketing.

SIC lacked correspondent relationships with the big five life insurance companies. However, it maintained a stable of medium-sized insurance companies, including Transamerica, Manhattan Life of New York, and Security Life and Accident of Denver. These relationships were expected to be continuous and exclusive over time. As long as the local mortgage banker produced a supply of high-quality mortgages, both profited from a long-term and stable relationship.

In the mid-1960s, the ability of independent mortgage banking firms like SIC to obtain sufficient capital to fund their operations became increasingly difficult. The company entered into negotiations with Colorado National Bank to obtain access to the commercial paper market through the bank's holding company. But the rise in interest rates and the softness of the local real estate market caused the negotiations to end. However, in 1969 the firm's management was contacted by Denver US National Bank. The purchase of SIC by Denver US National was hailed on Seventeenth Street, Denver's financial center, as a major coup by this fine old firm. I joined SIC during this transition period.

The acquisition resulted in the diversification of Denver US Bancorp, the parent company of Denver US National Bank, and started the company on a growth path to becoming the state's leading residential mortgage banking firm. In the early 1970s Denver US Bancorp launched a new branding campaign, changing its name to United Banks of Colorado. All of its affiliated banks and financial services companies adopted the United name, leading SIC to be renamed United Mortgage Company. Colorado did not yet have branch banking; each individual bank had its own charter and conducted business at only one location. But the new branding resulted in the appearance of branching and a single, statewide market identity.

Because of United Banks of Colorado's broad reach of affiliates across the state and the anticipation of hosting the 1976 Winter Olympics, United

Mortgage Company utilized its construction loan and capital markets expertise to establish its presence as one of the major lenders in financing the state's ski areas. The company provided financing for major condominium projects in Aspen, Snowmass, Steamboat Springs, Vail, and Winter Park. In 1973 United Mortgage Company negotiated the largest delivery of loans to Freddie Mac in the firm's history to that date and the state's largest issue of a Ginnie Mae mortgage-backed security.

This was an exciting period for me. In 1971 United's senior management assigned me additional responsibilities in the company's capital markets. My role was to facilitate the delivery of loans to investors and organize their inspection trips to the various projects throughout the state. I assembled and prepared loan files for the investors' review, organized the inspection trips, created maps showing the locations of all properties, and provided economic information about the communities in which the properties were located. Some investors appreciated being wined and dined, others wanted to return to their hotel, and a few were delighted to be brought to my house for a home-cooked dinner.

The company sold whole loans and loan participations directly to investors or through New York mortgage brokers. A large swing in interest rates and weakness in the economy and local real estate markets caused it to suffer substantial marketing losses in 1974 and 1975. Norwest Corporation, a large Minneapolis-based bank holding company, acquired United Mortgage, along with all United Bank affiliates, after it recovered from the economic downturn. Norwest later merged with San Francisco–based Wells Fargo Bank.

BENEFITS OF COLLABORATION

From the early years of the twentieth century to the present day, the mortgage banking industry's senior management has attended the annual Mortgage Bankers Association (MBA) convention to meet with each of the institutional investors, primarily life insurance companies. Depending on economic conditions, a younger career-track member of the firm might be invited to accompany a senior member to the convention. The senior representative and the junior associate arrived loaded with state and city economic data, legal opinions on foreclosure, information on taxation and business laws, and promotional material from their builder customers.

Both industry and insurance companies' representatives came to the convention prepared with their projected investment needs for the following year as well as several years into the future. Based on their market analysis, investors would negotiate the volume of loans they expected from each of their local correspondents, along with the yield and the terms on the loans and particularly property types. This was done by contract and a term sheet that also included whether the loans would be FHA insured, VA guaranteed, or low loan-to-value ratio conventional mortgages. The contracts also stipulated the ratio between new construction and existing properties. In addition, certain investors preferred specific neighborhoods.

A rating system measured a neighborhood's quality, including pride of ownership, reputation of the local school system, proximity to primary employers, and overall quality of local public services. Many investors also required a rating from a casualty insurance company on the quality of the local fire department, as well as the proximity of the property to the closest fire station and the distance to the fire plug. Most investors had stringent credit criteria, such as job stability of the principal breadwinner, character and reputation of the borrower, and a pristine credit record. Accessibility to transportation, shopping, recreation, and neighborhood and regional parks proved equally important to investors. Generally, investors looked at the total quality of life and reputation of the city.

Pride of ownership figured greatly in the valuation of residential real estate, both single-family and multi-family. Maintenance of the property meant maintaining its value; maintaining the value of individual property meant maintaining the property's appeal in the marketplace, which equated to a good loan. One long-term SIC investor would reject loans if, when he inspected the property, its "curbside appeal" did not meet his standards. For example, he deemed a motorcycle or motorhome parked in the driveway as unacceptable. One loan he rejected in 1969, located in Denver's Hilltop neighborhood, was for a newlywed couple in the process of purchasing their first home. He conducted his inspection during October. The couple had already made the required 25 percent down payment. In the process, they had drained the balance of their discretionary spending budget. So even though the grass needed mowing, the husband had opted to use their remaining funds to purchase snow shovels in preparation for the upcoming winter instead of a lawn mower. But without that information, the inspector interpreted the unkempt lawn as a lack of pride of ownership and rejected the loan. He later rescinded his objection following intervention by the president of SIC, who knew the creditworthiness of the borrowers who happened to be me—one of his employees—and my wife.

Appraisals on real estate are truly a value opinion based on market performance on a given date in history. Therefore, a major component of the analysis included the long-term economic and functional influences that promoted the long-term health and sustainability of the property as security for a long-term investment. A seasoned mortgage banker who grew up during the Great Depression once shared with me his most basic question regarding loan approval. He said, "Son, when you're going to make a loan on a piece of property ask yourself, can you sell it for what you've got in it?" For me, that one simple question became "Rosser's First Law of Real Estate."

The quality of the land and land-use regulations were equally important from a mortgage investor's standpoint beginning around the turn of the twentieth century and gaining momentum during the Coolidge administration. This began when Secretary of Commerce Herbert Hoover initiated a national conversation on good city planning. Strong zoning and building code enforcement, along with appealing architecture, ensures the longevity and sustainability of projects over time.

The better correspondents understood all of the influences that affected their markets. The more they understood, the better their relationships with the insurance companies would be over time. Notwithstanding the ups and downs of the economy, many of these relationships lasted for generations, and the quality of the real estate was the tie that bound them together. From the 1870s until the 1950s, most life insurance companies acquired their mortgage investments from correspondents. Beginning in 1932, as the volume of new mortgages shrank and foreclosures increased, the insurance companies supported their correspondents the best they could; failing that, they hired key individuals from among their correspondents to manage their mortgage and real estate assets, just as Prudential had hired my father away from WKH.

The correspondent's contract with the investor outlined the compensation and responsibilities in some detail. The correspondent received an origination fee or commission, typically 1 percent, and often earned an additional annual fee, usually about 0.5%, for servicing the loan—for collecting the payment and remitting it to the investor, plus maintaining and paying the property taxes and insurance. The correspondent also assumed responsibility for collecting delinquent payments and handling any foreclosures. Sometimes an investor required an annual drive-by inspection of the property, including photographs. Most mortgages or, in Colorado's case, deeds of trust included a "wasting clause" that gave the lender the right to foreclose in the event that the borrower did not maintain the property. These inspection duties were often assigned to a new intern or trainee in the correspondent's office. Almost all loans, whether FHA or VA insured or low-ratio conventional loans, received prior approved by the investor. Before the loans were bundled into portfolios, correspondents submitted loans on an individual basis by mail; the denial or approval, including closing conditions, would be returned to the correspondent.

Often, an employee of the insurance company would inspect each property and neighborhood before loan approval and purchase. Investor trips might last as long as a week, depending on both the number and dollar volume of the loans to be purchased. These trips proved to be quite valuable, as they cemented a relationship of trust and confidence between the investor and the correspondent that promoted the best interests of both parties. With the introduction of modern mortgage-backed securities for residential mortgages, there was no need to continue the inspection trips. As a result, the industry began to move away from relationships of trust and became transactional in nature.

While I was working at United Mortgage, the chief financial officer and I took an investor to dinner at Denver's Normandy Restaurant. Our wives and the investor's wife joined us. A competitor had hosted this prospective client for lunch at Denver's Playboy Club earlier that day. Unaccustomed to the altitude and perhaps because of an overly ambitious schedule, the gentleman suffered a minor seizure during dinner. After he was seen at a nearby hospital, we took him back to his hotel. The next morning, while relaying the incident to the president of our company, I informed him that I had adjusted our agenda for the day. As a precaution I had rearranged the schedule so the properties we were to inspect were all within a ten-minute drive of Swedish Hospital. Later that day the president's wife called her husband to ask why I was circling their neighborhood and had not acknowledged her when she waved. Simply stated, I was attentively observing the inspector the entire day. It was abundantly clear to me that nothing could end one's career more quickly than having a client's representative die during an inspection trip. Our concern for our client was amply rewarded over the years.

For the most part, the same basic principles of analysis applied to income property mortgages. While a residential mortgage used a market approach to estimate the value, the underwriting of an income property loan was a great deal more sophisticated. An appraisal or opinion of value must be supported by a number of economic, social, political, and environmental factors. Insurance companies can have complicated payment programs in which the developer of a property such as a shopping center might add an inflation "kicker" allowing the investor to share in any upside income produced by the property.

In the case of an income property loan, the owner/developer provided the investor with a current financial and operating statement for the ownership firm as well as for the specific property the loan covered. An annual inspection was also required. As industry knowledge and concerns about environmental issues arose, additional routine inspections may have been required to assure investor compliance with all the covenants of the mortgage.

To add to their stable of investors and capture new sources of funds in the capital-rich areas of the East, local mortgage companies turned to intermediaries associated with the thrift industry to help sell their loans. Discovering how to develop that new market created another challenge. The solution lay with the mortgage broker. In the 1950s the term *mortgage broker* had a dual meaning. Some mortgage brokers dealt directly with borrowers in the origination of loans; however, very few of these brokers were found in Colorado or Kansas during the 1950s. Most mortgage brokers dealt with institutions, many located in New York City, buying and selling mortgage portfolios.

Operating into the late 1980s, these New York firms, some of which were Wall Street investment banking companies, negotiated commitments to purchase FHA and VA loans. Utilizing the expanded lending powers provided by state and federal regulators, they also bought conventional loans on a nationwide scale. One such company was Salomon Brothers, another was Wallace and Associates. Highly respected in the New York savings bank community, Selma Wallace and her staff introduced mortgage bankers throughout the West to New York and Middle Atlantic investors and assisted them in building a portfolio with a number of banks in the New York area. For most mortgage bankers this was a less cumbersome and bureaucratic method of selling loans than was selling them directly to Fannie Mae. In addition, the New York broker provided assistance in maintaining long-term relationships to encourage repeat sales.

United Mortgage was always envious of its competitor, First Denver, because of its membership in the Massachusetts Purchasing Group, which represented savings banks in Massachusetts and other states in the Northeast. Headed by a retired savings bank executive and industry regulator, the group made funds available to purchase FHA and VA loans in the Carolinas, Texas, Utah, California, and Colorado. These activities by eastern savings banks were greatly facilitated by certain unrestricted investment exemptions for government-insured loans. During 1948 and 1949, many eastern states began allowing their local institutions to engage in nationwide investing. By 1955, almost half of the mortgage loans in New York's savings banks' portfolios were on out-of-state properties.[35]

---

35 Saul B. Klamen, *The Postwar Residential Mortgage Market* (Princeton, NJ: Princeton University Press, 1961), 149–50.

6

Early Twentieth Century Urbanization and Associationalism

The Farmers' Alliance and the Rural Credit Movement followed by the Populist and the later Progressive movements all represented reactions to the changing economic circumstances of American farmers. The Industrial Revolution provided the technology for the nation's farmers to move beyond subsistence-based agriculture into for-profit commercial agriculture. The opportunity to enter the global market as a major exporter of farm products existed. Yet during the closing decades of the nineteenth century, farmers throughout the Midwest, West, and South felt stymied by the lack of affordable financing needed to expand their operations so they could fully participate in the fast-growing global economy.

Farmers were also frustrated by higher farmland prices and falling crop prices, the marketing agencies' methods of public land disposal, and the economic and political power amassed by large corporations, especially the railroads and banks. By the 1880s the railroad companies had gained enormous wealth as a result of the Pacific Railway Act. Farmers complained that

DOI: 10.5876/9781607326236.c006

the companies added to that wealth by charging unjustifiably high freight rates to transport farm products to market, thus reducing the farmers' profits. The Populists argued for government control, if not outright ownership, of the railroads based on their social purpose of providing public transportation and communications and transporting mail. Another basis of their argument was that the government had already invested millions of dollars of the public's money in the railroads through subsidies, grants, and bonds.[1] The Populists and Farmers' Alliance members' dissatisfaction with the banks revolved around currency issues and, more important, the lack of available farm credit and its higher cost compared with other regions of the country. What they apparently failed to understand or consider was the banks' fiduciary obligation to invest money as prudently as possible, thereby limiting their depositors' risk as well as that of larger investors such as insurance companies and their policyholders. Banks limited the loans they provided to farmers and charged more for those loans because of the higher risk of failure of western farms.

Dissatisfaction with the government's apparent lack of interest in the farmers' plight motivated members of the Farmers' Alliance and other dissident groups to formally organize the People's Party, also known as the Populist Party, in 1892. While its candidates enjoyed success at the state level in the 1894 election, they failed to gain the support needed for success in the 1896 national election.[2] The Populists' hopes for a federal solution in support of the farm mortgage industry would have to wait another twenty years. Yet one important legacy of the movement was the adoption of the public trustee system in Colorado, a unique public transfer system that assures protection for both the lender and the borrower through its use of a third-party system to determine the lender's right to foreclose.

Other attempts at change also failed. A move to license loan agents fizzled. In 1881, the Kansas Loan Agents Association was formed. The intent was to organize industry members to provide uniform mortgage interest rates throughout the state. This pre-antitrust effort to stabilize and "fix" rates also ended in failure. The concern that the purchasers of Kansas mortgages— primarily insurance companies and private investors—would be subject to

---

1   Charles Postel, *The Populist Vision* (Oxford: Oxford University Press, 2007), 146–47.
2   Postel, *Populist Vision*, 12–14.

double taxation on investment profits, owing taxes to their home state as well as Kansas, also remained unresolved.[3]

Renowned economic historian Kenneth A. Snowden explains that as early as 1908, Progressives led by President Theodore Roosevelt took up one of the concerns raised by the earlier Populists—the issue of insufficient availability of agricultural credit. Roosevelt organized the Country Life Commission to begin examining interregional differences in the distribution of farm mortgage credit. The volatility in commodity prices and the corresponding volatility in land values, coupled with the recessions and repeated cycles of foreclosure during the 1890s, caused great concern about the stability of American agriculture. The commission concluded that the lack of affordable credit to fund the purchase of additional land for cultivation and new equipment to improve production, compounded by the lack of a system for credit distribution, were the principle impediments to agricultural expansion.[4]

The discussion of promoting American agriculture and attracting capital for its growth continued through the Taft administration. In 1912, the Southern Commercial Congress formed the American Commission to explore agricultural credits in Europe.[5] In 1913, soon after his inauguration as president, Woodrow Wilson formed the United States Commission. Composed of members of Congress, its task was to cooperate with the American Commission in exploring the different agricultural finance systems employed by various European countries.[6]

The members of both commissions sailed to Europe. They spent three months conducting their investigations and preparing recommendations for submission to Congress in November 1913. Congress debated several proposals during numerous hearings. Ultimately, it focused on the merits

---

3   Bogue, *Money at Interest*, 147–50. Many investors—individuals, mortgage banking companies, and insurance companies—were headquartered in the eastern states and subject to those states' laws. Consequently, they feared being taxed by the state in which they resided as well as by the states in which they conducted business.

4   Kenneth Snowden, *Research Institute for Housing America Special Report: Mortgage Banking in the United States, 1870–1940* (Washington, DC: Mortgage Bankers Association, 2013), 29.

5   The Southern Commercial Congress was an organization of business leaders whose purpose was to promote agriculture, trade, and commerce in the southern states.

6   James B. Morman, *Farm Credits in the United States and Canada* (New York: Macmillan, 1924), 1–2.

of three different plans to resolve the problems related to the distribution of affordable agricultural credit across all areas of the country. The first, supported by most farm groups, called for a direct loan program offered through the US Department of the Treasury with funds raised by the sale of US government–backed mortgage bonds. The second promoted the "creation of a federal farm loan bank system to charter small, local associations" of borrowers whose loans would be funded by debentures secured by the mortgaged properties. The third plan called for a series of "federally chartered, privately financed joint-stock land banks" to manage the equitable distribution of farm loan funds. The banks were to be formed by groups of farmers who purchased stock, or shares, to fund the bank. They would require a minimum capitalization of $10,000 and would be limited to lending only on in-state farms.[7]

The eventual compromise, the Federal Farm Loan Act of 1916, created a new system that included elements of each proposal. The system required the establishment of locally based lending cooperatives with oversight by regional Federal Land Banks chartered and organized in a manner similar to the Federal Reserve System.[8] The legislation also created the Federal Farm Loan Board to supervise the land banks, especially their role in issuing bonds to fund the loans made by the cooperatives. While the loan parameters were broader than those offered by the major competitors, the individual life insurance companies, they were definitely restrictive compared with today's standards. One generous aspect called for a maximum loan amount of $10,000 with a loan-to-value ratio of 50 percent. A feature that resembled the European financing systems demanded a minimum term of five years, but loans could also be written for a maximum term of forty years. While the bill did not include a true or implied full faith and credit federal guarantee, interest rates were lower, capped at 6 percent, and for the first time applied equally across the nation. In addition, to encourage investors, the bonds used to fund the mortgage loans were tax-exempt.[9]

---

7   Snowden, *Special Report*, 30–31.

8   This model reappeared in 1932 when President Herbert Hoover created the Federal Home Loan Bank System.

9   Snowden, *Special Report*, 37–39.

PUBLIC-PRIVATE COOPERATION AND ASSOCIATIONALISM

The government's early-twentieth-century concern and the debate over agricultural financing occurred during a time of dramatic change as economics and politics clashed in a way never before seen. Prior to the hostilities of World War I in August 1914, the world felt secure in its belief that business and government networks united by technology, personal relationships, and professional societies that spanned international borders would prevent nations from engaging in armed conflict. The globalization of the world's major economies and the anticipated loss of vast fortunes in the wake of war deepened the sense of security that enveloped the people of most nations. Common wisdom dictated that no one would be foolish enough to engage in war. Cooperation would ensure peace and prosperity.

In the early years of the century, associationalism began as a major economic movement in the United States and continued to grow, building a cooperative spirit between government and business. The emergence of trade associations brought together the best minds, motives, selfless ideals, intellectual independence, and institutional cooperation that led to a New American System of greater prosperity. This is, in short, the vision of an associative state, or associationalism.[10]

The leading advocate and chief apostle of the gospel of associationalism was Herbert Hoover. His life experiences no doubt shaped his view of the relationship between the US public and private sectors. Certainly, a case can be made that Hoover was one of the most influential American politicians of his time. Joan H. Wilson, Herbert Hoover's biographer, characterized him as both the forgotten Progressive and a man of the world. The term *Progressive* would be disputed by some because in many ways he felt government should stay out of people's individual lives unless absolutely necessary. He eschewed deficit spending and expansive federal programs. As an alternative, he strongly advocated for government and industry cooperation.

Born in West Branch, Iowa, in 1874, Hoover experienced tragedy early in life. He was just six years old when his father died. Orphaned three years later following the death of his mother, Hoover experienced a transient existence for the next six years, living with various Quaker family members and family

---

10 Ellis W. Hawley, "Herbert Hoover, the Commerce Secretariat, and the Vision of an 'Associative State,' 1921–1928," *Journal of American History* 61, no. 1 (1974): 117–18.

friends until he moved to Oregon in 1889 to live with his uncle, Dr. John Minthorn, and his aunt Laura. It was during his brief two-year stay in Oregon that his mentor uncle exposed him to business. Hoover worked as an office boy in Minthorn's Oregon Land Company. Not only did he gain knowledge of real estate transactions, but he had the opportunity to meet Robert Brown, a mining engineer. That chance meeting ignited Hoover's interest in engineering and mining.[11]

Hoover's life may have lacked stability, but his Quaker upbringing filled him with a strong sense of community cooperation in which everyone gave their best effort for the good of the entire community. This approach to individual and community welfare, a balance between an individual's right to advance and the good of society—what Hoover later called "progressive individualism"—buttressed by his belief in Jeffersonian agrarian idealism,[12] obviously influenced his approach to public-private cooperation.

Herbert Hoover was a self-made man. A member of the first class to graduate from Stanford University, he became one of the institution's early trustees. He followed a successful career in the mining industry with a longer, more successful career in public service. He made his name as a humanitarian and built a strong reputation as a man of action while dealing with the famine in Europe and Russia after World War I. Hoover served as secretary of commerce for eight years under Presidents Warren Harding and Calvin Coolidge before being elected US president in 1928.

Industrialization had begun in the United States a century earlier, but it hit its stride following the Civil War in the second half of the nineteenth century. By the time Hoover became commerce secretary, the United States had emerged as the strongest world power with a mature and productive economy, primarily as a consequence of World War I. In many ways the associative state had already taken root in American agriculture, finance, and manufacturing. Recognizing the need to encourage, reward, and support the values of hard work and self-reliance, Hoover believed institutions needed to be stimulated, encouraged, and nurtured. Cooperative institutions such as mutual insurance companies, mutual savings banks, credit unions, and agricultural cooperatives, along with unions and business and professional

---

11 Joan H. Wilson and Oscar Handlin, *Herbert Hoover, Forgotten Progressive* (Boston: Little, Brown, 1975), 4–10.

12 Ibid., 6–7.

organizations, emerged to both advance and protect their respective interests and the interests of their members.

Hoover believed that a cooperative effort by these associations would create a "type of private government, one that would meet the need for national reform, greater stability, and steady expansion, yet avoid the evils long associated with 'capital consolidations' [monopolies], politicized cartels, and government bureaucracies . . . These newer institutions would preserve and work through individual units, committing themselves voluntarily to service, efficiency, and ethical behavior." The result would be a "new and enlightened leadership"[13] that would limit excessive oversight. Hoover envisioned an American society based on self-reliant smallholders, influenced by Jefferson's yeoman farmer ideal, and individualistic business owners who would protect Americans' ideals, lifestyle, and freedom; he realized that such a vision would require not only cooperation but also organization and standardization.

Attempts to organize and standardize the mortgage banking and real estate industries had begun as early as the 1890s with the formation of the first state associations. In Kansas, for example, the goal was to create a business model that promoted ethical lending standards and prohibited excessive fees while creating a self-policing model. Another organization came about in 1892 when the United States League of Savings Institutions (the League) emerged from the unification of many of the small national, state, and regional savings and trade associations. After the collapse of the national building and loans in 1893, the League tried to improve its image by cultivating a message of thrift and assisting members of the broad middle class in becoming homeowners.[14] True to the ideals of associationalism, most of these institutions were owned by their depositors, as evidenced by their purchase of shares or cash deposits in the mutual institution. The League's most important contribution to the associationalism movement was its support of the creation of the Federal Home Loan Bank System by President Hoover in 1932. The system created a regulatory framework and a vehicle to provide liquidity to local thrifts in much the same way the Federal Reserve provides liquidity to banks.

---

13 Hawley, "Herbert Hoover," 117.

14 Mason, *Buildings and Loans*, 86.

First convention dinner of the Farm Mortgage Bankers Association, October 8, 1914.
Courtesy, Mark Reidy.

A more prominent and long-lasting example of organization and standardization is the National Association of Real Estate Exchanges. Formed in 1908 by a number of local real estate exchange organizations, its goal was to bring order, discipline, and information to real estate markets and offices. In 1916 the organization changed its name to the National Association of Real Estate Boards. A key component of these real estate organizations was to provide a reliable source of information to both the industry and government organizations. Responding to the problems of the real estate and mortgage lending industry, the National Association of Real Estate Boards formed two institutes to promote industry professionalism. The first of these, created in 1932, was the American Institute of Real Estate Appraisers. The following year saw the foundation of the Institute of Real Estate Management. The National Association of Homebuilders did not materialize until 1942. In 1972 the National Association of Real Estate Boards changed its name once again, to the National Association of Realtors (NAR).[15]

---

15 National Association of Realtors, "Mission, Vision, and History," accessed April 8, 2007,
    https://www.nar.realtor/about-nar/mission-vision-and-history; Appraisal Institute, "Our

Yet it is the Farm Mortgage Bankers Association (FMBA) that perhaps best exemplifies the type of organization Hoover espoused. Many mortgage bankers became increasingly concerned as they witnessed the federal government's growing interest in the farm mortgage banking industry from 1908 into 1913, including the creation of the Federal Reserve System. As Congress began deliberating the recommendations submitted by the American and United States Commissions, the threat of intervention in the credit markets became more serious. Most mortgage bankers viewed the possibility of the creation of Federal Farm Loan Banks as particularly ominous. But some mortgage bankers anticipated the need for the industry to separate itself from rogue agents and identify itself as made up of reputable, professional financial institutions that provided a valuable service.[16]

To do so, in May 1914 a group of representatives from approximately forty-five well-established mortgage banking firms met at the Astor Hotel in New York to organize the FMBA. These firms represented institutional investors both at home and abroad, with nine representing firms from Kansas. During that initial meeting they drafted a constitution and by-laws for the association. To ensure the quality and professionalism of FMBA members, one of the by-laws dictated that membership in the organization would require a minimum capitalization of $50,000, but that amount was reduced to $25,000 the following year.[17] The preamble to the FMBA constitution stated:

In the belief that the formation of an association of individuals and corporations dealing in farm mortgage loans will in general promote their welfare and extend their influence and specifically accomplish this desirable object by 1) encouraging intelligent legislation affecting the business, 2) acquiring and disseminating correct information regarding the business, 3) aiding public discrimination between such securities and dealers therein and that should command confidence in those who should not, 4) securing uniformity of practice where uniformity is desirable, 5) affording opportunity for those engaged in the business to secure the benefits of personal acquaintance and interchange of ideas,

---

History," accessed April 8, 2007, https://www.appraisalinstitute.org/about/our-history

16 Lesley Hall, "The First Century," *Mortgage Banking's Centennial Special Edition* (October 2013): 8.

17 Robins, *Farm Mortgage Handbook*, 198. Using the consumer price index as a deflator, the required $25,000 in 1914 would have equaled $6 million in 2013 (Snowden, *Special Report*, 33).

both by individual contact and public discussion in various ways not herein enumerated, we submit a formal constitution and bylaws for such organization.[18]

This meeting and the founding of a national trade organization proved
to be a watershed moment for the mortgage banking industry. The express
purpose of the FMBA was to find a way to bring order to the chaos surrounding agricultural credit in the farm mortgage banking industry. It provided a
forum to unify the mortgage banking industry, to create a public voice and
maintain a seat at the public policy table, and to protect the correspondent
system, which has survived in various forms to this day. The new organization also established a code of conduct to guide its members' business practices. The FMBA adopted the constitution and by-laws at its first national
convention in Chicago, held a few months later in October.[19]

Colorado did not participate in the founding of the FMBA and did not
formally organize its own state association, the Denver Mortgage Bankers
Association, until 1956. However, that does not mean that Colorado's mortgage bankers acted independently or ignored the national organization. C. C.
Bennett represented Colorado's interests when he took a seat on the MBA's
Board of Governors in 1922. Others followed him in taking leadership positions, including Aksel Nielsen. The Centennial State has been a major player
on the industry's national stage since the late 1940s.

Clearly, as outlined in the preamble, the stated purpose of the FMBA was
to align the interests of the mortgage banker with those of the investor. The
group sought to speak with one voice when dealing with the array of issues
that had been simmering since the 1890s. As in many organizations, members held varying opinions about the potential threats posed by the creation
of a Federal Farm Loan System. Some felt it was an opportunity to create a
new investor class, while others feared a substantial government intrusion of
questionable constitutionality into their business.

The October 9, 1914, edition of the *Chicago Daily Tribune* reported on the
FMBA's offer to assist with legislation governing farm credits. It attributed the
FMBA's promise of "cooperation" with Congress to meet the credit needs
of American agriculture by providing rural credits in a prudent manner to

---

18 Hall, "First Century," 8; Robins, *Farm Mortgage Handbook*, 197.
19 Robins, *Farm Mortgage Handbook*, 197.

George Ramsey, the first chair of the organization's legislative committee.[20] Because farm mortgage bankers from the 1880s through the 1920s operated in underserved markets by building the correspondent system that channeled private and institutional money to agriculture, many members resisted adapting to structural changes in the industry. Scattered across the rural West and Midwest, member firms had built a substantial presence in their local markets by providing real estate brokerage, insurance, and property management services as well as mortgage banking to their communities. Exercising their entrepreneurial spirit, they committed themselves to protecting the businesses and the correspondent system they had worked so hard to develop.

Given the economic circumstances of 1914, the greatest demand for farm mortgage credit and the largest presence of farm mortgage banking firms was in the state of Kansas. It held the distinction of being the "wheat state" and breadbasket of the nation, and it also produced an abundance of alfalfa and other crops. Kansas obviously had an abundance of agricultural products but lacked the capital to be truly successful. New England possessed plenty of capital, so the issue became how to bring these two regions together.[21] Prior experience with farm mortgages and their performance during panics and recessions in the period 1873 through the 1890s had made eastern capital leery of rural credits. Many investors had not been sufficiently discriminating or had not done the proper due diligence regarding the risks of agricultural credits. Unlike many other investments, agricultural credits rely solely on income, and eastern investors had little understanding of the unquantifiable risks presented by the region's environmental issues. The FMBA hoped to define the risks and inform the investing public of the opportunities in rural Kansas and other western states.

A strong connection existed between Kansas and New England dating back to the 1850s. Contrary to common public knowledge, the Civil War started in Kansas long before guns fired on Fort Sumpter. Violence between abolitionist immigrant settlers from New England, including John Brown, and proslavery interests from neighboring Missouri began almost before the ink had dried on the Kansas-Nebraska Act that created Kansas Territory in 1854. In 1855 Isaac Goodnow, who figured prominently in the development of Kansas,

---

20 "Mortgage Bankers Offer Congress Aid," *Chicago Daily Tribune*, October 9, 1914.

21 Hall, "First Century," 9.

and the New England Emigrant Aid Company established the anti-slavery community of Boston in Riley County, Kansas. A few months later a group of emigrants from Ohio joined them, and the town was renamed Manhattan. The majority of the county's settlers opposed slavery, with some espousing abolitionism. According to Riley County historian Cheryl Collins, members of Beecher Bible Church, just a few miles from Manhattan, imported rifles and ammunition hidden below layers of Bibles in crates shipped from Massachusetts. The troubles of "Bleeding Kansas" created headlines across the country and foretold the Civil War that divided the nation.[22]

During its first decade of operation, the association limited its membership only to institutions actively engaged in making farm mortgage loans. In fact, one of the FMBA's by-laws prohibited membership of firms that invested in city mortgages. Perhaps as a reflection of the increased competition provided by the Farm Loan Act of 1916 or the agricultural recession of the early 1920s or the industrialization of the country, the organization changed its name to the Mortgage Bankers Association of America (MBA) in 1927 and began recruiting city mortgage bankers as members. By 1933, 80 percent of the membership was engaged in investing in city mortgages, and only 20 percent was still involved in farm mortgages.[23]

The alignment of the interests of mortgage bankers and investors formalized their existing relationships, with benefits accruing to the borrower, the mortgage banker, and the investor. Mortgage banking companies that had managed their business operations and relationships with their life insurance company investors well survived the 1890s and were well positioned to prosper as the nation entered the twentieth century's age of commercial agriculture. Successful mortgage bankers possessed the ability to achieve attractive enough yields to accumulate mortgage portfolios suitable for potential investors. In exchange for the assurance that good credits were provided, mortgage bankers aggressively serviced the loans and verified that the obligations of the contract were fulfilled. Under those circumstances, when market conditions changed and communities began to grow, requiring additional funding for city/urban mortgages, a platform already existed to fill those needs. Those

22 Riley County Historical Museum, "History of Riley County," accessed May 2, 2017, http://www.rileycountyks.gov/441/History-of-Riley-County; E. Michael Rosser, telephone interview with Cheryl Collins, May 8, 2017.

23 Hall, "First Century," 11.

relationships would serve all parties well when the Great Depression took hold of the United States following the stock market crash in October 1929.

Ironically, many of the farm mortgage bankers' fears about the success of the Farm Loan Bank System never materialized. Some imprecise language in the enabling legislation contributed to the slow development of Federal Land Banks and joint-stock land banks during the first fifteen years following passage of the law. The *Smith v. Kansas City Title and Trust Company*[24] lawsuit created a constitutional challenge to the tax-exempt status of the bonds of joint-stock institutions and contributed to the delay, even after the Court ruling in February 1921 upheld the constitutionality of the Farm Loan Act.[25] Nevertheless, by 1930 the federal land and joint-stock land banks held 18.7 percent of the nation's mortgage debt while insurance companies held 21.9 percent; 49 percent was funded by "others," including individuals and mortgage companies.[26] The continued strength of insurance companies and mortgage bankers is attributable to the strong correspondent relationships that had previously developed between them. These relationships exemplified the type of working relationships advocated by Hoover to advance urban lending and led the industry away from its focus on farm mortgage lending and toward more urban lending in the post–World War I era.

When sworn in as commerce secretary in 1920, Hoover brought an engineer's discipline to the government. He began an ambitious campaign to transform a dusty backwater bureaucracy into an agent of change. His appointment of John M. Gries to head of the newly formed Division of Building and Housing proved one of Hoover's most important appointments that affected middle America. The new agency was charged with designing the tools and providing the resources to increase public interest and participation in homeownership. Its stated purpose was to provide economic research and education to the public regarding house plans, methods of purchasing and financing homes, and encouragement of zoning to protect housing values. In addition, Hoover advocated for the standardization of building materials and the organization and training of the building trades—actions that would require cooperation among a number of interests including materials producers and fabricators,

---

24 255 U.S. 180 (1921).

25 Larry E. Yackle, "Federal Banks and Federal Jurisdiction in the Progressive Era: A Case Study of *Smith v. Kansas City Title and Trust Co.*," *Kansas Law Review* 62 (2013): 255.

26 Snowden, *Special Report*, 43.

tradespeople, architects, engineers, and urban planners. He also fought for the availability of affordable credits for borrowers as well as for slum improvement and rehabilitation. At the same time, Hoover demonstrated his strong belief in self-reliance by affirming that he did not "feel that a government financial subsidy to home-building was either desirable or necessary."[27]

Hoover's commitment to the mission of the associative state occurred early in the administration of President Harding. One of his first initiatives focused on getting municipalities to recognize the need to reform their institutions and acknowledge the changing conditions of life in the 1920s. Cities and municipalities needed to provide adequate open spaces, parks, and playgrounds to help relieve the misery of tenant life. Transportation and street design, coupled with zoning laws, were needed to protect homeowners from encroachment by nonconforming uses. When Hoover started this initiative, only 48 municipalities in the country had zoning laws; by 1928 the list included 640. In a 1922 report to Congress, Hoover recommended systematic measures of cooperation with the appointment of a committee to formulate standard building codes. The committee submitted a draft for those codes to over 900 engineers, architects, and representatives of the building industry. Their feedback to the committee resulted in the publication in 1928 of the first formal standard building code.[28]

In addition to Hoover's advocacy for the reduced cost of homeownership by way of better city planning and zoning, he sought solutions to lowering the cost of mortgages. His strong belief in savings and self-reliance made him a strong supporter of the thrift industry. However, to accomplish these goals he needed a public outreach program. He found his solution in the Better Homes organization created by Mrs. William Brown Meloney in 1922. Meloney was the editor of *The Delineator*, a national magazine that claimed a committed readership of over 1 million women.

Hoover and Meloney, along with other key government officials and business leaders, developed a volunteer organization called Better Homes in America, which promoted a nationwide campaign to expand homeownership and home improvement through education. In addition to articles printed in *The Delineator* and newspapers across the county that offered advice on house

---

27 Herbert Hoover, *The Memoirs of Herbert Hoover: The Cabinet and the Presidency, 1920–1933* (New York: Macmillan, 1952), 92–93.

28 Ibid., 94–95.

styles, decorating, and home improvements, the organization published its own pamphlets and provided materials to assist new homeowners in the selection, purchase, and financing of new homes. The volunteer organization raised $75,000 to $250,000 annually in support from private sources. At its height, Better Homes registered 9,000 active committees, with a nationwide membership of 30,000. Together with the National Association of Architects, the Better Homes organization sponsored an annual design competition for houses priced from $3,000 to $9,000.[29]

Whether Meloney had studied the houses offered in the Sears, Roebuck and Company (Sears) catalogs will never be known. But if she did, they may have provided the inspiration, at least in part, for her creation of the Better Homes in America movement. This iconic Chicago company had been a leader in the home building and mortgage business since 1908. Part of the attraction of the Sears homes was their simplicity and affordability for the emerging American middle class. Even before the Better Homes in America movement attracted Washington's attention, the American desire for ownership and financial security was beginning to transfer from the farm to urban and suburban America. Sears contributed to making this dream a reality and in many ways contributed to the future direction of housing across the country. Part of the company's success can be attributed to Sears's famous consumer promise, still proudly displayed at the entrances to its stores, "Satisfaction Guaranteed or Your Money Back."

Sears introduced its first *Book of Modern Homes and Building Plans* in 1908. It contained forty designs priced from $495 to $4,115. Although it had been advertising building materials in its catalog since 1895, marketing and selling a kit home through the catalog was a monumental achievement. By the early 1920s Sears *Modern Homes* catalog included 144 pages displaying 90 home styles with options for garages, outhouses, and chicken coops. Sears also offered a schoolhouse kit for $11,500.[30]

By 1914 the company was marketing complete precut kits that could be assembled by a homeowner who had even marginal construction abilities. To demonstrate the economy and savings of Sears homes, the company staged various demonstration events. One such event in 1921 centered on

---

29 Ibid., 93; Janet Hutchison, "The Cure for Domestic Neglect: Better Homes in America, 1922–1935," *Perspectives in Vernacular Architecture* 2 (1986): 168.

30 Rosemary Thornton, *The Houses That Sears Built* (Norfolk, VA: Gentle Beam, 2004), 3–5.

a race between construction of a house using traditional building practices and assemblage of a comparable Sears kit house. Of course, the Sears house was built in considerably less time.[31]

Sears made the purchasing process simple. For one dollar the customer would receive a complete set of building plans. Beginning in 1911 Sears offered mortgages on an easy payment program. Once the prospective homeowner demonstrated that he held clear title to the building lot and completed a simple one-page order/loan application form, the kit would be shipped in two railroad boxcars, ready for assembly. Qualification for the loan was based on just one question—the applicant's vocation. The loans, written at 6 percent interest, required a small monthly payment and were the first stated income loans.[32]

As World War I came to an end in 1918, housing analysts' estimates determined that the nation needed an additional 1 million to 2 million homes.[33] Sears stepped up to meet that need. Success followed Sears homes across the country until the Great Depression. In 1929 sales crested at just over $12 million, but by 1932 the company was losing money; sales dropped 40 percent in one year alone. In 1933 sales dropped to a meager $3.6 million, causing the company to close its Modern Homes Department the following year. During its history in the home building business, Sears sold approximately 75,000 mail order homes based on nearly 400 different designs and options.[34]

"In 1934, Sears liquidated more than $11 million of their home mortgages. At the time . . . the average Sears house cost well under $3,000."[35] Assuming an average loan amount of $2,500, this represented delinquencies and foreclosures on approximately 4,400 homes. Most likely, these loans were taken over by the Home Owners Loan Corporation. Sears received a black eye in the media for foreclosing on its best customers.

One unique Colorado example of a Sears house is the saga of the Kouba family's purchase. Helen Kouba purchased a Sears home kit in 1910 for $3,000 and waited another thirteen years for it to be assembled on the family's ranch in what is now Sedalia, southwest of Denver. Forty-seven years later, when the Kouba's grandson, Pat Allis, and his wife moved into the house, they

---

31 Ibid., 11.

32 Ibid., 3–6.

33 Ibid., 5.

34 Ibid., 7–9.

35 Ibid., 6.

The Kouba family in front of their Sears mail order house, ca. 1923. Courtesy, Allis Ranch Winery, Sedalia, CO.

found it in a deteriorating state of neglect. They spent the next twenty years making improvements to the house and filling the surrounding gardens with flowers. After Pat's death in 1991, the family sold the house and the ranch's 840 acres to Colorado Open Lands, which created the Allis Ranch Preserve.[36]

By 2004 the house had again been subject to such neglect that it was all but unlivable. Margaret and Dave Rhyne, who owned the adjacent lot, convinced the other homeowners within the preserve to add the house to the Rhyne's property in exchange for the responsibility of restoring the building. After gutting the interior down to the studs, an engineer determined that the house was structurally sound. The Rhynes then installed new heating and electrical systems and replaced the drafty windows that Pat had long ago stuffed with newspaper with visually identical but energy-efficient ones. They refinished the original wood floors they discovered beneath carpeting that hid layers of linoleum. They hand-milled base and window trim to match the profile of the original materials. Capped off with new paint and a new roof, this delightful little Sears house has been fully restored and is probably in better condition than ever.[37] Today the Allis Ranch Winery uses the house for its offices, public tasting room, and production facility.[38]

36 Margaret Rhyne, "Alexis' House at Allis Ranch" (unpublished, available at Allis Ranch Winery, Sedalia, CO, 2015).

37 Ibid.

38 Margaret Rhyne, "History of Allis Ranch and Allis Ranch House," Allis Ranch Winery, accessed September 17, 2015, http://www.allisranchwinery.com/scripts/historyPg.cfm.

The restored house, ca. 2005. Courtesy, Allis Ranch Winery, Sedalia, CO.

Looking back on the quality of Sears homes over the last 110-plus years, the kit homes have withstood the test of changing times, tastes, styles, and fads. Rosemary Thornton cited an article in the September 13, 2001, edition of the *Washington Post* that reported the recent $816,000 resale of "a modest Sears home in Chevy Chase, Maryland."[39] An informed estimate today would value the property near $1.3 million, assuming it is in good condition. Rarely mentioned is the fact that President Richard Nixon's boyhood home in Whittier, California, is a Sears home.

Hoover's influence and the country's rapid urbanization led mortgage bankers to become much more involved in both commercial and residential urban lending during the 1920s. In 1924 the Service Investment Company (SIC) of Denver was established to invest the surplus funds of smaller financial institutions and private individuals in home mortgages and to make construction loans to individual builders in the city. Many

---

39 Thornton, *Houses That Sears Built*, 3.

neighborhood and ethnic thrift associations also made loans to their members. Hoover recognized that his goal of expanded home ownership depended on adequate financing. At the same time, he also recognized the dangers presented by the common practice of borrowers with insufficient savings using second mortgages to supply funds for the down payment. Such loans charged a higher rate of interest than first mortgages and often required repayment within a very short time frame, most in as few as five years. This additional layer of risk was responsible in part for the high rates of foreclosure during the Great Depression of the 1930s and the more recent Great Recession of 2008.[40]

In 1931, then President Hoover opened a conference to study and discuss the nation's housing problems. The conference focused on two primary issues—creation of a credit system that would allow borrowers who enjoyed steady work, sound character and credit, and an earnest desire to own a home but without sufficient funds to meet the required 50 percent down payment many lenders demanded to buy a home and second, the need to improve the blighted areas and slums of the nation's cities. The conference yielded a number of papers that included recommendations to address these complicated issues. Some of the papers' titles were *Planning Residential Districts, Slums and Decentralization, Home Finance and Taxation, Home Ownership, Farm Housing, Negro Housing,* and *Housing Objectives.* These publications helped set the standards for the nation. Hoover initiated a program of national action for new methods and community cooperation. A further outcome was the establishment in 1932 of the Federal Home Loan Bank System, which ultimately served as the first step toward today's complex mortgage system.[41]

From its inception in 1914 through the mid-1930s the FMBA, then the MBA, dedicated itself to political action. During the economic recovery from the farm recession of the early 1920s, the industry fought for removal of the tax-exempt status of federal securities and the restrictions on the interstate sale of securities. In 1927 the MBA became a strong advocate for a uniform standard of title and mortgage laws, as well as national servicing standards.[42] Throughout the period, the organization exerted enormous influence by advocating for public policies to solve many of the nation's economic

---

40 Hoover, *Memoirs*, 95.

41 Ibid., 258.

42 Hall, "First Century," 10.

problems. The MBA actively engaged in promoting and guiding the structure of the FHA and Fannie Mae. As the MBA's engagement in policymaking increased, so did the intensity of the federal government's involvement.

The MBA actively opposed public housing legislation, preferring a more public-private partnership. As an alternative, it urged the FHA to use its funds to rehabilitate blighted areas instead of using government credits to force interest rates down. In addition, the organization expressed concern about the encroachment and expansion of the government in the field of farm mortgage lending. The MBA also advocated further efforts to standardize mortgage documentation and improve foreclosure procedures nationwide.[43] Its industry advocacy at the federal, state, and regional levels continues to sustain Hoover's belief in associationalism.

In his memoir, President Hoover wrote about his experiences in government service. He acknowledged and took some pride in the success of his efforts to improve American housing—the increase in the number of detached homes and the improvements made in multi-family apartment projects. During his time in Washington, not only the quantity but also the quality of housing increased.[44]

President Hoover's forgotten legacy is twofold. First was his dogged determination to advance urban revitalization through new development and slum clearance. By the 1920s more than half of the American population had left the farm and moved to the cities. Rapid industrialization had brought slums and overcrowded tenements to urban America. Hoover strove to remedy the housing conditions of the 30 percent of the American public who lived in housing that "was below the ideals of decent family life."[45] Robert and Helen Lynd's classic study of American life in the mid-1920s revealed that just under half of all homes had central heat provided by a furnace. Their study also found that approximately 25 percent of American homes lacked running water; occupants brought water inside from a backyard well, and a "privy," also in the backyard, served as the only toilet.[46] In most older homes, especially those occupied by working-class families, there simply was

---

43 Ibid., 14.

44 Hoover, *Memoirs*, 93.

45 Ibid., 92.

46 Robert S. Lynd and Helen M. Lynd, *Middletown: A Study in American Culture* (San Diego: Harcourt, Brace, 1957), 96–97.

no space to add a bathroom. Where city water and sewage systems *were* available, the new "bathroom" was often a lone toilet installed in the cellar, under a staircase, or inside an existing closet.[47]

During his time in Washington as a member of the cabinet and as president, Hoover laid the groundwork for the modern American city. His second and more lasting contribution was as an advocate for city planning, building codes, and the home mortgage finance system. The considerable success of the US mortgage finance system, envied around the world, is largely a result of the plans and programs of the man from West Branch, Iowa.

It might be an overstatement to say that what Hoover accomplished for the urban middle class and housing by providing an opportunity for ownership and a financial stake in the success of American society is comparable to Jefferson's advocacy of the yeoman farmer. But Hoover should certainly be credited for his leadership in creating a culture of good planning and design and supporting the associations and institutions that promoted economic sustainability.

FEDERAL FARM LOAN ACT OF 1916

The history of the Federal Farm Loan Act (FLA), its context, and the reasons for its passage were outlined earlier. The Federal Farm Loan Program, created by the act, became the first modern government-sponsored enterprise (GSE). As defined by Investopedia, "A government-sponsored enterprise consists of privately held corporations with public purposes created by the US Congress to reduce the cost of capital for certain borrowing sectors of the economy. Members of these sectors include students, farmers and homeowners."[48] Not surprisingly, the GSE was met with a decidedly mixed reaction. Also discussed earlier, concern about the pending legislation prompted the 1914 founding of the FMBA, whose members considered government action an intrusion into the private sector. Privately, many members questioned the constitutionality of the FLA but publicly agreed to work with Congress.[49]

---

47 Alison K. Hoagland, "Introducing the Bathroom: Space and Change in Working Class Houses," *Building and Landscapes* 18, no. 2 (2011): 16, 28–30.

48 Investopedia, "Government-Sponsored Enterprise," accessed February 24, 2016, http://www.investopedia.com/terms/g/gse.asp.

49 "Mortgage Bankers Offer Congress Aid."

In 1913, in response to the nation's history of financial panics, Congress passed the Federal Reserve Act authorizing the creation of the Federal Reserve System (the Fed). Driven in part by the need to support the growth of industrial agriculture, the Fed loosened the restrictions on real estate lending by commercial banks, but only slightly. Nevertheless, banks continued to stay away from real estate lending as a policy matter.

For the next three years Congress continued to debate the conditions and language of the proposed FLA. During that process, legislators received input from the American and United States Commissions and a variety of interest groups, including the FMBA. Strong lobbying by the Farmers Union and the National Grange in driving social policy contributed to the successful adoption of the FLA. Still, Congress correctly anticipated strong opposition on constitutional grounds.

In 1918 the FMBA joined Charles E. Smith, a stockholder and director of the Kansas City Title and Trust Company, in a constitutional challenge of the Farm Loan Act by filing a suit in the Federal District Court in Kansas City. The case was later appealed to the US Supreme Court. In a "friendly suit," Smith sought an injunction against his own company to prohibit the use of corporate funds to purchase tax-exempt bonds issued by the Federal Land Banks or the joint-stock banks created by the FLA. Smith's theory was that the trust company's charter permitted investments only in lawful securities and that the bonds in general and the tax-exempt status of the bonds in particular were unjustified and illegal under any of Congress's enumerated powers.[50]

Boston University law professor Larry E. Yackle provided an excellent explanation of the suit and its consequences in an article published in the *Kansas Law Review*. The decision in the case of *Smith v. Kansas City Title and Trust Company* was not exactly straightforward. The issue went back to the case of *McCullough v. Maryland*[51] almost a century earlier in 1819 when Chief Justice John Marshall expansively interpreted the power granted to Congress by the US Constitution by upholding Congress's authority to establish the Second National Bank of the United States. Marshall's opinion asserted that the validity of these federal banks could be best assured by empowering them to hold

50 Yackle, "Federal Banks," 255–60.
51 17 U.S. 316 (1819).

public money and to administer the government's finances, however slight or insignificant.[52] Therefore, Marshall's US Supreme Court ruling in *McCullough* enabled the Court to affirm Congress's ability under the US Constitution to create government-sponsored credit facilities for farmers. Defending the legislation, Justice Hughes wrote, "Congress has the power to create a corporation whenever it would be appropriate to assist in the execution of any authority vested in Congress." He continued, claiming that "the Farm Loan System is an aid to the development of agriculture through the whole United States, and hence provides for the general welfare" as allowed by the US Constitution.[53] The ruling in *Smith v. Kansas City Title and Trust Company* thus validated the Farm Loan Act, establishing the precedent for the creation of the Federal Home Loan Bank System in 1932 and Fannie Mae in 1938. GSEs later expanded to include loan programs for homeowners and students, among others.

A previous precedent-setting case in 1907, *Kansas v. Colorado*,[54] involved a dispute over Arkansas River water rights. The case affirmed the federal government's power to promote the development of agriculture.

As for the joint-stock farm loan banks, about eighty-seven were created over the life of the program, and most were profitable through World War I.[55] During the ensuing depression of the early 1920s, many of these institutions suffered. In 1923, Congress curtailed their authority by limiting the size of loans they could make and restricted their business to agricultural projects. Compounding the problems of the joint-stock banks, Congress provided a bailout for the land banks following the great crash in 1929 but not for the joint-stock banks, signaling their eventual demise. According to Yackle, "The Emergency Farm Mortgage Act of 1933 created a number of new federal institutions to supply rural credit but provided for the liquidation of all of the joint-stock banks still standing."[56]

In 1933, President Roosevelt abolished the Federal Farm Loan Board and transferred supervisory responsibility to the newly created Farm Credit Administration. Over succeeding decades, numerous reorganization plans

---

52 Yackle, "Federal Banks," 265.
53 Quoted by William M. Bullitt, speech at the Farm Mortgage Bankers Association National Convention, Kansas City, MO, September 19, 1918, 34.
54 206 U.S. 46 (1907).
55 Yackle, "Federal Banks," 310.
56 Ibid., 311.

perpetuated the system. The Agricultural Credit Act of 1987 collapsed the land banks into the Farm Credit Banks. The act also provided for the establishment of another GSE, the Federal Agricultural Mortgage Corporation, also known as Farmer Mac. Formally established in 1988, this GSE pools loans from institutional lenders and issues securities with the guarantee of timely payment of principal and interest in the same manner as the Government National Mortgage Association (Ginnie Mae).

During the early 1970s, life insurance companies remained active in agricultural lending, funding everything from family farms and ranches to meat-packing operations such as the Monfort facility in Greeley, which combined cattle feedlots with facilities that slaughtered and processed the carcasses into smaller units for distribution to retailers. In testimony before the Subcommittee of Agricultural Credit and Rural Electrification of the Senate Committee on Agriculture and Forestry in May 1971, Everett Spelman of Denver, president of the MBA, testified that life insurance companies held over $5.8 billion in farm loans and that private institutions, excluding federal agencies, held 57 percent of all farm mortgage debt.[57] He also spoke about the role of the GSEs, particularly regarding their impact on farm mortgage banking. Spelman referenced a prediction made by Frederick P. Champ, a prominent farmer mortgage banker, in a 1965 article published in the journal *Mortgage Banking.* Champ asserted that any agency subsidized by exemption from paying federal income tax would ultimately dominate and monopolize the field in which it operated.[58] As predicted, over time, insurance companies would move away from financing family farms, gravitating to larger, more industrial corporate farms—a move that escalated both the corporatization of American agriculture and the advancement of the American dream of homeownership, especially in the ever-expanding suburbs, through mortgage bankers' increased attention to the residential sector.

57 Miles Colean and Columbia University Oral History Review, *A Backward Glance—an Oral History: The Growth of Government Housing Policy in the United States 1934–1975* (Washington, DC: Research and Educational Trust Fund, 1975), 46.

58 Everett Spelman, "MBA's Testimony on Farm Credit Proposals," *Mortgage Banker* (July 1971): 49.

Part III

GOVERNMENT HOUSING PROGRAMS AND THE EVOLUTION OF MORTGAGE BANKING

7

The Federal Housing Administration and the Housing Act of 1934 and Beyond

One of the most successful programs for attracting increased investment in the mortgage industry was, and continues to be, Federal Housing Administration (FHA) mortgage insurance. The National Housing Act of 1934 contained a provision for an FHA mortgage insurance program designed to stimulate the rehabilitation of existing properties while encouraging the construction of new, modern homes. It was designed to create jobs and to fulfill President Franklin D. Roosevelt's desire for a privately funded government initiative without the use of tax dollars. It was hoped that government insurance would increase lending activity by mitigating the cost of foreclosures to lenders. The purpose of Title I of the act was to create insurance on loans for renovation. Title II provided mortgage guarantee insurance for long-term mortgages, both single-family[1] and multi-family properties. In later years, FHA Title II also insured mortgages on hospitals, senior housing, nursing homes, and condominiums. In short, the FHA is an insurance

---

1   The FHA Section 203b program includes single-family homes, duplexes, triplexes, and four-plexes in the single-family building category.

DOI: 10.5876/9781607326236.c007

company. It is composed of four separate funds, the largest of which is the Mutual Mortgage Insurance Fund.

The promise of a safe and decent home for every American was the goal of the 1949 Housing Act. That goal, whether stated in the letter or the spirit of the law, became entrenched as part of subsequent housing acts and remains an essential part of America's social fabric. In Miles Colean's oral history of his career, which lasted from the 1920s through 1975, a common thread runs through the performance of the government's role in housing. That thread is the delicate balance between the program's social purpose and sound fiscal management.[2]

A MULTITUDE OF FINANCING PROGRAMS

Over its history the FHA has been a laboratory for developing loan programs with the social purpose of meeting the varying needs of America's homeowners. The home equity conversion mortgage (reverse mortgage) is a good example; it is a program that allows seniors to stay in their homes, aging in place, without the burden of a monthly mortgage payment. Other examples of the successes include FHA Section 203b, the standard homeownership program; the 203k home rehabilitation program, the 207 multi-family program, the 221 affordable housing program, 221(d)4 that supports single-room occupancy housing, and the 242 program that provides mortgage insurance for hospitals. Many of the programs the FHA developed have enjoyed long-term success, at times interspersed with short-term failures. The FHA 245 graduated payment program enjoyed some short-term success but in the long run turned out to be a passing fad. There have also been notable failures, including the massive subsidized housing projects Cabrini Green in Chicago and Pruitt-Igoe in St. Louis, the well-intended but failed FHA Section 235 loan program of the 1970s, and the seller-assisted down payment programs of the early 2000s. One of the long-term goals that existed, and in some cases still exists, in all these programs is an effort to ensure economic and program sustainability.

---

2   Miles L. Colean and Columbia University Oral History Review, *A Backward Glance—an Oral History: The Growth of Government Housing Policy in the United States 1934–1975* (Washington, DC: Research and Educational Trust Fund, 1975), 46.

Homeownership programs such as Sections 235 and 221(d)(2) shared the goal of expanding homeownership opportunities through payment subsidies and zero down payment programs. Neither program lasted. Section 221(d)(2) required a down payment of only $200. Of the roughly 100,000 mortgages insured through the program in 1970, 36 percent went into foreclosure and became claims against the Mutual Mortgage Insurance Fund. Lower down payments result in the borrower having less equity in the property and generate riskier mortgage loans. In a falling real estate market, the lack of equity encourages a strategic default in which the borrower abandons the property even when he or she can afford to make the payments.[3]

The FHA's underwriting guidelines had allowed borrowers to receive a gift for the down payment on their home purchase. A typical gift letter stated that the borrower(s) received the down payment funds as a gift, not a loan that needed to be repaid. Generally speaking, the source of the gift would have to prove that it had the surplus funds to donate to the borrower. In addition, some down payment assistance programs utilized locally funded grants and silent seconds that enabled individuals who were unable to accumulate enough funds through savings to get into a home. However, the seller could not "fund" the down payment. Still, seller incentives became a widespread business practice, particularly with new construction.

This issue generated vigorous discussion beginning in 1999 when so-called seller-funded down payment assistance programs emerged. Using a loophole in the regulation, a seller would make a gift to a nonprofit charity. The charity would then provide the down payment. In practice, the selling price of the house would be marked up to cover the "charitable contribution." Fannie Mae, Freddie Mac, and all seven mortgage insurance companies declined to participate in these programs because of the obvious risk.[4]

The FHA found itself in conflict with another government agency, the Internal Revenue Service (IRS), over this practice. Over time, the agencies established regulations determining that such "charitable contributions" did not violate the 501(c)(3) provisions of the tax code. Even so, the FHA's regulation on the sources of down payments was hotly disputed. A local IRS district office approved the tax-exempt status of the program, but in May 2006 the

---

3   Thomas Herzog and Alexander S. Majlaton, "FHA's Costly Experience with Seller Funded Downpayments," *Mortgage Banking* (October 2010): 98.

4   Ibid., 100.

Country Club Gardens and Towers, Denver, 2014. Courtesy of the authors.

Washington, DC, office of the IRS ruled that these charitable organizations did not qualify.[5]

The FHA multi-family programs have provided rental housing for vast numbers of Americans. The FHA 207 program facilitated the development of classic apartment communities such as Country Club Gardens in Denver. A consortium of five Denver banks provided the construction financing and received a commitment from Prudential for an $850,000 permanent loan. This three-story walkup apartment project was built on a five-and-a-half-acre site across from the Denver Country Club. Throughout the planning and construction phases, a mountain of correspondence grew among the local Denver architectural firm, the local FHA office, and the FHA's Washington, DC, architectural firm.[6]

---

5   Internal Revenue Service, "IRS Targets Down-Payment-Assistance Scams; Seller-Funded Programs Do Not Quality as Tax-Exempt," accessed May 4, 2006, https://www.irs.gov/uac/irs-targets-down-payment-assistance-scams-seller-funded-programs-do-not-qualify-as-tax-exempt.

6   E. S. Gregory, letter to Fisher, Fisher, and Hubbell, Architects, June 15, 1938, Van Schaak and Company Archives, Special Collections WH1293, Western History Department, Denver Public Library, Denver, CO.

Detailed discussions between the architects and the sponsors covered wide-ranging details such as the floor joists, the slope of the roofs, doorways and entrances, kitchen hardware, floor coverings, and more. Many of these conversations appear to have delayed the beginning of construction. In the end, it was the Connecticut General Life Insurance Company that provided the financing. Country Club Gardens remains one of Denver's iconic apartment residences, but in 2014 a proposal by the current owner called for a significant redevelopment, including a second high-rise tower.

The FHA Section 608 program created in 1942 allowed the FHA to insure mortgages on rental properties, thereby drawing more investment capital into rental property development for war workers. In 1946 Congress amended the law, giving priority to providing rental housing for veterans and their families over war workers. With the war over, few people, if any, objected to the focus on veterans. But the legislation redefining the mission of Section 608, "to further stimulate production of housing and extension of mortgage credit for veterans," also included a change in language that opened the door for possible financial abuses. Under the original 1942 law, to qualify for FHA insurance, mortgages could not exceed 90 percent of what the FHA estimated as "the reasonable replacement cost of the completed project."[7] The 1946 bill changed "reasonable replacement cost" to "necessary current cost." The wording change resulted in widespread abuses. As demonstrated by the media, the public believed developers were collecting excessive profits by inflating their construction costs. The resulting public outcry led Congress to insert changes in the 1954 Housing Act requiring developers to certify their actual construction costs to qualify for FHA insurance.

Palmer Park Gardens in Colorado Springs was just such a project. Built in 1949 with financing under the FHA 608 program, Palmer Park is a 200-unit apartment complex. In the early 1950s, at the height of the scandal, journalist Pasquale "Pocky" Marranzino wrote a series of columns in the *Rocky Mountain News* about excess profits and other issues in the 608 program. I remember that my father was very upset because the mortgage finance company he worked for, Jordan Mortgage Company, was the target of these articles. The challenge the builders and the FHA confronted in the immediate

---

7   Klaman, *Postwar Residential Mortgage Market,* 53–54.

Palmer Park Gardens, Colorado Springs, 2015. Courtesy of the authors.

postwar era was finding ways to access supplies of quality building materials since the industry had not fully adjusted following the war. Later examinations proved that Palmer Park Gardens was built in compliance with the 1946 legislation allowing for necessary current costs, and the FHA's construction standards were maintained. Many of the projects built under 608 remain today, including Palmer Park Gardens. It has been renovated and updated, but the core of the complex remains intact—a testament against the unfounded criticism it received early on.

Public housing, by and large, was a new experience in America. While city planners, architects, and sociologists worked diligently to design safe and livable homes for the poor, problems still existed; Denver was no exception. The initial screening of tenants was often inadequate. Maintenance expenses often ran high. Brick and concrete structures replaced those with deteriorated and damaged oak flooring and plaster walls. Notwithstanding all the hard work of city officials and community leaders, the projects lost their welcoming, home-like appearance and assumed a more institutional feel. The evolution created an environment conducive to crime, vandalism, and poor schools.

Spurred on by Jane Jacobs, urban activists, architects, planners, and developers began to seek out new solutions to the public housing problem.[8] Supported in part by insurance companies and civic-minded leaders from the mortgage banking industry, some communities adopted an entirely new philosophy when replacing and rebuilding public housing projects. One of the leaders of this new movement was Professor Oscar Newman of New York University.

Newman demonstrated that the use of thoughtful architecture and design could lower crime rates in public housing. By designing buildings in such a way that neighbors could become acquainted, they would have the ability to recognize who belonged on the property and challenge those who did not, effectively developing a "neighborhood watch" to protect their homes. Newman's criticism and public pressure led to a rethinking of what public housing should look like.[9]

In many ways, it was a conflicted time. The entire issue of subsidized housing became very controversial in the late 1970s, particularly in the area of public housing and some of the subsidized homeownership programs. Growing public resistance to subsidized housing originated from multiple sources, but the primary reason was probably the failure rate of these developments. The public had witnessed a virtual revolving door of initiatives. Whether as a result of poor program design, poor construction, poor management, or outright waste and corruption, far too many failed and everyone in the industry sought a solution. For my part, in conjunction with the Mortgage Bankers Association's (MBA) examination of the urban lending initiative, I invited Newman to speak at the association's 1978 conference in New York City.

During Newman's talk, he generally agreed with the audience that many of the subsidized housing programs could be reexamined, reformed, or in some cases completely eliminated. He stated that the largest subsidized program that could be curtailed or dropped completely was the home mortgage interest tax deduction. That was not a solution designed to warm hearts in a

---

8   Jane Jacobs, *The Life and Death of Great America Cities* (New York: Random House, 1961).

9   Oscar Newman, *Defensible Space: Crime Prevention through Urban Design* (New York: Collier Books, 1973).

roomful of mortgage and real estate executives. The subject of the mortgage interest tax deduction is still controversial and remains a subject of negotiation when discussing tax reform.

One of the programs in the 1968 Housing Act, designed to expand home-ownership through an interest rate subsidy to low-income borrowers, drew particular criticism. The FHA 235 program created a government subsidy of the interest rate charged on loans down to as low as 1 percent based on a calculation of the borrower's income. The borrower's income had to be re-verified every year to determine the level of subsidy. The program was universally abused, and investigators revealed many cases of fraud and misrepresentation. The FBI aggressively tracked down instances of fraud. The investigations led to the arrest of several individuals in the real estate and mortgage community in Denver, Detroit, Chicago, and other cities. The scandals brought the viability and purpose of the FHA into question. Not since the 608 program of the late 1940s and early 1950s had there been such a public outcry.

Expressing the frustration of many Americans and housing experts, MBA staff member Robert Gray complained that the 235 program did not solve the problems associated with public housing: "Public housing never provided a complete answer to the problem of housing the poor and never gave anyone a stake in the capitalistic system."[10] The program was ill conceived because, like the 236 program, the subsidized interest did not reduce monthly payments to any meaningful degree. In addition, those who did qualify were inadequately prepared for homeownership—something the Housing Act had tried to address by requiring counseling systems, but those systems were inadequately funded.

Section 237 of the 1968 Housing Act called for pre-purchase counseling for prospective homeowners. Everett Spelman, a Denver mortgage banker and president of the MBA, testified before Congress that underfunding of the Section 237 home buyer counseling program contributed to the failure of the FHA 235 program. Spelman commented in his testimony before the Senate Appropriations Subcommittee that the $9 million Congress allocated for the program was completely inadequate given the size and scope of the project.[11]

Following the conclusion of a number of studies, the Research Institute for Housing America (RIHA) published a paper in 2011 that reported on the

---

10   Robert Gray, "Good Counseling: The Answer in Successful 235 Housing," *Mortgage Banker* (August 1971).

11   Ibid.

effectiveness of home buyer counseling and education programs in predicting loan outcomes. The paper demonstrated that the programs achieved, at best, mixed results. However, those results may have been skewed because of the lack of desire or ability to conduct double-blind studies. In addition, unanticipated changes in individual or family circumstances almost certainly contributed both positive influences and negative impacts on home buyers' success at managing their loans and avoiding foreclosure.[12] Nevertheless, the mortgage banking industry and its leadership strongly supported home buyer education and counseling and do so to this day. Because of its industry support, HUD has continued to fund mortgage counseling, particularly for a number of its high-risk programs.

The FHA 235 single-family program was yet another case of the "social purpose" being misapplied and mismanaged. Yet one lesson learned from the 235 and 237 debacle found its way into a special program created for Colorado Springs–based Otero Savings and Loan. Regulators approved the authority of thrift institutions to provide checking accounts in the early 1980s. With the support of PMI Mortgage Insurance Company, Otero partnered with the Federal Home Loan Bank of Topeka in the unique affordable housing program using $3 million in community investment funds. As the national accounts sales manager for PMI, I worked with the senior staff at Otero Savings to develop a program using a residual income calculation formula pioneered by the Veterans Administration (VA) loan guarantee program. That program had been highly successful in all but the most severe regional or national economic recessions and served as a great model for this experiment. The program measured how much income a family had left after making its mortgage payment and paying other debt obligations, including Social Security and other taxes. Then a determination was made as to whether the family could live on that leftover income. During the Great Recession of 2008, it was found that VA loans, which did not require a down payment, performed at the same level as conventional prime loans. One ingredient that led to the success of this VA program was a pre-purchase counseling program called Mortgages for Beginners.

The program involved small-group counseling sessions with pre-approved applicants who demonstrated a willingness to save and to pursue

12 J. Michael Collins and Collin O'Rourke, *Homeownership Education and Counseling: Do We Know What Works?* (Washington, DC: Research Institute for Housing America, April 26, 2011), 43–46.

homeownership. The borrowers were given a course in the responsibilities of homeownership, including a basic course in home repairs and maintenance. A retired US Army sergeant (with the kind of organizational skills, sensitivity, and direction for which army sergeants are known) conducted the course. This proved invaluable for prospective homeowners. One issue many first-time home buyers face is having to deal with problems such as replacing a water heater or furnace and not having the proper financial reserves or experience to solve the problem.[13] Mortgages for Beginners gave many first-time home buyers the skills necessary to become successful homeowners.

This program for home buyers reaffirmed my belief, acquired in graduate school during the 1970s, that homeowner education can have a positive impact on long-term mortgage performance. The foreclosure crisis of the Great Recession only confirmed my views on the effectiveness of such counseling programs, even without the benefit of extensive outcomes research.

I also believe the large servicers, having local knowledge and expertise, should capitalize on that advantage to assist troubled homeowners. Local staff members know their borrowers' neighborhoods. They can visit distressed borrowers in their homes, a more comfortable and less intimidating environment in which to discuss their financial situation. There, as experienced loan originators and underwriters who deal with the various program guidelines every day, they can speak frankly to explain the borrowers' options and provide appropriate advice to families facing foreclosures. As a strong believer in counseling and counseling agencies, these individuals can not only answer questions, they can also help borrowers assemble the proper information for a lender to make decisions on whether to modify, forbear, or move toward foreclosure.

By 1973, the public's widespread frustration with the FHA forced President Richard Nixon and HUD secretary George Romney to place a moratorium on most subsidy programs. As a result, many of the pilot voucher programs launched after passage of the 1970 Housing Act were permanently adopted in 1974 and have proven to be very successful. Administered by HUD, these programs allocated different voucher programs to participating states. In Colorado the vouchers are distributed to qualifying individuals and families by the Colorado Division of Housing. One such program, the Section 8 Voucher program, provides rental assistance to low- and moderate-income families

13   Richard Fischman, "'Mortgages for Beginners': An Early Success in Flexible Underwriting," *Federal Home Loan Bank Board Journal* 14, no. 8 (1981).

(those earning less than 80 percent of the state's median income). The 112-unit Grand Manor apartment complex in Grand Junction, which is owned and operated by the nonprofit Rocky Mountain Communities, is one of many projects that participates in the program. Section 8 and other direct subsidy programs have proven to be much more successful at providing financial assistance than were the inefficient indirect interest rate subsidies of the 235 and 236 programs. They also helped restore the public's confidence in the FHA.

In 2014 the FHA celebrated eighty years of providing housing opportunities for growing numbers of first-time home buyers and middle-class Americans by providing access to mortgage capital. Today, the FHA is strengthening its balance between social purpose and fiscal responsibility by continuing to revise its plans and programs because of the challenges it faced during the Great Recession. It has played an important role in providing ownership opportunities. The FHA will remain the primary source of mortgage credits for young adults, seniors, first-time home buyers, and minority families. In addition, home buyer pre-purchase and post-purchase counseling will remain important components of FHA programs.

CREATING A SECONDARY MARKET FOR MORTGAGES

The 1934 Housing Act also enabled the creation and supervision of national mortgage associations to provide capital and liquidity for FHA-insured loans.[14] As designed by the act, these national mortgage associations and institutional investors such as insurance companies would purchase large portfolios of mortgage loans from mortgage bankers with the assurance that these were quality loans made on quality properties. The mortgage bankers would then use the proceeds of those sales to make more mortgage loans, thus expanding ownership across the nation.

The program had been designed for commercial banks, thrifts, and insurance companies, but many of these lenders were reluctant and slow to act because of concerns about the conflicting role of the insurance program and its "social purpose" or "social mission" nature. This conflict has raged throughout the industry from its inception through the Great Recession of 2008 to the housing policy legislation of 2014.

---

14 Morton Bodfish, "Government and Private Mortgage Loans on Real Estate," *Journal of Land and Public Utility Economics* 11, no. 4 (1935): 406.

In January 1937, President Roosevelt declared that a third of the nation was poorly housed. An initiative was launched to appropriate federal money to local housing authorities for the purpose of creating affordable housing. Unfortunately, discussions regarding possible solutions soon stalled as the nation's attention turned to the international crisis of World War II. Housing concerns diminished as the country focused on winning the war. But the return of US soldiers revealed an even more critical pent-up demand for housing that could no longer be ignored. The result was the Housing Act of 1949.

The goal of this new legislation was to provide "a decent home and a suitable living environment for every American family."[15] For example, "The 1950 Census found that 29 percent of American homes lacked a flush toilet."[16] Veterans returning from World War II needed jobs and housing. And a growing consensus among Americans dictated that something had to be done about the nation's slums. Pushed by Senator Robert Taft, a conservative Ohio Republican, the law was finally passed and signed into law on July 15, 1949. With it, many of the New Deal housing programs were firmly established.

The housing shortage that engulfed the nation in the years immediately following the end of World War II caused home prices to climb. As a consequence, in an effort to dampen the inflation of home prices, new policies were introduced to restrict the activities of both the FHA and Fannie Mae. In October 1950 the Federal Reserve, with the blessing of the administrator of the Home and Housing Finance Agency, implemented Regulation X. It reduced the level of loans that Fannie Mae could purchase and simultaneously reduced the level of insurance that could be written by the FHA. As a matter of sound fiscal practice, much of the authority to administer these programs through various control mechanisms lasted for years. At about the same time, the FHA commissioner had the power to set the interest rate rather than allow the rate to float with the market. That power helped control the production of FHA loans.[17]

Early in its history the FHA recognized that for a sustainable mortgage insurance program to be successful, it needed the assistance of architects

---

15 "Housing Act of 1949/Public Law 171–81st Congress," Government Accounting Office, accessed October 10, 2014, https://bulk.resource.org/gao.gov/81-171/00001EE4_595076.pdf.

16 James R. Hagerty, *The Fateful History of Fannie Mae: New Deal Birth to Mortgage Crisis Fall* (Charleston, SC: History Press, 2012), 29.

17 Klaman, *Postwar Residential Mortgage*, 58–60.

and planners who would work with lenders, builders, and communities to construct economically sustainable neighborhoods. The first order of business was to assemble an underwriting manual that would establish parameters for the agency's single-family and multi-family programs. To protect the FHA's reserves in the Mutual Mortgage Insurance Fund, minimum property, subdivision, and architectural standards needed to be drafted. The FHA Underwriting Manual, published in 1936, provided those standards.

The 1947 FHA Underwriting Manual revised previous publications and adapted itself to the new postwar environment of suburbia. For new homes to be approved for FHA insurance, not only did the house plans need approval but so did the subdivision as a whole. Plans, specifications, and subdivision maps had to be filed with the FHA field office. There, a team of architects and appraisers analyzed the subdivision for street layout; installation of curbs, gutters, and sidewalks; and open space. Water availability from either public or private water systems, along with storm water and wastewater systems, were also part of the subdivision analysis and approval. The FHA even required home buyers to plant a tree or provide a tree letter from a nursery as part of the approval and closing process. The underlying goal was to provide the American public with quality homes in quality neighborhoods.

Once the subdivision and house plans were approved, a so-called D Binder was created demonstrating the project's acceptance by the FHA. Then, as construction progressed on the subdivision and the individual properties, an FHA inspector made three trips to the site to assure that the construction met the minimum property standards. Upon completion, the properties were appraised and the value determined for their eligibility for mortgage insurance. In 1947 the maximum loan amount was $16,000 and the minimum required down payment was 10 percent of the acquisition cost. In most cases the owner was required to live in the house. Some non–owner-occupied loans were allowed, but they were limited to a loan-to-value ratio of no more than 80 percent.[18]

In the early 1970s, construction quality came under increased scrutiny. A first inspection was conducted when the foundation was poured, a second during the middle of construction, and the final inspection before closing of the loan. Most of the time, inspectors required only minor corrections because

---

18 FHA, *Underwriting Manual*, Sections 332–334.

House in Manhattan, Kansas, owned by a Rosser family relative, 1938. Courtesy of the author.

builders understood the construction quality requirements from the outset. Only once did I encounter a serious situation. An out-of-state builder, of questionable background, had not been diligent with his supervision of construction. During the second inspection the FHA inspector wrote "reframe" on the report because of poor workmanship and noncompliance with the plans and specifications. That inspection was only the beginning of a long series of problems with the project. But it did get our attention and gave us an early warning about the capability and integrity of the builder's organization.

The quality of the standards and requirements of the FHA's single-family programs have withstood the test of time. Many of these postwar-era subdivisions remain more than fifty years later as beautiful neighborhoods with desirable, well-maintained homes. Yet controversy abounds regarding the success, or lack thereof, of slum clearance and urban renewal. The evidence is mixed. Most successful programs can attribute their success to the commitment of the city's leadership and the strength of public-private partnerships. Two good examples are the Skyline Urban Renewal Project in Denver and the Embarcadero Center in San Francisco. Both projects found vigorous support in strong city administrations and the commitment of local private

Original 1938 FHA inspection report. Courtesy of the author.

institutions. But in terms of urban renewal failures, one cannot argue with statistics. Between 1949 and 1968, an estimated 425,000 units nationwide fell to the wrecking ball, but only 125,000 replacement units were built—many of which were luxury apartments.[19]

---

19 Roger Biles, "Public Housing and the Postwar Urban Renaissance," in *From Tenements to the Taylor Homes: In Search of an Urban Policy in Twentieth-Century America*, ed. John F. Bauman, Roger Biles, and Kristin M. Szylvian (University Park: Pennsylvania State University Press, 2000), 153.

In the 1920s, encouraged by President Hoover's Better Homes campaign, the mortgage banking industry began studying new ways to make housing affordable to larger segments of the American public. Following World War II the industry recommitted itself to the cause under the influence of President Eisenhower's Advisory Committee on Government Housing Policies and Programs. By the 1970s many policymakers at the national, state, and local government levels saw affordable workforce housing as an important component of job sustainability and economic growth. To address the housing issue, many states began to take full advantage of Title VII of the New Communities Act of 1968 by forming state housing finance agencies.[20]

Even though several types of state finance agencies exist, they all perform as mortgage bankers in one way or another. Some purchase and fund loans, which are then delivered to the capital markets for resale. The agencies may or may not retain the servicing rights, but if they do they charge a fee for performing those services. In addition, they may receive direct or indirect federal government subsidies for various housing programs. Furthermore, most state housing finance agencies are authorized to issue tax-exempt bonds. The proceeds from the sale of the bonds are then used to fund individual mortgage loans that meet the qualifications of the FHA's various affordable housing programs. The housing agencies often work with mortgage bankers or other real estate lenders to originate such loans. Some states have granted their agencies special powers, such as the ability to establish state building codes. And some agencies function as land-use regulators by establishing growth and community development plans.[21] But the common denominator is that all are reliant on tax-exempt financing.

WHAT CAN HAPPEN WHEN SOCIAL OBLIGATIONS AND FISCAL MANAGEMENT COLLIDE

One example of a conflict between the FHA's social purpose and fiscal management is the unfolding of events following a series of episodes at the Rocky Flats Nuclear Weapons Plant. As a result of conflicting information from other federal and state agencies, the FHA struggled with how to handle the

---

20 James Kozuch, "State Housing Finance Agencies: Their Effect on Mortgage Banking," *Mortgage Banker* (October 1972): 12–13.

21 Ibid., 16.

warnings of potential health risks while protecting the real estate market and its own mortgage insurance programs.

The often repeated theme in the history of real estate finance is that mortgages are risky. Mortgage lenders understand and accept credit risk. They spend enormous amounts of time and money determining the creditworthiness of borrowers and evaluating each individual property. More important, mortgage bankers and investors alike constantly monitor the strength and viability of the markets in which they invest their funds. Institutional investors, government-sponsored enterprises (GSEs), private mortgage insurance companies, and the FHA all employ actuarial models to forecast the performance of the loans in their portfolios. These models are used to establish the underwriting guidelines that determine the amount of risk each institution is willing to take. These risks are, by and large, quantifiable and reasonably accurate.

Yet catastrophic losses can and do occur, often as a consequence of events or activities originating beyond the economic realm. Sometimes they result from unknown or unanticipated environmental events. A series of such accidents and incidents of mismanagement occurred at the Rocky Flats Nuclear Weapons Plant during the 1950s and 1960s. The location of the facility, fifteen miles northwest of downtown Denver, was later deemed to pose a potential hazard to the entire metropolitan-area population in the event of a nuclear accident. The fact that there were two fires at the plant, one in 1957 and another in 1969, that resulted in off-site nuclear contamination was not publicly known for many years. Fortunately, the fast action of the employees who responded and a lot of good luck averted what could have developed into a major disaster.

The consequence of the incidents at Rocky Flats could have led to a collapse of the regional real estate market, with foreclosures and a massive abandonment of properties surrounding the facility. Some special hazards such as hurricanes and tornadoes have a certain predictability that can be accounted for in the actuarial models. But environmental hazards such as the ones presented by the activities at Rocky Flats cannot be forecasted.

The story of Rocky Flats begins in 1951 when the Atomic Energy Commission, now known as the Department of Energy (DOE), selected the 2,600-acre site northwest of Denver bridging Jefferson and Boulder Counties. The site would eventually expand to encompass 4,600 acres. This $45 million facility was seen as an important generator of jobs, as it greatly enhanced the size and scope of the region's scientific and academic employment base. It also significantly validated the area's national reputation by its contribution to national security and defense.[22]

It is important to note the historical context behind the construction of the plant and its role in national defense. The year 1948 brought heightened tensions with the Soviet Union and the ramping up of the Cold War. It began when the Soviet Army sealed off access to the city of Berlin, prompting the United States and its allies to respond with the Berlin Airlift. The airlift was followed in 1949 by the successful Chinese Communist overthrow of its nation's government and the Soviet Union exploding its first nuclear weapon. In 1950 the United States became embroiled in the Korean War to thwart further expansion of communism. The public was fearful of a so-called nuclear exchange. For those of us who lived through these times, this was an era of "duck and cover" air raid drills and listening for the civil defense radio named CONELRAD (CONtrol of ELectronic RADiation). Palpable anxiety enveloped an American public fearful of nuclear war with the Soviet Union as well as conflict with the new People's Republic of China. That anxiety increased dramatically with the disclosure that some Americans had shared nuclear secrets with the Soviet Union.[23]

For many years the general public was not aware of what was actually going on at Rocky Flats. I remember going to Boulder in the early 1950s to do appraisal inspections with my father and seeing the plant far off in the distance. I remember it as highly secretive and somehow very mysterious. At the time it was comforting to know that it was there, protecting us from the Soviets, even though it was surely a target of the Soviet Air Force.

The contract for the Rocky Flats operation was awarded to the Dow Chemical Company. Dow had a reputation as a good company for which to work. An economic generator for the region, the plant created jobs and stimulated growth in the real estate industry in Jefferson and Boulder Counties. With the first phase of development completed, the company began operations at the facility in 1952. Within a year, one of its primary functions was building plutonium triggering devices. Throughout the early 1950s Rocky Flats expanded with the construction of new buildings, and in 1956 Dow

---

22 Patricia Buffer, *Rocky Flats History* (Self-published, 2003), 6, published online by Office of Legacy Management, Department of Energy, July 2003, accessed September 2, 2016, https://www.lm.doe.gov/WorkArea/linkit.aspx?LinkIdentifier=id&ItemID=3026.

23 Ibid., 8.

Chemical was honored by the National Safety Council for completing 3 million hours of work without a disabling injury.[24]

However, in 1957 things began to change. On September 11 of that year a fire erupted in one of the hundreds of glove boxes on the fabrication line in the plutonium-processing building, resulting in a contamination leak. The general public was not aware of the fire and did not learn about it until years later.[25] A virtually identical event occurred twelve years later on Mother's Day, May 11, 1969. Once again a spark in a glove box set off a fire, but this time it escalated quickly. Only three firefighters were on duty that day, so other employees were called in to assist them in containing and extinguishing a fire that engulfed two buildings, numbers 776 and 777.[26]

Kristen Iversen documents the events of the day in *Full Body Burden*. She describes the chaos, the frightening and dangerous conditions, and the desperation of the men who fought the fire. She tells of two men in particular, security guards with only a rudimentary knowledge of firefighting, who reentered Building 777 multiple times despite direct orders not to do so from the radiation monitor. No one was there to relieve them.[27]

When efforts to extinguish the blaze with the mandated CO_2 failed to slow the inferno, let alone put it out, the guards opted to employ the only other weapon at their disposal—water. However, water was the one thing they had been told never to use to fight a plutonium fire. Unbeknownst to the guards, the real firefighters, tackling the fire from the other side by attacking Building 776, made the same decision. Spraying water on the ceilings of the buildings may have contributed to saving the roofs from collapse. But what really saved the facility from a major catastrophe was an accidental power outage, resulting in the shutdown of the exhaust system that had been feeding air to the blaze. The fire slowed. The roofs of both buildings held as the fire continued to burn. Meanwhile, black radioactive smoke billowed into the sky. It took the 1969 Mother's Day "incident" a little over six hours to unfold.[28]

---

24 Ibid., 9.

25 Ibid.

26 Kristen Iversen, *Full Body Burden: Growing Up in the Nuclear Shadow of Rocky Flats* (New York: Crown, 2012), 24–25.

27 Ibid., 30–38.

28 Ibid., 32–40.

Only a brief article in the *Rocky Mountain News* the following day reported on the fire. Since the article appeared on page twenty-eight, the editor certainly did not consider it a major event. According to the article, a plant spokesman claimed that the radioactive contamination was minimal and was "contained to the site."[29]

But that was not true. The Mother's Day fire allowed toxic materials to escape into the atmosphere. To make matters worse, the complex was no longer the remote location it had been in 1951. All of metropolitan Denver, particularly the Denver-Boulder corridor, had experienced unprecedented growth. Area residents did notice the plume of radioactive smoke escaping from the plant but paid little attention, perhaps because they knew so little about its activities.

Apparently, no disaster plan existed to guide employees or local authorities. The local fire departments had not been advised, trained, or equipped to deal with an emergency at the plant. The 1969 fire is remembered as the largest industrial accident in the country's history up to that time, costing over $70 million and consuming over $20 million in plutonium.[30] And yet the earlier fire in 1957 had resulted in significantly more radioactive plutonium release and contamination.[31] Many of the details of both fires continued to remain a secret.

The Colorado Department of Health monitored the facility for background radiation, but there was little public awareness, certainly not in the greater real estate community, about hazardous materials escaping until 1974. That year Colorado elected two stalwart environmentalists—Richard Lamm as governor and Timothy Wirth to represent the state in the US Congress. Both men committed themselves to discovering and dealing with the hazards presented by Rocky Flats.

At the time, developers were proposing a number of subdivisions to be developed near the plant. Arvada in particular was rapidly expanding northward, and a number of subdivisions were being planned and built by Denver's large home building companies. As more information became available, controversy erupted about the hazards posed by the plant. On May 13, 1975, the *Denver Post* reported that the Jefferson County commissioners had rejected

---

29 Ibid., 40.

30 Ibid., 43.

31 John E. Till, "Technical Summary Report for the Historical Public Exposure Studies for Rocky Flats Phase II," September 1999, 29.

a request for residential development near Rocky Flats because of possible plutonium contamination.[32]

Complicating the issue further was the fact that since many of the subdivisions throughout the metropolitan area had been financed using FHA programs, the Department of Housing and Urban Development (HUD) and the FHA were caught in the middle of the controversy. The FHA had very strong underwriting standards for subdivision approval. There was concern not only about approving new construction projects in the area but also about the existing portfolio. In short, what were the implications of possible massive defaults and abandonment of properties for the FHA insurance fund?

A *Rocky Mountain News* article in May 1977 reported that discussions were held between Paul Smith, head of the radiation branch of the Denver Region 8 EPA office, and HUD officials in which Smith proposed that homeowners in the area be provided with an impact statement disclosing the potential radiation hazard generated by Rocky Flats.[33] Walt Kelm, regional environmental quality chief for HUD, indicated that the most HUD could do was require builders to notify FHA borrowers of the potential hazard posed by the plant. Plutonium contamination could have enormous financial consequences for both borrowers and investors. The mortgage banker's role is always to represent the best interest of investors and to protect them against loss. If mortgage bankers started backing away from making loans near Rocky Flats to safeguard their investors, they could have triggered a real estate collapse. Economically, everyone was caught in a Catch-22—protect the regional economy by conducting business as usual or red-flag the area against a potential but unknown and unverifiable environmental health risk.

The dilemma was complicated further when the *Rocky Mountain News* reported that HUD had hired three researchers to make a risk evaluation.[34] Their findings showed that area residents had more to fear from bathtub falls or car crashes than from operations at Rocky Flats. The Department of Energy told HUD the same thing, stating that there was only a 1-in-10,000 chance of a fire that could cause a dangerous event. In addition, HUD officials

---

32   "Jeffco Rejects Flats-Area Development," *Denver Post*, May 13, 1975, B17.

33   Allen Cunningham, "EPA Official Seeks Radiation Warning," *Rocky Mountain News*, May 19, 1977, 6.

34   Myron Levin, "Agencies at Odds over Giving Information EPA Advised to Tell Flats Homebuyers [about] Risks," *Rocky Mountain News*, May 10, 1978, 12.

expressed concern that builders and developers would drop FHA programs if forced to notify their buyers of an emergency response plan.

Iversen recalls that for years potential homeowners, including her parents when they purchased a home in 1969, were asked to sign a waiver acknowledging the possibility of plutonium soil contamination if the property was within ten miles of Rocky Flats. Buyers affirmed that they had been warned of the risk but were also told that the level of contamination was deemed safe by the government. However, in 1979 HUD and the FHA approved and implemented a mandatory disclosure about possible plutonium contamination. The Rocky Flats Advisory Notice stated: "This notice is to inform you of certain facts regarding United States Department of Energy Rocky Flats Plant which is located within ten miles of your prospective residence. You should be aware that there exist within portions of Boulder County and Jefferson County, Colorado varying levels of plutonium contamination of the soil. However, according to the information supplied by the Department of Energy, the soil contamination in the area in which your prospective residence is located is below the limits of the applicable radiation guidance developed by the Environmental Protection Agency (EPA)." The notice also required that potential buyers be notified of the emergency response plan. The waiver was required for all properties located within ten miles of the Rocky Flats facility.[35]

Then, just three years later, in March 1982, at the urging of real estate developers, HUD and the FHA rescinded the Rocky Flats advisory notice.[36] As a result, building and development continued to move forward. Notwithstanding the off-site contamination resulting from the fires of 1957 and 1969, to date the home building, real estate, and mortgage industries have not experienced any long-term economic impact from the operations of the Rocky Flats Nuclear Weapons Plant, but they could have experienced major upheaval. Obviously, the industry and the public are relying on the studies conducted by the DOE and the Colorado Department of Health and Environment to reveal any long-term health hazards that can be attributed to the operations that transpired at Rocky Flats. But throughout the period it has been obvious that fiscal concerns outweighed the social mission of ensuring safe housing.

---

35   Iversen, *Full Body Burden*, 40–41, 163, 203.

36   Ibid., 203.

Production activities at Rocky Flats ceased in 1989. The DOE then installed a contractor to undertake the demanding process of decontamination and restoration, which it completed in 2005 at a cost of $7 billion.[37] As a result, the DOE and the Colorado Department of Public Health and Environment have declared the area "completely safe."[38] Carl Spreng, supervisor of the environmental cleanup at the site for the Colorado Department of Public Health and Environment, participated in a promotional video in 2009. In it he claimed: "These lands have been essentially protected for many years because they were part of the buffer zone of Rocky Flats, and it's an example of some pristine prairie areas . . . The land is a jewel."[39]

The land surrounding the facility has been returned to the public domain; ownership resides with the US Department of the Interior. The US Fish and Wildlife Service manages the complex as the Rocky Flats National Wildlife Refuge and is currently restoring the landscape's habitats to fully support the native plants and animals that have historically lived there. The refuge is currently open to the public on a limited basis, but plans call for it to eventually include a visitor center and an extensive trail system for hiking, cycling, and horseback riding.[40]

---

37 US Fish and Wildlife Service, "Rocky Flats National Wildlife Refuge," accessed July 7, 2015, http://www.fws.gov/refuge/Rocky_Flats/about.html.

38 Iversen, *Full Body Burden*, 333.

39 Ibid., 333–34.

40 US Fish and Wildlife Service, "Rocky Flats."

8

Government-Sponsored Enterprises, 1916–1968

> The fundamental problem is that the GSEs are private companies
> with a public mission—a very difficult construct to balance. Unless
> GSE activities are constrained by appropriate legislation and strong
> regulation, their predominant motives will always be to reward
> their stockholders at the expense of taxpayers and consumers.
>
> —FM Watch, GSE Mission Creep

As far back as the Farm Loan Act of 1916, the primary public policy justification for the establishment and continued operation of mortgage government-sponsored enterprises (GSEs) has been the need to provide farmers and home buyers with access to affordable mortgage financing. By linking local mortgage markets with regional and national financial markets, interregional interest rate disparities have been moderated, if not eliminated, and interest rates for borrowers in general have been reduced. The result is that

DOI: 10.5876/9781607326236.c008

the functions of the GSEs have made farm credit and homeownership available to a greater number of American families.[1]

In essence, GSEs are financial services corporations. Created by the US Congress, GSEs seek to improve the availability of low-cost credit in certain financial markets. Congress established the first mortgage GSE in 1916 when it chartered the Federal Farm Loan Program discussed in chapter 2. Today, the two most widely known examples of mortgage GSEs are the Federal National Mortgage Association (Fannie Mae) and the Federal Home Loan Mortgage Corporation (Freddie Mac). In addition to Fannie and Freddie, another popular GSE is the Government National Mortgage Association (Ginnie Mae). A separate group of twelve Federal Home Loan Banks also works as a mortgage GSE and as discount banks.

The history of GSEs has been mixed at best. The same economic and credit cycles apply to GSEs as to any other financial institution. Many studies have been written by academics, politicians, think tanks, and the industry to suggest modifications and reforms of these organizations to create some level of immunity from normal business cycles. But GSEs behave differently than many business organizations because of their social purpose. Fundamentally, they lack market discipline.

The social purpose of the housing GSEs is to expand the availability of credit and more favorable terms to underserved groups. To serve more people, the credit and financial requirements of borrowers are relaxed, but that increases the risk to the investor or taxpayer without providing a greater return to compensate for the additional risk. The social purpose and fiscal discipline often conflict. Finding the right balance between increased availability of credit and maintaining sufficient standards to assure the creditworthiness of borrowers is crucial. Only the Federal Home Loan Bank System has been economically successful because it has kept tighter control of financial guidelines and requirements while attempting to meet the social mission of as many of its members as possible.

---

1   June E. O'Neill, *CBO Testimony on Assessing the Public Costs and Benefits of Fannie Mae and Freddie Mac: Statement of June E. O'Neill* (Washington, DC: Congressional Budget Office, 1996), 1–2.

RISK CREATES MULTIPLE CHALLENGES
FOR MORTGAGE FINANCING

As the Great Depression set in following the stock market crash in 1929, the number of foreclosures across the country skyrocketed. Miles Colean, a major figure in the mortgage banking industry from the 1920s through the 1970s, once observed that "mortgages are a risky investment."[2] Conditions in the 1930s certainly proved him correct. In an oral history that documents a series of interviews he gave, Colean often discussed the conflicts between the public/social policy of expanding homeownership and the maintenance of sound fiscal management.[3]

The mortgage finance system quickly responded to the financial challenges. The first piece of legislation designed to turn around the housing and construction markets created the Federal Home Loan Bank System in 1932. Congress followed up in 1934, passing the Homeowners Loan Act and the National Housing Act. While it can be argued that the programs instituted under these laws did not have an immediate effect, over the long term many proved to be quite beneficial, and they did stabilize the US mortgage and real estate markets.

Loss of income during the Great Depression, as in all other economic downturns, stands as the single greatest contributor to any mortgage foreclosure—residential, multi-family, commercial, or industrial enterprise. If income is generated from industrial enterprises, borrowers will, generally speaking, make their payments. In recent years, many experts and policymakers have prescribed regulations for larger down payment amounts and other ways to mitigate foreclosures. However, local, national, and global economic factors, often beyond the control of policymakers or individual borrowers, play a larger role.

Traditionally, many mortgage guaranty insurance companies collect data to determine the reasons for foreclosure. In addition to the obvious cause of loss of income, other reasons for mortgage default include death, divorce, major illness of the borrower or a family member, and overextension of credit. None of these factors is predictable when a loan is originated.

---

2   Miles L. Colean and Columbia University Oral History Review, *A Backward Glance an Oral History: The Growth of Government Housing Policy in the United States 1934–1975* (Washington, DC: Research and Educational Trust Fund, 1975), 29.

3   Ibid.

However, predictive models have been developed with the intent of minimizing or even eliminating unduly risky loans. Yet it is impossible for a lender to predict with certainty the future performance of individual mortgage loans. The decision to extend credit can only be based on the applicant's past performance as evidenced by his or her credit score and meaningful income verification, typically provided by tax returns.

As stated before, real estate mortgages are risky. When any combination of risk factors comes together simultaneously, the lender can suffer the greatest impacts. Fluctuating interest rates create capital market risk. If the interest rate rises after a borrower locks in at a lower rate, the value of the loan decreases, creating a loss for the lender if not properly hedged. Every loan contains some credit risk since it is impossible to predict if the borrower will maintain his ability to pay. During economic declines like the Great Depression and the more recent Great Recession, real estate risk escalates. If the borrower loses his ability to pay and property values decline, the borrower may not be able to sell the property for the value of the loan, or it may not sell at all. Even if the borrower retains the ability to pay, he may choose to strategically default and abandon the property, a recurrent theme since 1890s Kansas. The lender can lose the property outright when a borrower makes all mortgage payments but fails to pay the associated property taxes. Finally, hazard and environmental risks apply if the property is located on an earthquake fault or in a wildfire zone or, as in the case of New Orleans's Ninth Ward, if it lies in an area subject to hurricanes and flooding. When there is inadequate or unobtainable insurance coverage to pay off the loan, the borrower may elect to strategically default and walk away from the property.

Historically, most institutional lenders including insurance companies, state-chartered banks, and building and loan societies limited loans to a maximum of 60 percent of the appraised value of the property, thus requiring down payments of up to 40 percent. Unfortunately, borrowers who did not have sufficient funds for the down payment often obtained a second mortgage for 20 percent or more of the property's value to purchase the home. Second mortgages usually commanded a higher interest rate and had a short term compared with the first mortgage. When the borrower lost his source of income, necessitating foreclosure, the first mortgage holder hoped the second mortgage holder would step in and redeem the property, but that rarely happened. The mortgage industry refers to these layers of debt as risk stacking. Risk stacking generally involves a very low or no down payment, a FICO score lower than 660, an adjustable-rate or interest-only loan, an investment property or vacation home, or a borrower without income or asset verification, along with the presence of a second mortgage that enables the borrower to withdraw the equity in the property. The practice led to a huge default rate in the early 1930s and again during the more recent Great Recession.

During the Depression era, the inability to pay caused by a combination of loss of income, consumer debt, and home mortgage debt constituted the greatest risk for lenders of home mortgages. Another challenge was the short-term nature of most mortgages and the inability of borrowers to refinance or obtain a loan extension. Most loans followed the pattern established by earlier farm mortgage lenders: short-term, interest-only loans requiring that all principal be paid at the end of the term in one balloon payment. At the time, typical residential loans were written for terms of five to seven years and may or may not have included a renewal clause. Because of the liquidity crisis that existed during the Depression, most lenders were unable or unwilling to extend the loans. Living on savings (that may already have been exhausted) as a result of loss of income, most borrowers did not have the funds to make the final balloon payment; in that case the borrower lost his home and the lender gained an unwanted property.

PRESIDENT HOOVER'S RESPONSE AND THE CREATION OF THE FEDERAL HOME LOAN BANK SYSTEM

Immediately after the stock market crash, building activity stopped, initiating a sharp downward spiral in real estate activity. Unfinished buildings testified to lost construction jobs, and liquidity in the mortgage markets dried up. As many as 40 percent of the loans across the country defaulted. Beginning in late 1929 when the term of loans expired, lenders refused to renew them because of the liquidity crisis caused by the stock market collapse. President Hoover, who believed that homeownership created civic responsibility and built personal moral character, recognized an urgent need to rescue the housing market.

As early as 1921, Hoover recognized many of the flaws in the home mortgage finance system. While serving as commerce secretary, Hoover held multiple conferences dealing with promoting homeownership. Through these conferences he cultivated what developed into a long relationship with the thrift industry and its trade association, the United States Savings and Loan League (the League).[4] The League resulted from the merger of a number of small trade associations representing savings banks, cooperative banks, savings and loan associations, and building societies.[5] Under the leadership of Morton Bodfish, a strong advocate and spokesman for the organization, the League grew and gained significant influence in Washington. An unfailing protector of the thrift industry,[6] Bodfish played a key role in formulating Depression-era housing policy, advocating strongly for the Federal Home Loan Bank (FHLB) system created during Hoover's administration.

Bodfish was an equally vocal opponent of the creation of the Federal Housing Administration (FHA) and Fannie Mae, as he was an advocate for the creation of the Federal Home Loan Bank System. History gives Bodfish mixed reviews. Certainly, he deserves enormous credit because the FHLB System has been a strong and viable institution. In retrospect, some of his opposition to the creation of Fannie Mae has strong merit. In contrast, his misplaced opposition to the creation of the FHA has been refuted by its continued success.[7]

As early as 1919, the League began advocating for a central bank for savings and loans and building and loans, more broadly known as thrift institutions, similar to the Federal Reserve for commercial banks. The League continued to lobby the US Congress for a central mortgage credit bank. Many industry members were apathetic toward the idea, while others were strongly opposed. Nevertheless, by 1922 the housing market had recovered, and by 1928 the League withdrew its support for a central mortgage credit bank. But all of that changed following the stock market crash in 1929.

Hoover had advocated for such a facility during the 1928 presidential campaign against Al Smith of New York. The problem facing the industry was twofold. As the economy worsened, depositing members of savings and loans withdrew their savings. At the same time, their mortgages were going into default on the other side of the ledger. In addition, thrifts relied on commercial banks as a source from which to borrow money, and in turn

---

4   Mason, *Buildings and Loans*, 78.

5   Ibid. 6.

6   Ibid., 78.

7   Ibid., 95.

the commercial banks provided thrifts with checking accounts. When the commercial banks failed, thrifts, like every other customer, lost their money because the Federal Deposit Insurance Corporation (FDIC) and the Federal Savings and Loan Insurance Corporation (FSLIC) had not yet been created to insure the funds customers deposited into their accounts.

Bodfish and other leaders of the League met with Hoover and recommended that the thrifts be allowed to join the Federal Reserve System so they could obtain the liquidity necessary to meet their obligations. The League saw this as a quick and easy solution, given the extent of the crisis enveloping the nation. Hoover objected strongly because he felt Congress would not approve tampering with the Federal Reserve. A informal survey of congressional members affirmed Hoover's position of not expanding the role of the Federal Reserve. Instead, Hoover presented League members with a proposal outlined to the National Association of Real Estate Boards to create a central mortgage reserve bank.

As President Hoover envisioned it, the plan called for a mortgage discount bank system that encompassed all members of the industry, including commercial banks, thrifts, mortgage bankers, and insurance companies. They would be enabled to purchase mortgages below the actual face value of the loans. By purchasing loans below actual face value, discount banks receive a higher yield and are better able to sell the loans later for a profit or to use them as collateral to fund other loans. Finding the president's plan the best possible solution, Bodfish began rallying League members to support the creation of the Federal Home Loan Bank System. However, the proposal faced stiff opposition from members of the Congressional Finance Committee, who had little interest in supporting the thrift movement.[8]

The US House and US Senate debated the role and mission of Hoover's plan over a three-year period. Controversy raged in 1932 over the need for such an entity, particularly the need to stimulate new construction given the nation's overbuilt housing supply. Many mortgage bankers feared the creation of this proposed new federal system would be inflationary and would not contribute to the recovery of the housing market.[9] Finally, using an obscure parliamentary maneuver, Congress passed the Federal Home Loan

8   Ibid., 78–82.
9   Snowden, *Special Report*, 83–84.

Bank Act and President Hoover signed it into law on July 22, 1932, thus creating the second GSE.

The Federal Home Loan Banks (FHLB) were created as a parallel institution to the Federal Reserve Banks for the express purpose of facilitating and expanding mortgage lending activities. The FHLB had a structure similar to that of its sister organization, the Federal Farm Loan Bank System, created in 1916. The FHLB System is a cooperative owned by its member institutions, which include building and loan associations, savings banks, and insurance companies. Those entities select individuals from among their membership to serve on the board of directors. The Federal Home Loan Bank Board, whose members are appointed by the president, oversees the twelve regional FHLBs. Just as key members of Congress had been instrumental in locating the Federal Reserve Banks, they also contributed to the placement of the FHLBs. In an effort to decentralize control, Congress located the Federal Reserve Banks serving the Midwest in St. Louis and Kansas City; Congress designated Des Moines and Topeka for the region's FHLBs.

For the new banks, their time had come and none too soon, given the administration's assessment of the severe nature of the housing market. Nevertheless, the Mortgage Bankers Association (MBA) and its insurance company correspondents raised serious opposition to the plan,[10] possibly because many mortgage bankers had hoped to gain access to the Federal Home Loan Bank System. This dream was not realized until passage of the Bank Holding Company Act in 1956. That law enabled commercial banks to buy mortgage banking firms, granting mortgage bankers access to the FHLB through their bank's membership. Even today, mortgage bankers are still not direct members of FHLBs.

Four major institutional events have left their mark on the FHLBs since their inception. First, the creation of the Home Owners Loan Corporation (HOLC) in June 1933 institutionalized the fixed-rate amortized mortgage. An amortized loan requires regular periodic payments, usually made monthly, to gradually pay the principal, interest, and other loan costs such as insurance and property taxes. Second was the establishment of the FSLIC, a critically important component of the 1934 Housing Act that provided insurance on depositors' accounts. The third event, and one of the most controversial

---

10   Mason, *Buildings and Loans,* 85–86.

for the thrift industry, was the creation in 1934 of the FHA and its mortgage insurance programs. Bodfish and other League members vehemently opposed the idea of the FHA. The founding of Freddie Mac in 1970 marked the final event.

HOME OWNERS LOAN CORPORATION

Established in 1933, the goal of HOLC was to provide immediate relief to homeowners in danger of losing their homes. It was further charged with giving aid and assistance to lending institutions.[11] In modern terminology, HOLC was known as a bad bank because it purchased delinquent loans from thrifts and other lenders in the hope of working them out by refinancing or restructuring the debt utilizing new loan practices.[12]

HOLC introduced the practice of extending mortgage terms to twenty years with an amortization schedule of monthly payments that included a commensurate reduction in principal. This change proved critical to the development of sound lending practices for the industry and was equally beneficial to borrowers. Another innovation was the introduction of escrow/impound accounts that reserved funds from the monthly payment to pay real estate taxes and hazard insurance premiums. Until then, borrowers had lost their homes when they failed to pay the associated taxes, even if they were current on their mortgage loan. Many lenders and certainly the FHA and HOLC programs began requiring escrow accounts and prohibited risk stacking.

Similar to the events of the Great Recession, during the Great Depression housing prices fell 30 percent to 40 percent, triggering a sharp rise in foreclosures and the failure of many financial institutions. An unemployment rate of 25 percent compounded the problems. As the driving factor in mortgage foreclosures, the long-term loss of employment/income contributed to the mixed results of the HOLC. Much like its twenty-first-century counterpart, the Troubled Asset Relief Program (TARP), HOLC functioned as a troubled-asset relief program. Funded by US government bonds and guaranteed only for the payment of interest at 4 percent, by 1935 the program had made 924,000 loans to individual homeowners totaling approximately $2.7 billion.[13]

11 Mason, *Buildings and Loans*, 112.
12 Bodfish, "Government and Private Mortgage Loans," 403.
13 Ibid., 404.

Under the program, a *troubled* borrower seeking to refinance an existing mortgage with government funds could apply at a local HOLC office. A nationwide network of local offices not only approved loans but serviced them as well. If approved, HOLC would issue a government bond for up to 80 percent of the appraised value of the property to the existing lien holder in payment of the old debt. According to Bodfish, many borrowers capable of making their payments to private institutions strategically (voluntarily) defaulted on their mortgages to obtain the more preferential government financing intended for genuinely distressed citizens. Bodfish asserts that many of these borrowers still had equity in their properties.[14] Nevertheless, the program succeeded in its goal of stabilizing real estate markets and keeping people in their homes.

James Nelson, CMB, CRE, and former president of the MBA, related the organizational structure of HOLC and how it operated.[15] Nelson's father, also a former MBA president, worked for HOLC in Minneapolis during the 1930s. At its peak, the agency had 458 regional and local offices staffed with individuals experienced in mortgage lending.

Generally speaking, loss of income and property neglect made foreclosure inevitable. However, even though most loans in 1933 were more than two years in default, many lenders had postponed initiating foreclosure proceedings because state mortgage foreclosure moratoriums often influenced forbearance policies. Not only had borrowers stopped making mortgage payments, but the property taxes often went unpaid as well. HOLC financed the first large-scale home modernization program responsible for rehabilitating more that 500,000 homes and launching a new industry. It reconditioned up to 40 percent of the neglected properties it refinanced to make them habitable and added the cost to the loan balance.[16]

Nationwide, HOLC rejected over 800,000 loans for various reasons, but for borrowers whose loans *were* approved, staff in a local office collected the loan payments just as local agents and correspondents had done for eastern and foreign investors fifty years earlier. The senior Nelson made regular

---

14   Ibid.

15   E. Michael Rosser, interview with James Nelson, Denver, CO, 2012.

16   Price V. Fishback et al., "The Influence of the Home Owners' Loan Corporation on Housing Markets during the 1930s," *Oxford Journals* (2010): 1788, accessed October 25, 2014, http://frs.oxfordjournals.org/.

visits to borrowers' homes, payment book in hand, to collect scheduled payments and verify that property taxes and insurance premiums had been paid. Having a local representative with neighborhood knowledge and frequent personal contact with borrowers was an important part of the HOLC program. Regular face-to-face contact with borrowers provided a much clearer picture of family circumstances and ultimately led to better decisions regarding whether to forbear or to proceed into foreclosure.

HOLC was dissolved in 1951; its remaining portfolio was sold and its operations ceased. During the organization's lifetime, over 20 percent of its portfolio entered foreclosure. Individuals who had expected immediate results from HOLC in resolving the foreclosure problems became frustrated by the burden of the process and the high incidence of loans that eventually entered foreclosure. I observed the same disappointment in many people who expected better results from the 2006 Hope Program and the Colorado Foreclosure Prevention Task Force. In contrast, those who took a long-range view, with the understanding that job recovery was the key to the housing recovery, could take great pride in its accomplishments—striving to maintain and preserve family stability, property values, and the health of local government services.[17]

HOLC did make significant contributions that changed the face of mortgage lending for decades. It served as a laboratory for new lending practices, laying the groundwork for the techniques that led to the creation of the FHA and the modern risk management principles of mortgage finance. First among the major changes was the extension of mortgage loan terms to fifteen and even twenty years. Another was the inclusion of "direct reduction payments" that combined amortization of the principal with the interest payment. As the principal declined, so did the interest payment, a feature that created equity at a faster rate, in effect creating a forced saving program. By introducing the amortizing feature, HOLC created the first successful high-ratio loan program.[18]

Perhaps most significant was the introduction and use of property security maps to evaluate loan risk. HOLC used maps to assign letter grades to classify neighborhoods: A = desirable, B = stable, C = definitely declining,

---

17   Ibid., 1789.

18   Mason, *Buildings and Loans*, 113.

and D = undesirable. This new appraisal system analyzed property using three fundamental approaches—cost, income, and comparable sales or market conditions—in addition to an evaluation of the neighborhood and pride of ownership. This new method employed scientific data and quickly took precedence over the opinion-based approach. One effect of this new scientific approach was that a neighborhood's racial characteristics were included in the data. Appraisers used that information to justify value adjustments and to determine whether neighborhoods were improving or declining. Today, this type of risk evaluation would be interpreted as redlining.[19]

Redlining was reinforced by the FHA's concern with "inharmonious racial or national groups." The 1938 and 1947 FHA *Underwriting Manual* recommended "subdivision regulations and suitable restrictive covenants" to prohibit African Americans and other groups from living in FHA-eligible housing. The 1948 decision in the US Supreme Court case *Shelley v. Kraemer*[20] ruled the practice unlawful, but it took until February 1950 for the FHA to stop insuring mortgages with such covenants included in the property deeds.[21] For example, Denver's North City Park and Clayton Park neighborhoods originally had such covenants, but following the Supreme Court decision they became racially mixed. Restrictive covenants prohibited Jewish families from purchasing homes in certain neighborhoods as well.

Even though redlining had been outlawed for over a decade, as late as the 1960s at least one California life insurance company still engaged in the practice. While working at the Service Investment Company (SIC), I learned this story about the company in question. On a visit to purchase loans from SIC, a mortgage loan officer drew a red line around an east Denver neighborhood and stated that his firm would not buy loans in that community. The president of SIC, Fred E. Kirk, called the investor's representative into his office and informed him that it would be difficult to do business with his company if that policy remained. That was a brave move, considering that SIC had a commitment to sell the loans at a firm price; if the investor did not rescind its policy of redlining, SIC could have taken a loss when selling those loans

---

19 Ibid., 114–15.

20 334 U.S. 1 (1948).

21 Kenneth T. Jackson, *Crabgrass Frontier: The Suburbanization of the United States* (New York: Oxford University Press, 1985), 208.

to another investor. The company reversed its policy, and SIC retained a long and profitable relationship with the investor.

This situation presented itself repeatedly over the years within the confines of the SIC. The corporate ethic conveyed to company employees stressed that our job was to provide our investors with good loans awarded to properly approved borrowers, regardless of race, creed, or national origin.

THE FEDERAL NATIONAL MORTGAGE ASSOCIATION (FNMA)–FANNIE MAE

The National Housing Act of 1934 provided for the creation of the FHA and European-style national mortgage associations or regional mortgage discount banks. These banks were to issue debentures, most commonly in the form of bonds, and function as a secondary market and liquidity source for FHA Title II (single-family and multi-family) mortgage loans. Although the National Mortgage Association (NMA) greatly resembled its predecessor, the Federal Home Loan Bank program, Congress granted it a few unique differences. These private associations were authorized not only to sell mortgage-backed debentures, but they could also buy and sell FHA mortgages and, later, VA mortgages or hold them in portfolios.

However, its creators applied the lessons learned from the Federal Farm Loan models. While creating a broad secondary market for the fully amortized loans, the associations were prohibited from becoming direct lenders and originating loans, just as the joint-stock farm loan associations had been denied those functions. The national mortgage associations were to be totally funded, with a minimum capital requirement of $5 million, more than six times the minimum requirement for the district banks under the Federal Farm Loan System and equal to the requirement for the district Federal Home Loan Banks.[22]

The NMA concept failed to generate interest. Some in the industry feared further nationalization of the residential mortgage finance market. Others expressed concern about the upcoming sunset of the federal guarantee of FHA debentures, set to expire in 1937. Investors feared purchasing FHA debentures and NMA obligations, knowing that without an extension the federal

---

22 Snowden, *Special Report*, 80–81.

guarantee would soon end. With FHA Title II loans eligible for purchase by the Reconstruction Finance Corporation (RFC) and the Federal Reserve, few saw a need for an additional agency. In addition, the FHA insurance program had not generated enough volume.[23]

Notwithstanding the objections of some members of the financial community, the American Bankers Association supported the proposal for the NMA. Some members raised concern about the size and scope of the proposal that would create a new banking institution the size of the national bank system. The League also saw the proposed NMA estimate to possibly equal as a competitive threat and voiced vigorous opposition. A major objection of the League focused on the NMA's tax-exempt status.

Jesse Jones, a Houston, Texas, businessman and entrepreneur, headed the RFC from 1933 until 1939. Created during Hoover's administration in 1932, the goal of the RFC was to deliver the economy out of the Great Depression by providing funding support for banks, agriculture, industry, and railroads and thereby reducing unemployment. With the force of his personality and the backing of President Roosevelt, Jones pushed the National Mortgage Association of Washington through Congress in 1938. Congress assigned this new association the express goal of building and maintaining a secondary market for home loans originated by private lenders and insured by the FHA. In less than two months, the entity's name changed to the Federal National Mortgage Association, commonly known today as Fannie Mae or simply Fannie. As chair of the RFC, Jones oversaw the RFC Mortgage Corporation and Fannie Mae. He expressed disappointment at the strength of the opposition from private funding sources that refused to invest in an NMA. While Jones did create an NMA, the League claimed success in placing barriers and restrictions on it; Fannie Mae was the only National Mortgage Association established that year.[24]

When Congress approved the Wagner-Steagall Housing Act in 1937, it created the United States Housing Authority, a precursor to today's Department of Housing and Urban Development (HUD). When Fannie Mae was created the following year, the Housing Authority assumed oversight of the new entity.

---

23 Ibid., 81–82.

24 Mason, *Buildings and Loans*, 116.

In 1944 Congress passed the Servicemen's Readjustment Act, more commonly known as the G.I. Bill, which enabled the Veterans Administration (VA) to guarantee home mortgage and business loans for members of the service returning from World War II. These loan programs were part of a larger entitlement program conducted by the VA that included education, training, and health benefits, among others. In 1948 Congress expanded Fannie's authority by allowing it to purchase those guaranteed VA loans. So instead of acting simply as a backup discount bank, Fannie Mae put the federal government in direct competition with private institutional investors. Fannie Mae's activities made it a key contributor to the financing of the postwar housing boom and caused the government to become deeply entrenched in the housing business, where it remains to this day.[25] By the end of 1956, VA loans represented 28 percent of the nation's mortgage flow. Mortgage flow is the amount of new capital invested in mortgages in a given time period, usually one year. The VA loan program experienced a 1,400 percent increase in volume between its inception in 1945 and 1956.[26]

During the Truman administration, in 1947 the Housing and Home Finance Agency (HHFA) replaced the US Housing Authority and took over as Fannie Mae's regulator. A 1950 reorganization removed Fannie Mae from "ownership" by the RFC, but the HHFA retained oversight until enactment of the 1968 Housing Act. The new legislation created HUD, which assumed responsibility for oversight of Fannie Mae.

But it did not take long for concern to arise about the proper role of Fannie Mae in the mortgage market, which ultimately led to President Eisenhower's appointment of a special advisory committee to study the government's housing policies and programs. One of the issues focused on the unanticipated political power gained by local housing authorities and beneficiaries of federal money resulting from Fannie's expanded activities. These entities became strong advocates and political supporters of Fannie Mae.[27]

The mortgage banking industry's worries about Fannie's changing role began to receive media attention. A story that could have been printed in a 2014 edition of the *Washington Post* appeared in a 1950 edition of the paper. R. O. Deming, president of the MBA, stated that he did not seek Fannie's

---

25 Hagerty, *Fateful History*, 25.

26 Klaman, *Postwar Residential Mortgage*, 33.

27 Hagerty, *Fateful History*, 25.

demise but felt that "the agency should revert to being a standby source of money when other sources dried up, *not* [be] a constant provider."[28]

Deming was highly respected in the industry. He had started his career as a farm mortgage banker in Kansas. His father was one of the original founders of the FMBA. Deming had long been involved in public policy discussions affecting the industry. The nationalization of many industries in Great Britain and the explosion of the size of the US government during his twenty years in the mortgage industry caused Deming and others in the industry great concern about the socialization or nationalization of American housing and housing finance systems.

In 1952 the United States elected Dwight D. Eisenhower president. One of his goals was to bring order and definition to the perceived chaos of the multiple, often conflicting housing programs and to address the housing needs of postwar America. At this point in the history of national housing policy, two individuals emerged who would have an enormous impact on the mortgage finance system for decades. A Columbia University architect from Chicago and a Danish immigrant from Denver started a major shift in US housing policy and became the founders of a great reformation movement. At this same time, the MBA began to gain greater influence in the halls of power.

Miles Colean attended the University of Wisconsin and was a fraternity brother of Phil La Follette, son of a Wisconsin senator. This friendship and the Washington network it produced would become valuable as Colean became a major housing policy and finance figure during and after the Great Depression. As America prepared for World War I, Colean transferred to Columbia to pursue studies to become a journalist. While there he met a young Smith College graduate and, as any astute mortgage banker would, he had the good sense to marry the young woman. Colean abandoned his thoughts of journalism to pursue a career in architecture. Following graduation, he worked for a Chicago architectural firm for several years before establishing his own firm. As the economy turned downward, he began to search out other opportunities. While attending the American Institute of Architects' convention in Washington, DC, he reconnected with friends from his days at the University of Wisconsin. The connections helped him become an influential advocate for shaping US housing policy.

---

28 Quoted in ibid., 32–34.

The second individual, Aksel Nielsen, arrived in Denver from Denmark in 1910 at age nine to live with an uncle. The Denver Public Schools denied him admission because he did not speak English. Nielsen attended night school at the YMCA to learn English and worked during the day at the Morley Mercantile Company. He became a naturalized citizen in 1922. Nielsen worked for a short time at the Parker Realty Company before joining the Landon Abstract/Title Guaranty Company as a mortgage loan solicitor in 1925. Like many immigrants, Nielsen was a hardworking, ambitious young man. The Dowd family of 750 Lafayette Street in Denver hired him as a book-keeper and financial adviser.

While on vacation in San Antonio, Texas, the Dowd's daughter, Mamie, met her future husband, a young US Army officer and West Point gradu-ate, Dwight D. Eisenhower. Returning to Denver frequently with his bride, Eisenhower met the family bookkeeper. That was the beginning of a lifelong friendship between the Danish immigrant who became a Denver civic and business leader, a university trustee, and a mortgage banker and the young army officer and later a five-star general, the Supreme Allied Commander during World War II, president of Columbia University, and president of the United States.

One story tells of Nielsen receiving a phone call from US Army headquar-ters in Washington directing him to report to Lowry Army Air Field that afternoon. When the general's plane, the *Columbine*, arrived, the mortgage banker and the general slipped away for two quiet days of fishing at Byers Peak Ranch on the Fraser River before Eisenhower left to plan the invasion of North Africa.[29] Once asked if he was seeking a position with the govern-ment, Nielsen famously remarked, "No, the President deserves a friend who doesn't want anything."[30]

The only recorded formal educational achievement of this YMCA night school student is an Honorary Doctor of Public Letters degree awarded to him in recognition of his service as chair of the board of trustees of the University of Denver.

When the war ended in 1945 and the economy began to reorient itself to meet pent-up consumer demand, it became apparent that swift action

---

29 Colean, *Backward Glance*, 100–101.

30 Ibid., 111.

needed to be taken to fulfill the nation's housing needs. By the time Truman relinquished the presidency to Eisenhower, Fannie Mae was in great disfavor. Its original purpose of building and maintaining a secondary market for home loans had been pushed aside because of the "limitations and demands put upon it by federal agencies."[31] As a consequence, the availability of mortgage credit decreased. Concern still abounded that the federal government would become a direct funder of residential mortgage credit. The National Association of Real Estate Boards advocated for HOLC to be made permanent. Meanwhile, the American Bankers Association sought the establishment of a series of federally chartered mortgage insurance companies that would be supplemented by a reserve discount facility for home mortgages similar to the Federal Home Loan Bank model. Almost everyone recognized that the housing finance system was broken. President Eisenhower characterized it as a "monstrosity."[32]

The New Deal had left a spider web of alphabetic agencies with conflicting roles, missions, and responsibilities. In early 1951, when it became apparent that Eisenhower would run for president the following year, he sought out his friend Nielsen for advice regarding his administration's housing policy. Eisenhower asked Nielsen to form a committee to evaluate the federal government's role in housing and make a report to him. Nielsen and Colean, then the policy and economic consultant to the MBA, interviewed and hired Albert M. Cole, a former member of the US Congress from Kansas, to chair the committee. Cole was asked to "re-examine the whole housing program" and deliver "suggestions on what the future set up would be" to the president.[33]

The immense importance Eisenhower placed on housing is evidenced in his inclusion of Nielsen in what is referred to as the Eisenhower Ten. In actuality, the group consisted of nine men; one, administrator-designate for the Emergency Transport Agency Frank Pace Jr., resigned and was replaced. As the Cold War escalated, the president recruited these individuals in 1958 and 1959 to run the government in the event of a catastrophic event resulting in a national emergency. Recognizing not only Nielsen's expertise regarding the housing industry but also his trustworthiness, the president named him

---

31 Ibid., 100.

32 Ibid., 100, 102.

33 Ibid., 101.

administrator of the Emergency Housing Agency.[34] Other emergency agencies would be created to oversee censorship, communications, manpower, food, production, energy and minerals, and stabilization. The letters documenting these assignments were declassified in 1996.[35]

President Eisenhower understood early the need for a clear and settled housing policy that streamlined and controlled the federal government's fragmented intrusion into the housing market. After taking office in 1953, the president began implementing changes. He appointed Albert M. Cole administrator of the Housing and Home Finance Agency (HHFA), which replaced the United States Housing Authority. While in Congress, Cole had voted against the 1949 Housing Act because of what he saw as an overreach into the housing industry by the proposed policies. Over time he changed his mind and became a supporter of the HHFA.

In September 1953, Eisenhower established the President's Advisory Committee on Government Housing Policies and Programs, with Cole as its chair. Cole created several subcommittees to investigate specific topics. The most influential, the Subcommittee on Housing Credit Facilities, explored ways to level the uneven distribution of credit flows and encourage financial institutions to operate on a nationwide basis. These had been the same goals assigned to the Federal Farm Loan Banks in 1916. Aksel Nielsen did not head the subcommittee but was its most influential member. What had become apparent to the mortgage banking industry in the 1950s was similar to the problem faced by farm mortgage bankers in the early years of the twentieth century: how to manage credit risk and still provide adequate capital on favorable terms to borrowers across the nation.[36]

The 1949 Housing Act brought about a major effort to eliminate slums and tenements in American cities. It was designed to replace urban blight with modern, safe, and affordable housing while simultaneously attacking the roots of vandalism, crime, and poverty. However well intended,

34 Dwight D. Eisenhower, "Administrator-Designate Letter to Aksel Nielsen," 1958, Box 1 of the collection NIELSEN, AKSEL, Records, 1956–59, folder "Official Correspondence, 1957–1959," Dwight D. Eisenhower Presidential Library, Abilene, KS.

35 CONELRAD, *The Eisenhower Ten* (1999–2008), accessed May 20, 2015, http://www.conelrad.com/atomicsecrets/secrets.php?secrets=05.

36 *The President's Advisory Committee on Government Housing Policies and Programs: A Report to the President of the United States* (Washington, DC: Government Printing Office, December 1953), 348–49.

implementation of the act's programs revealed multiple problems. As early as 1953, Eisenhower's Advisory Committee report highlighted faulty aspects of the urban renewal program that needed to be remedied.[37]

The Urban Renewal Subcommittee of the president's committee was made up of such housing luminaries as James Rouse, chair and developer of Columbia, Maryland; Robert Moses of the City of New York; Otto Nelson of the New York Life Insurance Company, as well as Nielsen and Colean. The subcommittee made seventeen recommendations. In general, the group advised keeping the major goals of the Housing Act but sought changes to federal funding and advised expanding the breadth, scope, and role of city planners. In addition, it recommended a number of loan guarantees and other incentives to encourage urban redevelopment. As a result, life insurance companies began investing in urban development.

The subcommittee argued that urban redevelopment demanded a more comprehensive approach. It sought a Federal Urban Renewal Service to provide technical aid to city governments. More important, the committee recommended that the role of the FHA be expanded. The mission of FHA insurance was to generate more favorable financing terms in urban renewal areas that would match those generally available in other areas of the market. The purpose was to incentivize the purchase and construction or rehabilitation of rental and owner-occupied housing. The subcommittee insisted that communities develop more modern building codes to prevent the spread of blight and increase the enforcement of health, sanitation, and safety codes. For the FHA to insure long-term mortgages, cities agreed to upgrade their ordinances appropriately and assured enforcement to maintain the long-term viability of redevelopment projects.[38]

Many of the Advisory Committee's recommendations were included in the subsequent National Housing Act of 1954. Those recommendations included the reconfiguration of Fannie Mae. The new legislation dictated that Fannie Mae become a quasi-public corporation and, wherever possible, be financed by private capital. The corporation was to be managed with the goal of purchasing marketable FHA and VA loans. The legislation also required that Fannie's chair would also serve as the administrator of the

---

37   Ibid., 113.
38   Ibid., 118–19.

Housing and Home Finance Agency. This individual would have the authority to appoint officers and directors whose terms of service would be long enough to eliminate undue outside influence and political pressure. Its affairs were to be conducted in a manner that would permit the sale of its obligations in credit markets on favorable terms, but the obligations would not be guaranteed by the US government.[39]

Eisenhower felt strongly that Fannie Mae should remove government funds from its secondary marketing operations. To do that, he believed Fannie should be reorganized to more closely resemble the Federal Home Loan Banks. Fannie Mae's customers would then be required to purchase stock in the organization in proportion to the size of their servicing portfolios. Eisenhower hoped that over a period of time the users of Fannie Mae's services would completely privatize the company, thereby allowing the Treasury to retire its holdings of Fannie Mae preferred stock.[40]

In addition, the 1954 act revised Fannie Mae's charter granting it government agency status, thereby making it exempt from state and local income taxes. It also directed the Federal Reserve Banks "to perform various services for Fannie Mae, and specified that Fannie Mae was to provide 'special assistance' for certain kinds of mortgages, a precursor to the 'mission' regulation of [the] 1990s and 2000s."[41]

A critical distinction must be explained. Even though the act specifically stated that the obligations were not guaranteed, investors acted on the basis of an "implied guarantee." In other words, the investment community believed the government would not allow Fannie Mae to fail. They believed that in a worst-case scenario, the government would cover any losses incurred by Fannie Mae. So the implied guarantee, interpreted as a full faith and credit US government guarantee, created a moral hazard.

From 1954 until 1968, the government's guarantee on Fannie Mae remained secure because the underlying mortgages did have a full faith and credit guarantee provided by the FHA. Not withstanding that FHA loans had 100 percent coverage, the mortgage banker had skin in the game because the FHA had the option to pay for any loan that defaulted either in cash or in debentures,

---

39 Ibid., 31–32.

40 Ibid., 32.

41 Viral Acharya et al., *Guaranteed to Fail: Fannie Mae, Freddie Mac and the Debacle of Mortgage Finance* (Princeton, NJ: Princeton University Press, 2011), 183.

and then HUD assumed ownership of the defaulted property. Today, HUD homes available for purchase are the direct result of this type of transaction in which the FHA acquires defaulted properties.

Mortgage bankers approved to sell loans to Fannie Mae and service them were required to buy stock in the quasi–public-private corporation on a pro rata basis based on their loan sales and servicing portfolio, typically 1 percent of the portfolio's value. These were not publicly traded securities. However, similar to the shares of the Federal Home Loan Banks, some firms benefited from the after-market sale of odd lots (1 or more shares but fewer than 100 shares) of Fannie Mae stock.

9

The Colorado Housing and Finance Authority

Colorado also recognized the importance of making homeownership available to first-time home buyers and other underserved communities throughout the state. Appreciating the challenges, leaders from the mortgage banking, savings and loan, home building, and real estate communities began advocating for the creation of a state housing finance authority. In 1973 the Colorado General Assembly passed the enabling legislation authorizing the establishment of the Colorado Housing and Finance Authority (CHFA). It called for a nine-member board of directors to oversee the agency. The board was to include the state auditor, a member of the Colorado General Assembly, a member of the governor's cabinet, a mortgage banker, an architect, at least one individual with urban and regional planning experience, and others with in-depth real estate knowledge. CHFA's board of directors has since been expanded to eleven members.

Charles W. Henning, the executive director of the Savings and Loan League of Colorado, was elected the first chair of the board; Robert G. Boucher, president of First Denver Mortgage Company, was elected treasurer. State

DOI: 10.5876/9781607326236.c009

Representative Betty Ann Dittermore, a sponsor of the enabling legislation, was also a founding board member.

CHFA commands broad powers to lend on single-family and multi-family properties. As a state-chartered government-sponsored enterprise (GSE), it can borrow money at tax-exempt (lower) rates than can private lenders; thus it has the ability to provide low-cost mortgages to communities not traditionally served by other mortgage institutions. It has the authority to buy, own, and sell properties related to the mission of expanding affordable housing. The originating legislation granted the new agency $300,000 in startup capital that enabled CHFA to issue $90 million in bonds for the initial single- and multi-family loan programs. In addition, the agency makes small-business loans to promote economic development.

Unlike some state housing finance agencies, CHFA does not have explicit land-use regulation authority. However, it can exert some influence over land-use and building codes through its loan underwriting standards. Complementing CHFA, the Colorado Division of Housing assumes some of the responsibilities of supporting various federal affordable housing programs.

Working with the board, CHFA's first executive director, Walter Kane, led an ambitious agenda to implement the powers granted to CHFA by the legislation. The first task involved locating an appropriate space to house the new agency. He chose the upper floors of the Grant Mansion at 1115 Grant Street. Perhaps not coincidentally, Lenders Mortgage Company, a consortium owned by five of Denver's largest banks, occupied the lower level. Lenders Mortgage hired Fred E. Kirk, formerly of United Mortgage, to head the organization. Kirk was tasked with addressing the business community's concerns about decaying neighborhoods and with increasing homeowner education. The presence of Kirk, Henning, and Boucher, plus the experienced staff of Lenders Mortgage, provided ready access to the state's mortgage institutions and was instrumental in getting CHFA off to a quick start.

Once Kane had selected the office space, he went about hiring investment bankers, bond counsel, and other staff. He developed rules and regulations for administering CHFA's loan programs and for gaining agency approvals from the Department of Housing and Urban Development (HUD) and the Federal Housing Administration (FHA), to name a few. Selection of specific projects for financing and development followed.

In December 1974 CHFA financed its first major endeavor through the sale of $11,550,000 in eighteen-month notes. It used the proceeds to finance the construction of six apartment projects in the Denver metropolitan area, Loveland, and Fort Morgan under the FHA 236 program, an interest rate subsidy for multi-family properties. In all, eighteen lenders participated, and the projects included 470 units. Upon completion, First Denver Mortgage Company replaced the construction loan with a permanent loan that it placed in a mortgage-backed security guaranteed by Ginnie Mae at a below-market interest rate. Between late 1974 and 1976, CHFA issued bonds equaling almost $45.5 million to support its single-family homeownership program. In addition, during its first full year of operation, CHFA accessed HUD's Section 8 Rental Certificate program to produce an additional 2,000 units of rental housing for low- and moderate-income families. By 1980 CHFA had provided over 7,100 loans to borrowers in forty-eight Colorado counties, forty of which were rural. To accomplish that goal it worked with ninety-two lending institutions, including thirty-nine savings and loans, thirty commercial banks, and twenty-three mortgage banking firms.[1]

During its first forty-plus years of operation, CHFA has provided more than 84,000 mortgages to first-time and low- and moderate-income borrowers. Not only did CHFA provide the financing, it also worked diligently to help homeowners keep their homes. In 2005 it joined a coalition of over twenty nonprofit home counseling agencies across Colorado in establishing the Colorado Foreclosure Prevention Task Force. The task force and CHFA have helped provide home buyer counseling for almost 98,000 families and individuals across the state. Those services included assisting troubled borrowers in refinancing their mortgages or securing other loan modification options that enabled them to stay in their homes. Since 2008, CHFA has been awarded $12.1 million in outside funding to support foreclosure prevention efforts in Colorado.[2]

---

1 Colorado Housing and Finance Authority, *Summary of 1975 Operations, Colorado Housing and Finance Authority 1975 Annual Report* (Denver: Colorado Housing and Financing Authority, 1976), 6.

2 Colorado Housing and Finance Authority, "Celebrating 40 Years of Financing the Places Where Coloradans Live and Work," Colorado Housing and Finance Authority, accessed May 2, 2015, http://www.chfainfo.com/Pages/chfa-40th-celebrating-40-years.aspx; Colorado Housing and Finance Authority, "Foreclosure Prevention," Colorado Housing and Finance Authority, accessed May 3, 2015, http://www.chfainfo.com/homeownership/Pages/prevent-foreclosure.aspx.

Furthermore, CHFA increased the available affordable housing inventory in Colorado by financing a total of 58,628 rental units. Along with its commercial enterprise financing programs for small and medium-size businesses, almost 50,000 jobs have been generated and sustained. Added together, over its forty-plus-year history CHFA has contributed $10 billion to the Colorado economy.[3]

In 1977 David W. Herlinger succeeded Kane as the executive director of CHFA. Formerly head of CHFA's housing operations department, Herlinger brought an entrepreneurial culture to the organization. Early in his tenure he succeeded in establishing a stable revenue source for the agency and achieved a AA bond rating. During his time as executive director, the Colorado General Assembly never failed to increase CHFA's bonding authority. Given the agency's broad vision, powers, and mission, CHFA was able to establish a strong financial reserve position and to selectively use those reserves to produce and preserve more affordable housing units. CHFA's board of directors felt a strong obligation to repay the state for its initial capital investment made in 1974. In 1976 CHFA made the first installment payment of $50,000 to Governor Richard Lamm. An additional $100,000 in seed capital was returned to state coffers by 1980. The following year CHFA made the last payment to fully reimburse the state for its original investment of $300,000.[4]

CHFA's prudent fiscal and real estate asset management practices led the Colorado General Assembly to authorize new broadened powers for the agency in 1991. As a consequence, it acquired nearly 1,000 multi-family units. Over the next several years it purchased additional units from the Resolution Trust Corporation (RTC). Congress had created the RTC to dispose of assets generated by the collapse of the savings and loan industry during the 1990s. The RTC sold those apartment properties at liquidation prices, and CHFA had the resources to preserve them as affordable housing. Known as the Rental Acquisition Program, this ownership venture allowed the properties to be rehabilitated and upgraded. During 2010–11, many were sold to private nonprofit housing providers and local housing authorities.

---

3   Colorado Housing and Finance Authority, "Celebrating 40 Years."

4   Colorado Housing and Finance Authority, *Colorado Housing and Finance Authority Annual Report, 1999* (Denver: Colorado Housing and Finance Authority, 2000), 3.

Major distinctions of affordable housing for low- and moderate-income families and individuals (those earning less than 80 percent of median income) are the lack of reserves or savings available to apply to the down payment and consequent low equity levels, and the higher leverage and expense ratios of the nonprofit owners. Another benefit of CHFA's sound fiscal management and reserve funds was its ability to dedicate those funds to such in-house ventures as the Housing Opportunity Fund, to provide gap financing to help sustain struggling multi-family nonprofits. The use of the multi-family tax credit programs provides a feasible financing vehicle for the development of new affordable housing projects.

Natural disasters create particularly acute housing problems. In 1976, Colorado's centennial year, the Big Thompson River flooded, leaving hundreds of residents of Larimer and Weld Counties homeless. CHFA stepped in and provided funding to repair and rebuild apartments in those areas. Later, CHFA worked with the Colorado Division of Housing to relocate 600 households from Louisiana to Colorado following Hurricane Katrina and stepped up again to assist numerous households after the September 2013 floods along the South Platte River.

One characteristic of CHFA's loan portfolio is financing properties of cultural and historical significance. Its commercial division's economic development program financed the Durango and Silverton Narrow Gauge Railroad. When the Denver and Rio Grande Railroad gave up ownership of the line, my father, a prominent Denver mortgage banker and son of a railroad conductor, commented that "it was too bad the D&RG gave up the line because it was the only profitable passenger train they ever ran." In my opinion, it remains the nation's greatest tourist railroad.

CHFA's loan portfolio also contains numerous diverse housing projects of cultural and historical significance. One, Sakura Square, is a twenty-story FHA 236–insured project. It lies within Denver's Skyline Urban Renewal District, in the city's old Japanese neighborhood on Larimer Street between Nineteenth and Twentieth Streets. First Denver Mortgage Company and the First National Bank of Denver provided a construction loan totaling $3.9 million for the project. They then arranged for the long-term FHA 236 forty-year mortgage in 1974 with the Metropolitan Life Insurance Company as the investor. The FHA 236 multi-family program was an interest rate subsidy program in which the government would subsidize the difference between the interest rate on the loan—in the case of Sakura Square, 7 percent—and the base amount of 1 percent. The intended effect was to lower the rent for tenants, but the concept proved unworkable.[5]

In 2014 the Tri-State Buddhist Church, sponsor of Sakura Square, paid off the project's forty-year FHA 236 loan. The event marked the closing of a very rich chapter in the history of one of Denver's unique ethnic neighborhoods. Since the early days of the twentieth century, the northwest corner of downtown had been the heart of the city's Japanese community. Restaurants such as the Twentieth Street Cafe and the Akebono were favorite dining spots of Denver's downtown business community for decades. Small shops and grocery stores catering to Japanese residents prevailed on upper Larimer Street. Everyone knew the neighborhood as Japan Town.

The first Japanese immigrants arrived in Colorado during the mid-1880s, first to work in the mines and later in farm fields. As they assimilated and prospered, many found their way to Denver, where they began entering the professions and established a variety of retail shops and other family-owned businesses such as landscaping, gardens, and truck farms along the Platte River north of the city.

Just as the Italian Catholics in North Denver had founded Saint Catherine of Siena Parish to celebrate their religion, the Japanese brought their Buddhist faith with them and established the Denver Buddhist Church in 1916. As the number of Buddhists grew, the church's ministers traveled throughout Colorado, Wyoming, Nebraska, New Mexico, Texas, and Oklahoma to conduct religious services and support Japanese culture. In 1931 the members opened their first permanent church on Market Street.[6]

After World War II, Denver's Japanese population exploded, as many of the 7,000 former "detainees" from the Granada War Relocation Center, also known as the Amache Internment Camp, in southeastern Colorado chose to make the city their new home. A courageous decision by Colorado's wartime governor Ralph Carr to welcome these refugees from the Pacific Coast proved to be a highly controversial act that ruined his political career.

---

5   E. Michael Rosser, interview with Roger Hara (Sakura Square Management Corp. board member), Denver, CO, December 19, 2016.

6   Noel, *Denver's Larimer Street*, 148; Judith Simmer-Brown, "Encylopedia of the Great Plains: Denver Buddhist Temple," University of Nebraska–Lincoln, accessed February 15, 2015, http://plainshumanities.unl.edu/encyclopedia/doc/egp.asam.009.

Yet the long-term consequences proved to be an enormous benefit to the city and the state. This example of ethical, inclusive leadership resulted in a vastly expanded Japanese community, as nearly 20,000 individuals moved to Colorado in the years immediately following the war. In the coming decades many of those immigrants made major contributions in medicine, education, and business and, perhaps more important, set a moral standard of civic leadership.[7]

To serve this new influx of immigrants, community members collected $150,000 to purchase land for a new church at Nineteenth and Lawrence Streets. The church, dedicated in 1949, flourished; and soon the congregation created a regional organization called the Tri-State Buddhist Church. Robert Cameron, head of the Denver Urban Renewal Authority, approached the church's board to determine if it would be interested in acquiring the entire block bounded by Larimer and Lawrence Streets between Nineteenth and Twentieth Streets. At that time, during the 1960s, the neighborhood was changing radically. The recommendation of the Urban Land Institute for constructing a freeway that would have bisected lower downtown had been abandoned. And Dana Crawford was spearheading the restoration of buildings at the opposite end of Larimer Street, known as Larimer Square. After considerable deliberation, in 1970 the church purchased the 1900 block from the Denver Urban Renewal Authority for $188,000. While the land price was greatly discounted from its previous value, the purchase was a substantial commitment for the church's members. At about the same time, the Denver Buddhist Church took the name Denver Buddhist Temple.[8]

The Reverend Yoshitaka Tamai, along with many other community leaders, expressed concern about housing for the elderly and particularly housing for the Japanese community. After purchasing the block, the board of the church set out to build the twenty-story apartment building later named Tamai Tower. Sponsored by the Japanese Association, the building included 204 units, a penthouse community room, and a large parking garage. Retail businesses occupied the two lower levels, with stores that included the Granada Fish Market and the Pacific Mercantile Company. When completed, the terrace level held a large Japanese-style garden. The garden triggered

---

7   Noel, *Denver's Larimer Street*, 148–49; Simmer-Brown, "Encyclopedia of the Great Plains."

8   Simmer-Brown, "Encyclopedia of the Great Plains."

the naming of the complex as Sakura Square, which translates to Cherry Blossom Square.[9]

One of the basic flaws of the FHA 236 program was that the subsidy criteria were locked into the terms of the forty-year loan and failed to allow for increasing operating expenses. Over the years it became increasingly difficult to build adequate reserves to maintain the property. In 1997 the stewardship of Sakura Square applied for and received supplemental funding under the Low Income Housing Preservation and Rehabilitation Act of 1997. The purpose of this act was to help stabilize FHA 236 projects by preserving affordability and habitability. This subordinated loan provided funding for rehabilitation and remodeling of the project. Many of the units in Tamai Tower were converted to Section 8 vouchers under President Nixon and Secretary Romney's reform of mortgage subsidy programs.

Not long before the final loan payment was to be made, discussions began between Tri-State Buddhist Church Apartments, Inc., the nonprofit that owns and manages Tamai Tower and its retail space, and the board of the Tri-State/Denver Buddhist Temple, which owns the temple, to explore various options for the tower, including its possible conversion into market-rate apartments. After much debate, they decided to move forward with conversion. However, HUD, CHFA, and City of Denver regulations required that tenants using Section 8 vouchers to subsidize their rent be given a one-year notice of the change before enactment. Consequently, conversion to market-rate rentals was not completed until 2015. Now, former Section 8 tenants who continue to reside in Tamai Tower receive tenant protection vouchers from HUD.[10]

First Denver Mortgage also backed the construction of the Volunteers of America Apartments project in lower downtown, again with financing from the FHA 236 program. High-rise multi-family developments were not common in Denver during the 1960s, in part because they were a challenge to finance but also because the city imposed a height restriction on buildings. These and other projects made First Denver a pioneering leader in generating

---

9   Bill Hosokawa, *Colorado's Japanese Americans: From 1886 to the Present* (Boulder: University Press of Colorado, 2005), 165.

10   Rosser, interview with Roger Hara; Dennis Huspeni, "Aging Sakura Square Faces Challenges," *Denver Business Journal*, October 26, 2012, 1–2, accessed April 12, 2015, http://www.bizjournals .com/denver/print-edition/2012/10/26/aging-sakura-square-faces-challenges.html.

FHA multi-family loans. These properties remain as examples of the community's commitment to sustainable affordable housing and the way public-private partnerships can succeed with strong and capable management.[11]

The FHA 236 program rested on the theory that a lower interest rate would provide enough subsidy to reduce rental rates for low- and moderate-income tenants. When the program was put into practice, however, lower rental rates did not materialize. As a result, several Band-Aid approaches designed to keep the projects viable were attempted. One called the rental assistance payment program, created in 1974 and not to be confused with CHFA's Rental Acquisition Program, was later replaced by the Section 8 voucher system. However, several projects in Denver, including Sakura Square, did receive financing through the 236 program.

Denver has benefited from other FHA-insured multi-family projects, both new construction and renovations of existing buildings under FHA's 221D-4 program. The Barth Hotel serves as one of the best examples of a rehabilitated property. Originally built in 1882 and used as a warehouse, by 1890 it had been converted into the elegant Union Hotel. But by the time the nonprofit Senior Housing Options purchased the property in 1980 with financing provided by CHFA, the structure had become an old skid row flophouse. The nonprofit organization enabled its preservation and rehabilitation as a single-room–occupancy senior citizens' facility. The building was added to the National Register of Historic Places in 1982. In 2005 the building underwent a $1.3 million historic restoration of the windows, pressed tin ceilings, and other original interior and exterior features and materials and became the Barth Hotel. The Colorado Division of Housing provided funding for this extensive project.[12]

Another historic, late-nineteenth-century structure is the Boston Building, constructed in 1890. After the Boettcher family purchased the building, it housed their various enterprises, including the family's investment banking business and the philanthropic Boettcher Foundation. Remarkably, the building has survived wide swings in Denver's real estate economy. Watson Bowes, one of Denver's most distinguished mid-twentieth-century real estate

---

11 E. Michael Rosser, telephone interview with Joe Kelso, Denver, CO, April 16, 2014.

12 Senior Housing Options, "The Barth Hotel Assisted Living: The History of the Barth Hotel," accessed February, 8, 2015, http://seniorhousingoptions.org/wordpress/wp-content/uploads/The-Barth-Hotel-History-Sheet2.pdf.

appraisers and a member of the Appraisal Institute, appraised the building in 1948. His assessment determined that the building had outlived its usefulness and should be replaced with a modern office structure. Bowes estimated the demolition cost at $40,000.[13]

In November 1957 Bowes appraised the Boston Building again; his previous recommendation for demolition had not been acted upon. This time he estimated the value of the property at $568,500, of which $462,500 was allocated as the value of the land and $106,000 for the building. The low value of the building was based on the fact that the momentum of downtown had shifted east. The two banks that had occupied spaces across Seventeenth Street, Denver National Bank and US National Bank, had merged and moved into William Zeckendorf's Mile High Center, designed by renowned architect I. M. Pei, at Seventeenth Street and Broadway. Zeckendorf had agreed to purchase the old May Company store, just a block from the Boston Building, as part of a redevelopment plan at Sixteenth Street and Court Place. The project also included Courthouse Square, the May D&F store, and the Hilton Hotel. The Colorado National Bank remained as the only major business in the area.[14]

Colorado National stayed in its Seventeenth and Champa Streets location. During the late 1950s it added three more floors to accommodate its growing business. The bank also purchased the Ernest and Cranmer Building at Seventeenth and Curtis for drive-up windows. The decision to reinvest in that area of lower downtown probably contributed to the decision by the owners of the Boston Building to renovate and update their building.

But by the 1990s the Boston Building and the adjacent and equally historic Kistler Building sat vacant. National Boston Lofts Associates, LLP (National Properties) purchased both buildings. It allied with the Denver Urban Renewal Authority (DURA) to link the buildings and transform them into a mixed-use complex of loft-style apartments anchored by retail space. By working with DURA, the project was eligible for $944,000 in sales tax increment financing assistance. Of the 158 one- and two-bedroom apartments, 32 were designated as affordable housing, while the rest were market-rate units.

---

13 Watson Bowes, "Appraisal of the Boston Building: 828 17th Street," AG Bowes and Company Archives, Collection reception number 362, client reference number 509, Stephen Hart Library, History Colorado, Denver.

14 Ibid.

In 1998 the $23.4 million investment resulted in the new Boston Lofts. As with the renovation of the Barth Hotel, the developers preserved many of the buildings' original features and materials. In addition, both buildings are listed on the National Register of Historic Places.[15]

Developers and investors can utilize two important tax credit programs for the preservation of historic buildings such as the Boston Building and the Denver Dry Goods store. The IRS provides tax credits if the redevelopment of a historic building includes low-income housing. Historic preservation tax credits are also available. They can be sold to partnerships if they create enough equity in the properties to allow CHFA to use its bonding authority, supported by the FHA risk share credit enhancement (loan guaranty), to preserve the historic buildings.[16]

Additional innovations over the years have been the introduction of a home improvement loan program, energy-efficiency upgrades for existing properties, and energy-efficient purchase money mortgages that allow the costs of energy-saving improvements to be included in the property mortgage without having to apply for additional financing. CHFA is also involved in the federal mortgage credit certificate program that returns 20 percent of the mortgage interest paid to the homeowner at tax time.

Needless to say, CHFA has assisted numerous developers and nonprofit housing agencies to increase the quantity and quality of affordable housing for low- and moderate-income individuals and families across the state. In the process it has contributed to the revitalization of Denver through the preservation and rehabilitation of some of the city's historic buildings. CHFA's thorough understanding and utilization of the vast array of available financing options has contributed to its ongoing success.

15　Denver Urban Renewal Authority, "The Boston Lofts," accessed February 9, 2015, http://www .renewdenver.org/redevelopment/dura-redevelopment-projects/downtown-denver/the -boston-lofts.html.

16　E. Michael Rosser, interview with Henry K. Burgwyn, Denver, CO, January 13, 2014.

10

The Age of Great Developers and Changing Land Uses

An old axiom among city planners and other policymakers asserts that people hate either density or urban sprawl or, in most cases, both. The two FHAs, the Federal Housing Administration and the Federal Highway Administration, are often but unfairly blamed for the growth of suburbia that is at the heart of these scorned conditions.

During the last sixty years, three monumental developments have affected urban land use in the United States: the explosion of suburbs, the emergence of planned developments, and neighborhood gentrification. These changes have been facilitated by a number of government policies and programs dating back to the formation of the United States Housing Authority (forerunner of the Housing and Home Finance Agency) in 1938 and the Department of Housing and Urban Development (HUD) in the 1960s. Partnering with government to implement these policies were mortgage bankers and large institutional real estate investors. If there was a catalyst for this change that married government policy with vast sums of real estate capital, it was the report of President Eisenhower's Advisory Committee on Government

DOI: 10.5876/9781607326236.c010

Housing Policies and Programs.[1] That report and the recommendations it contained have influenced virtually every piece of housing legislation since 1954. Financial institutions and government policymakers responded to the desire of the American public for a home, good schools, and, eventually, a garage that housed two cars.

THE GROWTH OF SUBURBIA

The first postwar trend, facilitated by FHA insurance programs and Veterans Administration (VA) loan guarantee programs, ushered in the nationwide explosion of the suburbs. The new suburbs were built to meet the needs of the growing population and veterans returning from World War II, who readily participated in the VA's GI zero down payment loan program. The sociological demand for homeownership grew from its roots in the Progressive movement of the 1890s and has continued unabated for the last 100-plus years. The new and rapidly expanding highway system, sponsored and funded by the Federal Highway Administration, also fueled suburban growth. Freeways made commuting into the cities easy and fast. Simultaneously, the creation of automobile access to and from urban business districts accelerated the demise of the closer streetcar suburbs of earlier decades.

Most historians credit the origins of this tidal wave of suburbanization to William Levitt, his brother, Alfred, and their father, Abraham. Together they developed the first mass-produced planned suburban residential neighborhood, Levittown, on Long Island, New York. Many of the features the Levitts incorporated into their houses as they evolved over time became the accepted standard for suburban homes. However, Levittown is also often criticized for its sterile blandness.

CHANGING LAND USES AND THE NEW TOWN MOVEMENT

In response to the cookie-cutter ordinariness of the numerous "Levittowns" that sprang up across the American landscape, the second postwar change in land use was the planned development of entirely new towns or communities such as Reston, Virginia, and Columbia, Maryland, both suburbs

---

1   Albert M. Cole, *President's Advisory Committee on Government Housing Programs: A Report to the President of the United States* (Washington, DC: Government Printing Office, 1953).

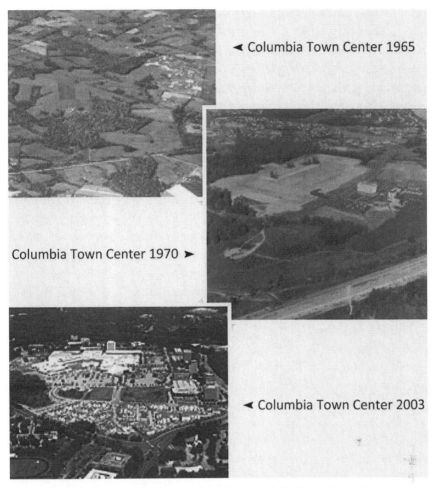

◄ Columbia Town Center 1965

Columbia Town Center 1970 ➤

◄ Columbia Town Center 2003

James Rouse initiated nearly forty years of development of the planned New Town community of Columbia, Maryland. Courtesy, Columbia [MD] Association.

of Washington, DC. These developments went far beyond being just residential neighborhoods. They incorporated areas for retail and commercial businesses, schools, libraries and other community services, and parks and open greenbelt areas in conjunction with housing. These new towns were designed to be self-sufficient; they were not just bedroom communities in support of nearby urban centers.

Robert E. Simon, the developer of Reston, is credited with triggering the New Town movement in America. He was followed closely by James Rouse, the developer of Columbia, Maryland. However, I argue that the real credit for the large-scale New Towns of the 1960s and beyond belongs to the J. C. Nichols Company of Kansas City, Missouri. Led by the company's founder, Jesse Clyde Nichols, the goal was to "develop whole residential neighborhoods that would attract an element of people who desired a better way of life, a nicer place to live and would be willing to work in order to keep it better."[2] The company's development of the Kansas City Country Club District began in 1907. This original new community grew out of a hog farm and a creek bed that frequently flooded. The comprehensive project included Moorish architecture, graceful tree-lined streets, inviting homes, and the world's first automobile-friendly shopping center, the Country Club Plaza Shopping Center, which opened in 1922. This development laid the groundwork for sustainable urban design that has endured for over 100 years. The housing, retail, commercial, and hospitality industries continue to thrive in the Country Club District. Also part of the New Town movement is my enduring memory of getting on the streetcar at the Brookside Shopping Center, more commonly known as Sixty-Third and Brookside, and taking a short ride to the Plaza. Sixty-Third and Brookside set a standard for other Nichols neighborhood shopping centers, including Prairie Village situated across State Line Road in Kansas City, Kansas. Brookside was financed by the Teachers Insurance and Annuity Association of New York. Investment in Nichols's developments was highly sought after by Metropolitan Life, New York Life, and Kansas City Life.

The New Town movement emerged from the recognition of people's desire for quality places of their own. At the same time, the leaders of the movement acknowledged the complaints of critics about the lack of creativity and amenities in America's suburbs. Already an industry leader when he was appointed to Eisenhower's advisory committee, Rouse emerged as the driving force in the New Town movement during the 1960s.

Like Nichols, Rouse was a visionary. When his education was delayed by the Great Depression, he worked nights at a parking garage to save enough money to put himself through law school. After working for two years in the Baltimore office of the FHA, he worked in the mortgage department of

---

2   J. C. Nichols Company Records (ca. 1886–2007), State Historical Society of Missouri Research
    Center–Kansas City, accessed April 10, 2015, http://shs.umsystem.edu/kansascity/manu-
    scripts/k0106.pdf.

a commercial bank for another two years. Soon after that he opened his own mortgage firm. Rouse also formed a second company, Community Research and Development, Incorporated, as his development arm. He earned a reputation as a successful shopping center developer. His credits include the Cherry Hill Mall in New Jersey, the first totally indoor, climate-controlled shopping center on the East Coast,[3] and Washington, DC's Union Station redevelopment. Rouse was an ardent and passionate advocate for urban renewal.[4]

In 1963, plans began to take shape to build a new town named Columbia on 17,000 acres in rural Maryland between Baltimore and Washington, DC. Rouse's idea was to build a completely self-contained and sustainable community that included employment opportunities, neighborhood and regional shopping centers, parks, open space and trails, environmentally sensitive neighborhood design, integration of single- and multi-family development, along with economic and social diversity. In November 1964 Baltimore papers carried the headline "A New Town for Howard County." The accompanying article included maps, architectural renderings, and photos of parks and a shopping mall. Rouse is quoted: "The idea that a whole new town might provide better and more complete answers to many of the problems of growth stems largely from a study of the way in which people live . . . Columbia is an opportunity for the growth of America to change course away from the needless waste of land, sprawl, disorder, congestion, and mounting taxes to a direction of order, beauty, financial stability, and sincere concern for the growth of people."[5]

Convincing the Howard County Board of Commissioners to issue a change in the zoning and subdivision regulations to allow for the development and construction of a new town posed the major land-use issue challenge for Rouse to overcome. Joshua Olsen summarized the situation in his biography of Rouse: "Many of the no growth advocates in the county preferred to keep their half-acre zoning for residential use. Rouse pointed out that such zoning allowed for almost 30,000 homes on his land containing about 100,000 people spread evenly over one half-acre lot after another. A new town would

---

3   Joshua Olsen, *Better Places, Better Lives: A Biography of James Rouse* (Washington, DC: Urban Land Institute, 2003), 113.

4   J. W. Anderson, "A Brand New City for Maryland: A Big, Bold Dream in the Making," *Mortgage Banking Magazine* (December 1964): 29.

5   Olsen, *Better Places,* 177.

accommodate the same amount but in a manner that would avoid low density monotony."[6]

The Rouse organization experienced great success conducting a series of talks with small groups to explain the overall concept and plan for Columbia. In all, they gave over 500 presentations. The developers often walked into a schoolroom, hearing chamber, or living room where the air was thick with opposition; after the meetings they often walked out to a standing ovation. The anti-growth Howard County Citizens Association began to see the wisdom of Rouse's proposal and later gave its qualified support. By 1965 many of the legal obstacles had been overcome and construction could begin moving forward.[7]

The next challenge for the Rouse Company was to find a lender or group of lenders willing to invest in what the vernacular of the time called "patient money"—money placed in long-term investments that may not realize profits for an extended period of time. Obtaining the land, then acquiring the necessary subdivision filings and zoning modifications along with the construction of streets and water and sewer systems required partners with a long-term strategic view and a willingness to see the return on their money over many years. Simons, who started a similar project in Reston, Virginia, a year earlier, had partnered with the Gulf Oil Company.

Rouse's reputation as a leading mortgage banker enabled him to assemble a group of lenders and investors who understood the project and had the patient money to fund the buildout of Columbia. Teachers Insurance and Annuity Association invested $15 million, Chase Manhattan Bank agreed to loan $10 million, Howard Research and Development made a $25 million investment for the construction of roads and sewer lines, and joint owner Connecticut General Life Insurance Company, which made the land loan, agreed to stay in the project. The total indebtedness stood at $50 million. The Howard Research and Development Company held title to the land.[8]

Rouse had hoped to have the program up and running by the summer of 1996, but at that point little had been done except work on the installation of sewer lines. A temporary post office finally opened on August 15, 1966, and the first postmark from the new town was issued. Rouse worked with Ryan Homes Companies of Pittsburgh to build 1,500 single-family homes. In

6   Ibid., 179.
7   Ibid.
8   Ibid., 79–182.

addition, unable to find an apartment developer, he began developing those units himself. The Columbia Parks and Recreation Association also received funding from Connecticut General Life Insurance Company and the Teachers Insurance and Annuity Association to fund its early operations. Securing a grocery store and other tenants for the village center proved equally difficult. To lure retail businesses, the Rouse Company agreed to subsidize rents until the population grew enough to support the first retailers. The company did successfully solicit Hittman Engineering, which announced its intention to open a research and development facility in Columbia and purchased a fifty-acre site in one of the community's industrial parks.[9] It may have taken longer than expected to materialize, but Columbia finally began to take shape.

However, Columbia was not the largest FHA subdivision project at the time; in fact, there were 173 larger projects. But it was the most innovative. The concept of a totally new town of Columbia's size and scope, with its full menu of public and private services fully integrated into the community, was totally unique.

Across the river in Reston, Virginia, Simon was developing 7,400 acres into a community with a population of 70,000. While Gulf Oil appeared to be a good choice for a partner, when the money dried up in 1966 the partnership began to fray, and Simon eventually left the project. Regrettably, Reston never lived up to original expectations. Nevertheless, it remains a remarkable development.[10]

In large measure, the success of Columbia, Maryland, can be attributed to the intellect, dedication, and determination of Rouse and his team. Benefiting from the lessons learned there, Rouse and others worked with HUD secretary George Romney on the 1970 Housing Act. This legislation contained a number of special assistance, loan guarantee, and insurance programs that expedited the building of other New Towns.

The New Town movement also recognized that, in addition to these new financing tools, city planners required training to manage and implement the new programs. Under Title VII of the 1970 Housing Act, graduate programs were established at Virginia Technical University and the University of Northern Colorado for executive-level working professionals to train in the

9 Ibid., 185–88.

10 James Bailey, ed., *New Towns in America: The Design and Development Process* (New York: John Wiley and Sons, 1973), 16–17.

basics of urban and regional planning and public administration. This was the program from which I earned my master of arts degree.

Colorado also participated in the New Town movement. The first such designed community was Montebello. On September 12, 1965, the venture partners purchased and Denver annexed almost 3,000 acres of grazing land northeast of downtown. Separated from the central section of the city by Stapleton International Airport, planners designed the new neighborhood to be relatively self-sufficient while enabling residents to enjoy the benefits of being part of the Rocky Mountain region's economic and cultural hub. Like Rouse's Columbia in Maryland, Montebello developed as a complete mixed-use community with a variety of housing options, from rental apartments to single-family homes, for moderate- and middle-income families. Just a year after annexation, the first group of houses was ready for occupancy. Home prices ranged from $15,150 to $22,250 and were eligible for FHA financing and no-money-down GI loans.[11]

Within a few short years, multiple housing subdivisions rose, accompanied by ample parks, greenbelt areas, shopping centers, hotels, and restaurants. Aesthetics and functionality went hand in hand. Montebello was the first area of Denver to be built with all of its utilities installed underground, and its graceful curved streets contrasted with the classic grid system found throughout much of the city. But Montbello's economic engine was the Montebello Industrial Park, which occupied 510 acres. Housing such firms as Samsonite Corporation, then the world's largest luggage manufacturer, by 1972 around 7,000 individuals worked at the growing complex. When fully developed, Montebello was projected to provide jobs for up to 12,000 commercial and industrial workers and to be called home by as many as 45,000 people.[12]

Two other highly successful new communities developed in Colorado. The first, Vail and its ski mountain, entered the planning phase in 1957 through the initiative of several ski enthusiasts who had served in the Tenth Mountain Division during World War II. The other is Highlands Ranch, located south of Denver in Douglas County.

World War II drastically changed the Colorado economy. Men and women came from all parts of the United States. Many of the soldiers who trained

---

11 W. Haselbush, "'Magic' Changes Montbello Scene," *Denver Post*, October 2, 1966, 73.

12 Ibid.; "Montebello Industrial Park Success Noted," *Rocky Mountain News*, May 11, 1969, 42.

at Camp Carson near Colorado Springs and at Lowry Field east of Denver for the US Army Air Corps decided to return and settle there. The World War II training facility for the US Army's Tenth Mountain Division at Camp Hale near Leadville on Tennessee Pass introduced the soldiers to the surrounding mountains and their potential for winter recreation. Some of its members, including Peter Seibert, returned to the area after the war. Seibert spearheaded the development of Vail Mountain into a world-class ski resort. He assembled a group of investors to create Vail Associates to develop the mountain for skiing and established the town of Vail as a base area to provide support services for the mountain, which opened to skiers in 1962. The early stages were financed largely by a consortium of banks led by the First National Bank of Denver and United Bank (formerly Denver US National Bank, now Wells Fargo).

During the 1960s, rising incomes and greater mobility dramatically increased the potential of outdoor recreation in Colorado. As the state grew, citizens concerned about maintaining Colorado's quality of life and protecting its environment turned away from so-called dirty industry. Instead, they looked to expanding tourism. Until the end of the war, Colorado's tourism industry had been based largely on summer visitors. The long-popular tourist communities such as Estes Park and Grand Lake had provided access for people visiting Rocky Mountain National Park. Cascade and Green Mountain Falls near Colorado Springs invited visitors to explore Pike's Peak, the Manitou Cliff Dwellings, Royal Gorge, and other area attractions. Each attraction offered a welcome respite from the summer heat and humidity for visitors from Texas and the Midwest. But in the 1960s the market began to change as skiing began to grow in popularity. Ski areas, previously limited to a few near Denver, began to spring up across the state. The building of Interstate 70 through the mountains to the Western Slope opened up a wide range of new opportunities for ski-area development.

The winter recreation department of the US Forest Service had analyzed potential ski-area sites within the White River National Forest and other national forests in Colorado as far back as the late 1930s. George Cranmer, manager of Denver's Department of Parks and Recreation, had been instrumental in developing the Winter Park ski area that opened in 1940. Winter Park was especially attractive because of its location at the west portal of the Denver and Rio Grande Railroad's Moffat Tunnel. The now famous

"Ski Train" provided easy, stress-free transportation to the ski area. Aspen Mountain and Arapahoe Basin ski areas emerged later in the decade. Aspen was probably the first postwar ski resort to capitalize on the nation's rising prosperity, as well as on the quality of the mountain's terrain and the quantity of its snow.

The broader Aspen area offered exceptional development possibilities. In 1957 preliminary discussions began with a number of investors for what became known as the Aspen Snowmass area. Over the next seven years the Forest Service conducted feasibility studies and submitted its report to Washington in the fall of 1964.[13] At its recommendation, four distinct ski areas would eventually dot the mountainsides above the valley floor—Aspen Mountain, Aspen Highlands, Buttermilk, and Snowmass. Vail, which opened in 1962, was taking off at the same time.

The burgeoning ski industry led to a shift in, or at least to an additional use of, Colorado's public lands. For decades, the primary economic use of the federal lands in the state was for extractive industries. Whether the mining of the various minerals hidden beneath the soil or the harvesting of lumber, almost all of these activities took place on public lands. However, the ski industry significantly broadened the use of public lands, as most of the skiing terrain of the new resorts was on mountains leased from the US Forest Service. Simultaneously, people discovered other outdoor recreational activities—fishing, hiking, backpacking, whitewater rafting, and kayaking, to mention just a few—most of which took place on public lands and waterways. This broader use of the public domain, assisted by the construction of Interstate 70, brought more people into the mountains and greatly diminished the isolation of the once sleepy communities of the central mountain and Western Slope regions. Recreation opened the Colorado high country, brought economic investment, and, for better or worse, opened previously untapped areas to real estate development.

By the late 1960s, Denver's large commercial banks and their mortgage banking affiliates began to recognize the investment opportunities arising from the exploding winter recreation and skiing businesses. Resort devel-

---

13 Paul I. Hauk, "Chronologies of the Ski Areas on and Adjacent to the White River National Forest," Manuscript Collection #WH1304, Rg 17B, Section 3, Box 2, Denver Public Library, Denver, CO.

opers needed financing to buy equipment and construct buildings. Ski-area owners faced the challenge of providing lodging and other services for the new resorts. Sun Valley in Idaho had been owned and operated by the Union Pacific Railroad. It had the capital to develop the ski area and cover overhead costs for the lodging. While the early developers in Colorado had access to private capital, few, if any, had deep enough pockets to make investments in lodging facilities that would be occupied only during the winter ski season.

Some people owned summer cabins. But most were located within easy access of Denver and other Front Range cities, not deep in the higher mountains where the new ski resorts were being developed. Further, they were not designed or built for winter use. Few people had the opportunity for year-round ownership of a place devoted to winter as well as summer recreational pursuits. The answer to the resort lodging problem arrived in the form of the second-home phenomenon and the rise of condominiums.

The condominium concept had been virtually unknown in the state until the 1960s. After the Colorado General Assembly passed the Condominium Ownership Act in 1963, it became the solution to the ski-area lodging problem. The act allowed for the sale of individual units of condominium complexes, thus transferring the vacancy risk from ski-area developers to individual owners. Soon, United Bank of Denver became a significant construction lender in Aspen and Winter Park and the new communities of Vail and Snowmass Village.[14]

United Bank of Denver financed Crestwood Condominiums, one of the early condominium projects in Snowmass. United's mortgage banking affiliate, United Mortgage Company, provided permanent financing to unit owners. But for most, lending in the mountains during the 1960s and early 1970s was seen as a challenge. For a large number of borrowers, the possibility of financing a second home or mountain condominium was virtually nonexistent. However, Aspen and the new area of Snowmass had particular appeal for institutional investors. A select group of high–net-worth borrowers solved the mortgage affordability problem. Some of the borrowers, particularly in Aspen, possessed star quality. The first loans for condominiums in Crestwood were issued to such borrowers. Jack Kemp, the former

---

14 Orten, Cavanaugh, Richmond, and Holmes, "Introduction to the Colorado Condominium Ownership Act" (Denver: Orten, Cavanaugh, Richmond, and Holmes, March 17, 2011), 2.

Los Angeles Chargers and Buffalo Bills quarterback, congressman, and later HUD secretary, is one such example.[15]

The initial investor in the Crestwood project was the Manhattan Life Insurance Company of New York. The company established very strict underwriting criteria. The units had to have "ski-out" access to the mountain. The down payments required a 30 percent cash investment from the buyer, and interest rates were higher than those for a primary residence loan. Sale prices ranged from $30,000 to $50,000. Comparable units in Breckenridge and Winter Park sold in the $20,000–$25,000 range, with similar mortgage terms.

Ironically, as Colorado's ski resorts were entering their boom years, many areas of the country were experiencing slow growth, which decreased investment opportunities in those areas. As a result, thrift institutions throughout Kansas, Iowa, and Illinois, whose management personnel had vacationed in Colorado, found second homes and condominiums in the ski areas very attractive for their mortgage portfolios. I accompanied several thrift institutions' representatives during their trips to survey potential investment opportunities. As long as the units were in well-established ski resorts that possessed a substantial base area with attractive amenities such as restaurants and shops, these loans performed very well for their investors over time.

By the mid-1970s Vail Associates had reached the final stages of permit approval with the US Forest Service for the Beaver Creek Ski Area. This world-class site was supposed to host the alpine events of the 1976 Olympic Winter Games, which were rejected by voters in 1972 in part because of concern about environmental impacts and overdevelopment not only at the Beaver Creek site but also along the Front Range. But even without the Olympic Games, Beaver Creek moved forward. Lifts were installed on the mountain as lodges, restaurants, shops, condominiums, and luxury homes rose. The resort opened for the 1981–82 ski season.

While working on the Beaver Creek permit application during my year with the Land Use Commission, I was a strong supporter of the resort and the Olympics. When voters rejected the games, I believe it negatively impacted Colorado's image. Subsequently, when issues regarding the exorbitant cost of hosting an Olympics, not only in Colorado but at later sites around the world, became evident, I changed my mind about the advisability of hosting

---

15   E. Michael Rosser, email communications with Jim Wahlstrom, senior planner for the Town of Snowmass, October 21, 2015.

Olympic Games. However, I still think the Beaver Creek Ski Resort is a good development.

In 1972 Colorado's legislature recognized the potential for developments in the state that would resemble Columbia, Maryland, and Reston, Virginia. To that end, it passed the Planned Unit Development (PUD) Act. The law recognized the ability of local governments to maintain existing zoning ordinances while providing enough flexibility for the development of quality, large-scale projects that included extra amenities. The PUD Act outlines ten purposes for large planned unit developments (PUDs), such as Highlands Ranch and the Stapleton redevelopment. It specifically encouraged more efficient land use, innovative development, and the integration of commercial, residential, recreational, and educational facilities.[16]

Highlands Ranch, just south of Denver in Douglas County, had been owned by the Phipps family for several decades prior to its purchase by Denver billionaire oilman and philanthropist Marvin Davis. At one time Davis owned several companies, including the Aspen Ski Company and 20th Century Fox. Almost immediately, he sold the property to the Mission Viejo Company of California, a subsidiary of Philip Morris Credit Corporation. The company had developed two large communities in Southern California—Mission Viejo and Aliso Viejo—and a small residential project, also called Mission Viejo, in Aurora, Colorado.[17]

Given the capital resources of Philip Morris, the vision for Highlands Ranch called for a buildout over a twenty-year period. From the beginning the plan included wide streets, numerous parks and trails, and substantial areas designated for natural open space. The company was instrumental in providing the financing for the first school and acquiring and building the water and wastewater systems. When the first subdivision opened, the interest rate stood at 14.5 percent. Still, buyers flocked to view Highlands Ranch to see for themselves this much-touted property with its rich local history.[18]

---

16 Donald L. Elliott, ed., *Colorado Land Planning and Development Law*, 9th ed. (Denver: Bradford, 2012), 90–91.

17 "Highlands Ranch History," Highlands Ranch Metro District, accessed May 4, 2017, http://highlandsranch.org/community/history/.

18 Highlands Ranch Historical Society, "Images of America: Highlands Ranch" (Charleston, SC: Arcadia, 2016), 53, 59, 67.Highlands Ranch Historical Society, *Images of America: Highlands Ranch* (Charleston, SC: Arcadia, 2016), 53, 59, 67.

Mission Viejo documented every promise it made to the county with periodic updates, which assured the company's credibility with the local political leadership. In the first years the company adhered to its established practice of building all the houses. But it soon became evident that demand could not keep up with Mission Viejo's production capacity, so it recruited three of the region's premier homebuilders—the Writer Corporation, Sanford Homes, and Richmond Homes—to join in the construction effort. The Highlands Ranch development was facilitated and financed with the resources of the Philip Morris Credit Corporation. With its 10,000 acres of permanently protected open space, Highlands Ranch has been recognized as one of the nation's leading and most successful New Towns.

The Stapleton redevelopment by Forest City is the latest New Town in Colorado. Known for its open space and mixed-use urban design, it is another example of James Rouse's vision.[19] These New Town community developments proved to be successful because of the developers' ability to implement a long-term plan and attract investors with patient money who shared their vision. The exception is Battlement Mesa; it did not become the self-sustaining community that was originally intended to support the oil-shale industry, but it is now a well-established community and home to many Colorado retirees.

Prior to the New Town movement taking hold in Colorado, much of Denver's growth during the immediate post–World War II era met with heated resistance. Many individuals in Denver's political and business establishment did not want to see things change. Life in Colorado had been easy and simple, but change was inevitable. Returning servicemen, the establishment of a large federal government workforce (at one time Denver ranked second behind Washington, DC, in the number of federal employees), and Stapleton International Airport becoming a major cross-country airline hub transformed Denver into a bustling city.

Long-simmering discussions between Denver's business community and its city government finally found resolution with plans for the revitalization of downtown Denver through redevelopment. Most came to understand that redevelopment was necessary to avoid the urban blight that would infect many of America's urban cores.

---

19 Forest City Stapleton, Inc., "Stapleton Sustainability Master Plan 2004," accessed May 3, 2015, https://www.stapletondenver.com/wp-content/uploads/2014/12/Stapleton_Sustainability_Plan.pdf, 12.

A redevelopment organization with international reach is the Urban Land Institute (ULI), founded by J. C. Nichols and others in 1936. A unique global organization, its mission is "to provide leadership in the responsible use of land and in creating and sustaining thriving communities worldwide."[20] With offices in Washington, DC, London, and Hong Kong, the ULI has had a global impact on real estate finance and development.

One mission of the ULI is to provide advising services to communities. Known as ULI Advisory Services panels, teams of experts travel to specific cities. After analyzing a designated land-use problem for several days, the panel crafts a variety of recommendations for solutions to enable the community to make a good decision.

Prompted by many leaders, particularly Aksel Nielsen and Bruce Rockwell of Colorado National Bank, the newly formed entity Downtown Denver, Incorporated, engaged the ULI in 1955 to assemble and bring a group of real estate experts to Denver to conduct such a study to guide the city's development. The panel was charged with holding public meetings and conferring with officials in addition to conducting whatever surveys and studies it deemed necessary prior to making its recommendations. In conjunction with a citizens' committee of seventy-five members, the resulting report contained a set of recommendations that would guide the city into the twenty-first century.[21]

Members of the ULI Advisory Services panels are selected from the institute's membership and vary depending of the type and scope of the proposed project. Panels may include capital investors, developers, private and public urban planners, architects, and other professionals. Many panels also include a university graduate student who works with panel experts on site-specific projects and contributes to the recommendations. The ULI maintains a strong reputation for fairness and neutrality; therefore, its recommendations bring great credibility and objectivity. It certainly promotes active discussion and can be a catalyst for constructive dialogue and change.[22]

One of the Denver panel members was Urban A. Denker of Wichita, vice president of the Wheeler Kelly and Hagny Investment Company. Through

---

20 Urban Land Institute, "Mission and Priorities," accessed April 20, 2017, https://americas.uli.org/about-uli/mission-priorities/.

21 "Downtown Denver: A Report to Downtown Denver, Inc.," Urban Land Institute panel (Washington, DC: Urban Land Institute, April 1955).

22 Urban Land Institute, "Mission and Priorities."

my knowledge of Denker as a family friend, I had great respect for his expertise and industry insight, as well as the contributions his company had made to real estate development and mortgage banking.

On April 30, 1955, the ULI Advisory Services panel presented its final report during a meeting held at the Cosmopolitan Hotel. Many of its recommendations dealt with both public and private organizational issues, as well as the city's tax structure. The ULI panel envisioned maintaining the central business district as the region's retail center. At that time there were three department stores in Denver: the Denver Dry Goods Company, the May Company, and the Daniels and Fisher Company. Among other things, the ULI report specifically recommended a major new department store development as well as a 700-room hotel.[23]

William Zeckendorf and the Webb and Knapp Company took up the challenge. They developed the new retail/hotel complex on the old site of the Arapahoe County Courthouse, known as Courthouse Square, at Sixteenth and Tremont Streets. Upon its completion, Denver boasted a new Hilton Hotel, and the retail space became the flagship property of the May D&F Company created by the merger of the May Company and the Daniels and Fisher Company. Zeckendorf also helped shift land use on Seventeenth Street, home of Denver's financial district. Known as "the Wall Street of the West," it moved farther east with the construction of the Mile High Center, which incorporated a twenty-four-story office tower, plaza, and the conversion of the Sears and Roebuck store into the headquarters of the Denver US National Bank.

The panel also recommended that legislation be passed at the state and city levels. One recommendation advised changes in land-use laws that would eventually allow for urban rehabilitation that incorporated the growing twenty-first-century popularity of lofts. Such legislation enabled Denver's Urban Renewal Authority to take advantage of the provisions of the 1954 Housing Act to ignite redevelopment of Denver's blighted area between Curtis Street and Union Station. This area would later encompass the Skyline Urban Renewal District. Approved by voters in 1968, its completion can now be celebrated with the redevelopment and reopening of Denver's historic Union Station during the summer of 2014.[24]

---

23 "Downtown Denver: A Report," 26.

24 Ibid., 34.

The ULI also dealt with issues of traffic, parking, and freeway construction. Vigorous discussions analyzed the need for mass transit and the role of the privately held Denver Tramway Company, which later became the multi-jurisdictional Regional Transportation District (RTD). Surprisingly, the ULI report paid little attention to a rail system in Denver. However, such a system was discussed at the meeting, and several recommendations were voiced about potential rail line locations. Ironically, years later the buildouts of the RTD's light rail southeast corridor and the west corridor are virtually identical to those unadopted recommendations. Other recommendations in the report, which fortunately were not followed, included creation of the Market Street, Columbine, Skyline, and Colorado Boulevard freeways.

Certainly, one criticism of the 1960s and 1970s was the expansive scope and influence of the Federal-Aid Highway Act of 1956, popularly known as the National Interstate and Defense Highways Act (Public Law 84–627), enacted during the Eisenhower administration. Critics such as Jane Jacobs attacked the disconnect between neighborhood conservation and protection and the random displacement of communities by the building of freeways and turnpikes.[25] The controversy surrounding the construction of Interstate 70 and the destruction of Denver's Globeville and Swansea neighborhoods has been mostly forgotten, but the placement of the freeway that split the North Denver community in half remains a scar on the landscape. Over the last sixty years the location of Interstate 70 through Denver has been recognized as a terrible mistake, and efforts are being made to mitigate the impact of that long-ago decision.

Alternatively, the placement of the Valley Highway, also known as I-25, acted as a catalyst for growth in Denver's northern and southern suburbs, especially the Denver Tech Center. George Cranmer, Denver's manager of parks and improvements, initiated the project in the late 1940s during Mayor Benjamin F. Stapleton's administration. While the new highway did divide some neighborhoods, its route followed city-owned land previously acquired from delinquent property tax payers. Fortunately, one proposed project of that era was not built: the Skyline Freeway, designed to connect downtown with the southwestern suburbs. The proposed route went through downtown Denver along the Larimer and Blake Street corridors. It

---

25 Jane Jacobs, *The Economy of Cities* (New York: Random House, 1969); Jacobs, *Life and Death of American Cities*.

would have eliminated the later possibility of the Lo-Do neighborhood and Coors Field. Downtown Denver remained intact and, after the 1965 flood and construction of the Chatfield Dam, the area became safe for intensive development.

In 1965 the ULI issued a technical bulletin that assessed the results of the city's implementation of the recommendations of the earlier *Panel Study*. Almost immediately after receiving the 1955 report, the city followed its advice by establishing the Downtown Denver Improvement Association, a nonprofit organization to guide and oversee Denver's redevelopment. The association undertook projects including a street lighting system, street improvements, zoning changes to allow for residential properties, and better code enforcement—all of which contributed to increased property values. The bulletin also reported that in 1957 the city's Planning Department, in conjunction with the improvement association and others, invited architects to submit sketches of their visions of how downtown could look. The creativity of the submissions "sparked creative thinking" and led the Denver City Council to create the Downtown Denver Master Plan Committee. The resulting development guide detailed an improvement program to be implemented over a twelve-year period. Among other things, it called for further transportation and parking improvements, "accelerated expansion of Stapleton International Airport," the development of an urban university, and planning for a new convention/exhibition facility.[26]

During the ensuing decades, all of these recommendations and others have become realities. The Auraria campus just west of lower downtown is now home to Metropolitan State University and the Denver campus of the University of Colorado. In 1987 Denver commissioned the ULI to conduct another panel study, this time to make recommendations for possible sites for a new convention center complex in the city. The final recommendation, to build on Fourteenth Street near the heart of downtown, turned out to be farsighted. The new Denver Convention Center, built just blocks from the Denver Center for the Performing Arts, has replaced the outdated Currigan Exhibition Hall. The activity generated the construction of a new 1,100-room Hyatt Regency Denver Hotel, a Renaissance Hotel, and a Hilton Garden Inn. In addition, attendance increased at the Performing Arts Center and

---

26 Mechlin D. Moore, "Downtown Denver—a Guide to Central City Development," Technical Bulletin 54 (Washington, DC: Urban Land Institute, 1965), 15–17.

retail sales in Larimer Square rose dramatically. A completely new center of activity grew out of the ULI Advisory Services panel. Denver International Airport, which replaced the outdated and undersized Stapleton International Airport, has supported the vision of the ULI and the city's leadership by making Denver and Colorado as a whole more accessible.

Smaller local and regional land-use and development projects were also reviewed. A recent transit-oriented development (TOD) site in Aurora, next to an abandoned shopping center, was evaluated and recommendations were made for its redevelopment. While still in progress, the site has been declared a blighted area and been designated an urban renewal area. This is part of the ULI's mission of preservation and creating resilient communities.

Prominent ULI member Jonathan Rose and his partner, Chuck Perry, spearheaded the redevelopment of North Denver's old Elitch Gardens Amusement Park into an affordable housing community. This attractive, mixed-use community represents the ideal form of redevelopment opportunity that cities seek. The project received financing from the Colorado Division of Housing, CHFA, and several other institutional investors.

Mortgage bankers and their correspondent life insurance companies have actively participated in redevelopment because of their very high concern about the health and vitality of America's urban centers and business districts. Before the banking activities were addressed with the Community Reinvestment Act (CRA) of 1977, the life insurance industry initiated the Urban Initiatives Program in 1971. It made a significant effort to find the best urban redevelopment projects to meet the needs of specific cities. Because FHA-insured apartment loans were eligible for inclusion in Ginnie Mae mortgage-backed securities, Robert Wilson, a Chicago mortgage banker, strongly advocated their use as ideal vehicles for the insurance industry as part of the Urban Investment Program, which encouraged investment in pioneering redevelopment projects, such as Denver's Sakura Square. Also in Denver, the Skyline Urban Renewal Project provides a good example of private-public partnerships and cooperative financing. Many of the city's mortgage banking firms, having established relationships with large insurance companies, participated in these developments.[27]

---

27 Robert H. Wilson, "Another Tool to Fund Life Insurance Companies' Urban Investment Program," *Mortgage Banker* (May 1971): 98–101; E. Michael Rosser, interview with Thomas J. Wrattan (former president of Principal Commercial Acceptance Corporation), May 5, 2017.

An additional project in the Denver metro area is the urban infill redevelopment of Lowry Air Force Base. Prior to 1938, the property housed the Phipps Tuberculosis Sanitarium. In 1939, the Denver Chamber of Commerce and others played a key role in convincing the US Army Air Corps to acquire the real estate and build a training facility. The base became the primary training facility for the pilots and crews of the B-25 and B-29 bomber aircraft. It also served as a training center for US Air Force intelligence but reached its academic peak in the mid-1950s as the first home of the United States Air Force Academy. Lowry became a victim of the Defense Base Closure and Realignment Act of 1990. Overseen by the Lowry Disposition Authority, the new community contains the same attributes as Columbia, Maryland, but on a smaller scale.

While Highlands Ranch and Lowry were immediate successes, the build-out of Battlement Mesa as a New Town took decades because of its economic foundation in the oil and gas industry. Oil shale had long been a will-o'-the-wisp dream that was only the next energy crisis away from becoming fully operational. However, teams of scientists, petroleum engineers, economists, and the major oil companies—including Atlantic Richfield and Exxon—had found the development of this resource unfeasible. After my second day on the job at the Land Use Commission, where I was assigned the task of developing new community guidelines, Atlantic Richfield announced that it had sold its oil shale interests to the Exxon Company of Houston, Texas, preferring to develop its tar sands holdings in Canada.[28]

Exxon was one of the original Standard Oil group of companies. The Humble Oil and Refining Company was the controlling member when Carter Oil and others combined to form Exxon. Exxon had high hopes for oil shale and began developing the resource using pillar and tunnel mining methods for the excavation. As part of the Naval Oil Reserve, there had been an experimental retorting facility near Rifle, Colorado, on the Western Slope. Retorting is a process of heating shale rock to extract the petroleum the rock contains. When Atlantic Richfield pulled out, Exxon acquired not only its resource facilities but also the Battlement Mesa New Town project.

Exxon assembled a first-rate development team for Battlement Mesa. The executive management and members of the Exxon Board of Directors flew

---

28   Ed Marston, "Life after Oil Shale," *High Country News* 15, no. 7 (April 15, 1983): 13.

into Grand Junction and spent several days touring the area, analyzing the extensive capital investment needed for both oil-shale extraction and the new town. A group of lenders and representatives from Fannie Mae also toured the Exxon mining operation and the Battlement Mesa community. We then began designing a menu of mortgage products for the workers.

Simultaneously, the Colorado Mortgage Lenders Association, the Association of Realtors, and the Home Builders Association formed the Mortgage Corporation of Colorado to act as a conduit to deliver high-quality fifteen- and thirty-year fixed-rate loans to the Colorado Public Employees Retirement Association (PERA). PMI Mortgage Corporation was hired as the master servicer to oversee the approximately eleven participating institutions. All of this occurred during a period of high double-digit interest rates, so this agreement with PERA filled a unique niche in the market. Because of the income and credit qualifications, there was a high degree of interest among Exxon executives moving into the area.

Local and San Francisco–based senior PMI management became more than a little anxious when Fannie Mae began renegotiating some of the parameters for the workers' mortgage product menu. The level of warranties and credit protection signaled that Fannie Mae saw Battlement Mesa as a very high-risk investment. So five days before the agreements were to be signed with Fannie Mae and before the closing of the loans that would go to PERA, Exxon abruptly shut down the facility and pulled out of its investment. Exxon employees returned to Houston without purchasing their homes in the area, and Battlement Mesa became a retirement community. The New Town guidelines were never formally adopted statewide, and Western Slope oil-shale development remains a will-o'-the-wisp venture.

CHANGING LAND USE AND GENTRIFICATION

The third land-use change is the gentrification of the urban central core and streetcar suburbs. This is the process of individuals and investors buying property in declining neighborhoods and renovating those properties, thereby improving the areas and attracting businesses such as restaurants and retail stores. The Skyline Urban Renewal Project of the early 1960s saved Denver from being criss-crossed with highways and having its distinct neighborhoods broken up. In the process it made these areas, especially lower downtown, prime for gentrification. The construction of Coors Field proved the catalyst for redevelopment of the area beginning in the 1990s. Gentrification in and around Denver has accelerated dramatically in recent years, driven by the lifestyle demands of millennials and baby boomers.

Today, lenders are financing development companies' projects to convert older inner-city office and warehouse buildings into residential and retail properties; others are built from the ground up. We have given examples of several such developments in Denver, including the Barth Hotel and the Boston Lofts. Aging baby boomers and maturing millennials increasingly desire the rich cultural environment and convenience of living in downtown neighborhoods—access to mass transit, parks, and recreation venues; opportunities to attend artistic, educational, and sporting events; and excellent, affordable restaurants offering a diverse variety of cuisines are just a few of the attributes of urban living. Others find similar benefits living in the former streetcar neighborhoods just beyond the urban core.[29]

As individual houses and apartment buildings have been upgraded in neighborhoods like Denver's Highlands, new business and investment opportunities have expanded. The gentrification of this neighborhood, facilitated by a Neighborhood Reinvestment Corporation program called Neighborhood Housing Services, began in the early 1980s. The program was a partnership among the city government, a consortium of mortgage lenders, and community members. Working together, they set priorities for neighborhood improvements, including housing rehabilitation, parks, schools, and transportation. To assist in the project's success, they developed special mortgage programs for home buyers in the community.[30]

At some point millennials may have children of their own and opt to follow in their parents' and grandparents' footsteps by moving to the suburbs and becoming homeowners. But trends over the last twenty years have demonstrated that this may not happen, at least not yet.[31] The institution of marriage is on the decline, and household formations are dramatically different

29 Alan Snel, "Downtown Redo: Historic Has-Beens-Reborn as Chic Housing," *Denver Post*, February 23, 1997, B1.

30 "Highland Neighborhood Plan; General Recommendations," *Denver Planning and Community Development*, April 28, 1990.

31 Tim Ahern, "Millenials May Be Forging Their Own Path to Homeownership," *Fannie Mae*, August 9, 2016, accessed May 9, 2017, www.fanniemae.com/portal/media/business/millennials -080916.html, 1–7.

from just a generation ago. Urban life is much safer and healthier than it was twenty years ago. The trend toward loft apartments, condominiums, and transit-oriented development that began in the late 1990s is now firmly established and growing in Colorado. Today's builders, developers, and lenders are committed to serve the new urban demographic that refuses to work a 9 to 5 schedule and then get in their cars for an hour (or longer) to drive to homes in the traditonal suburbs.

In Denver, the conversion of the central business district land use from commercial to residential started in the 1980s and escalated in the 1990s with the preservation, redevelopment, and rehabilitation of the Neusteter's and Denver Dry Goods stores into multi-use properties. Photographs of Denver's Sixteenth Street retail center and Seventeenth Street financial district taken in 1990 and 2015 show little change. For the most part, the outward appearance of the buildings remains the same, but the land use has changed from department stores and banks to hotels, rental lofts, and condominiums. The American National Bank Building, Joslin's department store, the Colorado National Bank Building, and the Railway Exchange Building (home of the FHA's Denver offices for fifty years) are now hotels. Downtown living, first pioneered by Brooks Towers, is now commonplace, as evidenced by the Bank Lofts, Boston Lofts, and Midland Lofts. US National Bank/Guaranty Bank, Boettcher and Company and the Boettcher Foundation, and Midland Federal Savings, respectively, once occupied these buildings that now provide the downtown living experience.

Denver had two iconic department store buildings—Daniels and Fisher, with its tower modeled after the Campanile in the Piazza San Marco in Venice, Italy, and the Denver Dry Goods store. Both were famous for their tearooms. From the 1920s through the 1950s, Denver mothers made the obligatory pilgrimage to one of these stores so their children could have their annual photograph taken while perched on Santa Claus's lap. The Denver Dry tearoom was a savory gathering place for many Denver businessmen to enjoy the restaurant's famous Chicken à la King. Round community tables reserved for singles provided an opportunity to engage in conversations about business, politics, and the decades-old speculation of how long it would take for major league baseball to come to Denver. The Daniels and Fisher building, except for the tower, gave way to demolition under urban renewal after the company merged with the May Company. Before the building fell to the wrecking ball, the tearoom's sad legacy was providing lunch for the young men taking their Vietnam draft physicals at the Old Customs House across the street. Sadly, several of the men I took my draft physical with never returned from Vietnam.

I witnessed all of these changes and more during my twenty-five years of working in downtown Denver. The evolution of the city saddened me as I watched iconic buildings disappear, but I was simultaneously excited and invigorated by the anticipation of what was to come.

After the energy collapse of the late 1980s and the consolidation of both of the downtown department stores and the Seventeenth Street banks into larger national chains, the central business district became an unattractive investment for both developers and lenders. Earlier, the historic Daniels and Fisher store had merged with the May Company. Later, the May Company purchased Associated Dry Goods, which owned Denver Dry Goods. Shortly thereafter it closed both of its downtown stores in favor of new suburban locations. The Denver Technology Center followed by the Inverness development combined to create a second downtown in the southeast suburbs. Unfortunately, Denver could not entertain the idea of incorporating this area into the city and county because of an amendment to the state's constitution approved by voters in 1974. Known as the Poundstone Amendment, it was designed to harness Denver's power by limiting the ability of counties to annex adjacent communities.[32]

A new generation of civic leaders emerged in the 1990s. They committed themselves to preventing the kind of urban decay seen in other cities. The Denver Chamber of Commerce and Downtown Denver, Incorporated, recognized that preserving the urban core would require substantial private-public partnerships involving business, government, and community organizations. Working with Historic Denver, Inc., one of the nation's leading nonprofit historic preservation organizations, created one such collaborative. These groups' efforts have successfully preserved several historic homes, schools, and other buildings as well as the Paramount and Mayan Theaters.

Denver Dry's downtown store had been vacant since April 1987. The unofficial recommendation on Seventeenth Street called for demolition of

---

32   Tim Hoover, "GOP Activist Freda Poundstone, 'a Giant' in Colorado Politics, Dies at 84," *Denver Post*, November, 18, 2011, http://www.denverpost.com/2011/11/08/gop-activist-freda-poundstone-a-giant-in-colorado-politics-dies-at-84/.

the building. But newly elected mayor Federico Peña had a strong interest in historic preservation and saw preserving the historic downtown store as an opportunity. Seizing the moment, after consulting with his planning department in the Denver Urban Renewal Authority, Peña flew to the May Company headquarters in St. Louis. While there, he negotiated the purchase of the building for $6 million. A number of partnerships formed to accomplish the purchase and rehabilitation of the building, one of which included Women's, Norwest, First Interstate, and Dominion Banks.[33]

In 1988 the Denver Urban Renewal Authority (DURA) took the building over from the city. It began working with the planning department to study how to utilize the new historic preservation tax credits. DURA also issued requests for rehabilitation and development proposals. The project captured the imagination of a number of local and national organizations. Several proposed keeping it as a retail facility with small shops, a movie theater, and restaurants but no housing.

But all of this was happening at a time when securing financing in Denver was fairly difficult. The city, like much of the country, had been in recession for several years. Real estate had experienced a major downturn, and big investors were reluctant to invest in Denver. The Neusteter's building, next door to the Denver Dry Goods building, had been converted to condominiums but was in foreclosure. However, to its credit, Fannie Mae had approved Neusteter's and ultimately provided permanent financing.

The process of evaluating the many development proposals for the Denver Dry Goods building took time. The key component turned out to be housing. Everyone recognized that to make downtown function, it had to include a variety of permanent residence options. A New York developer, Jonathan Rose, collaborated with Chuck Perry, the project manager at DURA. Rose proposed a unique mixed-use arrangement with retail on the main floor and affordable housing distributed throughout other portions of the building. When his proposal was adopted, Rose and his company, the Affordable Housing Construction Company, became the developer and set Denver on a path to become an eighteen-hour city.[34]

---

33 Steve Raabe, "Denver Dry Revamp to Get Off the Ground —Transformation Should Be Complete by Fall," *Denver Post*, December 14, 1992, 1A.

34 E. Michael Rosser, interview with Chuck Perry, Denver, CO, December 30, 2014.

Recruiting candidates quickly was crucial. Rose convinced the Robert Waxman Camera and Video Company to move into the first floor on the Fifteenth Street side of the building. T. J. Maxx committed to leasing the second floor. Equally important, the Denver Convention and Visitors Bureau and DURA signed on to occupy space on the third floor.

The new city administration under Mayor Wellington Webb pulled together the disparate groups and hammered out an agreement for a $20 million renovation package. CHFA and Bank One (now J. P. Morgan Chase) agreed to a $6 million construction loan to cover 60 percent of the cost of renovation. CHFA also provided an additional $3 million FHA 540(c) risk share permanent loan. Rocky Mountain Investors, a union pension fund, provided an additional $3.4 million, HUD provided a $3.6 million urban development action grant, and Fannie Mae contributed another $3.4 million. The agreement with the mayor's office called for two floors of affordable housing containing fifty-one units; CHFA provided purchase financing for thirty-nine of the units as rental housing for low-income residents.[35]

Completed in three phases between 1993 and 1999, the total redevelopment cost of the preservation of the Denver Dry Goods store was $48 million. The project has won countless awards from organizations such as the American Institute of Architects, the National Trust for Historic Preservation, and the ULI. To restore this historic structure, twenty-three sources of financing were used, including traditional bank financing, low-income housing tax credits, historic preservation tax credits—some of which were purchased by Fannie Mae—and a CHFA HUD risk share loan. In addition, tax increment financing also played a key part in financing the project.[36]

All of these example projects demonstrate how evolving land uses serve to revitalize communities and occasionally rescue historic buildings from destruction.

---

35 Raabe, "Denver Dry Revamp," 1A.
36 Rosser, interview with Chuck Perry.

11

The Mortgage Bankers Association from the Postwar Era into the New Millennium

Leadership is not the manipulation of cogs in a machine. It
is the encouragement and stimulation of the creativity, the
energies and the potentialities of individual human beings.

Robert G. Boucher
MBA president, 1980

World War II inevitably brought about major changes to both the nation
and the mortgage banking industry. In 1939, with war clouds hanging over
Europe, mortgage bankers knew they would be affected when the United
States joined the conflict. The industry began planning and preparing for the
coming demands. For example, many industry members volunteered and
served actively during the war, while others were recruited and given direct
commissions to oversee the development and construction of defense instal-
lations. The Mortgage Bankers Association (MBA) studied defense housing
needs and helped develop and implement various programs to respond to
the impending crisis.

DOI: 10.5876/9781607326236.c011

In 1940 the MBA introduced a committee structure that remains in place today, surviving as a communications vehicle for members to help form the industry's public policy positions. In 1944 the industry lobbied heavily in support of the Servicemen's Readjustment Act. The law introduced the G.I. loan: a zero down payment, low–interest rate mortgage program for returning veterans. The program survives today as an entitlement for military personnel and veterans. From a credit quality standpoint, it remains the most successful of the government housing programs.[1]

By August 1945 the war was over, and recovery got under way. For the next three years the industry focused its efforts on G.I. loans, controlling interest rates, Federal Housing Administration (FHA) reform, and, perhaps most important, industry education and training. With the expansion of the housing industry, employment opportunities abounded in all areas, including mortgage banking. The MBA was especially interested in recruiting veterans and understood that education and training would be key for everyone's success.[2]

In June 1948, "the MBA held its first Mortgage Banking Seminar at Northwestern University's downtown Chicago campus."[3] The seminar met with great success. Just six years later Aksel Nielsen, the MBA president, and future president R. O. Deming Jr. from Oswego, Kansas, expanded the five-day seminar into a series of three weeklong sessions conducted throughout the summer months—and thus the School of Mortgage Banking was born.[4] The MBA continued its relationship with Northwestern's School of Management for several decades. The school gained enormous popularity and prestige throughout the industry. The program was so successful that the organization introduced a second one at Stanford University; it, too, continued for several decades. In addition, the MBA sponsored a senior executives' conference held annually in New York City in conjunction with New York University's business and economics faculty.[5]

Throughout much of its history, the industry had been composed of family-based businesses providing mortgage funds in their local communities. The

---

1   Hall, "First Century," 14.

2   Ibid., 16.

3   Ibid.

4   Ibid., 18.

5   E. Michael Rosser, "Educating an Industry," *Mortgage Banking* (Centennial Special Edition), October 2013, 51.

leadership of the MBA has reflected that aspect of mortgage banking over the years. R. O. Deming Jr., co-founder of the School of Mortgage Banking who became president in 1950, was the first son of three father-son pairs to lead the MBA. His father served as president in 1924, the year the organization held its national convention in Denver. In 1934 W. Walter Williams of Seattle became the MBA's president. During his tenure he witnessed the birth of the FHA and Fannie Mae. Forty years later his son, Walter B. Williams, assumed the lead and was one of the major figures responsible for creating the industry's highest professional designation, the Certified Mortgage Banker (CMB). In 1957 Walter C. Nelson, a CMB from Minneapolis, became the MBA's president; in 1991 his son, James W. Nelson, CMB, followed in his father's footsteps.[6]

Like other national organizations, the MBA established a series of awards to recognize outstanding achievements. In 1950 the Aksel Nielsen Distinguished Service Award was given in recognition of an individual's professional reputation and commitment to the mortgage banking industry. By the late 1960s Nielsen's name had disappeared from the award, and in 2004 the award was renamed in honor of Andrew Woodward, another former MBA president. The association did not create another award named for a member until the establishment of a lifetime achievement award in education, in honor of this book's principal author, at the 2013 annual convention. The MBA's Burton C. Wood Legislative Service Award, established in the 1990s, recognizes members for their contributions to the industry's public policy initiatives.

In the early 1950s, education programs, including the School of Mortgage Banking, began serving the industry on a greatly expanded basis. The MBA's School of Mortgage Banking became the industry's principal management training program. In a way, it was analogous to the military's officer candidate schools. Not only did junior managers need exposure to all aspects of the industry, but they also needed a broader understanding of public policy and policy formation as they affected real estate finance.

POLITICAL ACTIVISM—A CORNERSTONE OF THE MBA

As the 1950s moved into the new frontier of the 1960s, the housing boom continued. With the FHA always at the top of the MBA's policy agenda, the

---

6   Ibid., 53.

organization fully supported the agency's adoption of a thirty-year fixed-rate mortgage. The primary benefit of the longer term was that it made mortgages and therefore home purchases more affordable. The benefit to mortgage bankers was the expansion of the market.

Throughout its modern history, the MBA has had extensive legislative and regulatory affairs committees. Issues percolate up to the leader of the legislative committee and are throughly analyzed by the staff and senior management. Grassroots activism took hold more strongly in 1972 and 1973 with the formation of the Mortgage Bankers' Political Action Committee.

In the mid-1980s the committee operated with a budget of $100,000; by 2015 it had evolved into a $2 million bipartisan political action committee. Over the years, the industry's primary concerns have been maintenance of the FHA insurance programs, the government-sponsored enterprises (GSEs) Fannie and Freddie, securities regulation, licensing, maintenance of the homeowner interest deductibility, and affordable housing issues.

Throughout its history the head of the FHA, the Federal Housing commissioner, has held the power to set the interest rate on FHA mortgages. In 1964 interest rates began to move up to keep mortgages competitive with other investments. The MBA supported the increase because it kept investors in the mortgage market.

To give some historical perspective, in November 1934 when the FHA was established, the interest rate was set at 5 percent. A short time later it rose to 5.5 percent. In 1935 the interest rate fell back to 5 percent and remained at that level until August 1939, when the FHA adjusted the interest rate down to 4.5 percent. The rate held steady through the 1940s but experienced a slow decline through the first half of the 1950s. Then the tide turned and interest rates started to climb. By 1961 the interest rate again stood at 5.5 percent, and by 1966 it had reached a record 6 percent, then surged to 6.75 percent. Amazingly, fifteen years later, in September 1981, the FHA interest rate stood at an unthinkable 17.5 percent.[7] These rate movements reflected market conditions. However, the FHA interest rate was highly political and only changed when FHA loans were sharply discounted to achieve a market yield that would attract investors. When discounts became so excessive

7   "FHA/VA Maximum Interest Rates Sec 203B Home Mortgages," Mortgage Bankers Association, Economics Department, August 1992. The FHA stopped setting the interest rate on November 30, 1983; the VA continued to set its rate until 1992.

that sellers—required by regulation to pay the discount—refused to do so, the result was a slowdown in the housing market. According to Santi and Newell, "The term discount refers to a dollar amount expressed as a percentage of the loan amount. A point is 1% of the loan amount."[8] For example, if a seller accepts a contract to sell his house for $100,000 and is obligated to pay five points, he is, in essence, reducing or discounting his selling price by $5,000.

On the other hand, discounting increases the yield to the investor. Using the above example, the $5,000 paid by the seller would be delivered to the investor, thus reducing his purchase price of the loan from $100,000 to $95,000. However, he still collects interest and fees based on the original $100,000 amount.

Over several decades the MBA lobbied aggressively to deregulate the FHA rate so it would float with market conditions. During the early 1980s, when the rate was still set by the FHA commissioner, the economy experienced a period of acute hyperinflation. When the FHA interest rate soared to 17.5 percent in 1981, the MBA redoubled its lobbying efforts and in 1983 finally succeeded in getting the FHA interest rate to be determined by capital markets, thus removing it from political influence. Locally, the Colorado legislature repealed those parts of the Uniform Consumer Credit Code that effectively operated as a usury law to allow mortgages to be written with interest rates at levels higher than 12 percent. However, the Veterans Administration (VA) rate continued to be regulated until 1992.[9]

In 1963, fiscal and monetary policies in the United States began to change. With interest rates moving up and discounts falling, the housing market began to freeze. Disintermediation occurred; institutions that relied on deposits to fund mortgages lost those deposits to other investments. This cycle repeated itself in the late 1970s. Mortgage bankers began to reassess their business models and search out new sources of capital. The MBA's president-elect in 1963 was C. C. Cameron of the Cameron Brown Company of Raleigh, North Carolina. Speaking to the graduates of the School of Mortgage Banking, he urged them to seek ways to diversify their organizations. He feared the VA program would soon disappear. He believed the FHA program needed

---

8   Santi and Newell, *Encyclopedia of Mortgage and Real Estate Finance*, 86–87.

9   Oliver H. Jones, "An MBA Editorial, What Ails the Mortgage Market," *Mortgage Banker* (July 1970): 4–7.

serious revision and that the mortgage banking industry needed to diversify. He advised firms to build their income property lending, land development, urban renewal, small-business lending, and private placement activity. Private placement involves the assemblage of a group of loans, such as apartment building loans or affordable housing loans, and selling them as a unit to a lender. But the industry would have to find new sources of mortgage credit to fund such an expansion.[10]

Cameron was also concerned with what he called a "supermarket of finance" and the fact that the mortgage banking industry was undercapitalized to fulfill this expanded role. Mortgage bankers' day-to-day operations are financed with short-term borrowings from local commercial banks. Because of the capital requirements and bank regulations, the volume of loans severely handicapped mortgage bankers' ability to continue to serve the booming housing market. The heavy volume of activity outstripped the capacity of the banks to fund mortgage bankers' operations, forcing them to seek new sources of capital for short-term borrowings.

If mortgage banking firms could become members of a bank holding company, they could fund their daily operations with low-cost commercial paper issued to that company. Under those conditions, well-managed companies could continue to grow in size and profitability and meet the needs of their builder and realtor clients. As the face of the MBA, Cameron and the Cameron Brown Company took the lead. The company purchased First Union Bank of North Carolina, a highly unique but legal acquisition. In 1956 the Bank Holding Company Act expanded banks' abilities to enter other "banking related finance businesses," including mortgage banking. This ability of the banks to enter into full mortgage banking operations marked the most significant event in the industry since passage of the Federal Farm Loan Act in 1916 and the National Housing Act in 1934. These new laws played a major role in the consolidation of mortgage lending into the hands of the ten largest commercial banks in the United States.

From its earliest days in 1914, the goal of the MBA's public policy capital markets effort has been to find new sources of long-term investment. A new and greater acceptance of mortgages among traditional investors as well as among profit-sharing, employee welfare, and pension funds—particularly if

---

10 C. C. Cameron, "A Hard Close Look at Mortgage Banking's Future," *Mortgage Banker* (October 1963): 15.

the loans were government insured—gradually developed. But the process of selling loans to those institutions was bulky, cumbersome, and inconvenient. A new vehicle was needed to facilitate the process. Largely as a result of the MBA's lobbying efforts, Ginnie Mae was formed in 1968 as a guarantor of issuers to assure the timely payment of principal and interest on FHA loans placed in thirty-year-mortgage–backed securities. These mortgage-backed securities relieved the pension fund from having to underwrite each individual loan. The introduction of Ginnie Mae mortgage-backed securities helped create greater efficiency and helped the industry deal with the increased volumes of loans, particularly for the baby boom generation.[11]

As the 1970s came to a close, the MBA celebrated a milestone event. As with many other industries, the mortgage finance world had been dominated by men. But women had been entering the field for some time, and some were attaining positions in middle and upper management. In 1979 one such woman, Donna Pillard of Carruth Mortgage in New Orleans, became the first woman to receive the CMB designation. By 1987 Pillard held the position of senior vice president of Mellon Finance Services.[12]

For the MBA, the decade formally ended at the 1979 convention, at which Johnny Cash performed. Who could forget the man in black? "Good evening everybody . . . I'm Johnny Cash . . . Hear that train a rollin'!" The day's worried discussions about increased regulation and increasing use of technology were forgotten by me and everyone else when Cash took the stage.

The 1980s ushered in an age of technology. Contour Software introduced the first loan origination system written for an Apple II computer; it required an entire 5.25-inch disk for each loan. Expensive mainframe computers tracked loans, but the IBM Selectric typewriter was still in use. The adoption of technology was neither swift nor wholeheartedly welcomed. But the MBA recognized that computerization had the ability to greatly improve efficiency and developed a software program for its members called MISMO.[13]

---

11 GNMA Mortgage-Backed Securities Dealers Association, *The Ginnie Mae Manual* (Homewood, IL: Dow Jones-Irwin, 1978), 3–7.

12 Hall, "First Century," 24; "Certified Mortgage Bankers: The Women at the Top," *Mortgage Banking* (August 1987): 43.

13 Hall, "First Century," 24–26.

The conventional loan rate stood at 18.5 percent in 1981.[14] Because of disintermediation and the need to allow the thrift industry the flexibility to enter into new kinds of businesses, the Garn–St. Germain Depository Institutions Act of 1982 gave thrifts the power to make commercial and agricultural loans on the same basis as national banks. However, most of the savings and loans were unprepared for such a dramatic institutional change. Many of these institutions lacked sufficient staff with the expertise to be successful at making either commercial or agricultural loans. Some, such as Silverado Savings and Loan in Denver, invested in land and joint ventures with developers, but their business practices included a variety of questionable and illegal activities.

The savings and loan crisis began to emerge in 1985 and lasted another six years. Failure of regulators such as the local district Federal Home Loan Banks to adequately oversee and manage the expanded powers of the industry contributed to the crisis; so did the Tax Reform Act of 1986. The repeal of the accelerated depreciation provisions from the tax code, which had been the basis for underwriting commercial loans, made those properties economically unfeasible to operate, causing them to enter foreclosure. Many of those loans were made to various limited partnerships composed of groups of unsophisticated investors. Unlike the general partner who was the borrower, these investment groups held no personal liability for the mortgage. As a consequence, many of those loans went into foreclosure. Furthermore, a reduction of the reserve requirements for thrifts and other accounting treatments, combined with the problems described above, led to the failure of the savings and loans, which disappeared as housing lenders.

Community development and the National Housing Act of 1987 gave rise to the last new program of the 1980s. The act created the FHA Home Equity Conversion Mortgage, also known as a reverse mortgage. This program allowed seniors sixty-two and older to use the equity in their homes, as calculated by a mortality table, to age in place. Robert G. Boucher of First Denver Mortgage, president of the MBA, advocated strongly for this new program. Paulette Wicsh, a senior officer at First Denver Mortgage, was instrumental in working with the US Department of Housing and Urban Development (HUD) to develop the guidelines.

---

14 Ibid., 26.

Finally, in 1989 the Financial Institutions Reform, Recovery, and Enforcement Act established the Resolution Trust Corporation (RTC). The RTC closed hundreds of insolvent institutions and created the Office of Thrift Supervision as the new regulator. In addition, Freddie Mac, until then owned by the Federal Home Loan Bank and its members, was re-capitalized as a public company.

The MBA Board of Governors closed out the twentieth century by adopting a policy statement on the matters of most concern to the industry regarding the conduct of the GSEs. The organization reaffirmed the vital role the GSEs play in maintaining liquidity in the secondary market. Yet given their substantial growth the policy statement advocated for the regulation of the GSEs by a strong and independent regulator. It called for the regulator to have the ability to enforce its findings and for the cost of the inspection to be borne by the respective agencies. Many individuals recommended that what was needed was more focus on the GSEs' financial safety and soundness, compliance with their charters, meeting their specific housing goals, and fulfilling their missions.[15]

The twenty-first century ushered in new leadership in the industry. At the MBA, Regina Lowry, a Philadelphia-area mortgage banker and CMB, became the organization's first woman to take the helm as president. Under Lowry's leadership the MBA sponsored a number of initiatives to make homeownership available to a wider group of working-class Americans. The association partnered with the National Council on Economic Education to create workshops for consumers and first-time home buyers; many community investment loan programs required pre-purchase counseling. At the same time, President George W. Bush did his part by signing the American Dream Downpayment Act of 2003. The law supports the NeighborWorks HomeOwnership Program and others working to increase the minority ownership participation rate from 44 percent to 50 percent.[16]

The industry has been a longtime supporter of mortgage programs that provide housing opportunities for all Americans, including first-time home

---

15 Mortgage Bankers Association of America, "GSE Policy Statement" (unpublished, August 1999), 1–6.

16 George W. Bush, "President Bush Signs American Dream Downpayment Act of 2003," White House archives, accessed May 10, 2017, https://georgewbush-whitehouse.archives.gov/news/releases/2003/12/print/20031216-9.html.

220 GOVERNMENT HOUSING PROGRAMS AND THE EVOLUTION OF MORTGAGE BANKING

buyers and members of minority groups. Many members of the industry, myself included, believe homeownership, as part of the American character, should be expanded to embrace underserved communities and that the GSEs have a role to play.

During the post-Depression–World War II era, 1940 to 1960, the overall homeownership rate grew substantially, from 43.6 percent to a rate of 61.9 percent. But over the next thirty years the rate grew by less than 3 percentage points, to just 64.2 percent. In the last decade of the twentieth century, many industry members cautiously supported the goal of increasing the homeownership rate to slightly above the 70 percent mark. The industry and policymakers were particularly concerned with underserved segments of the population, namely, the African American and Hispanic communities who garnered rates of 43.9 percent and 42.4 percent, respectively—rates significantly lower than that for white Americans, 72.4 percent. A goal was set for the GSEs to raise the rate of homeownership among African Americans and Hispanics to above 50 percent.[17] The energy, incentives, and political pressure behind this goal prompted virtually all of the institutions in the market to seek ways to support the initiative.

In October 2000 HUD published its affordable housing goals for the years 2001 through 2003.[18] While many members of Congress and affordable housing activists were concerned about the never-ending conflict between fiscal management and social purpose, a heightened awareness developed about whether the GSEs, specifically Fannie and Freddie, were doing enough to reach underserved markets, particularly given the benefits and subsidies provided in their respective charters. Conversely, others both within and outside the industry began to voice concern that the GSEs had gone too far. Critics, such as FM Watch, would later write that the establishment of these goals and the lack of oversight, particularly given the accounting scandals that emerged beginning in 2002, were major contributors to the foreclosure crisis of 2008.

But at the time, the common wisdom or group-speak among the majority of the industry clearly aligned with the early goal of the Bush administration's

---

17 Christopher E. Herbert et al., *Homeownership Gaps among Low-Income and Minority Borrowers and Neighborhoods*, US Department of Housing and Urban Development (Cambridge, MA: Abt Associates Inc., 2005), 85.

18 *Issue Paper: GSE Affordable Housing Goals, Department of Housing and Urban Development, Final Regulation* (Washington, DC: Mortgage Bankers Association of America, October 31, 2000).

program of a wealth-building society. Public and private economists agreed that homeownership was the answer for a growing population, based on both births and immigration. The administration supported that goal until some early signs of financial weakness and credit problems at the GSEs began to emerge. Those early indicators prompted the administration and some members of Congress to begin the effort to rein in the GSEs. Republican senator Richard Shelby of Alabama led the charge. At one time he served as chair of the Senate Banking, Housing, and Urban Affairs Committee.[19]

Simultaneously, some members of the MBA, much like the independent group FM Watch, had serious concerns about the duopoly on several fronts. First, they questioned how the affordable housing goals were calculated. They also had reservations about the GSEs' entry into the primary mortgage market and the potential implications for deteriorating credit quality. The primary market is defined as constituting the origination, processing, underwriting, and servicing of loans to the investors that are the funding sources. Those funding sources make up the secondary market. The GSEs saw the primary market area of the mortgage industry as an opportunity to integrate vertically and increase profitability. Fannie Mae went so far as to seek a minority interest in a small savings bank in Buffalo, New York, and explored entry into title and mortgage insurance. Like many in the industry, it, too, sought a countercyclical enterprise to smooth out its earnings. However, most industry participants outside the GSEs correctly perceived the GSEs' ability to control and profit from other primary market services, such as title and mortgage insurance, as contrary to their federal charters and designated mission.[20]

Both Fannie Mae and Freddie Mac had been experiencing record profits for a number of years. These years cultivated significant sentiment throughout the industry that this profitability should be used to expand affordable housing programs and create an affordable housing investment fund that would supplement the work of the Fannie Mae Foundation. The foundation provided assistance to numerous nonprofits, some of which were strong political advocates and supporters of influential members of Congress who backed the GSEs, especially Fannie Mae. However, those sustained profits

---

19 Morgenson and Rosner, *Reckless Endangerment*, 176–80.

20 Gerald L. Friedman, "Mission Creep: The Threat to American Consumers," *FM Watch* (March 2001): ii–iii, 26.

sounded the alarm about potential accounting problems when Freddie Mac restated its earnings for the 2000–2002 fiscal period. The company explained that it was trying to even out earnings and by doing so had originally understated its earnings. Concern spread to Fannie Mae. But when asked if Fannie was experiencing similar accounting problems, Frank Raines, the company's CEO, asserted that Fannie had no such problems.[21]

However, contrary to Raines's vehement denial, Fannie Mae did have accounting problems, and they were much more severe than Freddie Mac's. In July 2003 an internal audit revealed a lack of accounting controls that might have impacted the company's financial statements by as much as $155 million. The *Washington Post* reported that Fannie Mae's problems constituted one of the largest financial restatements in history. Further investigations found that the company had "refrained from booking nearly $200 million in estimated expenses, allegedly to maximize management bonuses."[22]

Against this backdrop of what originally appeared to be minor problems with the interpretation of accounting rules, the MBA recognized the need for an industry examination of the GSEs' affordable housing goals and their implementation. In May 2003 it formed an Affordable Housing Task Force. While the charge of the task force was to study the affordable housing programs and the issues surrounding the operations of Fannie Mae and Freddie Mac, the intrusion of the GSEs into the primary market became the ever-present topic overhanging its mission. I was a member of the group, and we met regularly in Washington and through telephone conference calls. Senior executives of both Fannie Mae and Freddie Mac attended some of the meetings, during which they outlined their goals and objectives, their strategies for implementation, and the expectations they had for each of their mortgage banking customers.

The task force attempted to address the competitive threat posed by the GSEs and to find ways to effectively utilize and distribute their profits to benefit low- and moderate-income families in the form of a housing trust fund. In 2000 Congress set the benchmark for determining "moderate" income

21 Gretchen Morgenson and Joshua Rosner, *Reckless Endangerment: How Outsized Ambition, Greed, and Corruption Led to Economic Armageddon* (New York: Time Books, 2011), 238–39, 244–45.

22 David Hilzenrath, "Fannie Mae Warnings Documented," *Washington Post*, March 13, 2006, accessed September 8, 2015, http://www.washingtonpost.com/wp-dyn/content/article/2006/03/12/AR2006031200799.html.

for the purpose of financing home ownership at 81–100 percent of an area's median income. "Low" income was set at 61–80 percent and "very low"–income families at 60 percent or less of the area's median income. Those formulas, employed throughout the industry, also enable compliance with the Community Reinvestment Act.[23] For families and individuals in the very low–income bracket, debt-to-income ratios, loan-to-value ratios, and employment stability are insufficient to sustain home ownership.

HUD secretary Andrew Cuomo proposed stretching the goals to provide mortgage financing for 7 million new low- and moderate-income families. According to his plan, financing would be distributed as follows:

- Low and moderate income = 50 percent of total number of units financed
- Very low–income families in low-income areas = 20 percent of the total number of units financed
- Geographically targeted = 30 percent of total number of units financed.[24]

To meet these goals, a disproportionate share of units were multi-family. Some institutional lenders felt crowded out of the multi-family market because of these aggressive GSE goals. The distinction between properties and units is important because of the manner in which the goals were tabulated. A single loan on a 400-unit FHA 221(D)(4) single-room–occupancy project scored 400 points, one for each unit, instead of just one point for the overall loan. This anomaly, while understandable, created an industry scandal when Freddie Mac bought a number of multi-family loans from Washington Mutual to fulfill its affordable housing goal with the provision that once the GSE goal at the end of the year had been met, Washington Mutual would buy the loans back. This transaction was one the Affordable Housing Task Force studied and represents one of many such issues in the HUD- and congressionally mandated goals that came before us during the task force's three years of service.[25]

The MBA recommended that separate goals be established for single and multi-family programs. The need to separate the goals was of particular importance to multi-family lenders. They had seen the market for apartment

---

23 *Issue Paper*, 5.

24 Ibid., 5–11.

25 Morgenson and Rossner, *Reckless Endangerment*, 247–49.

loans absorbed by the GSEs at the expense of private market investors such as insurance companies, real estate investment trusts, and thrifts.[26] In addition, extensive discussions addressed the type of loans that should be included when calculating the market. For instance, second-home loans and some State Housing Authority bonds were excluded from the calculation. Loans receiving full credit included HUD/FHA reverse mortgages, FHA 248 loans for properties on tribal lands, and FHA 184–insured loans issued to Native Americans. Rural Housing Service programs were also eligible.[27]

The Affordable Housing Task Force continued to meet through 2005. During this period, issues began to surface regarding the accounting and risk management practices of Fannie and Freddie. At the same time, three reform bills were introduced in Congress, all dealing with the actions and business practices of the duopoly. Cracks were beginning to emerge.

In retrospect, while the mortgage banking industry was very concerned with mission creep as well as the financial stability of the GSEs, few people were completely aware of the impending crisis and its ramifications. It is easy to look back now and see the signs of trouble, but the focus then was on issues such as how to distribute financing to underserved communities and establish distribution percentages. Simply put, the management of the technologies and systems that would affect the long-term health of the housing market was not high on the consciousness level of more than a handful of individuals in the industry or in government.

A CLOSER LOOK AT MBA EDUCATION AND
LEADERSHIP DEVELOPMENT

The MBA also responded to the need to develop a leadership training program for the association and the industry as a whole. In 1951 it established the Young Men's Activities Committee (which actually included one woman). Member companies selected individuals for the committee to participate at the highest levels of the industry's policymaking events. During its three decades of activity, the organization changed its name to the Young Mortgage Bankers

---

26 Department of Housing and Urban Development, "Comment Letter, Office of the General Counsel US Department of Housing and Urban Development, Subject: Proposed Regulation of Fannie Mae and Freddie Mac," May 8, 2000, 2–7, copy in author's possession.

27 *Issue Paper*, 9.

Committee (YMBC). Many individuals from the Young Men's Activities Committee/Young Mortgage Bankers Committee went on to hold significant leadership positions within the MBA and its member companies.[28]

YMBC chapters also developed in many of the individual state MBAs, particularly in the late 1960s as the role of state governments grew. As these chapter members attended national meetings and conferences, many were recruited for the national committee. For those who were selected, exposure to the inside workings of the association and the industry was invaluable. To encourage participation by younger members of state associations, the MBA established a national award to recognize a state chapter's success. The award was named for M. William Donnelly, an MBA staff member who coordinated the committees' activities. The award recognizes significant contributions to industry leadership and community service. The Michigan YMBC took home the first Donnelly award in 1975.

Locally, by 1968, amid the continued growth of the Denver Mortgage Bankers Association (DMBA), a group of emerging middle-management leaders formed the Young Men's Activities Committee of the DMBA. The committee soon followed the national directive and changed its name to the YMBC. The Young Mortgage Bankers took on a number of philanthropic activities. One project involved preservation of the Smedley House in the Ninth Street Historic Park on the Auraria higher education campus. Other undertakings included providing construction financing for member companies to teach high school students to design, build, and sell houses. Their efforts earned the group the second Donnelly award in 1976.

During the 1970s, an annual September board of governors and national committee leadership meeting was held in Washington, DC. After a number of sessions and briefings, the attendees traveled to the Federal Reserve to meet with its board of governors or went to Capitol Hill to meet with US House and Senate leaders. Dinner followed, with a speaker of national reputation, one being former speaker of the House Thomas "Tip" O'Neill. Several MBA presidents started out as chair of the Young Mortgage Bankers Committee. James W. Nelson of Minneapolis is one example. Because of a change in the MBA's organizational structure and budgets, the YMBC was dissolved in the 1980s.

---

28 Hall, "First Century," 18.

In 1996, MBA president Ron McCord brought back the YMBC, restructured and renamed the Future Leaders Program. More reflective of the time and requiring intensive participation, the Future Leaders Program embodies the best traditions of the MBA. The program enhances participants' skills with three hands-on sessions geared toward political activism, business analysis, problem solving, and collaboration. Network building and peer group interaction are key ingredients of today's executive development. In 2013 the Future Leaders spent a day at the Lincoln Leadership Institute in Gettysburg, Pennsylvania. There, they focused on leadership in a stressful and changing environment: Gettysburg College, in the shadow of the Civil War battlefield. The institute offers a dynamic and inspiring look at how the lessons of history can guide leaders today.

"Man's Flight through Life Is Sustained by the Power of His Knowledge" is inscribed on a statue at the US Air Force Academy in Colorado Springs. Those words, which inspire cadets, also reflect the MBA's long-standing commitment to education and to improving the professionalism of the mortgage industry. During the last seventy-five years, the MBA has responded to the needs of its members and the markets by providing both broad-based and specialized programs that address the extraordinarily complex nature of the industry.

In a 1971 issue of *Mortgage Banker*, Louis Kerwood, the MBA's director of education and training, described a conversation he had with a young student at the School of Mortgage Banking about the importance of continuing education. Throughout our organization's history, he told the student, the path to upward mobility has been, and always will be, ongoing education. Kerwood pointed out that scientists and engineers must keep abreast of changes in their fields or risk being rendered obsolete. He argued that change is inevitable and that more than anything the mortgage banking business is subject to growth, change, reversals, and uncertainty. Not surprisingly, the knowledge required to make an FHA loan in 1964, when the MBA celebrated its fiftieth anniversary, bears no resemblance to the knowledge needed to negotiate the vast menu of programs available to today's consumer.[29]

While training and education are equally important, they are vastly different. Training involves the acquisition of specific task skills, such as learning which forms comprise a mortgage loan application package and how to

---

29 Lewis O. Kerwood, "The Importance of Continuing Education," *Mortgage Banker* (September 1971): 4.

assist borrowers in completing those forms. Education for managers who wish to advance includes gaining an in-depth understanding of such topics as the interrelationships among investors, bankers/lenders, and borrowers; the purpose and operation of capital markets as they relate to real estate investment; and differing approaches to public policy, land-use, and zoning regulation development and implementation.

The MBA offered its first educational program, a mortgage clinic, in 1939. These clinics later evolved into three national conferences dedicated to examining the latest issues and trends affecting the industry. The conferences were held in various locations, beginning in the East, then moving to the Southeast and the West over the course of a year. The regional programs enjoyed great popularity and over time attracted the participation of 1,000 MBA members. The MBA also offered a farm mortgage seminar, but as the composition of members changed and farm lending declined, that program ended in 1947.

The Great Depression of the 1930s had an enormous economic and psychological impact on mortgage bankers, their investors, and the entire real estate industry. Then as today, many in the industry thought education would be the solution to the majority of the economic and housing problems of the time. They also believed such education would help build a knowledge base that would avoid similar problems in the future. Many insurance companies and other mortgage investors, in cooperation with the National Association of Real Estate Boards, worked to establish two organizations to provide professional education and training. One, the American Institute of Real Estate Appraisers, formed in 1933, dealt with increasing the knowledge and raising the standards of real estate appraisers. The other, the Institute of Real Estate Management, was created to train property management professionals, as well as those who were operating and managing investment real estate assets. These institutes and their founding members represented some of the industry's best minds, those with insight into the needs of the institutions involved in real estate and mortgage lending. The staffs of many, if not most, mortgage banking firms of any size included at least one member of one of these two institutes.

Many leaders of the MBA and other real estate organizations during this era did not have the benefit of a university education. The establishment of industry-sponsored training was critical to the success of these individuals and their firms. Acquisition of the professional designations provided by the Institute of Real Estate Appraisers (Member of the Appraisal Institute) and the Institute of Real Estate Management (Certified Property Manager) were seen as significant professional and academic achievements. Many MBA leaders and officers throughout this period were members of one of these organizations. Advertisements in *Mortgage Banker* attest to the importance of having one or more institute members on a firm's staff.

With the growth of the US economy after World War II, the association grew to 1,205 member firms by 1948.[30] Responding to this growth, two annual senior executive conferences were held—one at New York University and a second at Southern Methodist University in Dallas. These conferences, aimed at senior management, featured top-flight faculty including representatives from the industry and government, as well as university professors. Topics ranged from economic outlooks and forecasts to the impact of government policy on real estate finance and current management practices.

Not to be overlooked, in 1961 the MBA introduced a series of correspondence courses. Similar to the home-study assignments given at the School of Mortgage Banking, these courses provided specific information regarding various industry topics. Today, the MBA offers a wide range of online and correspondence courses covering a multitude of subjects that affect the industry. Meanwhile, in 1975 a course was offered at Ohio State University on underwriting conventional loans for the secondary market and on Fannie Mae's new conventional programs.

Other specialized classes and programs responded to the growing needs of an expanding industry. Along with the regional conferences and senior executive conferences, for many years Michigan State University conducted a one-week intensive course on income property finance. The university soon added an advanced income property course to the curriculum. Another example of the MBA's response to the needs of its income property–focused members was the awarding of more than \$1 million in grants in 2000 to educate and train undergraduates in commercial real estate finance at five universities throughout the nation: the University of Wisconsin, Texas A&M, the University of San Diego, the University of Nebraska–Omaha, and Colorado State University.

---

30 Hall, "First Century," 16.

THE SCHOOL OF MORTGAGE BANKING

Chicago's Northwestern University introduced the MBA's new program in 1948. That year it hosted a five-day mortgage banking seminar. Nearly 200 professionals attended. Its success led to the creation of the School of Mortgage Banking.[31]

As mentioned, many leaders in the industry did not have a university education. Recognition of that fact made the MBA educational programs even more important. The School of Mortgage Banking became an important step in the career paths of industry and corporate leaders. Throughout the 1960s and 1970s, Northwestern and Stanford Universities hosted the school. The complete program included three courses. Each intensive week-long course included lectures and study groups that began early in the morning and lasted late into the evening. Wednesday nights were set aside for recreation, and Thursday and Friday nights were consumed by preparation for the final exam, originally taken on Saturday mornings. Students dedicated time over the next several months to complete home-study exercises that reinforced what they had learned. They could not advance from one course to the next without successfully completing the home-study assignments.[32]

Course I included a general overview of all aspects of mortgage banking, with instruction provided by industry leaders and university faculty. Then as now, the course emphasized the role of the various departments in a mortgage banking firm and the firm's relationships with the various institutions and agencies of the industry. At that time, Course II emphasized income property finance. Case studies were analyzed and presentations were made demonstrating how to underwrite multi-family housing, office space, and big-box retail outlets such as K-Mart and Sears using so-called credit deals. These are deals in which one all-inclusive loan is made for multiple facilities based on the credit of the borrower. For example, in 1938 Prudential and Safeway struck a deal to build new stores in Colorado and southern Wyoming. Each of the approximately twenty-five stores shared the same uniform footprint, architecture, and interior design, thereby eliminating the need to approve each building. Course III provided instruction in strategic planning and financial management, along with an overview of the MBA's

---

31 Ibid.

32 Rosser, "Educating an Industry," 50–52.

legislative and political activities. The week culminated with an examination and graduation ceremony. Students then went home to assume leadership positions within their organizations.[33]

While Course I has changed little over the years, Courses II and III are different today, reflecting the changing dynamics of the industry. Much more emphasis is given to simulation modeling and the financial performance of mortgage banking firms than was the case in the past. Course III now provides the students with essential tools to develop and implement a strategic plan for the firm, in addition to covering the MBA's legislative and political affairs. Course III also includes a final comprehensive exam and the much-anticipated graduation ceremony.

Graduation ceremonies are special occasions, and part of the long-standing tradition of the School of Mortgage Banking is honoring a recipient of the Willis Bryant Award for academic excellence. Bryant was a mortgage banking pioneer in the 1950s, a longtime member of the school faculty, and author of the book *Mortgage Lending: Fundamentals and Practices*. To qualify for the Willis Bryant Award, a student must achieve a grade of excellent on all exams and demonstrate exceptional qualities of leadership with fellow students in the classroom.

Other aspects of the School of Mortgage Banking have changed. In addition to the curriculum changes made to meet the industry's changing needs, the school is no longer held on college campuses. Now it is more technology driven and offered regionally in various cities. Today, the school is divided into the Residential School of Mortgage Banking and the Commercial School of Mortgage Banking. Both still feature expert and experienced faculty from the industry. The MBA and the school also recognize teaching excellence. Those who receive student ratings of 90 percent or better over a period of time are recognized with a Faculty Fellow or Master Faculty Award.

CERTIFIED MORTGAGE BANKER DESIGNATION

In 2013, as we celebrated the 100th convention of the Mortgage Bankers Association, we also celebrated the 40th anniversary of the Certified Mortgage Banker (CMB) designation, as well as the 10th anniversary of the formation

---

33 Information in this and the following paragraphs comes from the principal author's experience.

---

of the Society of Certified Mortgage Bankers. The society is a formal organization within the MBA and replaces the informal CMB Committee of the first thirty years. Today, the society boasts more than 1,100 members representing all areas of the real estate finance industry—commercial mortgage bankers, residential mortgage bankers, financial analysts, mortgage insurers, investors, and a wide range of consultants.

The history of the CMB designation is interesting and not without controversy. Professional real estate designations go back to the 1930s, when there was a recognition that the appraisal and property management fields needed a demonstrable standard of competence and professionalism. In 1971 the MBA's education committee organized a subcommittee to look into a professional designation for mortgage bankers. Robert Peterson of the Aetna Life and Casualty Company chaired the subcommittee. The MBA is unique in the real estate area because its members are firms and not individuals. At the time, some thought personal recognition was not necessary or warranted.[34]

In 1973, MBA president W. Walter Williams recommended acceptance of the subcommittee's recommendation in favor of a designation and the formation of the CMB Board of Review. In October 1973 the MBA executive committee approved the designation and put in motion its implementation. The MBA's immediate past-president, Everett Mattson, gave the organization's members formal notice that the designation was ready to be granted to qualified applicants. Mattson summed up the establishment of the CMB program: "The recognition of professional capability and the establishment of standards for measuring individual competence are increasingly important today in the field of real estate finance. The CMB designation sets out industry criteria for measurement and impetus for individual achievement."[35] One criterion set forth by the CMB Board of Review was that the designation could be recalled for a violation of the MBA's Code of Ethics.

In October 1974 James L. Starnes, chairman of Phipps Harrington Corporation of Atlanta, became the first individual to receive the CMB designation. An award ceremony at the 61st annual convention in Miami Beach featured the first class of twenty-five CMBs. Robert Peterson and MBA education director Louis Kerwood, who was also secretary of the CMB Board

34   Rosser, "Educating an Industry," 45.

35   Everett Mattson, "Certified Mortgage Banker: A Professional Standard for the Mortgage Industry," *Mortgage Banker* (December 1974): 46.

of Review, studied and examined the applicants' credentials. They conducted a thorough review of each candidate's background and experience. A one-hour oral examination followed an eight-hour written test. Among those in the first class of CMBs was future MBA president James F. Aylward, the president of Sherwood and Roberts Company of Seattle. He was the first CMB to serve as the national president of the MBA. Since then, forty other CMBs have led the organization.[36]

At the time of the establishment of the CMB designation, most firms provided a full range of residential and commercial mortgage banking services. Many also serviced loans for their investors. During the 1970s and 1980s, most individuals who earned CMB status were entrepreneurs who either owned an independent mortgage banking company or worked for a major financial institution; some were investors and others held significant senior management positions with life insurance companies. In 1999 the MBA Board of Directors appointed a task force to evaluate the status of the CMB designation and recommend one of two options: either adapt the designation to a new environment or discontinue the MBA's commitment to it. Over a two-year period, the task force met in person and through numerous conference calls before submitting a final report.

The task force recognized that mortgage banking had become a global business that required expanded knowledge and a different skill set than before. The task force hired an industry certification consultant to evaluate the existing status of the designation and make recommendations for improvement and future development. The consultant interviewed active and inactive CMBs as well as Course III students from the School of Mortgage Banking and members of the Future Leaders Program. The results of the consultant's research were compelling. Those surveyed demonstrated a high degree of loyalty to the CMB designation and felt it carried an element of prestige. Most viewed it as a significant personal and professional achievement. Nevertheless, it became clear that changes needed to be made to bring the designation fully in line with current industry practices.[37]

Members of the task force also interviewed the leaders of other real estate–related designations. They found that others recognized and valued the CMB

---

36 Rosser, "Educating an Industry," 45.

37 Michael Hamm, "Report and Recommendations: Certified Mortgage Banker Designation" (internal document submitted to the MBA, February 29, 2000), survey results, 14–18.

designation and that its stringent requirements were consistent with other professional designations in the real estate industry.

The consultant recommended that the MBA recognize the trend toward greater specialization within the industry. In February 2001 the task force submitted its formal report and recommendations to the MBA Board of Governors. Following the consultant's advice, the task force recommended the creation of a Residential Certified Mortgage Banker designation and a separate Commercial Mortgage Banker designation. The board approved the recommendations, and today the MBA offers a number of additional specialized certificates and designations for commercial and residential servicing as well as residential underwriting. Furthermore, a Master CMB designation was established that reflected the desire of individuals to be certified in both residential and commercial real estate finance.[38]

A commission, the CMB Board of Review, governs the CMB Society. It provides oversight governance for the society and ensures the integrity of the designation. The society also bestows the Society Fellow Award to an individual for recognition of his or her long-term commitment to the CMB designation. The award represents and fosters the highest ideals of the organization. Former MBA president Jim Murphy received the first Society Fellow Award.

In 1954 the MBA received a substantial financial gift from a former association president, Milton T. McDonald, for the specific purpose of forming an educational and research arm for the MBA. His donation allowed the formation of the Research and Educational Trust, a nonprofit 501(c)(3). Known today as the Research Institute for Housing America (RIHA), the organization provides stipends for academic research on issues that affect real estate finance and the mortgage banking industry. In addition, RIHA provides annul diversity scholarships to individuals employed by MBA member firms for various educational programs, including attending the School of Mortgage Banking. The trust also provides scholarships for academics to attend the School of Mortgage Banking to receive a hands-on review of the operations of a modern mortgage banking firm from renowned industry practitioners.

---

38 Ibid., 18–20.

THE COLORADO MORTGAGE LENDERS ASSOCIATION, 1956–2015

The Colorado Mortgage Lenders Association originated in 1956 as the Denver Mortgage Bankers Association (DMBA). Prior to its formation, an informal group of mortgage banking executives met weekly for lunch at the Albany Hotel, located at Seventeenth and Stout Streets in the center of the city's financial district. Most mortgage banking firms were within two blocks of the hotel, and the Albany offered the group a quiet corner table at the rear of the restaurant. Unfortunately, little is known about those private discussions.

Kansas attempted to start the first statewide mortgage association in January 1881. It tried to unite members of the mortgage banking industry to lobby the state legislature on the various interests that affected loan agents, brokers, and mortgage bankers. The Kansas association attempted to set standards of professional conduct, defined as integrity and honesty in handling borrowers' money. Members also sought to get industry members to agree on standard rates and fees to be charged to borrowers. This occurred before passage of the Sherman Antitrust Act in 1890 outlawed price fixing, a common practice in all industries prior to the act. This effort ended in failure when some agents began to cut prices, particularly as volume began to shrink.[39]

Ironically, little has been written about the Kansas state association except to note that the Kansas legislature attempted unsuccessfully to license the industry in 1893. However, active statewide associations also existed in Texas and North Carolina at about the same time. Even though Colorado lagged behind, not organizing the DMBA until 1956, the state's associations have long been seen as leaders, with a history dating back to the 1890s.

Nielsen, the first national MBA president from Colorado, led the organization almost a decade before the state association was founded. Because of his close relationship with President Dwight Eisenhower, he conducted virtually all of his industry work at the national level. Locally, he participated actively in many business, civic, and community organizations, including the University of Denver, the Denver Chamber of Commerce, Presbyterian Hospital, Empire Savings, United American Life, and United Airlines. Certainly, he was a supporter of local mortgage bankers, but he also provided unqualified endorsements for two of his senior managers for national leadership positions. In turn, one of those senior managers, Robert

---

39 Bogue, "Land Mortgage Company," 26–27.

G. Boucher, enthusiastically mentored not only myself but others as well in achieving national leadership positions in the MBA.

Before the organization held elections for officers my father, Ed Rosser, served as unofficial chair. Claire "Bus" Bacon of Mortgage Investment Company became the first president in 1957. Eleven years later he was elected president of the MBA. Since Nielsen's elevation to that post in 1949, Colorado-based mortgage banking firms have produced four additional national presidents: Bacon, Everett C. Spelman Sr., Boucher, and Debra Still.

Bacon had moved to Colorado with his parents at the age of twelve. A few years later the family moved from Leadville to Denver, where he graduated from East High School. While a student at the University of Denver, Bacon became an all-conference guard and fullback. His football career highlight came in the 1936 rivalry game against the University of Colorado. Bacon stopped All-American and future Supreme Court justice Byron "Whizzer" White on two critical plays, enabling the Pioneers to emerge victorious.

During Bacon's tenure as leader of the DMBA, he oversaw a very collegial group of members. While they competed for business, they shared a strong unity of purpose in the conduct of affairs affecting the industry. They knew who the good players in the city were and who to avoid. They understood and generally agreed on most policy issues, only disagreeing at the margins of some issues. The cooperation has continued under his successors.

In 1956, the founding year of the DMBA, the term on FHA loans was extended from twenty-five years to thirty years. Nationwide, Fannie Mae purchased $315 million in mortgages, which it added to its $3 billion portfolio. Nationwide, the market originated mortgage loans totaling $24 billion. The country was experiencing a robust period of growth, and so did Denver.

At that time, Denver was still a comparatively small city. Without a National Football League team, the big rivalry game pitted the University of Denver against either the Colorado Buffs or the Aggies from Colorado State College (now Colorado State University). Basketball was limited to the AAU teams. The Denver Bears Baseball Club of the Western League was the only professional sports team in the city. Passenger trains departed daily from Union Station bound for San Francisco, Portland, Los Angeles, Kansas City, and Chicago. Five airlines—United, Continental, Braniff, TWA, and Frontier—served Denver's Stapleton International Airport. The average family income was $5,200. The Urban Land Institute was discussing but came short of recommending that the

City of Denver develop a rapid transit system (light rail) to replace the street-car system that had been abandoned a few years prior. Ironically, many of the possible routes the institute contemplated were selected fifty years later for the Regional Transportation District's Fast Tracks light rail system.

The DMBA moved from the corner table at the Albany Hotel to the Denver Athletic Club. The organization limited membership to the presidents of mortgage banking companies or the ranking member of their mortgage department. Similar to the national MBA, over the nearly sixty-year history of the DMBA, its primary purpose has been to represent the mortgage banking industry to state government policymakers. Over the years, issues of interest on escrows, licensing, regulation of business practices, foreclosures, and recession have garnered the DMBA's attention.

In the 1970s the DMBA began to grow into a statewide trade association when Colorado Springs lenders started to participate. Intermountain Mortgage Company of Colorado Springs was the leading independent firm in the area. Its president, Norman Petersen, became the first DMBA board member from Colorado Springs. First National Bank of Colorado Springs had a significant mortgage banking department representing many institutional investors, including major life insurance companies. At one time First National was among the largest servicers of mortgages among commercial banks in the country.

In 1971 Everett C. Spelman Sr. of Western Securities Company was elected the third MBA national president from Colorado. Known along Seventeenth Street as "Mr. Mortgage Banker," the industry held him in the highest esteem. In 1972, an issue came before the Colorado General Assembly about paying interest on escrow accounts. This had been an issue at the state and national levels for several years. The bill would have seriously impacted mortgage bankers' ability to use lines of credit from their commercial banks to fund their mortgage closings. By that time the MBA's legislative committee had grown to include not just senior officers but also those who had supervisory or management responsibilities with specialized knowledge. Spelman, known as an expert on the subject, worked with the committee.

The interest on escrows issue presented the DMBA with its first major legislative challenge. To deal with the issue the association hired Charles Rhyne, a partner in the law firm Gorsuch, Kirgis, Campbell, Walker, and Grover, as its legal and legislative counsel. Rhyne had been a member of the Arvada

City Council, was instrumental in forming a metro-area wastewater district, and served as counsel to the Regional Transportation District. The firm also represented a number of financial institutions, local governments, and real estate firms as well as the Colorado Association of Realtors.

Through three long years of fighting these bills in the legislature, Rhyne, along with Spelman, was instrumental in blunting this detrimental legislation. After months of hard work and lobbying, the bill was defeated. The DMBA was fortunate that Spelman, an expert on the topic, came to its legislative committee to present his paper on the interest on escrows and to help Rhyne formulate the committee's position.

A gentleman in every sense of the word, Spelman was a self-made man. Spelman reacted with a flash of anger during a DMBA legislative committee meeting when one of the members stated something to the effect that "we shouldn't be making loans to women." His reaction stunned us all. He emphatically told the man that he had obviously never worked in servicing and had never dealt with women who were struggling to take care of their children and keep a roof over their heads. Widowed or divorced or abandoned, they worked hard and they would make their payments. Such a strong admonition, coming from such a highly recognized national leader, created a palpable feeling of discomfort in myself and everyone else in the room. The individual who elicited that response never attended another committee meeting. In fact, I never crossed paths with him again.

I only learned the trigger for that emotional response fifty years later while reading an old issue of *Mortgage Banking* that contained the annual profile of the incoming president. In the article Spelman described his childhood and his respect for his mother: "I have been on somebody's payroll continuously since I was 11 years old. My father died when I was 14. My mother, a strong Scotch-Irish quietly efficient woman[,] held the family of seven children together."[40] Many years after the incident, I learned a valuable lesson about judging individuals' actions.

By 1974 the industry had grown, and the DMBA began taking in new members from around the state. The board of directors elected to change the name to the Colorado Mortgage Bankers Association (CMBA). The first convention was held at the Broadmoor Hotel in Colorado Springs. The board

---

40 Everett Spelman, "Meet the New President," *Mortgage Banking* (December 1970): 10.

authorized a series of awards named for the past national presidents of the MBA from Colorado. The Aksel Nielsen Award acknowledges a member's contribution to committee service, the C. A. "Bus" Bacon Award gives recognition of CMBA presidential leadership, and to this day, in my opinion, the association's most prestigious award, the Everett C. Spelman Mortgage Banker of the Year Award, recognizes the individual who made the most significant contributions to, and demonstrated leadership in, the industry.

The 1970s ushered in a more activist state government and the first of the Young Mortgage Bankers to serve as CMBA president, Terry Jones of Moore Mortgage. For the first time in the industry's experience in Colorado, it received scrutiny from the press and the media. For many years the DMBA had retained Charles Rhyne as its legal and legislative counsel. One of the city's leading real estate attorneys, Rhyne was widely respected in city and state government. The CMBA also hired Governor John Vanderhoof's former chief of staff, Hank Kimbrough, as a lobbyist. Both men served the CMBA well for many years.

A long relationship had existed with the attorney general's administrator to deal with consumer issues and compliance. In response, Robert Ferguson, vice president of the CMBA, suggested to Terry Jones that the CMBA set up a consumer helpline and an ethics committee. Acting on Ferguson's recommendation, Jones set up a protocol with the CMBA vice president and chair of the ethics committee to determine the nature of consumers' complaints and provide the chief executive officer of the offending firm(s) with a written report alerting them to the problem and asking for resolution. The resolutions of consumer complaints were shared with the attorney general's office. This program became a model for the industry and remained in place for years.

The Colorado Uniform Consumer Credit Code, administered by the Colorado attorney general's office, licensed several statewide lending activities, including second mortgages. However, the code also capped the interest rates on first mortgages at 12 percent. As a consequence, Colorado mortgage bankers were almost forced out of business when interest rates in the state climbed to 17.5 percent in the 1980s. Rhyne and the legislative committee worked diligently to have first mortgages exempted from the interest rate cap.

In 1980 Robert G. Boucher became Colorado's fourth MBA national president. Boucher served in the military during World War II. After graduating from Middlebury College and while on his way to California, he stopped in Denver to visit friends. During the visit he was introduced to Aksel Nielsen. Instead of continuing on to California, he began working for Nielsen's United American Life as the company's treasurer and chief investment officer. Later, he joined the Mortgage Investment Company as a senior vice president.

Boucher assisted Nielsen on President Eisenhower's Advisory Committee on Government Housing Policies and Programs. He conducted much of the research for the committee. A man with a strong sense of social responsibility, Boucher joined Nielsen in advocating for the development of plans to bring the federal government and private enterprise together to build low-income housing. He was recognized as a national leader in the origination and servicing of FHA multi-family loans and for his leadership in fair housing and anti-discrimination efforts. In addition, he helped create the Colorado Housing and Finance Authority. After acquisition by First National Bank of Denver, Mortgage Investment Company became First Denver Mortgage Company. Boucher and First Denver Mortgage provided virtually all of the FHA multi-family housing financing in Colorado for many years.

In recognition of Boucher's vast contributions, the Colorado Mortgage Lenders Association (CMLA) created the Robert G. Boucher Award for Commitment to Furthering Public-Private Partnerships in Support of the Free Enterprise System.

The industry experienced a downturn in 1966 but nothing compared to what began with the collapse of the energy industry in Colorado in 1985 and 1986. The infamous COLT states—Colorado, Oklahoma, Louisiana, and Texas—experienced a near Depression-level decline in real estate values, which led to Colorado's worst foreclosure crisis since the Great Depression. The collapse of the housing market in Colorado eventually exceeded that of the more recent Great Recession. The CMBA tried to mitigate the problem by initiating a foreclosure counseling program called "Don't Walk" and launching a media campaign to promote the program. Still, many of the state's savings and loan associations failed, were taken over by regulators, and were liquidated.

Along with the failure of the savings and loans, Reliance Funding—a prominent Denver mortgage banking company with offices across the state—collapsed, leaving the industry with a black mark. The situation energized Colorado's legislature to seek a licensing law for mortgage bankers, but it did not gain enough support for passage. The failure of Reliance Funding also motivated the CMBA to work with the title insurance industry on what were called "good funds" (cash or cash equivalents) to develop a newer architecture to protect lenders and title agencies during the closing and sale of loans in the secondary market. By that time, CMBA president Dave Harder and Rhyne had hired Doug Huddleston and Evan Goulding as lobbyists. Huddleston was an institution at the state capital. In those days, long-serving members of the Colorado State House and Senate crafted most legislation, often with industry input. Huddleston could frequently be found at "Nicks" on East Colfax after legislative sessions, "building relationships" with multiple legislators.

Goulding became the primary lobbyist for the CMBA when Huddleston died tragically in a plane crash on his way to a Rural Electric Association board meeting in Montrose. Goulding had graduated from Brigham Young University Law School and served as the state's agriculture commissioner under Governor Richard Lamm. He was a highly capable and thoughtful representative for the industry. In a business with arcane language and a puzzling vernacular, he deftly steered the industry through the change and crisis period of the 1980s and 1990s to get the story told. Known for his integrity and knowledge, he trained a generation of mortgage bankers on the operations and processes of the Colorado General Assembly.

The goal of mortgage banking firms from the early years, beginning in the 1850s, through the 1980s was to build the firm's servicing portfolio of loans. These were loans serviced for investors, for which the mortgage banker received a fee. Rarely did mortgage bankers sell loan servicing rights. The income from servicing loans provided an annuity and was the primary source of profits for the company. Much of that changed in the mid-1980s when companies, forced to raise capital as a result of the pressure of the local real estate recession, began selling their servicing rights. As a result, the level of customer service declined and customer complaints escalated. In response, Charles Rhyne and Terry Jones collaborated to draft new servicing guidelines that were adopted nationally in 1988.

One mantra of the organization over its sixty-year history has been to be ready and able to adapt to change. Colorado always had a few mortgage brokers, though not more than a handful. But by the early 1990s many independent loan originators were opening their own mortgage brokerage companies. An economic benefit could be realized from the pairing of mortgage bankers and the newly minted mortgage brokers. Originating loans is rarely profitable. The mortgage banker's goal is to build a servicing portfolio. If a mortgage banker can obtain loans from a broker without the overhead expense of loan origination, this can be a cost-effective way to build servicing. In addition, a mortgage broker might be able to offer a wider menu of products to consumers by signing a broker agreement with a number of companies. As the broker channel began to grow, for the first time ever the CMBA faced an industry competitor. Mortgage brokers had established their own trade association, Colorado Association of Mortgage Brokers (CAMB), which found itself at odds with the CMBA, particularly on the licensing issue. Peter Lansing, president of the CMBA, opened an outreach effort to recruit brokers and overcame an obstacle by changing the name of the organization to the Colorado Mortgage Lenders Association. This was an effort by the organization to create a more inclusive membership. The name Colorado Mortgage Lenders Association (CMLA) remains in place today.

As the 1990s progressed, the Denver real estate market recovered. Through true merger or acquisition, the large bank-owned mortgage companies, having significant capital, entered the Colorado market. They saw mortgages as a way to permanently tie in customers. Many of the large banks had a cross-sell goal of four to seven banking products to offer customers as a retention strategy.

The large banks functioned as strong originators, investors, and competitors to independent mortgage bankers. They all utilized a three-pronged loan acquisition strategy. First, with the advent of national branch banking, Wells Fargo, US Bank, and Chase developed a strong retail mortgage presence. They also purchased loans from mortgage brokers, a practice called wholesale lending. Third, they purchased closed loans from independent mortgage bankers in what is called the correspondent channel. Because the originator of the loan did not intend to service the loans in wholesale lending or the correspondent channel, the originating lender received compensation for giving up the servicing fee. The big banks limited their support of the CMLA and instead devoted significant resources to cultivating relationships with mortgage brokers, but these efforts were unsuccessful.

These resources sustained the CAMB and enabled it to lobby for strong licensing laws, which the association believed would put it on equal footing with mortgage bankers and allow it to gain respectability. Many Capitol Hill observers suspected that the real reason the association supported licensing was to restrict others from entering the business.

Under Colorado statute, any measure to regulate a business must go through a lengthy research, hearing, and legislative procedure and, once passed, be signed into law by the governor. The Colorado Department of Regulatory Agencies (DORA) uses a process called the Sunset Review. In 2001, after much research, DORA recommended that the mortgage business not be licensed by the state of Colorado. In coming years the state would be criticized for not having enacted licensing, with claims that the failure was a contributing factor to the state's high foreclosure rate during the Great Recession.

A battle over the licensing of mortgage loan originators in the legislature during this time was led by the CMLA, particularly by Executive Director Chris Holbert and lobbyist Evan Goulding. Holbert had been in the industry and was a passionate advocate for the free market system. Goulding had been the association's lobbyist for several decades and knew the ins and outs of the legislature.

During the 2002 Colorado General Assembly, the CMBA proposed the registration of mortgage originators. That effort also failed. However in 2006, with the foreclosure crisis looming, a registration bill was passed and the director of the Colorado Division of Real Estate became the regulator of mortgage originators. Amid the storm surrounding the mortgage crisis, a licensing bill for mortgage loan originators was passed in 2007. The Board of Mortgage Loan Originators was established in 2009 and was granted wide-ranging oversight and rule-making authority.

During this time, the subject of predatory lending also became front-page news. Most legislation affecting mortgage lending involves federal laws and regulations in addition to the rules of business practices established by HUD/FHA along with Fannie Mae and Freddie Mac. In 2008 the US Congress passed the Housing and Economic Recovery Act (HERA). Title V of the act contains the Secure and Fair Enforcement for Mortgage Licensing Act of 2008 (the SAFE Act). The SAFE Act sets minimum nationwide licensing standards for mortgage loan originators and requires that they all be registered with the nationwide mortgage licensing system. Since the Colorado legislature initiated a regulatory program, it has implemented seven laws and approximately forty rules to maintain industry standards of conduct and to discipline violators of the act, all in the interest of protecting the consumer.[41]

Beginning in 2006, cracks began to appear in the Colorado housing market. The media, led by the *Denver Post*, started to pick up on that weakness and began reporting foreclosure statistics compiled by a firm that dealt in selling foreclosed and distressed properties. Debra Bustos, vice president and community reinvestment officer of Chase Bank, went to the Colorado Division of Housing (CDH) to urge the state government to take action. The CDH had been solicited by the Hope Now organization, based in Washington, DC. This coalition of industry and nonprofit organizations was beginning to implement nationwide strategies to provide assistance to borrowers and minimize the impact on neighborhoods. Hope Now wanted to partner with the CDH but would not provide funding because more severe foreclosure problems existed in other states, such as Indiana, Michigan, and Illinois.[42]

The State Housing Board staff, led by Executive Director Kathi Williams, formed the Colorado Foreclosure Prevention Task Force and the Colorado Foreclosure Hotline in 2006. The contract to manage the hotline was awarded to Brothers Redevelopment, a nearly forty-year-old housing nonprofit with a well-established counseling program. Brothers Redevelopment had provided foreclosure counseling in the 1980s and early 1990s. The CMLA became one of the hotline's early sponsors and financial contributors. The Colorado Association of Broadcasters and real estate industry firms and banks, along with their trade associations, also provided funding for the public service campaign that promoted the program. Numerous federal programs and local governments, including the City of Denver, also became financial supporters. The largest and earliest major gift was a $50,000 grant from Freddie Mac.[43]

One challenge the Foreclosure Prevention Task Force faced was the media reliance on out-of-state companies whose principal business was marketing

41 Colorado Department of Regulatory Agencies, "Colorado Real Estate Manual: Rules Regarding Real Estate Brokers," accessed May 23, 2015, http://www.sos.state.co.us/CCR/Generate RulePdf.do?ruleVersionId=6098&fileName=4%20CCR%20725-1.

42 Aldo Svaldi, "Colorado Tops in '06 Foreclosures," *Denver Post*, January 24, 2007, accessed March 15, 2016, http://www.denverpost.com/2007/01/24/colorado-tops-in-06-foreclosures/.

43 E. Michael Rosser and Kathi Williams (director, Colorado Division of Housing Foreclosure Prevention Efforts in Colorado), letter to Mortgage Lenders and Servicers, "Foreclosure Prevention Efforts in Colorado," November 15, 2006.

foreclosed properties rather than providing accurate reporting. Despite many attempts by the task force to provide accurate information, the media insisted on using these firms' flawed information. The CMLA and other industry partners lobbied the legislature, which passed a bill that made the Colorado Division of Housing the official reporting agency on foreclosure activity in the state. While a seemingly small, inconsequential piece of legislation, the bill proved extremely helpful in allocating resources to help troubled borrowers.

Once again, Colorado's leadership was recognized at the national level when Debra Still, president and chief executive officer of Pulte Financial Services in Englewood, became the second woman and fifth member from a Colorado firm to head the MBA. During her career at Pulte, Still was an agent of change. Quickly adapting to new-age business processes and technology coupled with implementation of a modern distribution system, she reorganized the company from a traditional business model into a streamlined manufacturing facility. Still accomplished all this change while winning top customer satisfaction ratings from J. D. Powers and Associates. Her structural knowledge of business processes and her emphasis on customer service are respected throughout the industry.

In October 2012, a time of monumental change within the mortgage banking industry, Still took over the helm of the MBA. The environment in Washington was hostile at best. As chair of the board and working with David Stevens, the organization's new CEO, she was able to bring her hands-on bottom-up experience in mortgage banking to work through the maze of Dodd-Frank and the thousands of pages of regulations affecting every facet of the industry while building a strong and credible relationship with the Consumer Financial Protection Bureau.

By 2013, the CMLA had gone under a corporate reorganization and formed a board of governors made up of company owners and other senior executives to function as a policymaking body for the organization. The board of governors established the Debra Still Award, to be presented to the outgoing chair of the board to recognize his or her industry service and commitment to principle-centered leadership.

Following the reorganization of the CMLA, it has become the go-to source for policymakers dealing with issues left over from the foreclosure crisis, including the introduction of improved technology for document transfers and for recording and processing foreclosures. The CMLA has also contributed to coordinating the legal and regulatory changes created by Dodd-Frank and the Consumer Financial Protection Bureau, state law, and the attorney general's office.

Part IV

THE CRISIS OF 2007

BACKGROUND, CAUSES, AND LESSONS

12

Government-Sponsored Enterprises after 1968

Public-Private Ownership, Control, and Political Impacts

Several congressional actions undertaken between the 1948 National Housing Act, which formally chartered Fannie Mae, and the 1968 National Housing
Act, which transformed Fannie Mae into a publicly traded corporation,
had significant impacts on mortgage bankers and their customers. Below-
market interest rates allowed Federal Housing Administration (FHA) and
Veterans Administration (VA) loans to be discounted, thus achieving yields
comparable to the interest rates/yields in the broader market. In 1953 the
FHA raised the interest rate from 4 percent to 4.5 percent, making FHA
loans more attractive to investors. In addition, the 1952 National Housing
Act had granted Fannie Mae access to $900 million to make advance com-
mitments for the purchase of defense, military, and disaster mortgages
under the so-called One-for-One program. The act also allowed Fannie
Mae to issue firm commitments to purchase non-defense or disaster-related
mortgage loans for one-year periods. Builders and mortgage bankers were
then able to obtain interim short-term financing for construction loans
and development. These loans carried a fixed 4 percent interest rate and

DOI: 10.5876/9781607326236.c012

required a commitment fee payment of 1.5 percent to Fannie Mae.[1] This program, although changed and revised several times, lasted over twenty years; it disappeared during the period of high interest rate volatility in the late 1970s and 1980s.

A number of other housing programs had been spread across the federal government to address problems associated with slum clearance, public housing, and rural housing. In 1943 the Housing and Home Finance Agency (HHFA) consolidated many of these programs. The next twenty-five years saw additional changes. President John F. Kennedy signed an executive order in 1962 establishing a policy of equal opportunity in housing, the first major effort to combine civil rights with housing. Two years later the US Congress passed the Civil Rights Act of 1964, which outlawed discrimination in housing programs. In 1965 President Lyndon B. Johnson expanded the cabinet with the creation of the Department of Housing and Urban Development (HUD). The Civil Rights Act of 1968 went further than the 1964 act by prohibiting discrimination in the sale, financing, and leasing of housing. Passage of the Community Reinvestment Act in 1977 had broad implications for all institutions in real estate finance, including those involved in conventional non-government multi-family and commercial loans.

The highlight of the 1968 Housing Act was the creation of the new publicly held Fannie Mae, which had the authority to buy, guarantee, and sell non–government-backed mortgages, commonly referred to as conventional mortgages. This change enabled Fannie to compete with other fixed-rate investments in the capital markets. In 1972 Fannie Mae began purchasing conventional mortgages originated by mortgage bankers. With significantly more long-lasting implications, Fannie, Freddie Mac (created in 1970 as the Federal Home Loan Mortgage Corporation), and the FHA became the principal investors, guarantors, and holders of conventional residential mortgages. At their peak before conservatorship in 2008, Fannie and Freddie held nearly 65 percent of the market share. Today, their combined market share is nearly 90 percent.[2]

---

1   Klaman, *Postwar Residential Mortgage Market*, 65–66.

2   Housing Policy Finance Center, *Housing Finance at a Glance: A Monthly Chartbook* (Washington, DC: Urban Institute, February 2016), 30–31.

When Fannie Mae converted to a public corporation listed on the New York Stock Exchange, the newly invested stockholders assumed its ownership. However, even though Fannie became a publicly traded company, Congress allowed it to retain its federal charter and all the benefits that went with it, including broad tax and securities laws exemptions. It also continued to enjoy the benefit of a United States Treasury line of credit. Furthermore, totally unique among publicly traded corporations, five members of the board of directors were appointed by the president of the United States. And HUD still retained regulatory oversight of Fannie Mae.

In 1992 Congress passed the Federal Housing Enterprises Financial Safety and Soundness Act, in part to protect taxpayers from the same circumstances that had created the earlier savings and loan crisis. It also sought to address Fannie Mae's four-year struggle to regain financial stability. The act required both Fannie and Freddie Mac to devote a percentage of their lending to support affordable housing. However, the change was not enough to mitigate a mild recession that began the following year. The recession, partly a response to the savings and loan crisis, caused the market to remain flat for approximately four years until it absorbed the excess real estate. The new law also created the Office of Federal Housing Enterprise Oversight (OFHEO) within HUD "to ensure the capital adequacy and financial safety" of both Fannie Mae and Freddie Mac. Through its function as the regulator for all federal housing government-sponsored enterprises (GSEs), OFHEO authorized a specific capital and regulatory regime that was more generous than that allowed to private financial institutions.[3] It was also tasked with developing a stress test to determine the GSEs' ability to withstand a financial crisis and establish proper levels of capital and risk management.[4]

Prompted by the 1992 act, organizations such as ACORN (Association of Community Organizations for Reform Now) encouraged and even pressured Fannie and Freddie for larger and larger commitments for affordable housing in underserved neighborhoods. Underwriting guidelines such as down payment requirements, debt-to-income ratios, and credit history records were loosened. Both GSEs wielded immense power that held OFHEO regulators at bay. OFHEO was so ineffective as a regulator that some observers judged it

---

3   Acharya et al., *Guaranteed to Fail*, 185–86.

4   Morgenson and Rosner, *Reckless Endangerment*, 24.

to be incompetent. For example, as a safety and soundness regulator, OFHEO never collected audit fees, something all such regulators charged the entities they regulated for the cost of their examinations.[5]

In 1977 a new Community Reinvestment Act (CRA) provided expanded goals for affordable housing loans and issued additional incentives to Fannie Mae for purchasing loans with alternative documentation and nontraditional credit. By 1994 technology was again on the mortgage industry's front burner. Fannie Mae and Freddie Mac introduced their Desktop Underwriter and Loan Prospector automated underwriting systems. These systems were designed to do more actuarial calculations as a predictive measure of loan performance rather than follow the traditional underwriting processes that had been industry practice for decades. The formalization of the affordable housing goals combined with the automated underwriting systems would become contributing factors in the collapse of the industry in 2008.

PREFERENTIAL STATUS, EXCESSIVE RISK TAKING, AND EXPANDING SOCIAL MISSIONS CREATE UNTENABLE PROBLEMS

In 1996, memories of the savings and loan collapse lurked in the minds of policymakers and leaders in the financial services community. In the void created by the collapse of the thrift industry, the GSEs Fannie Mae and Freddie Mac evolved into a huge duopoly that dominated the nation's secondary mortgage market. Concern grew about the duopoly's escalating power and influence. Memories of the government bailout of the thrift institutions generated heightened concern about the financial risk posed to the government, and therefore to taxpayers, if one or both of these institutions were to fail. The level of government subsidization employed to achieve lower interest rates and diminish the influence of regional disparities in mortgage pricing, particularly in the fluctuation of local real estate markets, added to the apprehensive mood.

At that time June O'Neill held the position of director of the US Congressional Budget Office. In testimony before the Subcommittee on Capital Markets, Securities, and GSEs of the Committee on Banking and Financial Services of the US House of Representatives in 1996, O'Neill acknowledged

5   Ibid.

that the housing GSEs' special privileges and exemptions provided immense savings and financial advantages. She stated, "One element of the true costs to taxpayers is that the housing GSEs save about $500 million a year from the provisions of federal law that exempt them from state and local income taxes and Securities and Exchange Commission registration fees. Those exemptions impose a clear cost on taxpayers, who must replace those forgone revenues with larger out-of-pocket tax payments."[6]

The charters of Fannie Mae and Freddie Mac also allowed them, with the backing of the federal government, to trade financial derivatives. The most popular of these derivatives is known as a credit swap, which is an insurance policy between a seller and a buyer. For example, someone wants to purchase a bond or a fixed-term investment that is highly rated by one of the credit rating agencies, but the buyer is worried about a possible incident such as a credit downgrade. In this case the buyer/investor would purchase an insurance policy, or credit swap, from an insurance company such as the American International Group (AIG) for protection against loss. Hypothetically, in this case there might be a counter-party risk in which a bond insurance or mortgage insurance company such as AIG could experience a downgrade in its credit rating; therefore, the investor would have a financial claim against the seller of the credit swap for a defined benefit.

Furthermore, both Fannie and Freddie could hedge their interest rate risk by entering the futures market and buying protection against wide swings in rates, in much the same way the farmer in the nineteenth century hedged his corn crop through the Chicago Board of Trade. If a wheat farmer is worried that the per-bushel price for his crop will fall before he harvests it, he can enter a contract whereby he agrees to sell the crop at a specific price. If the commodity price does fall, he will still be paid the contract price. If instead the price for wheat goes up, he must sell for the lower price and loose out on the additional gain. Clearly, one of the downfalls of Fannie and Freddie was their inability to properly account for the gains and losses on their positions in derivatives, to say nothing of managing their credit risk.

A popular protection against interest rate swings utilized by the duopoly is an interest rate swap, "an agreement between two parties where one stream of future interest payments is exchanged for another based on a specified

---

6   O'Neill, *CBO Testimony*, 6.

principal amount. Interest rate swaps often exchange a fixed payment for a floating payment that is linked to an interest rate. A company will typically use interest rate swaps to limit or manage exposure to fluctuation in interest rates, or to obtain a marginally lower interest rate than it would have been able to get without the swap."[7]

As publicly traded corporations, Fannie and Freddie were required by the Financial Accounting Standards Board to periodically value their portfolios. Both use a number of hedging devices to ensure against a loss in value. If interest rates climb above the interest rate on the portfolio, the loss is transferred to a third party—the individual on the other side of the hedge. If interest rates go down and the value of the portfolio goes up, then the GSE has made a profit. Accounting for these transactions is enormously complex. Accounting firms issue opinions on how these transactions are defined on the company's balance sheet. Part of the difficulties faced by Fannie Mae and its accounting firm involved the complexity of these transactions and the inability to issue accurate financial statements since 1998.

Another area of controversy surrounded Fannie and Freddie's ability to enter into off–balance-sheet transactions with other parties who saw such transactions as free of default risk.[8] In what was essentially an expanded credit swap, a third party would purchase a financial instrument or instruments plus an insurance policy against default. The seller of the asset would purchase and pay for the insurance policy. To hedge the loss, the insurance company would assess the risk and set an appropriate premium. The seller would profit if the losses were less than expected, but if the losses were greater than anticipated the insurance company, as in any insurance claim, would suffer the loss. In the cases I am familiar with, these activities were reviewed by various state insurance departments, law firms, and accountants regarding their legality; and the appropriate regulators of the selling institutions were fully informed of and approved the transactions.

With regard to subsidy benefit distribution, O'Neill affirmed that as publicly traded corporations, the managements of Fannie and Freddie held the power to determine how much of the subsidy benefit would accrue to mortgage borrowers in terms of lower interest rates and how much of that

---

7   Investopedia, "Interest Rate Swap," accessed March 16, 2015, http://www.investopedia.com /terms/i/interestrateswap.asp.

8   O'Neill, *CBO Testimony*, 2.

benefit would be passed on to executives, management, and stockholders. She further stated that because of the complex nature of both institutions' financial transactions, it was difficult to determine how much of the subsidy went to lower interest rates for borrowers and how much was retained by management and stockholders.[9]

Yet in 1995 the Congressional Budget Office had determined that this implicit federal government backing was worth $6.5 billion. Of that amount, it estimated that $4.4 billion flowed through to borrowers by way of lower interest rates. The balance, $2.1 billion, or nearly $1 for every $2 delivered to American homeowners, was retained for the benefit of the duopoly for political outreach, software development, and other functions including employee compensation and stockholder benefits.[10] Some industry economists believe these numbers were conservative and that it was more likely that these ratios were flipped, drastically reducing the benefit to homeowners and increasing the benefits to management.

The purpose of O'Neill's testimony was related to a study done on the possible privatization of Fannie Mae and Freddie Mac published by the US Department of the Treasury in conjunction with HUD, the General Accounting Office, and the Congressional Budget Office.[11] The issue at the time was whether to move toward full privatization of these two GSEs. In general, the privatization proposals would remove, over a period of time, government backing of the GSEs to limit the financial risk to the American taxpayer. Except for certain targeted programs, the level of the government guarantee would be greatly reduced. The consensus among GSE critics was that the increased competition anticipated from privatization would result in a widespread matching of the lower rates created by existing subsidies in the market. As a result, the benefits would be passed on to borrowers and not be retained by the GSEs for their executives and stockholders. How much homeowners truly benefited may never be known.

From the beginning, the oversight and regulation of Fannie Mae and Freddie Mac had been conflicted. The GSEs had clearly received a mixed

---

9   Ibid., 4–5.

10   Ibid.

11   US Department of Housing and Urban Development Office of Policy Development and Research, *Studies on Privatizing Fannie Mae and Freddie Mac* (Washington, DC: US Department of Housing and Urban Development, May 1996).

message from what Miles Colean called their special or social purpose mission and the need for prudent fiscal management. Which was more important, the mission or the method? Both GSEs were tasked with helping underserved low- and middle-income families achieve homeownership. Beginning in the 1980s, the social purpose goals took priority when Congress and HUD established more aggressive affordable housing goals, leading to a downward spiral in credit quality.

Then there were the financial safety and soundness regulations. While the ones applied to the GSEs were less stringent, they were the same type of requirements demanded of banks, thrifts, and other financial institutions. The Oil Patch Foreclosure Crisis of the early 1980s, combined with hyperinflation, created significant losses for Fannie Mae. In 1981 the US General Accounting Office, now the Government Accountability Office (GAO), estimated the market value of Fannie's net worth at negative $11 billion. Net losses of over $350 million accumulated from 1981 through 1985. In 1982 Congress passed a law granting Fannie favorable tax treatment for its losses, thus allowing it to maintain its preferred credit rating and below-market borrowing costs. A private firm in similar financial circumstances would be forced out of business and into bankruptcy or, at the least, be charged extremely high interest rates to borrow operating funds.[12]

The culture of Freddie Mac was decidedly different than that of Fannie Mae. By the 1990s it was no longer an arm of the Federal Home Loan Bank (FHLB) system, but it maintained the conservative business ethic of the FHLBs. It also remained detached from many of the clashes among Congress, the executive branch, and their traditional customer base—the savings and loans. That discipline remained until Freddie got caught up in competition with Fannie Mae for market share. Only then did it become more aggressive with its credit standards. However, the detachment did not preclude Freddie from seeking every possible avenue to meet its affordable housing goals and, in turn, its compensation benefits. In 2003 an OFHEO audit determined that Freddie had been understating its earnings to meet Wall Street's expectations, thereby mitigating the swings in earnings characteristic of the cyclical nature of mortgages and interest rates. As this accounting scandal emerged, Frank

---

12 US General Accounting Office, *Government-Sponsored Enterprises: The Government's Exposure to Risks* (Washington, DC: US General Accounting Office, August 1990), 9.

Raines, Fannie Mae's CEO, asserted that his organization did not have any such issues.[13]

DEFENDING THE FORT

Some members of Congress, the industry, and think tanks experienced the wrath of the GSEs' management. Fannie Mae could be especially zealous about demonizing those who expressed concern about what would happen if one or both GSEs failed or when it felt their social mission was under attack. The demonization would be expressed both in the media and in various public venues.

In 1997 Fannie Mae, First Union Capital Markets, and Bear Stearns launched the first publicly traded security composed of Community Reinvestment Act affordable housing loans. These loans carried the Fannie Mae guarantee for the timely payment of principal and interest. Two years later Fannie eased credit requirements further to encourage banks to extend terms on home mortgages made to individuals with impaired credit who could not qualify for conventional loans. At the same time, Congress repealed the Glass-Steagall Act, which further deregulated banks, insurance companies, and securities institutions. Fannie Mae was required to allocate 50 percent of its business to low- and moderate-income families and affordable housing projects. Growing concern in the industry about the increased credit risk and the potential for a housing bubble prompted a number of industry study groups to question the advisability of these extended guidelines.

The financial press reported on the importance of the affordable housing goals for the GSEs to maintain their preferred status and the financial benefits enjoyed by executives. By 2003 many industry groups were also aware of these issues. That year Freddie Mac almost missed reaching its affordable housing target goal by $6 billion. To avert disaster, Freddie approached Washington Mutual to search its multi-family loan portfolios in an effort to purchase enough loans to meet its corporate mission objective. Multi-family loans were unique in that each unit in a building counted toward meeting the goal. After paying a $100 million fee to Washington Mutual, Freddie purchased

---

13 Morgenson and Rosner, *Reckless Endangerment*, 248–49.

the needed loans under the condition that after a month, Washington Mutual would buy back the loans.[14]

In January 2004 Frank Raines played an instrumental role in the establishment of the Institute for Corporate Ethics within the business school at the University of Virginia. Less than a year later the Fannie Mae scandal broke; it proved to be worse than Freddie Mac's. The scandal provided the catalyst that triggered the downward spiral of the mortgage finance industry and ultimately led to its collapse in 2008. These scandals, along with the push by many members of Congress to move the safety and soundness regulator to the experienced management of the Department of the Treasury, led to the demise of OHFEO.

Timothy Howard, who first joined Fannie Mae in 1982 and served as its CFO from February 1990 to December 2004, writes that "in the late 1990s the US mortgage finance system was envied throughout the world." He relates that foreign leaders envied the role and position of Fannie Mae in the capital markets and its ability to provide thirty-year fixed-rate mortgages to the American public.[15] In that, he is not wrong.

In 1996 I traveled to Latin America on a trade mission with Angelo Mozilo of Countrywide Mortgage and Lyle Gramley, a former governor of the Federal Reserve and a chief economist for the MBA. We heard the same observation from housing industry leaders and central bank officials throughout Brazil, Argentina, and Chile. It was clear to me that these individuals saw the Fannie Mae and Freddie Mac system as a vehicle to transfer risk without having skin in the game. In these countries with credit and currency risk, I believed a more appropriate system would be something akin to the US Federal Home Loan Bank System, with strong institutions as participating stockholders having the prospect for earnings and appreciation of their stock in a mortgage discount bank. However, Fannie's reputation among many people, both at home and abroad, testified to its success, as long as one did not look too closely at the inside operations.

Having had a relationship with Fannie Mae and Freddie Mac that went back to the late 1960s, I was a strong supporter and advocate of their role in the mortgage industry. I had served on a number of industry committees

---

14   Ibid., 247–48.

15   Timothy Howard, *The Mortgage Wars: Inside Fannie Mae, Big-Money Politics, and the Collapse of the American Dream* (New York: McGraw-Hill Education, 2014), 263.

with Fannie Mae officials dealing with affordable housing issues, a matter of great concern to me. I had also served one term on Fannie Mae's Dallas-based Southwest Regional Advisory Board. Jamie Gorelick, former deputy attorney general and general counsel for the US Department of Defense under President Bill Clinton, resigned her executive position at Fannie Mae sometime before the collapse and before many of the problems began to surface. Gorelick had recruited me to run Fannie Mae's Colorado partnership office. I listened to her overtures primarily out of curiosity. Although I was greatly impressed by Gorelick, I felt the mission of the local partnership office was inconsistent with my vision of the role of the GSE. Furthermore, I had given my word to the senior management at United Guaranty that my position with them would be the last stop in my career.

At the time, I felt the duopoly GSEs, especially Fannie Mae, were reaching too far into the private sector, that their positions were more politically motivated instead of being strictly mortgage related. Had the job focused on being the local representative of Fannie Mae and its mortgage operations, it might have been appealing. But I had been reading of the growing concerns about its credit discipline. I was also very suspicious about the promised seven-figure compensation package to be earned within a relatively short time frame. Somehow, it just seemed inappropriate.

REPOSITIONING AND THE FIGHT FOR MARKET SHARE

David Maxwell assumed the helm of Fannie Mae in 1981, a position he held until 1991. I had only met him on a couple of occasions, one of which was Fannie Mae's fiftieth anniversary in 1988. During his tenure, Maxwell restructured Fannie Mae. While he kept the portfolio lending programs in place, he moved quickly to install risk management tools to avoid the problems the savings and loan industry had experienced with the interest rate mismatch. In addition, one of Maxwell's major contributions was to restructure Fannie Mae's advanced/forward commitment program. Mortgage bankers could pay a small fee to the company; in return, Fannie Mae would guarantee a specific dollar amount of available funds for purchase at a specified yield for up to a year. This vehicle provided a great benefit to mortgage bankers and builders alike because it delivered protection against interest rate volatility at a very low cost. Yet if rates went down, no loans were delivered to Fannie

Mae. If rates went up, all of the loans under the advance commitments would be delivered to Fannie, but they would not reflect current market interest rates; as a result, the compensation to the GSE for taking that risk was woefully inadequate.

Maxwell developed Fannie Mae's mortgage-backed security and guarantee fee programs to such a degree that within a short time Fannie became extremely profitable. Fannie Mae's numbers were so attractive that in 1988 Warren Buffett of Berkshire Hathaway visited Maxwell to discuss the possibility of taking a large position in Fannie Mae stock. Buffett purchased less than one fourth of the projected amount, however, and soon sold that initial stock purchase. He later acknowledged that had he done so during the housing boom years, he would probably have realized a gain of $1.4 billion in his portfolio.[16] Much of Fannie's success can be attributed to market timing and the mortgage-backed security with its built-in guarantee fees, which made Fannie one of the world's largest insurance companies.

The establishment of Fannie Mae's servicing fee at 0.50 percent, which included a 0.25 percent guarantee fee, was arrived at by a calculation of expected losses over time. In the late 1960s the calculation used by Ginnie Mae (the Government National Mortgage Association) set the servicing fee for its mortgage-backed security program at 0.50 percent. Of that amount, 0.44 percent was designed to compensate the mortgage lender for the cost of advancing principal and interest to security holders, regardless of whether the borrower made the payments. These advances could continue until the properties were foreclosed upon and liquidated. The balance of 0.06 percent was retained by Ginnie Mae as a guarantee fee, or G-fee, in the event that the lender for whom the agency guaranteed against default could not make advances of its securities to the investor. In addition, that amount would compensate Ginnie Mae if it had to take over a portfolio from a defaulted servicer, manage it, and place it with another servicer. Implied within the Ginnie Mae program was coverage by the government of any losses known in the industry as special hazards risks caused by earthquakes, fires, floods, and other natural disasters that would not be covered by the borrower or the servicer's insurance.[17]

---

16 Howard, *Mortgage Wars*, 29–30.

17 GNMA Mortgage-Backed Securities Dealers Association, *The Ginnie Mae Manual* (Homewood, IL: Dow Jones-Irwin, 1978), 30.

At the request of my friend and colleague Bill Wildhack, a former vice president of Ginnie Mae and a mortgage-backed securities consultant, we met with Fannie Mae's top officials as they designed their mortgage-backed security program. At the time, in 1981, I had just acquired a special hazard insurance policy from a AAA-rated company for a private label mortgage-backed security issued by Norwest Mortgage of Minneapolis. This was an extremely fortunate occurrence in my career because it happened while memories of California earthquakes were still fresh in the minds of investors and rating agencies; special hazard insurance from a rated company was therefore virtually impossible to obtain. The special hazard risk would compensate the lender against loss if properties went into foreclosure because they had been destroyed by some cataclysmic natural event. It was part of an inevitable risk mitigation calculation on a large pool of nationwide loans to protect investors' mortgage portfolios against certain acts of God and other adverse weather occurrences.

The guarantee fee risk equations for conventional loans packaged into mortgage-backed securities and government-insured FHA and VA loans in Ginnie Mae government-backed securities were generally similar except that the conventional loans were seen as having higher-quality borrowers with more equity in their homes. Therefore, the pools would have a weighted average loan-to-value ratio adequate to cover losses, even losses from high-ratio loans with private mortgage insurance. The pricing of Fannie Mae's 0.25 percent G-fee appeared adequate to cover the servicer or the investor in the event of a service default or the lender's inability to advance principal and interest, defaults covered by private mortgage insurance, or a special hazard event on the scale of the San Fernando or Northridge earthquakes or Hurricane Katrina.

A major concern, not discussed outside select members of the industry, was what appeared to be a suicide pact between Fannie Mae and Freddie Mac. Driven by the goal of acquiring more market share, the GSEs competed against each other by progressively lowering their guarantee fees to extremely low levels—levels below which the investors and taxpayers would not be protected in the event of a major financial crisis. would not protect the institutions and taxpayers. The rationale was that lower guarantee fees would translate into a larger market share and that increased volume would provide higher profits. They were right.

In reality, Fannie Mae's activities made it little more than the nation's largest savings and loan. In the short term it borrowed money, much as a commercial bank borrows from its depositors' checking or savings accounts, and used those funds to make long-term fixed-rate mortgages. However, the interest rates charged on the mortgages in its portfolio were lower than the rates it paid to borrow the money. As a result, Fannie Mae operated at a loss; on a mark-to-market value, Fannie Mae became insolvent in 1981. Fannie Mae's president, Allan Oakley Hunter, left the organization in 1981, replaced by David Maxwell, a former HUD attorney and founder of Ticor Mortgage Insurance Company. Maxwell restructured the corporation to become a guarantor of mortgages while still operating as a portfolio owner of mortgages and mortgage-backed securities, although to a lesser degree.[18]

GINNIE MAE AND FREDDIE MAC

The other side of the balance sheet of social purpose versus fiscal management and perhaps the most successful aspect of the 1968 National Housing Act involved the chartering of the Government National Mortgage Association (Ginnie Mae) to operate within HUD. Since the end of World War II, the industry had been searching for a way to finance both residential and commercial long-term mortgages using an instrument that could be purchased by pension funds and insurance companies that were not dependent on short-term consumer deposits. During the 1950s and 1960s, mortgage bankers had been working with a number of union pension funds in an effort to tailor an investment program suited to their needs. In addition, the industry sought a way to use existing programs to meet the housing needs of both active and retired union members.

The Ginnie Mae program guaranteed that the issuer of the mortgage-backed security would make a timely payment of principal and interest to the investor. Ginnie Mae guaranteed issuer performance and put in place a unique system of monitoring to ensure compliance. Bill Wildhack, a protégé of Indianapolis mayor Richard Lugar, spearheaded the formation of Ginnie Mae. With Bill Cumberland, Harvard-educated housing lawyer Cheryl Malloy, and policy analyst Warren Lasko, the team built a fiscally sound organization that guaranteed the survival of the thirty-year fixed-rate mortgage.

Ginnie Mae securities carry the full faith and credit of the US government and are unique because they support all FHA-insured loan products,

---

18 Acharya et al., *Guaranteed to Fail*, 17–18.

including mortgages for hospitals, apartments, co-ops, and nursing homes and reverse mortgages for seniors. VA-guaranteed mortgages are also included in the Ginnie Mae program. Ginnie Mae also assumed the "special assistance" responsibilities in financing various federal housing programs.

The 1970 Emergency Home Finance Act established the Federal Home Loan Mortgage Corporation (Freddie Mac) to compete with Fannie Mae and thus minimize Fannie's monopolization of the secondary mortgage market. The Federal Home Loan Bank System and its twelve member banks assumed ownership of this new corporation. The FHLBs, in turn, were owned primarily by their savings and loan association members. The members of the Federal Home Loan Bank Board also served as the board members of Freddie Mac. Preston Martin, former savings and loan commissioner of California and chair of the Federal Home Loan Bank Board, became the first chair of Freddie Mac. He later resigned to found PMI Mortgage Insurance Company. Martin eventually went on to hold the position of vice chair of the Federal Reserve.

In its first year of operation under the Housing Institutions Modernization Act of 1971, Freddie Mac created controversy through the way it purchased FHA- and VA-insured and guaranteed loans. The controversy centered on Freddie Mac's interpretation of its charter, which enabled it to limit its membership only to insured depository institutions—namely, savings and loans. The rationale was that the Freddie Mac organization could not exercise regulatory control over non-member or non-depository institutions. However, it failed to recognize that most purchases of government-insured mortgages were from mortgage bankers who possessed the ability, expertise, and systems to meet the servicing requirements of the FHA and the VA. All mortgage bankers were "regulated and audited" by Freddie, Fannie, and the FHA. Freddie Mac's limited membership had a serious negative impact on the availability of access to FHA and VA programs for qualified borrowers.[19]

Philip C. Jackson, president of the MBA, testified before a Senate subcommittee in early 1971 about the controversy and industry concerns over the

---

19 Philip C. Jackson, "Testimony Before the Subcommittee on Housing and Urban Affairs of the Senate Committee on Banking, Housing, and Urban Affairs Relative to Provisions of Senate Bill 1671 Dealing with the Federal Home Loan Mortgage Corporation and Savings and Loan Associations Lending Authority," *Mortgage Banker* (November 1971): 4–8.

Housing Institutions Modernization Act. What he said proved prophetic. Not only was Freddie denied access to the stable of traditional investors with which mortgage bankers worked, but the act also allowed savings and loans associations to invest 3 percent of their assets in real estate. Jackson believed this would lead to speculation in both land development and acquisition of residential real estate. He also expressed concern about the use of insured deposits to fund such enterprises. The use of consumers' federally insured deposits resurfaced again during the foreclosure crisis of 2008.[20]

According to Jackson, some savings and loans at the time operated non-profit service corporations for data processing and other services. Jackson also testified about his fear that the legislation would enable savings and loans to engage in other businesses, such as loan origination and non-mortgage investment activities, that would jeopardize their ability to invest in home mortgages. In 1988 his concerns were validated as the savings and loan crisis developed.[21] Jackson later became a governor of the Federal Reserve System.

Mortgage banking industry economist Oliver H. Jones expressed similar concerns about the savings and loan industry. Jones found the prospect of the savings and loans entering into new lines of business particularly troublesome. The issues of preferential tax treatment and capital requirements also emerged. The savings and loans' broadened lending and investment powers combined with their possible expansion into other fields of commercial and consumer financing greatly concerned the mortgage banking industry. As large purchasers of government loans, these other investment opportunities would drain funds from the home mortgage market.[22]

Mortgage bankers also voiced concern about what they perceived as a shortage of qualified commercial real estate lending experts among the savings and loans, as well as insufficient supervisory oversight of the thrift industry. This stew of conflicting issues—concerns about the continued supply of ample mortgage funds, expansion of the business practices of the savings and loans, and the unwarranted amount of direct subsidies to homeowners and builders—caused Jones to observe that these policies would have the same effect on the industry as did the Farm Loan Banks in the late 1920s by driving private market players away from mortgage finance. The widely held

20 Ibid., 7–8.
21 Ibid., 8.
22 Ibid.

view within the mortgage banking industry was that the thrifts in general were not properly prepared for the land development or commercial real estate lending businesses.[23] These dire predictions by Jackson and Jones in 1971 would surface again in 1988 and yet again in 2008.

Working with HUD, the FHA, and industry groups, Freddie Mac began to develop a secondary market for conventional mortgages. Soon, Freddie Mac stood second only to Fannie Mae in the amount of individual loans it purchased. Within a few years, under pressure from industry groups, Freddie Mac allowed mortgage bankers to participate in its secondary marketing programs but required them to pay half of 1 percent of the total loan delivery amount as a non-member fee to sell loans to Freddie Mac. When Freddie Mac was spun off from the Federal Home Loan Bank System, the surcharge was eliminated.[24]

In 1971 Freddie Mac also issued its first conventional mortgage–backed securities, called participation certificates. These certificates "identify the participating interest in a block or pool of [conventional mortgage] loans."[25] Freddie Mac's operational system was unique. Because the Federal Home Loan Banks owned Freddie Mac, its operations, underwriting, and marketing facilities were located within each of the twelve district banks. By contrast, Fannie Mae had only six, more widespread regional offices to serve its customers. Later, as a consequence of the collapse of the savings and loan industry, Congress changed the corporate structure of Freddie Mac to resemble that of Fannie Mae. As directed by the Financial Institutions Reform, Recovery, and Enforcement Act (FIRREA), passed in 1989, Freddie Mac became a publicly traded, stockholder corporation under the ownership of private shareholders instead of the FHL Banks, but it retained the regional offices for a number of years before advances in technology drove it to consolidate.

The year 1972 was magnificent for Colorado real estate and my employer, United Bank of Denver. The expanding market allowed the bank's mortgage banking affiliate to become one of the top five home mortgage lenders in the state. As an insured depository, United Bank of Denver was a member of the Federal Home Loan Bank of Topeka. Its secondary marketing team negotiated a $25 million sale to Freddie Mac, the largest sale to the GSE to that time.

23 Oliver H. Jones, "Easy Credit or Not, 1971 as a Critical Year," *Mortgage Banker* (March 1971): 10–13.

24 Ibid., 4–8.

25 Santi and Newell, *Encyclopedia of Mortgage and Real Estate Finance*, 276.

Meanwhile, I picked up the reins of a large sale of loans, packaged into a Ginnie Mae security, to Westside Federal, a New York City–based thrift institution. A calculation error in the loan schedule almost caused the deal to fail. By working with Bill Wildhack, the department vice president and major designer of Ginnie Mae's mortgage-backed securities, and Ginnie Mae's staff, we were able to engineer a proper correction. The completed sale was for approximately $10 million.

The introduction of these securities programs by Fannie Mae, Freddie Mac, and Ginnie Mae resulted in greater efficiencies in the capital markets of mortgage-backed securities. The pooling of mortgages with the credit enhancement provided by private mortgage insurance and the implied government guarantee opened new avenues for investors—including pension funds, insurance companies, and mutual funds. These changes allowed the market to expand and improved mortgage loan pricing. As a result, homeowners benefited from lower interest rates and a greater diversity of mortgage loan products tailored for a new age of borrowers and investors.

Fannie Mae and Freddie Mac provided support for residential mortgages in the capital markets until their demise in 2008, when they were placed in conservatorship. Ginnie Mae continues to be financially sound and to fulfill its mission as a guarantor of issuers of mortgage-backed securities made up of pools of FHA and VA loans.[26]

The great success of the 1968 National Housing Act was the Ginnie Mae mortgage-backed security program. It gave millions of people the opportunity of homeownership thanks to the efforts of those who figured out a way to capture Americans' invested savings and turn middle Americans into homeowners. Regardless of whether they realize its origins, Americans have never rejected the Jeffersonian republican ideal of aspiring to be freeholders—citizens who support American society by owning their own home, business, or both.

WHAT'S NEXT FOR THE GSES?

Early in the new millennium, mounting concerns about the increasing risks taken by the GSEs and the escalating size of their mortgage portfolios prompted the Bush administration to introduce legislation to transfer their

---

26 Acharya et al., *Guaranteed to Fail*, 17–23.

regulation from HUD to the Department of the Treasury. As a consequence of the deteriorating real estate market and the looming foreclosure crisis, the long-sought-after change in oversight came with the passage of the Housing and Economic Recovery Act in July 2008. The new regulator, the Federal Housing Finance Agency (FHFA), was given broadened powers to conduct examinations and oversee the GSEs' programs and policies. The FHFA acted on its ability to take over the direct management of both GSEs. The first exercise of its powers put Fannie and Freddie under conservatorship. The FHFA granted each a credit limit of up to $100 billion. In 2009 the Treasury increased the line of credit to $200 billion so Fannie and Freddie could remain solvent. In 2010, "Fannie Mae reported a staggering $127 billion in losses, exhausting its capital and causing it to draw $75 billion . . . [from] the Treasury in order to maintain a positive net worth."[27]

Also in 2008, the MBA formed the Council on Ensuring Mortgage Liquidity, aimed at examining the policy issues surrounding the roles GSEs would assume in the future. The council also studied private-label securities, affordable housing goals, and the new GSE regulator, the FHFA. With Fannie Mae and Freddie Mac operating under conservatorship, Washington looked for ways to restructure and reform the government's role in housing finance. Furthermore, the FHA's seller-assisted down payment programs caused excessive claims that absorbed its capital. Additional studies and recommendations for how to shore up the FHA's balance sheet and provide for the long-term financial viability and sustainability of the mutual mortgage insurance fund followed.[28]

In 2014 the bipartisan Johnson-Crapo Bill, a GSE reform effort made by the US Senate, passed out of committee but regrettably was not brought to the floor because of objections that the bill failed to address expanded opportunities in the affordable housing arena. The failure of this bill to get wide Senate support means GSE restructuring does not appear likely in the near future. I believe that if a slight recession occurs in the near term, another Treasury bailout of the GSEs will be required because they are inadequately capitalized to withstand another slowdown of the economy.

---

27 Howard, *Mortgage Wars*, 259.

28 Council on Ensuring Mortgage Liquidity, "MBAs Recommendation for the Future Government Role in the Core Secondary Mortgage Market," *Mortgage Bankers Association* (August 2009): 2.

13

The Housing Bubble (That Wall Street Built) Burst

Over the past 100 years, the financial architecture of government-sponsored enterprises (GSEs) has changed very little. From one organization to another, they share several common components. First, a mutual or cooperative corporate structure exists that requires stock ownership; therefore, GSEs are owned by their stockholding members. Second, they each have a board of directors consisting of stockholders and public interest members; some of these members are political appointees, and others are elected by the stockholders. Third, GSEs enjoy an economic advantage in pricing because of their tax-free status. Fannie Mae presents a perfect example; it pays no state income tax in the District of Columbia, where it is headquartered. Before the Great Recession, when earnings reached an all-time high, Fannie Mae's annual state tax liability in the nation's capital would have been nearly $400 million. A decade earlier, without the exemption status, its tax bill was computed at $313.8 million.[1] Those lost funds would have contributed to

---

1   Congressional Budget Office, *Assessing the Public Costs and Benefits of Fannie Mae and Freddie Mac* (Washington, DC: Government Printing Office, 1996), 24.

DOI: 10.5876/9781607326236.c013

improving Washington, DC's public schools, public safety, and other social services. But perhaps the most important commonality among GSEs, one that is of grave concern following the Great Recession of 2008, is the level of federal government guarantee and the concept of being too big to fail.

The idea of stock ownership is to have skin in the game, for members to have a financial investment in the enterprise. In some cases today, GSE stock is publicly traded and held by both individuals and mutual funds. For example, prior to 2008, stock in Fannie Mae and Freddie Mac was held by the public and traded on the New York Stock Exchange, and their debt obligations were exempt from Securities and Exchange Commission registration. Other GSEs, such as the Federal Home Loan Banks, require stock ownership by participating members and member institutions (banks, insurance companies, and thrifts / savings and loans) proportionate to their size and level of participation. Consequently, stock in the Federal Home Loan Bank System member banks is not traded. The stock held by member institutions is based on the institution's size and whether it has membership in more than one bank district. For example, Washington Mutual Savings Bank, the largest bank to fail in US history, was a member of both the Federal Home Bank of San Francisco and the Federal Home Bank of Seattle. Throughout the 1950s and 1960s, as recommended by the 1953 President's Advisory Committee on Government Housing Policies and Programs, mortgage bankers who sold loans to Fannie Mae were required to purchase shares determined by a formula based on the total number and dollar volume of the loans they serviced for the agency.

Every author, when telling the story of a specific historical event or a period in history, brings his or her own perspective, observations, and prejudices to the work. Having watched the mortgage industry crumble from the inside, I have a strong and credible opinion regarding the folly that led this important financial service to become a major worldwide crisis. My conclusions are not black and white. There is plenty of blame to go around. Contrary to the findings of the Financial Crisis Investigating Committee and its virtually unanimous view that Wall Street is solely to blame, I believe the crisis evolved from misguided policies and greed within the GSEs.

The affordable housing goals of the GSEs, set by Congress around 2003 and implemented by the Department of Housing and Urban Development (HUD), were too aggressive when combined with the lavish compensation programs awarded to the GSEs' senior management personnel. Without a system of checks and balances to enforce accountability or any sense of market discipline, the incentive system rewarded irresponsible behavior, thus creating an atmosphere of greed. Management had no moral compass.

However, that does not get Wall Street and the credit rating agencies off the hook. While Wall Street understood the risk-reward equation, it is guilty of a lack of transparency, along with the rating agencies, in assuring that the high rate of interest on these securities was justified. Institutional buyers must assume responsibility when they neglect to exercise proper due diligence of analyzing the underlying composition of the mortgage pools they purchase. The element of greed should never be discounted. Not every investor in these securities was naive or uniformed; they should have known better. Prudent investors in any security are legally required to conduct a thorough due diligence investigation and understand exactly what they are purchasing. They need to dig deeper than the pitch of Wall Street salespeople.

The idea that GSEs have become too big to fail played out in real life during 2008's Great Recession and left taxpayers paying for the bailout. The US taxpayer is subject to two levels of obligation with virtually all of these institutions. The first is the "full faith and credit" of the United States. US treasury bonds and Ginnie Mae mortgage-backed securities are full faith and credit instruments. In the event that either should default, the federal government, on behalf of its taxpayers, is legally bound to step in and cover the financial loss.

Similar to a full faith and credit guarantee is an implicit or implied guarantee, which we now know meant the same thing as a full faith and credit guarantee in 2008. An implied guarantee carries no legal financial commitment, as was the case with Fannie Mae and Freddie Mac before they entered conservatorship in 2008. The implied guarantee meant that the United States Treasury did not have to step in and honor Fannie's and Freddie's obligations. Nevertheless, no one believed that if Fannie or Freddie reached the verge of collapse, the US government would *not* step in to rescue them. The implied guarantee created a *moral hazard* that allowed management at the two institutions to operate in a reckless manner, which ultimately led to the government bailout.

Notwithstanding the opinion of "experts" in the media, the mortgage banking industry, and government, this collapse was neither a shock nor wholly unanticipated. Economic cycles, like earthquakes, happen. But this time its depth and breadth should have been foreseen. Some observers have noted that the seeds of this crisis were sown almost a decade earlier. At the core of the discussion is the role of a very vocal groupthink coalition of economists and mortgage industry insiders on public policy. The coalition's herd mentality reinforced faulty analyses that reached the conclusion "this time it will be different."

A great example of historical outcomes analysis comes from Professor Timothy Garton Ash of St. Antony's College, Oxford.[2] Ash discusses part of a lecture he gave at the Hay on Wye Book Festival to illustrate how easily an individual can interpret or misinterpret the events surrounding his or her actions. While he was conducting research for his doctoral dissertation in East Berlin, he believed the Stasi (the East German secret police) were spying on him. He also assumed that some of his friends and associates were reporting his activities to the Stasi. When the Berlin Wall collapsed and the Stasi files were opened, Ash returned to Germany to verify his conclusions. Some of his conclusions were correct, but others were not. The Stasi did have him under surveillance, and he had guessed correctly that the landlady in his apartment block was filing regular reports. He had also assumed that a close friend was reporting on him, based on her actions; he was wrong on that count. From what he could recall years later, Ash determined that the friends and associates who had reported on him occasionally provided information that was wrong, only partially correct, or lacking completeness. Ash's conclusion is that interpretation evolves over time as more facts and information become available. Evaluation of outcomes, like a fine wine, needs time to mature.

Blame for the mortgage crisis can be assigned to many quarters. A number of public policy decisions and perverse market incentives, all in the name of good social policy, share partial responsibility. The thought that the housing collapse and the foreclosure crisis were partially avoidable is correct. The nexus of the crisis resided in a number of actions that converged simultaneously to create the financial storm. Laws govern economics just as they govern physics. Attempts to "repeal" those laws generally fail. Economies go through cycles of expansion and contraction. When expansion goes on for too long, the subsequent contraction can be long and deep, as was the case in 2008.

---

2   Timothy Garton Ash, *The File: A Personal History* (New York: Random House, 1997).

I believe the housing crisis and the Great Recession, while many years in the making, evolved from a series of well-intentioned laws and regulations that created an environment of greed and political and financial corruption. When combined with an absence of critical analysis, an over-reliance on faulty prognostications, irrational assumptions, and bad arithmetic, the mix created a recipe for disaster. Yet the "smart guys" claimed everything was okay and we were going to be just fine. There was nothing to worry about.

This is the groupthink/herd mentality syndrome. I believe the GSEs were enablers and catalysts that allowed the subprime business to grow and prosper. The times fostered a climate of complacency based on the assumption that real estate values would always go up. It is not a stretch to state that the top executives at the Wall Street rating agencies and at the two most prominent GSEs, Fannie Mae and Freddie Mac, wrapped themselves in a blanket of imprimaturs and ex cathedras, meaning that nothing hinders and we are infallible.

As late as 2004, officials still denied the possibility of problems in the housing market. Speaking on behalf of the Federal Reserve Bank of New York, Jonathan McCarthy and Richard Peach asserted, "Home prices have been rising strongly since the mid-1990s, prompting concerns that a bubble exists in this asset class and that home prices are vulnerable to a collapse that could harm the US economy. A close analysis of the US housing market in recent years, however, finds little basis for such concerns. The marked upturn in home prices is largely attributable to strong market fundamentals."[3] Such was the groupthink mentality before everything came crashing down.

Gretchen Morgenson and Joshua Rosner chronicle the groupthink mentality. Media reports of potential home buyers engaged in bidding wars, cable television pitchmen's advice on how to get rich by purchasing properties with no money down, and loose credit standards invited the participation of amateur speculators. Much of the get rich quick, no down payment on investment properties phenomenon was fraught with fraud.[4]

The Federal Reserve Board (the Fed) also shares in the blame for the real estate meltdown. The Fed has two principle charges: first, to manage the money supply and second, to maintain wage and price stability. Nevertheless, in 2006 Ben Bernanke, chair of the Fed, "signaled the institution's [the Fed's]

3   Quoted in Morgenson and Rosner, *Reckless Endangerment*, 219.

4   Ibid., 219–20.

disinterest in identifying or reining in asset bubbles."[5] His refusal to take action to curb the rapidly escalating housing bubble may have been in part a response to the industry and public reaction following the 1992 publication of a study of discrimination by lenders, conducted by the Federal Reserve Bank of Boston.[6] Seen as highly credible, the report gave rise to relaxed lending standards for underserved markets and a new array of affordable housing programs offered by the GSEs. Perhaps Bernanke feared that taking any action to rein in the housing bubble would trigger a broader response, as it did in 1992, that could have negatively impacted the economy as a whole. Perhaps he was wrong.

The Boston Fed study relied on the Home Mortgage Disclosure Act, which compelled mortgage lenders to report information not only on the loan but on the borrowers themselves. Even if a borrower did not want his or her race reported, the lender was obligated to guess. The data were used to score the bank's performance under the requirements of the 1977 Community Reinvestment Act (CRA), which called for banks to lend on properties across their entire service area with the goal of eliminating redlining. Compliance with the CRA and a high performance score are critical measurements regulators use when evaluating banks. Using the HMDA information, the Boston Fed study claimed that black and Hispanic loan applicants were far more likely to be rejected by banks than were white applicants.[7]

This report sent a shudder through the industry, for it indicated the ongoing practice of redlining. While redlining had been instituted and sanctioned under the neighborhood scoring matrix of the Home Owners Loan Corporation in the 1930s and was a common practice for years, it had been outlawed by the US Supreme Court in 1948. Even though I had never experienced it in my professional career, I knew it existed. Nevertheless, attitudes about redlining had changed; most people disapproved of its use. From a business standpoint, it made no sense to decline a minority applicant who met the institution's credit guidelines and had demonstrated the ability to repay. Not only was turning down a borrower based on race illegal, but why would a bank risk losing a customer and not profiting by making a loan?

---

5   Quoted in ibid., 226.

6   Lynn E. Brown Munnel, James McEneaney, and Geoffrey M.B. Tootell, *Mortgage Lending in Boston: Interpreting HMDA Data* (Boston: Federal Reserve Bank of Boston, October 1992).

7   Morgenson and Rosner, *Reckless Endangerment*, 52–53.

From a public relations and profitability standpoint, engaging in redlining was totally illogical.

However, the fact that this study had been done by the Boston Federal Reserve Bank made it highly credible. The study researchers were seen as objective and nonpolitical. Since 1977 all banks, particularly those actively engaged in mortgage banking, were particularly sensitive to meeting their CRA goals. The risk of bad media headlines is critically important to banks; none want to be accused of discriminating. The Boston Fed report received considerable media attention, resulting in heightened sensitivity, particularly among the senior executives at Fannie Mae's headquarters in Washington. In the highly charged political environment of Fannie Mae, the report had the potential to be highly damaging, and it was.

Recognizing the political threat, Jim Johnson, Fannie Mae's chief executive officer, seized upon the Boston Fed study and began reaching out to the housing advocacy groups that were the company's financial beneficiaries. Johnson saw this as an opportunity to expand Fannie Mae's reach, not by making more loans but by developing strategies to streamline the home purchasing experience to cut costs.[8] Some of these outreach initiatives included local partnership offices to serve as focal points to cultivate state and local political leadership and build ties with affordable housing groups.

At this juncture, Johnson and his executives began to reshape the credit culture of Fannie Mae. His ideas and policies of "expanding creative financing" and utilizing other methods to make homeownership more affordable became the basis for President Bill Clinton's National Partners in Homeownership and the Fannie Neighbors program. Johnson's successor, Frank Raines, maintained his predecessor's approach. He was once quoted as saying, "We have to keep bending financial markets to serve the families buying the homes you [the construction industry] build."[9]

In the new world of more relaxed standards for mortgage financing created in the wake of the Boston Fed study, alternative credit histories were deemed acceptable. Statements from utility providers and other creditors could be substituted in lieu of a credit report. Credit scores based on this widened pool of information had gained full acceptance in the mortgage

---

8   Ibid., 33–35.

9   Ibid., 34–37.

industry during the 1980s. But from the mid-1990s on, the minimum acceptable credit score for loan approval steadily declined. As late as 2007 a credit score of 500 was acceptable for certain subprime loan products. Prior to that time the normal minimum score for a prime loan was 620; scores from 619 to 581 were considered subprime. Most applicants with scores of 580 and below were not approved. Taking into account other risk factors such as loan-to-value ratio, probability of the borrower's continued employment, and type of loan, the rate among subprime loans was two times greater than that of prime loans granted to those with credit scores of 620 and above. Default rates among borrowers with a score of only 500 reached four times those of prime borrowers.[10]

From the 1960s through the 1970s, almost all mortgage loans were based on a monthly payment ratio of 25 percent of gross income, and the total debt-to-income ratio did not exceed 33 percent. In the new world of mortgage loan approval, total debt-to-income ratios could rise to 40 percent, and in some cases the automated underwriting systems approved ratios as high as 60 percent. To assist low-income borrowers who had not been able to save money toward a down payment, down payment assistance programs also became commonplace. Many local government programs, nongoverment organizations (NGOs), and family members (with an appropriate gift or cash-on-hand letter) were deemed acceptable sources of a down payment.[11]

Seller-assisted down payment schemes, while not engaged in by Fannie or Freddie, were approved by the FHA. The seller of the house would raise the price and make a "donation" in the same amount to a nonprofit that would then provide the funds to the borrower for the down payment. These seller-assisted programs were responsible for a nearly 20 percent default rate in the FHA's portfolio.

After the Boston Fed study became public, my company, United Guaranty, instituted a thorough review process to ensure that we did not discriminate against any of our customers based on their race, gender, age, or any other discriminatory qualifier. Furthermore, we began discussions with our

---

10 Hollis Fishelson-Holstine, "The Role of Credit Scoring in Increasing Homeownership for Underserved Populations," BABC 04-12, Joint Center for Housing Studies of Harvard University, Working Papers (Cambridge, MA: John F. Kennedy School of Government, Harvard University, February 12, 2004), 3–5.

11 Morgenson and Rosner, *Reckless Endangerment*, 37.

customers who were regulated under the provisions of the Community Reinvestment Act to verify that our risk profile was consistent with theirs. Our senior management provided the necessary endorsement to assure proper implementation of our clients' needs. These face-to-face meetings provided an invaluable exchange of information. One such meeting with the chief credit officer of a large California bank proved particularly valuable. We had access to loan performance data and understood the bank's commitment to particular borrowers and neighborhoods. The products and profiles were consistent with prudent risk management, the loans were fully documented, and in some cases pre-purchase loan counseling programs were required.

The Boston Fed study was a significant event in what would lead to the mortgage crisis. The reputation of the study and the media attention it garnered set in motion a chain reaction with long-term implications. However, a year later *Forbes* magazine, along with a number of other critics both inside and outside academic circles and government, contended that the research was flawed. They were correct. One of the complaints purported that the study did not take into account whether an applicant met a lender's credit guidelines.[12] Had that information been included, the number of loan application denials based on race versus creditworthiness would have been reduced, possibly by a significant amount.

Alicia Munnell, the Boston Fed's research director who oversaw the study, stated in a 2010 interview that "she never intended her 1992 study to result in relaxed lending practices for minorities." She claimed, "It was not that they [bankers] were doing bad things to black people, they were doing nice things for white people so when you look at it statistically, race becomes a factor. We were never arguing that you should give loans to people who don't qualify."[13]

The role of the study cannot be understated. Dissenting voices arose across the political and economic spectrum. They included FM Watch, Peter J. Wallison and Edward Pinto of the American Enterprise Institute, and Professor Robert Shiller of Yale University, who won the Nobel Prize for economics in 2013. These men shared a concern about rapid inflation and deteriorating credit quality and loan documentation. In contrast, a broad industry consensus predicted an ever-increasing demand for housing and

---

12 Ibid., 35.

13 Quoted in ibid., 39–40.

homeownership among echo boomers. Immigration and other changing demographics also drove increased demand. Lower interest rates added to the frenzied speculation that housing prices would continue to climb.

Concerns about a housing bubble were not limited to conservative think tanks. Joshua Rosner's study "Housing in the New Millennium: A Home without Equity Is Just a Rental with Debt" correctly forecast the conse-quences of over-leveraged borrowers and an accelerated rate of foreclosures. At the time, others expressed concern about the large amount of equity extraction through refinancing, as well as home equity loans and piggyback second mortgages used as a substitute for cash or mortgage insurance.[14]

An important factor that has not been addressed is the link among lower interest rates, generally accepted accounting principles, and the ferocious rate of refinancing. Financial institutions that service loans are required to report the value of the income stream as well as the cost of the acquisition of new loans to the portfolio. The cost associated with that acquisition is amortized over the expected life of the mortgage, generally estimated to be a period of five to seven years based on the borrower selling or refinancing the property within that time frame. If the borrower refinances before the forecasted pay-off date, the servicer must write off the fee paid for acquiring the servicing of the loan. With the constant churning of loans through refinances, the ser-vicer must acquire new loans at a faster pace than existing loans are paid off to remain profitable. This accounting treatment can have significant negative impacts on earnings. If the replenishment of loans cannot keep up with the payoffs of existing loans, then the firm books a loss. To replenish the portfolio, the temptation exists to be more aggressive in originating new loans and to go further out on the credit curve. Combined with the "expert" groupthink, the competition, enabling, encouragement, and incentives created by the GSE duopoly through changing guidelines, manipulation of criteria, and under-pricing credit risk made the duopoly's collapse unavoidable.

These organizations completely dominated the market, particularly with their automated underwriting systems and the fact that virtually every enter-prise in the residential mortgage sector was heavily influenced in some way by Fannie and Freddie. These two GSEs commanded influential, aggressive, and ongoing lobbying campaigns. Both Jim Johnson, who succeeded David

---

14 In ibid., 220–23.

Maxwell as president of Fannie Mae, and Frank Raines, a Rhodes scholar who succeeded Johnson, maintained an extremely powerful web of relationships throughout Washington. Through the Fannie Mae Foundation and other initiatives, Fannie Mae's largess found its way into political campaigns on both sides of the aisle. Because of Fannie's and Freddie's friends in the US Congress, one leveled criticism at his or her peril.

As early as 2000, concerns arose about the operations of the GSEs and the potential threat to US financial stability. Especially troubling issues included the generous taxpayer subsidies, the implied government guarantee, and the companies' high 30:1 debt-to-equity leverage ratio (a rate double what was tolerated for strong AA-rated companies). Many analysts felt this high level of leveraging posed a threat to the US economy and to taxpayers. Several conservative think tanks, including the Heritage Foundation and the American Enterprise Institute, had been longtime critics of the housing agencies' accumulation of risk. But at the same time there was great support for the social missions of the GSEs in many academic quarters and among nonprofits.[15]

In response to these threats, several major financial institutions formed FM Watch to alert policymakers and the media to the danger of a potential taxpayer bailout of the GSEs. FM Watch sought to redirect the GSEs back to their appropriate role of providing liquidity in the secondary market, especially for low-income borrowers. Gerald L. Friedman, a renowned and respected industry leader who had run the Mortgage Guaranty Insurance Company, led FM Watch.[16]

FM Watch's attack was driven by the monopolistic actions of the GSEs to control business practices that enabled them to dominate the pricing and distribution of mortgage products by other players in the market. In essence, Fannie and Freddie threatened to loosen the market discipline of their private-sector competition to gain additional market power by using their proprietary technology platforms. The use of those platforms by the mortgage finance system would have been permitted by the sanction of a "permissible monopoly."[17] In 2001 awareness of the huge political influence wielded by the GSEs grew within the executive branch, Congress, the NGO community, and the industry. That concern was known and

---

15 FM Watch, *GSE Mission Creep*, iii.

16 Ibid.

17 Ibid., 1.

acknowledged but rarely verbalized. The fear of retribution was great. Any public response to the growing power and influence of the GSEs was carefully selected and measured.

Not only was FM Watch concerned about the threat to US taxpayers, it was equally worried that Fannie and Freddie, in their quest for additional profit opportunities, would vertically integrate much of the home buying process. Their low cost of capital and favorable tax environment would then allow them to enter into related businesses. Contrary to Fannie Mae's charter as a secondary market investor and guarantor, it explored the prospect of direct lending, thus creating a competitive threat to its current stable of customers. In addition, it expressed interest in reaching into the pool of discounted mortgage insurance products and the title insurance business, which includes real estate and loan closing functions. The opportunity to insure mortgages directly presented an appetizing prospect of a profitable revenue stream for both GSEs. To facilitate some of these activities, Fannie Mae invested in a small startup bank in Buffalo, New York. FM Watch and other industry observers characterized this initiative by the GSEs as "mission creep" to facilitate some of their diversification activities.

A Congressional Research Service report in 1996 deconstructed many of the operations of the GSEs. The report raised questions about what level of government subsidies accrued to home buyers and what amount benefited the GSEs' executives and stockholders. To remain profitable and meet the requirements of Wall Street analysts, the GSEs would have to enter new lines of business. Without expansion, it would be difficult for them to maintain their stock prices and average high rates of return of 25 percent based on a near-saturation rate of 70 percent homeownership. As to the real benefit to borrowers, the report estimated that about 67 percent of the subsidy benefit reached the American public.[18]

Furthermore, the most powerful strategic threats identified by FM Watch were the two technology platforms or automated underwriting (AU) systems, Desktop Underwriter and Loan Prospector, initiated in 2001. These systems definitely contributed to the housing crash in 2008. The duopoly

---

18 Ibid., ii–iii; Barbara Miles, "Government Sponsored Enterprises: The Issue of Expansion into Mission-Related Business," Congressional Research Service Report for Congress, January 19, 1999; James L. Bothwell, *Housing Enterprises: Potential Impacts of Severing Government Sponsorship* (Washington, DC: US General Accounting Office, June 12, 1996), 4–7.

practically forced everyone to use those programs because they would "only waive certain contractual requirements and offer extra financial incentives on loans run through their own AU systems."[19] The result was that if the AU system approved a mortgage loan, then the mortgage insurance company was almost always obliged to insure that loan, and the lender was obliged to make the loan. For example, in 2007, as the market continued to weaken, applications from borrowers with very low FICO scores—as low as 500—were approved, often under pressure from various community groups. Yet charging a risk premium on these loans became almost impossible for fear of accusations of violating the disparate impact laws that protect against discrimination. Later, when the economy went into recession, many of those same homeowners, approved by AUs that were applying very generous guidelines, suffered severe financial damage and lost their homes.

By 2003, the controversy sparked by the efforts of FM Watch had generated a furious response from the GSEs. Partly in response to the turmoil, the Mortgage Bankers Association (MBA) formed its Affordable Housing Task Force to help establish the industry's policy on the affordable housing goals of both Fannie and Freddie. At that time, HUD was ready to amend the housing goals, and the industry needed to exercise its influence.

The first reading in preparation for the working group meeting was a March 4, 2003, paper written by two economists, G. Donald Jud and Daniel T. Winkler, from the University of North Carolina at Greensboro.[20] It discussed changes in housing prices, employment, and mortgage rates. The paper also forecast that the possibility of a sharp housing market collapse appeared unlikely. This and other studies demonstrated the sanguine deniability of the deteriorating credit cycle as the goal of 70 percent homeownership was reached. At a subsequent meeting Lyle Gramley, a former Federal Reserve governor and MBA economist, expressed the opinion that a realistic, healthy homeownership rate was probably closer to 63 percent. The study by Jud and Winkler was not uncommon. Business and trade association economists were predicting a shortage of housing given the baby boom echo and greater immigration. But because homeownership throughout the past century had been seen as constituting wealth accumulation and contributing

---

19 FM Watch, *GSE*, 21.

20 G. Donald Jud and Daniel T. Winkler, "Some Thoughts on Housing Markets Cycles," paper prepared for and submitted to the MBA, March 4, 2003.

to community stability, almost unstoppable momentum was moving toward the bubble.

When Fannie Mae became aggressive, the industry responded in-kind. Given the imprimatur of the GSEs, the sector of the market outside their sphere adapted its policies and programs, with or without credit enhancements or mortgage insurance, to fill in the gap between the 60 percent market share controlled by the GSEs and the balance of the market. Because the GSEs had been given broader scope and leeway, many of the more aggressive programs could in turn be sold in the private mortgage–backed security market. They were then sold through the back door to Fannie, Freddie, and other institutional investors on Wall Street.[21]

The evolution of the private-label mortgage-backed securities market had its beginnings in the late 1970s when Bank of America offered the first issue of conventional loans sold with mortgage pool insurance from a AA-rated company. By the turn of the new millennium the private-label market had matured and represented a major outlet for loans that were above the eligibility limit for the GSEs.

One element of the foreclosure crisis has for the most part escaped public attention—the role of the credit rating agencies. Standard and Poor's Ratings Services is the largest and most recognized of these agencies, but Moody's Investors Service and Finch Ratings are equally well-known in the financial community. These organizations are paid by the issuer of the security, in this case a mortgage-backed security. The rating agencies' role is to render an opinion on the creditworthiness and risk profile associated with the security.

The agencies that perform these evaluations use a risk model rather than the analytical profile employed more often to assess corporate and municipal debt. A tape with the data is provided by the originators of the underlying loans. In the case of a mortgage-backed security, they feed data into the risk model to determine the possible frequency and severity of potential losses because of default in the entire pool of loans. Within these risk models are various attributes and assumptions about borrowers' credit behavior. The model compares those loans granted to borrowers with higher credit scores and therefore having a lower probability of default with those of borrowers

---

21   Acharya et al., *Guaranteed to Fail*, 21.

with low credit scores and then assigns a risk level. Built into the level model's analysis are assumptions about price appreciation for the properties that comprise the pool. Generally speaking, the categorical attributes in the risk model are confidential and proprietary. In providing a credit enhancement on a pool of mortgage-backed securities when mortgage pool insurance is used, a minimum of thirty-five variables of different weights is used in forecasting the probability of default.

The level model assumptions are confidential, but the industry is aware of some of the major components. Examples of a hypothetical issue would begin with the credit rating of the issuer. The issuer could be an institution such as a bank, a special purpose facility, or a mortgage conduit. Mortgage conduits and special purpose facilities obtain loans from numerous originators and issue a security against the pool of these loans based on the monthly cash flow. These facilities and conduits generally have a sponsor, such as a AA or AAA financial services company, and have their own ratings. To achieve a minimum AA rating, they must demonstrate adequate capital and experienced management.

Other factors affecting the evaluation include the type of loans contained in the loan pool—single-family houses, condominiums, townhouses, or some combination. All of these cases would be conventional loans, meaning they are not FHA or VA insured or guaranteed. The model also employs a weighted average loan-to-value ratio and a weighted average interest rate sufficient to cover the costs of issuance. Those costs include loan-level surveillance, trustee fees, and more. Costs of issue can also include legal and accounting fees as well as credit enhancements, such as mortgage pool insurance or a senior subordinated debt structure. The location of the properties covered by the loans is also important. Efforts are made to avoid a concentration of properties in any one market—usually no more than a certain percentage in any census tract, community, or neighborhood. If the issuer is also the servicer, that is less complicated than a case in which a separate servicer is used. If there are multiple originators and servicers, a master servicer must be hired, rated, and compensated.

While Standard & Poor's (S&P) dominated the market, Moody's was also a significant player. In 2002 Moody's built a mortgage risk assessment model that differentiated among three levels of data; primary, highly desirable, and desirable. Moody's required only primary data such as "loan-to-value ratios, property zip codes, borrowers' credit scores and whether a loan was a first or second lien" to rate the security.[22]

The amount of information in Moody's primary data category is totally insufficient to forecast portfolio default performance. Moody's did not require the submission of the two other levels of data; they were seen as a supplement to the primary data. Some of the secondary non-mandatory data could have helped the security achieve a more accurate and possibly a higher or lower quality rating had it been required. Such information included the borrowers' cash reserves and disposable income, regardless of whether the borrower was a first-time home buyer, and a history of bankruptcy or any other credit weakness, all of which are critical in mortgage analysis. Further, Moody's did not require information regarding borrowers' debt-to-income ratios. Two-income households that are highly leveraged, even with good credit scores of 760 and above, have a high propensity to default, particularly if one of the co-borrowers loses his or her job.

But perhaps the most egregious omissions from Moody's primary data were the type of appraisal used during the loan approval process and the identity of the company that originated the loan. That information fell into the desirable category.[23]

Three approaches to establishing property value—the market, cost, and income approaches—are employed in real estate appraisals. An experienced mortgage banker could also use a fourth approach by asking, can I sell this property for what I have invested in it? Moody's relied to a great extent on lenders who were not included in the company's risk-level assessment models and whose appraisals were generated by automated systems, not by an appraiser who actually visited the property. Such automated valuation systems can provide context for particular markets, but their information can often be outdated and inaccurate. It is difficult to drill down and extract all the necessary information to make a solid credit judgment on both the borrower and the property. It is even more difficult, in the absence of a complete file, to interpret the data correctly and make a sound credit judgment. Automated underwriting and decision systems, whether used by credit rating agencies or the GSEs, are no substitute for experience, insight, and judgment. So, the

---

22 Morgenson and Rosner, *Reckless Endangerment*, 160–61.

23 Ibid., 160–61.

assembly of the underlying mortgages of the mortgage-backed security could suffer from a weak analysis when key risk points are not properly assessed.[24]

The next key step for the security is to analyze all the players responsible for gathering the loans from the originator, doing the underwriting, and building the data set for the rating agency. Depending on the size and asset composition of the pool, each of the participating institutions, including the issuer, needs to have its own rating. This rating must be investment grade (AAA, AA, A) to meet international conventions on a financial institution's capital. For the issuer of a large mortgage-backed security, an important first step is to recruit and vet the other partners in the transaction. Strong partners are imperative because the important theory in rating agency parlance and analytics is to rate the "weakest link," also known as counter-party or third-party risk, in the transaction.

Consider a hypothetical security issue. A firm with a AAA credit rating plans to issue a mortgage-backed security based on a pool of loans in prime neighborhoods with stable economies, modest price appreciation, low interest rates, and fully documented files. After the issuer selects all of its transaction partners, an evaluation is made on each of the participants by a credit rating agency, based on the individual ratings. Unfortunately, the insurance company that provides a special hazard policy to insure against losses caused by a catastrophic storm or wildfire not covered by the homeowners' policies is only rated single A. Even though all the other participants have the same AAA rating as the issuing firm, the security will only receive a single A rating.

An additional concern for potential investors is third-party risk, one that, while not anticipated, might have been foreseen at the time of issuance as possibly able to affect the value of the security in the future. For example, when considering the above scenario, a sophisticated investor with a long-range view would look at the weakest link, the insurance company, and conclude that a hurricane of Katrina's proportions could cause the special hazard insurer to be downgraded to a B rating, which would be less than investment grade; hence, the investor would suffer a marketing loss. Needless to say, the investor would probably decline investing in that particular mortgage-backed security.

Knowledgeable investors know and recognize that the agencies' ratings are their opinions at a specific moment in time. Unsophisticated investors often

---

24 Ibid., 162.

fail to recognize that the assigned rating, particularly on a mortgage-backed security, is just one of many risk factors to consider when deciding to make an investment. The investor needs to read and understand the prospectus provided by the issuer. The investor must understand that a rating is neither investment advice nor a guarantee of future marketability.

In 2008, as the subprime market began to crash, securities formerly rated AAA lost their value virtually overnight. One of the failures of the Trouble Asset Relief Program (TARP), which was designed to support the market for these securities, was that it could not determine the price and marketability of the securities quickly enough. The market moved faster than TARP was able to determine the appropriate level of support. Consequently, the market determined the level of risk; as a result, the prices of the securities fell from ninety-five cents on the dollar to forty cents to twenty cents on the dollar in a matter of days.

Another failure of Moody's was that it did not conduct random samplings of the loans in the pools to verify the reliability of the data the issuers provided. In fact, the company provided a disclaimer that stated that it had "no obligation to perform, and does not perform, due diligence with respect to the accuracy of information it receives or obtains in connection with the rating process. Moody's does not independently verify any such information. Nor does Moody's audit or otherwise undertake to determine that such information is complete."[25]

A number of other issues existed surrounding the weaknesses and lack of discipline of the credit rating agencies, including their inability to, or lack of interest in, accurately assessing the level of risk and taking steps early enough to spot trouble. They were particularly negligent in assessing the credit and accounting weaknesses of Fannie Mae and Freddie Mac.

But it was the dominant S&P, not Moody's, that the Department of Justice targeted in a 2013 lawsuit accusing the firm of defrauding investors by inflating the ratings of residential mortgage-backed securities and collateralized debt obligations that masked the securities' actual credit risks.[26] Without admitting to any legal wrongdoing, S&P, along with its parent company,

---

25 Ibid., 161–62.

26 Department of Justice, "Department of Justice Sues Standard & Poor's," February 5, 2013, accessed February 6, 2015, http://www.justice.gov/opa/pr/department-justice-sues-standard -poor-s-fraud-rating-mortgage-backed-securities-years-leading.

McGraw Hill Financial, agreed to a $1.375 billion settlement in February 2015. Half of the funds were to be paid to the Department of Justice and the other half was designated to be paid to nineteen states and Washington, DC, which also participated in the suit.[27]

When Bank of America issued its first conventional mortgage-backed security, it needed the approval of one or more bond or credit rating agencies such as S&P, Moody's, or Fitch. For debt securities of any type to be marketable, investors require the opinion of such agencies as to the creditworthiness of the issuer and its ability to pay the obligation. For many investors, such as life insurance companies, pension funds, banks, and trusts, such debt obligations have to be rated investment grade by at least one of the three credit rating agencies. Investors seek not only the best yield on a bond but also the highest credit quality. The job of the rating agency is to give an accurate opinion of the issuer's credit quality.

The three agencies apply a standard assessment method based on a mathematical model called a "levels model." In the case of a mortgage-backed security, it forecasts the level of performance of the underlying loans that will cause the buyers of the security to suffer a loss of principal and interest or otherwise impair the value of the security. For those that provided a guarantee or credit enhancement, the use of the levels model was important for pricing the risk. Whether a first loss position on individual loans was purchased or an aggregated feature was used, the analysis proved to be dramatically flawed because the groupspeak assumptions were inherently wrong. While I was not directly involved in those transactions, I was fully aware that the actuaries in my company were unable to price the risk because our internal models (which I believe were by far the best in the industry) were forecasting a default rate of nearly 20 percent in the loan pools. That rate was four to five times higher than the normal expected default rate on high-ratio loans, regardless of whether they were insured by FHA or a highly rated (AAA) mortgage guaranty company.

From an insider's perspective, forecasting models have one serious flaw. The analysis assumes that all of the assumptions on which the models are

27 PRNewswire, "McGraw Hill Financial and S&P Ratings Reach Settlements with DOJ," February 3, 2015, accessed February 6, 2015, http://www.prnewswire.com/news-releases/mcgraw-hill-financial-and-sp-reach-settlement; M. Robinson and D. McLaughlin, "S&P Ends Legal Woes Paying $1.5 Billion Fine to US, States," *Bloomberg Business*, February 3, 2015, accessed February 6, 2015, http://www.bloomberg.com/news/articles/2015-02-03/s-p-ends-legal-woes-with-1-5-billion-fine-to-u-s-states.

based are complete and the numbers are accurate. Yet the models lack a way to evaluate any level of fraud or to account for an overreliance on credit scores as a measure of future loan performance. Credit scores measure how borrowers have performed in the past but, as we saw during the mortgage crisis, they cannot and do not predict future performance. Ironically, the executive in charge of one of the country's largest servicing portfolios is a behavioral psychologist.

The large seller servicers monitor their loan portfolios and measure certain predictive behaviors to anticipate possible defaults. While job loss and illness are major reasons for loan defaults, many borrowers during the late 1990s and early 2000s became overextended by using their high credit scores to access as many as ten or more lines of credit. Eventually, they could not meet their obligations and entered foreclosure. The case of borrowers having three lines of credit when they opened their mortgage and then establishing as many as seven or eight additional accounts to furnish the home and maintain a new and better lifestyle became commonplace. Some of these factors could have been built into the levels models, but many of the behavioral patterns, based on past history, could not.

The following case study is, in large measure, typical of conversations held with major national account customers of United Guaranty in the context of extreme conflict in the industry about relationships with business partners at the GSEs or the mortgage guaranty company.

In the spring of 2001, I had arranged the annual executive dinner with one of our company's senior executives and the president and chief executive officer of one of our firm's largest national accounts, the mortgage banking arm of a large international bank. The CEO was highly regarded and had received a number of awards for contributions to the industry and for his teaching excellence in industry educational programs. Harvard-educated and disciplined, this executive knew the numbers and how the business operated in great detail, particularly the loan servicing operation and loss mitigation department functions. The purpose of our meeting was to review our overall relationship and respond to several new initiatives for the expanded underwriting criteria for the bank's CRA portfolio included in the renewal of the annual contract with Fannie Mae. He believed that if properly executed, these expanded guidelines could be used prudently and the credit risk managed.

It is important to understand the context in which these discussions took place. First, because this firm was part of a large bank, there was significant pressure to meet the goals of the CRA. In addition, Fannie Mae exerted pressure on the mortgage company to adopt the expanded guidelines because of its status as a major seller servicer. Fannie Mae, under the Federal Housing Enterprises Financial Safety and Soundness Act of 1992, had agreed to these ambitious mission policy goals to support housing for low- and moderate-income households, particularly in underserved areas. Similar conversations and the attendant pressures were exerted every day inside most major financial institutions, whether they were depository or non-depository mortgage lenders. Bank regulators and the GSEs had the regulatory muscle and financial incentives to push the agenda for expanded homeownership opportunities as a matter of public policy. A system of incentives and punishments ensured the achievement of those goals. The pressure then partially shifted to the mortgage insurance partners to share the risk, without the appropriate risk-based compensation.

Second, some background on the CRA is important for context. In many ways the act is unfairly blamed for financial problems and is generally misunderstood. Simply stated, the goal of the CRA was to eliminate discrimination by requiring financial institutions to reinvest depositors' money back into the community from which those deposits were gathered. What is often not understood is that the CRA did not require investment in mortgages if the policy of the bank's board of directors was not to engage in mortgages. But at the time, most banks of any size offered real estate mortgages, either through the bank itself or through its affiliated non-bank real estate lending operations, as a way to satisfy customers' needs and tie them more closely to the bank. Offering mortgages also expanded banks' opportunities to sell their CRA loans in the secondary market.

Given the pressure on United Guaranty to assist customers to earn exceptional reports from regulators on compliance with the CRA and the GSEs' affordable housing goals, we had begun preliminary discussions to determine how we might respond to our customers' needs in a prudent and actuarially sound manner. To help them insure loans using the expanded guidelines mandated by the CRA and the annual contract with both GSEs, we needed to know more about the level of risk we were accepting. The market was moving aggressively in a new direction, and we had to deal with it.

Both Fannie Mae and Freddie Mac received these affordable housing goals[28] under the Federal Housing Enterprises Financial Safety and Soundness Act, and the goals expanded at an increasing rate until roughly 2005. In 2003 the aggressive subprime market began to expand with the entrance of Wall Street investment banks and other nontraditional mortgage banking firms, such as New Century. These firms packaged many of the high-risk loans into securities that found their way back into the portfolios of Fannie and Freddie, as well as to other yield-hungry investors.

My role as a corporate officer and senior sales executive with a mortgage insurance company was to manage the account strategy, seek to balance the risk, and maintain a profitable relationship with the client. The role of a mortgage insurance company is to take the first dollar loss on loans with a loan-to-value ratio greater than 80 percent. The company insures the lender up to a certain percentage of the loan. Typically, the top 25 percent to 40 percent of the outstanding loan amount is covered by a mortgage guaranty insurance policy. For example, a loan with an outstanding balance of $100,000 defaults. The terms of policy stipulate 25 percent coverage of the outstanding balance plus related foreclosure costs; in this case, the costs equal $15,000. The insurance company will pay the investor 25 percent of $115,000, or $28,750. Just because Fannie Mae had negotiated expanded guidelines with the lender, it did not necessarily mean United Guaranty would automatically adopt those guidelines, particularly if they were outside our risk tolerance parameters. Discussions surrounding this and similar topics were carried on in the euphoric environment of increased housing prices, full employment, and pre-9/11 national security. While all this transpired before the real deterioration of credit quality began, great concern permeated the industry regarding GSE mission creep.

In the language of the industry, the mortgage banker that deals with Fannie Mae or Freddie Mac is a seller servicer. The mortgage banker operates under a rather complicated contractual arrangement with the GSE, which spells out in great detail how both are to operate. These contracts—written on an annual basis—deal with technology interfaces, underwriting guidelines, performance measurements, compliance requirements, and, most important, compensation and financial incentives between the two organizations. For

---

28 See a list of the goals in appendix D.

this particular customer, acceptance of the expanded guidelines along with certain performance measurements could translate into a generous financial incentive to the seller servicer. Both GSEs capture a portion of the interest rate paid by the borrower and guarantee protection for buyers of their securities against loss as a result of foreclosures, a failure of the seller servicer, or a special hazard risk such as an earthquake or hurricane. Initially, the GSEs kept 0.25 percent of the interest rate as an insurance premium called a guarantee fee, or G-fee. The seller servicer's G-fee was dependent on its ability to make the GSE meet its affordable housing goals. As the duopoly began to compete for market share, it contributed by negotiating that fee to almost nothing to gain a larger share of customers' business; in some cases, G-fees were as low as 0.07 percent.

The question is posed, why would you cut prices? The answer is simple; the expanded guidelines were a reflection of the ambitious affordable housing goals set by the GSEs in response to their political masters. In turn, as the success of the GSEs in meeting these affordable housing goals increased, so did the financial rewards to the organizations' stockholders, employees, and executive compensation packages.

To continue the story of the customer dinner, I engaged in a discussion with the chief executive officer about how to respond to the expanded guidelines in a prudent way. At that point United Guaranty's president raised the issue of the prolonged credit cycle. We both realized that the nation's economy would soon experience a severe contraction, but the question remained, when would the cycle snap back and contraction occur? As we know now, the housing market continued to expand, particularly in the Sun Belt states, and housing values continued to rise. At the same time, the credit quality of large numbers of borrowers began to deteriorate as they added to their total debt level through the use of multiple credit cards.

We watched the prolonged escalation of real estate values without a correction for another five years. In addition, we faced a competitive threat from so-called piggyback loans. These loans are high-ratio (in excess of 80 percent loan to value) adjustable-rate second mortgages placed on homes in lieu of mortgage insurance. History from the 1929 stock market crash and subsequent Great Depression told us that risk stacking (one loan on top of another plus credit card consumer debt) was a prescription for financial disaster.

This delayed cycle was a matter of concern that caused us to pay closer and closer attention to our portfolio performance. Early payment defaults escalated; so did rapid refinances as borrowers cashed out the equity in their homes while simultaneously increasing their debt. All of these were signs of a weakening housing market. We began to step up face-to-face meetings with our customers to evaluate whether our opinions and observations reconciled with theirs and determine ways to mitigate our losses.

As more and more frequent requests were made for mortgage insurance coverage on the riskier expanded guidelines, another competitive threat arose. This time it came directly from the politically strong and media-savvy GSE duopoly of Fannie Mae and Freddie Mac. As part of mission creep, they began expanding their operations to the point that they started encroaching into our business on many fronts. They were seeking ways to get into our business and position themselves to capture our income in addition to their existing revenue streams. At that time, between 15 percent and 20 percent of the conventional mortgage market was in high-ratio privately insured mortgages, an area the GSEs wanted to access.

The MBA's policy statement expressed concern about mission creep and the need to draw a clear distinction between primary market and secondary market activities. The primary market activities into which Fannie and Freddie expanded included being a direct investment lender, owning a minority stake in a savings bank in Buffalo, serving as a mortgage insurance or title insurance company, and developing a proprietary technology platform.[29] The GSEs argued that offering these other services would lower costs for borrowers. The other side of the argument was that the GSEs were entering the primary market, which is disallowed by their charters. When combined with their monopolistic nature, such activities would defeat a robust competitive market, an essential factor in lowering the cost of home ownership.

During this time in the 1990s until 2008, the GSEs' power and influence in Congress and the executive branch were legendary. For example, through the Fannie Mae Foundation the organization was able to distribute funds to numerous local governments, community groups, and nonprofits that, in turn, became political allies. In addition, Fannie Mae had a superb political operation, both in Washington and regionally across the nation. Many

---

29 FM Watch, *GSE*, 25–26.

members of Congress found good internships for their college-age children at Fannie Mae. Fannie Mae as well as Freddie Mac also made contributions to political candidates whose views were shared by the GSEs' executives.

One personal example of Fannie Mae's reach came from its regional office in Dallas. It concerned the 1996 Colorado US Senate race between Congressman Wayne Allard and Denver attorney Tom Strickland. I received a call from the Dallas public affairs officer, asking for my assessment of the candidates' campaigns and wondering who I felt would win the race. I told him in the interest of full disclosure that Congressman Allard's father had been my first customer in the mortgage business and that I knew the congressman from his time in the Colorado legislature and from my involvement at Colorado State University, of which Allard was a graduate. I told the gentleman that Allard was quiet and unassuming and that he had been an effective member of Congress. He did his homework, had a superb staff, and represented the district well, with excellent constituent service. I predicted that Allard would win, explaining that "simply stated, many in Colorado won't vote for a Seventeenth Street lawyer." That abruptly ended the conversation. On election day the official called me again and said, "What the hell is going on with that senatorial race in Colorado? Our sponsored enterprise exit polls are showing that Allard is going to win." I thought to myself, why is he surprised considering our earlier conversation, and, more important, why is a GSE conducting exit polls?

Fannie Mae could also take revenge on what it perceived as its enemies. The Fannie Mae Foundation funded an enormous number of affordable housing and counseling agency nonprofits. However, criticism of Fannie Mae by individuals associated with a nonprofit could result in negative consequences. For example, a nonprofit affordable housing provider in Colorado had been promised a substantial grant to complete a financial package for a new urban-style multi-family project. Some members of the nonprofit were actively engaged in local and national discussions of GSE reform. Suddenly, the Fannie Mae Foundation withdrew its financial commitment, which delayed the construction of the project for a year—long enough that it opened in the middle of the financial crisis. The nonprofit survived only because of the intellectual strength of its lenders, staff, and board. A coincidence . . . ?

A second demonstration of Fannie Mae's reach revealed itself in early 2001. The month before, unbeknownst to me and against my explicit instructions, several mortgage banking industry leaders had forwarded my name to the Bush transition team committee to be named president of Ginnie Mae. I had told them frankly, but apparently not strongly enough, that I had given my word to United Guaranty when I accepted the national accounts position that I would not seek the Ginnie Mae job (notwithstanding the fact that it had been a long-term career goal of mine). I felt strongly that I could not go back on my word, particularly to the people and company I admired and respected.

I arrived in my hotel room in the nation's capital on January 18, 2001. I had inauguration tickets and a fistful of invitations to parties and other events over that weekend. The first telephone call I received in my room was from a Fannie Mae official telling me that my name was on the list for the Ginnie Mae position and that if I gave the word, Fannie Mae would go to work lobbying on my behalf. Before I could call anyone at United Guaranty to try to clear up the misunderstanding, the phone rang again. Fortunately, I was able to satisfy United Guaranty's senior management that I had not initiated the conversation or approved the action. To this day I am still puzzled about what Fannie Mae officials knew, how they learned it, and how they got my hotel room phone number.

14

Observations and Lessons Learned (or Not)

While not the worst financial crisis in American history, the 2008 Great Recession has had far-reaching implications beyond the distress to defaulting homeowners and the permanent damage to the mortgage industry. America's long-held belief that any problem can be solved by passing more laws and regulations was in part the source of the meltdown. Over the long run, the thousands of pages of new legislation and regulations resulting from the 2010 Dodd-Frank Wall Street Reform and Consumer Protection Act will do little to prevent the next foreclosure crisis. Another world-shaking event such as a terrorist attack, war, a sovereign debt default, or the collapse of commodity prices could impact domestic employment. The consequence could well be another foreclosure crisis. While those events are unpredictable from a domestic economic policy viewpoint, the medication needed to mitigate or inoculate against another financial crisis on the scale of the Great Recession lies in a series of sound government, fiscal, and monetary policies that promote economic growth and job creation.

DOI: 10.5876/9781607326236.c014

The foreclosure crisis caused the American tradition of homeownership to come under attack. The precipitous drop in housing prices beginning in 2007–8 and continuing in many markets into 2015 led many financial planning experts to claim that buying a house was not a good investment. Admittedly, in some cases the critics are correct. Yet ownership of a home is a forced savings program that leads to stable communities and families. As equity builds through appreciation and amortization of the mortgage, the homeowner accumulates wealth and financial security. Historically, many economists and members of the real estate and mortgage industry have viewed home equity as a family safety net. The ability to deduct mortgage loan interest payments on second mortgages granted by the 1986 Tax Reform Act and the loosening of bank regulations on second mortgages effectively removed the safety net. The home evolved from a forced savings account into an automated teller machine. This aspect of over-leveraging created numerous problems for both first mortgage lenders and financially distressed borrowers seeking to restructure their debt obligations.

Prescribing all sorts of remedies misses the often repeated but overlooked point that most home buyers, farmers, and apartment or office building owners take their mortgage obligations seriously. They work hard to make their payments as long as they have income. Helping them avoid becoming over-leveraged and establishing fiscal policies that ensure job growth remain the central challenges.

The expansive net of blame for the 2008 foreclosure crisis spreads far and wide. Obviously, the activities and programs of the government-sponsored enterprises (GSEs) played a big role. So did the credit rating agencies, commercial and investment banking institutions, mortgage bankers, loan originators, and appraisers. However, not enough has been said about the borrowers' responsibility. A significant number of borrowers also drank the Kool-Aid. The unchecked escalation of housing prices led many to believe they had to jump on the housing ladder right then or forever be left out. At the time I agreed with that sentiment because we were all following the advice of the "experts," even though my gut told me to advance cautiously.

Certainly, the effects of the collapse of the real estate bubble created havoc in the economy and resulted in the widespread job loss that caused many families to lose their homes. All but a few neighborhoods in America felt the impact. But many of those same borrowers engaged in questionable behaviors just as the GSEs and others had, albeit on a smaller, individual scale. But taken cumulatively, the consequences were devastating. For example, after being coached, borrowers misrepresented their financial positions and employment prospects. Loan originators were known to have said things such as "you need to make $100,000 a year to qualify for this loan. You do make $100,000 a year, right?" "Right." Most borrowers who followed such clues and overstated their income eventually got into financial trouble.

Many borrowers also failed to read the application before they signed. Federal law, included at the bottom of the application form used throughout the industry (Form 1004), admonishes borrowers not to lie or misrepresent themselves and clearly states the federal penalties for doing so.

Since 1965, the mortgage process has become more and more complex. However, the experience of home buying for the purchaser has not changed, even after two minor and two major recessions. When buying a home, most borrowers continue to be interested in knowing the answers to just three questions:

1. How much will my payment be, and when is it due?
2. How much money do I have to bring to the closing?
3. What is my interest rate?

They exhibit little interest in whether the loan will be assumable by a future borrower if they sell the property, whether any prepayment penalties apply, or what the process would be if they get behind in their payments. I found the lack of home buyers' interest in investigating and understanding the mortgage product to which they were obligating themselves very disappointing.

Wells Fargo, Citicorp, and Bank of America have predictive models that track loan performance in an effort to intervene and prevent a foreclosure. These institutions and others have been conducting behavioral psychology studies for many years, beginning long before the foreclosure crisis. But even after a risk has been identified, the challenge of getting a borrower to respond remains. In the period 2007–10 institutions mailed cellular phone certificates and offered gift certificates and other benefits to encourage troubled borrowers to call and seek assistance. The majority did not respond.

Notwithstanding reports in the media, mortgage servicers—those who collect the payments, forward the funds to the investor, and pay the taxes and insurance premiums—go to extraordinary efforts to contact borrowers and help them avoid foreclosure because, as we saw during the Great Recession, the consequences can be far-reaching. Families who lose their homes experience major dislocation from which many never recover. The mortgage banker loses money even if there is mortgage insurance from the FHA or a private company. A foreclosure leaves a vacant and abandoned property. If several foreclosures occur in close proximity, the neighborhood often enters a downward spiral of blight and decay. Local governments lose property tax revenue, resulting in reduced services, and schools suffer. Everyone loses.

The sad truth is that many borrowers go into denial and do not respond to mail, telephone calls, or direct contact from door knockers. Regrettably, many foreclosures and much long-term credit damage can be avoided by simply contacting the mortgage servicer early. In Colorado in 2007–9, foreclosure notices were nailed to the doors of delinquent properties with the number of the Foreclosure Prevention Hotline. (The hotline was an initiative of the Colorado Foreclosure Prevention Task Force.) That action resulted in a number of calls, and a corresponding number of borrowers were helped.

Beginning in 2006, the industry learned that many borrowers who had gone into default had tended to consume whatever savings they had after the loan was closed. While job loss is an important factor in loan default, overextension of credit became another major contributor. Many borrowers binged on their credit cards to furnish their new homes. Most began with a car loan and maybe two credit cards with reasonable balances when they obtained their mortgage. But within months they may have obtained up to ten additional debt obligations through major credit cards, individual store credit cards, or new car loans. Eventually, borrowers may have obtained a second or third mortgage in a futile effort to stay in their homes.

Much discussion continues regarding the effectiveness of borrower education provided through both pre- and post-purchase counseling. Unfortunately, the topic does not lend itself well to the kind of statistical research with control groups common in most areas of medicine and pharmacy. In many cases the data reach very contradictory conclusions because of the inability to establish a large enough population of buyers who receive counseling to compare against a similarly sized control group that did not receive counseling. Certainly, the more education available to the borrower, the better the chances for success. Regrettably, many borrowers who become sixty days' delinquent do not have adequate financial resources to prevent an ultimate foreclosure.

One of the early signs of impending trouble was the GSEs' removal of home buyer counseling from their Community Mortgage programs. The GSEs also removed the requirement that borrowers maintain a six-month cash reserve after closing. Presumably, the Dodd-Frank reforms have addressed those issues. However, the regulations promulgated new rules for borrower disclosures that are significantly more complex than the prior ones. The regulations took years to write and in the early stages did not provide borrowers with information that was both clear and meaningful.

Prior to the Equal Credit Opportunity Act of 1974, the principal borrower's income alone was used for loan approval. Now, in the case of a couple, both incomes are generally used to qualify. In some instances that means the co-borrower, who often has the weaker probability of continued employment, presents an additional element of risk. Because of the difficulty of predicting income stability over a long period, the need to maintain a cushion of at least six months' payments in reserves is prudent.

Sometimes, bad decisions lead to a loss of income. One homeowner I tried to help at a legislator's town meeting had a good job with a good company but did not like his immediate supervisor. His wife, a stay-at-home mom, cared for their two small children. In addition to some credit card debt, he had purchased a new, large four-wheel-drive truck. Without any forethought he abruptly quit his job before finding a new one at a time when the unemployment rate was skyrocketing. I watched as the couple drove away from the meeting. The recognizable fear on the wife's face at the prospect of losing her home is a lasting memory.

In another case, utilizing its own resources and the efforts of a local television station, the Colorado Foreclosure Prevention Task Force was able to help a troubled borrower meet the requirements of the loan modification program. As in the previous case, small children and a stay-at-home mom became ensnared in a set of tragic circumstances. Because the media covered the story about the couple's success in obtaining the modification, the husband's first wife was able to successfully claim for unpaid child support from the funds he had accumulated to meet the terms of the modification. An earlier intervention and a full disclosure of all the facts might have been sufficient to prevent this family from being dislocated. These are unfortunate cases, with so many lives permanently damaged.

These stories provide a tragic contrast to many who try to game the system. Unscrupulous and clever individuals often find ways to manipulate the system. Some have claimed they do not know who their lender is or that they do not understand the terms of their mortgage. Others challenge the lender's right to foreclose, and they manipulate the court system with endless delays. They all test the limits of patience and fairness.

But the fact remains that some borrowers commit fraud. When attempting to buy their dream house, many misrepresent their financial position. This was particularly true in the case of stated income and stated asset loans, known in popular industry parlance as liars' loans. The program description for these loans did not require verification of income or assets, leaving the door wide open to fraud; and many borrowers did take advantage of that opportunity. Lenders can verify income directly with the IRS, so phony tax returns are one method of fabricating income. Copies of bank investment account statements are harder to manipulate, but it happens. Many checks and balances have been put in place to catch fraud, but none are foolproof.

The approval method used for liars' loans was definitely preferable to filling out a typical application with fraudulent statements in regard to income and assets. Yet while liars' loans may only be appropriate in very limited circumstances, they created a huge opportunity for fraud and misrepresentation and ultimately played a large role in the foreclosure crisis. As discussed above, unethical loan originators, brokers, and real estate agents sometimes encouraged borrowers to lie about their assets and liabilities on their applications. In misstating such information, all involved parties were breaking federal law and became subject to prosecution, fines, and imprisonment. Regrettably, few who engaged in such behavior were caught and fewer still were prosecuted. Ironically, as early as the 1970s the FBI began aggressively investigating lenders and borrowers who were misstating incomes so they could participate in the FHA 235 program.

The heated real estate market also created an open invitation for criminal elements. Interestingly, a mortgage fraud ring operated out of the Colorado State Penitentiary. The participants were caught and successfully prosecuted; they are still serving their sentences. In another case an international criminal ring completely fabricated not only the borrower but the property as well. This phenomenon is not limited to certain individuals, institutions, and local rogues. In one of my former accounts, an employee was paid by a criminal fraud ring to fabricate fictitious files. His actions caused my firm to lose millions of dollars.

While the nation's attorneys general have been pursuing mortgage fraud by loan originators and brokers, little effort is given to prosecuting borrowers who have committed mortgage fraud. More media attention to borrower fraud would have a chilling effect on the behavior of those committing such acts. The guilty borrowers share some, if not equal, responsibility for the foreclosure crisis as a consequence of their bad behavior.

Yet despite all the negative publicity and media attention regarding the foreclosure crisis, the desire for homeownership remains strong. It has become ingrained in Americans' DNA. An editorial in the November 29, 2014, edition of the *New York Times* stated that despite the decline in the homeownership rate, from slightly over 70 percent in 2004 to 64 percent in 2014, the number of owner-occupied homes remained approximately the same during that period. The article also stated that occupancies by renters increased by nearly 25 percent. Much of that gain can be attributed to a dramatic demographic shift as well as population growth. Yet some of the increase in renters is an obvious result of the dislocation and loss of homes through foreclosure.[1]

The editorial states that notwithstanding the financial crisis and the decline in housing values, the net worth of homeowners over time has outpaced that of renters because of the forced savings for a down payment and the buildup of equity from the monthly amortization of the mortgage. It argues that the lesson from 2008 is not to devalue homeownership but instead to foster conditions under which the middle class can avoid foreclosure.[2] However, the editorial neglects to mention that financial illiteracy remains a national problem.

Regardless of the complicity of borrowers, first among the many problems of the 2008 crash and post-recession years was and continues to be the lack of regulatory oversight and enforcement of existing laws and regulations. Flawed policies and incentives sanctioned and even encouraged the

---

1   Editorial Board, "Homeownership and Wealth Creation," *New York Times*, November 29, 2014, SR8.
2   Ibid.

irresponsible behavior among subprime lenders and the GSEs that damaged homeowners and institutions alike. The term *moral hazard* had its modern debut in the late 1990s. Called a "get out of jail free card" by some, almost all of the bad behavior went unpunished. There were financial consequences for some individuals, but nearly all of them escaped the punishment they deserved. The executives of Enron were among the few who were tried, convicted, and sent to prison.

The media also bears some of the blame. With the exception of the *Wall Street Journal*, the media has failed to report on the activities of those both inside and outside the industry and government and chose to ignore the warnings regarding the fiscal and financial stability of the industry and of Fannie and Freddie in particular. The media's relative silence is inexcusable. The unbridled growth of subprime mortgages is very sad and speaks again to a moral weakness in US society. Yet where is the punishment? Subprime loans, properly underwritten and serviced, can be of great benefit to borrowers with less than pristine credit. They provide those borrowers with an opportunity to move into America's ownership society. However, those loans must be managed carefully. They require almost constant monitoring to track their performance. Strong personal intervention with the borrower, even before the loan becomes delinquent by just thirty days, is required for a subprime loan to be successful.

Across several presidential administrations, independent agencies and organizations inside and outside government—such as the Government Accountability Office, the Congressional Budget Office, and the US Department of the Treasury—pointed out weaknesses in the oversight and management of the housing GSEs, especially Fannie Mae and Freddie Mac. Conservative and liberal Washington think tanks—including the American Enterprise Institute, the Heritage Foundation, the Financial Services Roundtable, and FM Watch— had been sounding the alarm since the early 1990s. The Brookings Institution and the Center for Responsible Lending also expressed concern about some of the emerging trends, particularly those involving subprime loans and other predatory financing products.

The inattention of both major and minor players neglected the first rule of mortgage banking, which is to provide a good investment to the investor and in doing so to provide the best product and service to the consumer. The mortgage banker's fiduciary responsibility is to do the utmost to protect the investor's best interests from the closing to the payoff or, in rare cases, through a foreclosure and sale of the property. If the banker does the best job for the investor, he or she will also do the best job for the consumer.

Like many of his predecessors, President George W. Bush believed home ownership created wealth and contributed to a stable economy. Therefore, he supported an initiative to raise the Hispanic and African American home-ownership rate by at least 10 percentage points. When he took office, the ownership rate for these two groups stood in the low 40 percent range. Bush hoped to raise that number to the mid-50 percent range. To help accomplish his vision of an ownership society, Bush supported and signed the American Dream Downpayment Act in 2003 to provide lower-income borrowers with money for mortgage loan down payments and closing costs.[3] But his push for expanded home ownership may have given some the false impression that the administration served as an enabler and therefore was not in favor of increased oversight and regulation of the GSEs.

In reality, the administration was a strong advocate for oversight reform, and the concern became greater after the revelation of the GSEs' accounting scandals and their inability to produce accurate financial statements. The president refused to nominate appointees to fill the vacant seats on Fannie Mae's board, hoping his inaction would get congressional bipartisan attention and alert Wall Street and the credit rating agencies to the problem. The Republican US Senate also sought GSE reform, but the political opposition was too difficult to overcome.

Deregulation has often been cited as one of the primary causes of the Great Recession, but the issues are mixed. Clearly, passage of the Graham-Leach-Bliley Act in 1999 was ill-advised. It repealed the parts of the Great Depression–era Glass-Steagall Act that had barred commercial banks from the investment banking and insurance businesses for over sixty years. This opened the door for major mergers and acquisitions that created a number of mega-sized financial holding companies. Citigroup, established by the merger of Citicorp and Travelers Group, led the way, bringing into its fold multiple subsidiaries so it could provide its customers with banking, securities, and insurance services. Graham-Leach-Bliley also placed oversight of these holding companies in the hands of the Federal Reserve. Considering

---

3   Mark M. Zandi, *Financial Shock: A 360° Look at the Subprime Mortgage Implosion, and How to Avoid the Next Financial Crisis* (Upper Saddle River, NJ: FT Press, 2009), 151.

Fed chairman Alan Greenspan's aversion to regulation, preferring instead to let the market police itself, this, too, proved to be a mistake.[4]

History has taught us that it is ill-advised to borrow short and lend long. Long-term fixed-rate mortgages present serious portfolio management problems for deposit-based institutions because of the volatility of interest rates. Although a small fraction of loans last for their entire thirty-year term, the vast majority are prepaid through either a sale of the property or refinancing when interest rates fall. Yet economist Mark Zandi and other observers of the financial crisis failed to recognize that all deposit-based financial institutions, whether banks, thrifts, or credit unions, have limited appetites to hold deposit-based, long-term fixed-rate mortgages in their portfolios. These institutions and the American consumer benefit greatly from participating in the world's capital markets. That explains why mortgages, typically bundled into mortgage-backed securities, are traded in the capital markets to institutional investors and do not rely on deposit-based lending. Through most of their history, bank regulators have barred banks from real estate lending activities to protect depositors and avoid unsound lending practices.

Other observers believe the Basel II Accords, an international treaty that sets risk-based capital standards for banks, was another enabler. This agreement establishes global standards and minimum requirements for the amount of capital banks must hold to cover credit or investment losses by category or level of risk. In addition, arcane accounting rules were employed to evaluate various loans, investments, and securities. Basel II allowed for lower capital requirements based on the credit rating agencies' assessment of the borrower's financial strength. The questionable creditworthiness of some institutions and the flawed analyses by rating agencies allowed for an investment grade rating of AAA on private-label mortgage-backed securities, making them eligible for purchase by even the most conservative investors. Consequently, the capital requirements of Basel II incentivized banks to sell off their mortgages and invest in mortgage-backed securities that offered very attractive yields. But the true risk of those securities, which often contained high-risk subprime loans, was often disguised and minimized.[5]

---

4   Ibid.

5   Ibid., 119–20.

The widely held belief that selling off mortgages in the capital markets relieves the seller of responsibility is patently false. If the loan is sold to one of the GSEs and goes into default, the mortgage banker is, more likely than not, forced to repurchase that loan. These so-called put backs have become epidemic in recent years. It is not uncommon to have a loan "put back" on the seller after five or six years from a borrower with a perfect payment record and no history of late payments or default. In such instances an auditor may have found a "defect" that had no effect on the borrower's ability to repay. In one such case, an auditor disputed the calculation of a co-borrower's income and required the lender to buy back the loan. Another example that could result in a repurchased loan would be an appraiser's inaccurate analysis of a property's neighborhood.

Another area subject to intense scrutiny and criticism has been the role of financial derivatives such as credit swaps and off–balance-sheet structured transactions. These instruments and structures are critically important in maintaining the thirty-year fixed-rate mortgage because they transfer the risk of holding a long-term fixed-rate mortgage to an investor who is willing and able to accept the interest rate risk. This is particularly critical for many members of the American middle class, who need the insurance and comfort of an amortized, fixed-term, fixed-rate mortgage.

During my years of teaching at the School of Mortgage Banking I would ask my students, what is the coolest, newest, and most innovative mortgage program available that is best for the consumer? They often gave one of two answers—the pay-option adjustable-rate mortgage (ARM) or an interest-only loan. The correct answer is the FHA thirty-year fixed-rate mortgage. Virtually all of the "new" products have been tried at one time or another throughout modern mortgage banking history. The thirty-year fixed-rate loan has stood the test of time and become the staple home financing tool. However, it is unique in the world. The only other country that offers the same loan structure is Denmark. The thirty-year fixed-rate mortgage offers the middle-class home buyer a long-term, stable payment that gradually builds equity over time.

But while this loan product provides great benefits to borrowers, it carries multiple risks for investors. Bethany McLean and Joe Nocera explain these risks:

Though a thirty-year fixed mortgage may seem simple to a borrower, mortgages come full of complex risks for investors. Thirty years, after all, is a long time. In the space of three decades, not only is it likely that interest rates will change, but—who knows?—the borrowers might fall on hard times and default. In addition, mortgages come with something called prepayment risk. Because borrowers have the right to prepay their mortgages, investors can't be sure that the cash flow from the mortgage will stay at the level they were expecting. The prepayment risk diminishes the value of the bond [mortgage].[6]

Another consideration is the risk of having to reinvest the funds in a lower–interest rate environment if the mortgagee pays off the loan prematurely. The borrower has enjoyed the benefit of a stable, fixed payment over time while retaining the option to get out of the mortgage while the investor—an insurance company, pension fund, or other—has no option. Because the terms of a thirty-year fixed-rate loan give the prepayment option to the borrower, financial engineers on Wall Street began devising ways to minimize interest rate risk to investors by tailoring the cash flows through mortgage-backed securities. Investors could be partially insulated by creating various derivatives. By breaking up the cash flows into tranches or portions, the borrower still gets a long-term fixed-rate loan, but the cash flows meet the needs of short-term money market funds, investors seeking five- to seven-year protection, and long-term bond buyers.

It is critical to understand this transfer of both credit and interest rate risk. The bank or the mortgage banker who sells the loan operates under a complicated set of warrants, pledges, and requirements in the contract with the purchaser of the loan relative to the quality and due diligence of the borrower. If the loan suffers a first payment default, fraud is almost always the cause. In general, if a loan experiences an early payment default or a defect is discovered, even if discovery occurs years later, the originating lender is obligated to repurchase the loan. For many years some investors would buy these loans at a sharp discount and either hold them or sell them to a "scratch and dent" investor. The latter investors evaluated the risk and determined whether the defect was material; in most cases they could correct the defect. After 2008 the number of investors who would buy these loans decreased

---

6   Bethany McLean and Joe Nocera, *All the Devils Are Here: The Hidden History of the Financial Crisis Portfolio* (New York: Penguin/Portfolio, 2010), 7.

significantly, and now the originating lender often finds it difficult to resell such loans.

Another factor that contributed to the mortgage crisis was the increased use of credit scores as a measure of consumer credit risk. Their use continues to be an important tool in making a creditworthiness decision but should not be relied upon exclusively. A credit score is a predictive model, based on past history, that demonstrates over time how consumers have handled their credit. Credit scores range from a high of 850 to a low of 450. The higher the score, the better the creditor. In general, through 2009 a credit score below 620 was considered subprime; anyone with a score above 700 was considered a prime borrower. However, each lender set its own risk threshold levels, and many lenders used their own internal predictive models with mortgage loans, applying proprietary attributes of credit, income stability, appraised value, and local real estate markets to predict loan performance. Studies have shown that loans granted to borrowers with credit scores between 580 and 619 experience default rates two times greater than loans to those with credit scores of 620 and above.[7] No one should have been surprised by the escalation of foreclosures and the free fall of real estate markets following the boom in subprime loans.

However, one reform in 1989 removed the safety and soundness regulation of the savings and loans from the Federal Home Loan Bank to the newly created Office of Thrift Supervision (OTS) in the Department of the Treasury. But once again the regulator continued to fail in its oversight of the thrift industry. The failure of Seattle's Washington Mutual Savings Bank, an old and respected community institution, is a classic example. Its rapid and unrestrained growth coupled with its entry into the subprime business created a recipe for collapse. By its very nature, the relationship between regulator and regulated contains tension. The regulator needs to fully understand the enterprise it is regulating, understand and appreciate its business model, and interpret the regulations according to the law. Therefore, safety and soundness examinations should be conducted by seasoned professionals.[8]

---

7   Fishelson-Holstine, "Role of Credit Scoring," 276.

8   "Housing Finance: Potential Reforms to Mortgage Markets," Budget Model (Philadelphia: Penn Wharton University of Pennsylvania, November 22, 2016), accessed May 9, 2017, http://www.budgetmodel.wharton.upenn.edu/issues/2016/11/14/housing-finance-potential-reforms-to-mortgage-markets.

As stated earlier, prior to 2003 Fannie and Freddie's duopoly set the standard utilized by most investors as evidence that the GSEs' market share was approximately 65–70 percent of home mortgages written in the country throughout the 1990s. However, beginning in 2007, their share increased, reaching a peak of nearly 95 percent in 2009. By 2014 it had declined to an estimated 75 percent.[9] Regardless of whether the loans were eligible for purchase by these two GSEs, their standards became the roadmap for, and established the protocols of, the industry. Because the two agencies controlled such a large market share and were the beneficiaries of private mortgage insurance, they held significant clout over the mortgage banking industry and their approved seller servicer lenders. The publishing of Fannie Mae's underwriting criteria was seen and applied by the industry as gospel, "the 10 Commandments of underwriting."[10] According to a General Accounting Office (GAO) report to Congress, the GSEs' "federal ties caused investors to behave like insured depositors who believe their investments to be very safe."[11] Both factors contributed to the meltdown of the real estate market that triggered the Great Recession.

When the affordable housing goals expanded in response to actions taken by the Department of Housing and Urban Development (HUD) and the US Congress, Fannie and Freddie adopted more aggressive business practices, which created an unexpected paradox—lower interest rates in the capital markets. Consequently, to increase the revenue on their portfolios, both GSEs bought lower credit quality products within parameters the computer models asserted were safe from loss yet gave both agencies a higher yield to compensate for the higher risk. This paradox enabled the creation of the subprime opportunity and allowed others to enter the low end of the housing market with aggressive products that were unsuitable for middle-class wage earners. This, too, contributed to the real estate collapse and the broader economic catastrophe.

In 2005 speculative buying began to demonstrate cracks in markets such as Boston and San Diego. Flippers—speculators who purchase properties and then improve their appearance with new paint, appliances, and other

9   Ibid.

10   Acharya et al., *Guaranteed to Fail*, 21.

11   General Accounting Office, *Government Sponsored Enterprises: The Government's Exposure to Risks* (Washington, DC: General Accounting Office, 1990), 9.

relatively minor upgrades—found that the properties began to stay on the market for longer periods. A slight upward move in interest rates caused some borrowers, particularly flippers, to default.[12]

In general, most borrowers nearing default will try to preserve their home. However, that is not necessarily the case for properties with subprime loans, investment properties, and second homes. Many of these borrowers have little financial investment in the properties. If they find themselves struggling to make the payments on their primary residence, they will have little reservation about letting go of the second home or the investment property.

Some adjustable-rate loan products also contributed to the foreclosure crisis. For example, a 2–27 ARM began with a payment based on a low "teaser" interest rate that lasted for two years. Then the loan's interest rate, and the corresponding monthly payment, was routinely adjusted upward over a relatively short time frame until it reached the prevailing interest rate. Many of these loans were used to finance fix and flip purchases and other speculative ventures. Debt-to-income ratios were aggressive; and for two-income households any change in job, income, marital status, or health, as well as death, could cause the borrower to march right to the sheriff's foreclosure sale.[13]

Another mortgage product, the pay-option ARM, a World Savings product, is a classic example of a loan program that is sensible for only a very limited number of sophisticated borrowers. Like the 2-27ARM, it begins with a low teaser rate. But this loan allows the borrower the option of making the full monthly payment or paying a lesser amount; the difference is then added to the principal. This is an example of negative amortization. If the borrower elects to continually pay the minimum, the borrower's equity can evaporate in a short period of time. Both Washington Mutual and World Savings promoted this product heavily. During the initial evaluation of this product for World Savings, I was told that it was designed especially for upper-income borrowers, such as engineers and similar professionals. It was not intended for a typical small business owner-operator such as the proprietor of a nail salon.

When the principal stockholders and owners of Golden West Financial, the parent company of World Savings, perceived a change in the real estate

---

12 Zandi, *Financial Shock*, 16.

13 Ibid., 16–17.

market, the institution sold to Wachovia Bank. As the real estate markets collapsed and the negative amortization erased any equity in the properties, borrowers began to default en mass. Wachovia was so greatly weakened that the regulators merged this well-established southern bank into Wells Fargo.

Wachovia's strategy had been to buy a West Coast retail banking network, which World Savings provided. The apparent lack of a thorough due diligence examination of World's operation resulted in disaster. Instead of Wachovia gaining a national presence through a profitable acquisition, the red ink flowed and the outcome was a regulatory takeover.

Washington Mutual offered the same product and had the distinct honor of being the largest bank failure in American history. It was taken over by J. P. Morgan Chase. During the time I managed account relationships with both World Savings and Washington Mutual, it became apparent that World Savings was always looking to diversify and manage its mortgage credit risk with its selected partners. For many years, both World Savings and Washington Mutual maintained solid credit discipline, but, like many other institutions, they too drank the Kool-Aid. They believed that given the population growth and demographic changes, the housing market would continue to expand and demand would remain robust for many years.

So, what can be done to avoid many of these problems in the future? If a philosopher king ruled over mortgage banking, he would order a number of measures to better serve the consumer/borrower, the mortgage investor, and the US taxpayer. Unfortunately, there are as many prescriptions and remedies as there are industry observers.

SOLUTIONS

Voluntary Loan Modification and Principal Write-Downs

Mark Zandi recommends a number of options, many of which have been adopted by the Dodd-Frank legislation and the Consumer Financial Protection Bureau (CFPB). Yet many of his recommendations are not new; they have actually been industry practice for the past 150 years. Others such as a national judicial foreclosure law are totally impractical and damage both the industry and consumers. Colorado's unique public trustee system, which provides consumer protection with a judicial review, is a major contributing factor to the state's housing recovery beginning in late 2012.

A related contributor to the foreclosure crisis of 2008–12 is the 1986 Tax Reform Act, signed into law by President Ronald Reagan. The act eliminated the deduction of interest on all consumer loans except first and second mortgages. No longer could consumers deduct the interest they paid on car loans, credit cards, and other consumer debt. As a consequence, consumers looked for other ways to finance their larger purchases, and commercial banks gradually gained additional authority to make more aggressive second mortgage and home equity loans.

Beginning in the 1990s, homeowners could use the equity in their property as an automated teller machine. They extracted the equity value of their homes not just for home improvements but also to pay for education expenses, vacations, cars, and other expensive items. At the time, no one seemed to recognize the magnitude of the problems that could and did arise from these borrowing practices. As property values began to decline, overextended homeowners had little alternative other than entering into foreclosure. Together these two factors, overextended borrowers and declining property values, helped create a huge moral hazard and a major financial crisis.

When homeowners became overextended by accessing their home's equity that action impacted savings. The savings rate reached a twenty-five-year low, falling from 12 percent in the early 1980s to 0 percent by 2006. In fact, with the increased borrowing through home equity loans and credit card debt, the estimated savings rate for lower- and middle-income households dropped to –10 percent, resulting in reduced net worth and negative equity.[14] A problem that created enormous difficulty in developing programs to help distressed homeowners, such as the FHA Secure and Hope Now programs, was caused by second mortgage lenders who were reluctant to modify or subordinate their position and their unwillingness to allow loan modifications.[15]

A voluntary mortgage write-down program, in which a portion of the principal is written off or forgiven and the remainder is reamortized, can greatly benefit troubled borrowers, but each case must be judged individually. Remember that the investor is dealing in some measure with the savings of individuals and families, so write-downs should be used sparingly. Forgiveness of principal is an indirect gift from a saver to a borrower. Credit-savvy

---

14 Ibid., 218.

15 Ibid., 194–95.

investors know and understand such workouts. The challenge is to avoid a moral hazard by creating an environment that gives borrowers the option to leverage the benefits of increasing equity and thereby accumulate more debt or to easily walk away when the market turns and housing prices fall.

Zandi points out that while there is no easy solution, many of the available remedies for troubled mortgages involve a commitment by the government to provide taxpayer funds. Those who have such mortgages should not rely on government policy, however. Instead, the servicer, after a thorough examination of the troubled borrower's ability to meet the terms of a loan modification that reduces the principal amount owed, should make an informed recommendation to the investor regarding the borrower's prospects of meeting his or her obligations under the new arrangement with the investor. The reality was that many troubled borrowers were unable to meet the terms of their modification during the years of the Great Recession.[16] Often, those borrowers failed because their loan modification only reduced the interest rate; the modification did not reduce the principal to match the decline in property values.[17]

Home Buyer Counseling, Consumer Education, and Financial Literacy

The home buying process can be daunting, confusing, and a total mystery even to the most sophisticated buyers. The amount of regulation and the number of required disclosures have increased manyfold since the passage of Dodd-Frank and the establishment of the CFPB. The question remains, do borrowers understand the documents they are signing and the obligation to which they have committed themselves for the next thirty years?

Zandi makes a strong argument for financial literacy and home buyer education. Most members of the financial service industry agree that personal financial management should be a mandatory part of all high school curriculums and should be taught long before an individual acquires a student loan, a car loan, or the bigger responsibility of a home loan.[18]

---

16   Ibid., 233.

17   Ibid., 195.

18   Ibid., 236–37.

Beginning with the widespread use of counseling in the early 1970s, it has become an article of faith in the industry that counseling does work. The Research Institute for Housing America (RIHA) funded a study to look at the benefits of counseling to determine the success and failure of such programs. The resulting RIHA paper was a study of studies and reached the conclusion that research on the "effectiveness of counseling remains under-developed." The original goal of the programs was based on the assumption that education and information from a trusted source (HUD) would improve decision making and the ability to deal with issues that limit the borrower's ability to repay.[19]

HUD and the Neighborhood Reinvestment Corporation along with mortgage lenders and foundations have been financially supportive of home-ownership education. Along with home purchase, foreclosure, and default counseling (also known as post-closing counseling), programs also exist for housing rehabilitation, reverse mortgages, and homelessness.

Pre-purchase homeownership counseling was a key part of most community mortgage programs from the 1990s into the period 2003–5, when the programs were dropped by the GSEs for competitive reasons. At that time the programs began to change direction toward default counseling and foreclosure prevention.[20] Sometimes these pre-purchase counseling efforts were done late in the process, immediately before closing. Often, they lacked substance and were used only to comply with program guidelines; they provided little else.

However, the successful foreclosure prevention activities of the Colorado Housing and Finance Authority (CHFA) are impressive. Because of its business model and corporate structure, the organization has a key advantage over many lenders in that it knows its borrowers and can contact them quickly when signs of delinquency arise. CHFA can then implement strategies to keep its borrowers paying and in their homes.

Consumer Protection

Prior to Dodd-Frank and the CFPB, multiple agencies existed at the federal, state, and local levels to oversee the operations of the residential

19 Collins and O'Rourke, *Homeownership Education*, 7.
20 Ibid.

mortgage banking industry. Depository institutions fall under the purview of the Department of the Treasury and the Federal Deposit Insurance Corporation. National banks are overseen by the Office of Comptroller of the Currency, while the Office of Thrift Supervision regulates savings institutions. The Federal Reserve System, the states' attorneys general, and state banking authorities, along with product-specific regulatory agencies such as HUD, the Federal Trade Commission, and the Securities and Exchange Commission, all regulate residential mortgage finance in one jurisdiction or another.

HUD, through its various agencies including the FHA, Ginnie Mae, and now the Federal Housing Finance Agency, exercises considerable power as a regulator. As much as these agencies oversee and regulate the mortgage industry and its business practices, the contractual relationships with FHA, Fannie Mae, and Freddie Mac serve as hands-on "regulators" of the day-to-day activities of the mortgage banking operation. Notwithstanding the corporate structure—bank, thrift, credit union, or insurance company—the GSEs impact every aspect of the enterprise. All of these agencies were charged with the regulation, oversight, and ultimate protection of mortgage consumers and their institutional investors.

The Great Recession changed all that. In 2010 Congress passed, and the president signed, the Dodd-Frank Wall Street Reform and Consumer Protection Act. This legislation created two agencies designed to prevent a repeat of the 2008 financial crisis. The first is the Financial Stability Oversight Council. The council's role is (1) to examine the market and search for potential systemic or catastrophic risks to the economy and (2) to avoid the possibility of a "too big to fail" bailout. The act further requires institutions to develop a plan for their own liquidation in the event of another crisis.[21]

Second, and more important for the mortgage industry, the creation of the Consumer Financial Protection Bureau marked a major change. The bureau operates as an independent agency under the Federal Reserve umbrella, which eliminates congressional control and oversight. It also has extensive powers to oversee and regulate virtually every aspect of the mortgage industry. Yet because the CFPB has no oversight, its regulations are not vetted

---

21 Mitchel Kider, Michael Kieval, and Leslie Sowers, *Consumer Protection and Mortgage Regulation under Dodd Frank* (New York: Thomson Reuters/Westlaw, 2013), 3.

by the Office of Management and Budget. Its unlimited authority, lack of transparency, and zero accountability to Congress have caused great concern to many inside and outside the industry. With literally thousands of pages of regulations affecting every facet of mortgage lending, it will take several years and another housing cycle to truly assess the CFPB's effectiveness. In the meantime, the process of obtaining a mortgage will be more costly, time-consuming, and cumbersome.

One of the new rules promulgated by the CFPB is designed to protect borrowers. Lenders, notwithstanding the safe harbor provisions that set lending guidelines, must now determine and in fact "predict" the borrower's ability to repay—a worthy and prudent but unattainable goal. Nevertheless, if a loan enters foreclosure and it is determined that the lender did not exercise "proper due diligence" in establishing the borrower's ability to repay, the borrower may sue to have any related foreclosure vacated.

The first high-profile consumer adversely affected by the new CFPB was former Federal Reserve chairman Ben Bernanke. One rule of the CFPB, entitled "the ability to repay," delineates in great detail the processes a lender must employ to determine a potential borrower's ability to repay based on his job history. The rule states that the lender can face liability if he or she has made an error in determining the borrower's ability to repay, and the recourse for the borrower is to have a foreclosure set aside. One requirement for a self-employed person is a verifiable two-year history of financial success. Chairman Bernanke applied for his refinance a few months after his term at the Fed ended. His new career as a consultant had just begun. Unfortunately, he had not established a two-year pattern of financial success in his new role and therefore was declined by his lender.

The CFPB has great authority to levy fines and penalties against lenders for noncompliance with the aforementioned ability to repay rule. However, that rule is only one small part of the innumerable regulations to which institutions are required to adhere for compliance purposes.

AFTERMATH

Fannie and Freddie: A Eulogy

Conservatorship has put Fannie and Freddie on life support until Congress exercises their do not resuscitate clauses. While these two enterprises operate under their independent regulator, the Federal Housing Finance Agency (FHFA), and provide income to the Treasury, their final disposition is not clear. Numerous ideas exist about how big or how small the role of government should be within the housing finance system. Questions remain about the scope of the taxpayer guarantee and the level of any future potential bailout or replacement of either agency. How much private capital can move into the space formerly occupied by Fannie and Freddie, should they disappear and under whatever circumstances, is also unknown. Clearly, a conflict exists if the FHFA is also charged with setting standards and goals for affordable housing.

In 2014 Senators Tim Johnson, a Democrat from South Dakota, and Mike Crapo, a Republican from Idaho, sponsored legislation that would have phased out Fannie and Freddie and replaced them with a new government agency. The proposed new federal agency, the Federal Mortgage Insurance Corporation, would have issued the same guarantee function to investors that Fannie and Freddie do today. It would not have held a portfolio of mortgages, although it would have had an affordable housing component aimed at low-income and underserved markets. However, many Senate leaders voted against the Johnson-Crapo Bill because they felt the affordable housing component did not go far enough.

Had the bill been approved, the regulatory role of the FHFA would have become part of the Federal Mortgage Insurance Corporation. The corporation would have had the authority to set capital standards and regulate mortgage insurance companies and mortgage originators. Johnson-Crapo called for the phasing out of Fannie and Freddie over a period of five years. They were to be replaced with what is characterized as a securitization platform that would have resembled the current Fannie and Freddie conduits or special purpose entities.

Unlike the current architecture of Fannie and Freddie, the platform would have assumed no interest rate or credit risk. It would have issued securities, managed cash flows between servicers and investors, and performed master servicer and bond administrative functions, including surveillance and quality control. Private issuers would have had access to the platform. It would also have set industry standards on data and would have functioned as a utility. Cost savings would have been achieved by consolidating Fannie and Freddie's backroom operations and removing portfolio management from the Federal Mortgage Insurance Corporation's activities when the liquidation was completed.

Other proposals call for regional institutions much like the national mortgage associations proposed in the 1934 National Housing Act. Others have suggested reconfiguring the Federal Home Loan Bank System, a quasi retreat to the original purpose of Freddie Mac.

Resurrection of the GSEs

To use an automobile analogy, why would people replace broken-down vehicles (Fannie and Freddie) with an unproven new, expensive, and possibly high-maintenance vehicle (Federal Mortgage Insurance Corporation) if they already have a perfectly good second vehicle (Ginnie Mae) in the garage? Hiring and staffing a new government agency and building a new regulatory structure from scratch would be counterproductive and a needless expenditure of taxpayer dollars.

A program floated in the first decade of the twenty-first century, Ginnie Mae Choice, incorporates many of the ideas of the Federal Mortgage Insurance Corporation without building a new bureaucracy. Fannie and Freddie, as currently constituted, would be phased out in an orderly disposition over five years. Many of their systems and staff could be merged into organizations trimmed to meet the new mortgage-backed security system. In addition, the full faith and credit of the Ginnie Mae guarantee would stay in place. Guarantee fees would remain the same, and there would be a band of FHA insurance above any lower-level, first dollar lost, private mortgage insurance. As currently anticipated, a lower-cost, leaner guarantee system would be established that would be limited to credit risk that could be more accurately determined; interest rate risk, the cause of Fannie Mae's insolvency in the 1980s, would be eliminated.

In a 2002 study conducted by Susan M. Wachter on behalf of Freddie Mac, Wachter clearly states her opposition to Ginnie Mae Choice yet acknowledges the substantial benefits of Ginnie Mae as a single guarantor. Referring to the program, she claims that it "brings a high degree of standardization of products and securities available, limits both the types of mortgages and the types of systems of securities eligible for credit enhancement, reduces information costs for investors and creates more liquid markets. Standardization generally reduces investors' uncertainty and would tend to create more liquid markets and further reduces the investors' exposure to credit and systemic risk."[22]

In terms of being a prudent safety and soundness regulator overseeing the FHA, a new guarantor of mortgage-backed securities should be totally independent. If Ginnie Mae Choice, the Federal Mortgage Insurance Corporation, or something similar is revived as the eventual replacement for the GSEs, then this agency needs to avoid duplication and maintain functional independence from inside the Department of the Treasury.

CONCLUDING THOUGHTS

Through these pages we have told the story of the men and women of the mortgage banking industry beginning in the years following the Civil War. We have covered their progress to the present day as they have made significant contributions to America's businesses, individuals, and families—whether on the farm or in cities. Hundreds of thousands of professionals in the mortgage banking industry work every day to represent the best interests of consumers and mortgage investors. In doing so, they provide a valuable service. As former MBA president Frederick P. Champ stated, "Their [mortgage bankers'] success or failure depended upon the exercise of sound judgment in their efforts to bring the distant investor and local borrower together, to the end that ownership of real property might rebound to the benefit of all parties concerned."[23]

To this end, policymakers must understand that thousands of pages of new forms, regulations, and penalties cannot repeal the laws of nature, science, and economics. For borrowers in western Kansas who suffered through the droughts of the 1890s and the 1930s, for those who suffered through the Great Depression or the recessions of the 1980s that affected Detroit's auto industry and the oil patch states, those regulations and forms printed on mountains of paper would not have prevented the ensuing foreclosures. The real challenge is to understand and manage risk and, when the inevitable happens, to respond quickly to help distressed borrowers and preserve investors' capital.

22 Susan M. Wachter, "GNMA Choice: The Public Policy Issues," *FreddieMac*, accessed October 11, 2014, http://www.freddiemac.com/news/pdf/gnma_0318.pdf, 12.

23 Frederick P. Champ, untitled, *Mortgage Banker* (November 1970): 139.

Economic cycles, like the weather, are largely unpredictable. What is known is that loan performance is based on the borrower's employment and earning capacity. The loss of a job, a divorce, death, or a catastrophic health incident are virtually impossible to predict. Pages of regulations, laws, and penalties will not change the future except possibly to limit the opportunities for future generations.

That is why Miles Colean, respected housing economist, policymaker, and consultant to the MBA, accurately summarized that mortgages are risky.

Epilogue

This book could be classified under multiple genres—personal memoir, real estate finance, and several subcategories of history, principally western and economic. However, it is mostly a saga of people searching for a place of their own and the people who financed them. Place matters; it is critical to personal, family, and community identity and for both financial security and social stability. This book is a discussion of the evolution of an industry from agricultural lending on the frontier and urban real estate investment during the pioneer era to the quest for homeownership that emerged in the late nineteenth century and continues to this day. At the center of this story is the critical role of mortgage bankers in making development and home ownership possible.

During the second half of the twentieth century, the citizens of Colorado, particularly Denver, witnessed in quiet amazement the almost imperceptible changes in land use in the varying areas of downtown. Redevelopment found new purposes for older office buildings, hotels, and warehouses. Some found new life as residential properties, some were converted to retail, others were

DOI: 10.5876/9781607326236.c015

revamped into newer, more modern (at least on the inside) office spaces. New buildings stand in the place of some of the dusty vacant lots whose prior highest and best use for eight Sundays every fall was parking for fans attending Denver Bronco games. Gentrification has transformed neighborhoods, perhaps the most prominent being the Highland neighborhood just across the South Platte River from lower downtown.

Sorely missed is Elitch Gardens, the summer home of some of America's greatest bands, and the Elitch Theater where Douglas Fairbanks, Sarah Bernhardt, and Tyrone Power were among the earliest performers to take the stage. Others followed, including Grace Kelly, Robert Redford, and Lana Turner, with the final performance starring Victor Borge. But change also brings many delights. In 1996, after Elitch Gardens had reopened in its current location, Perry Rose LLC, a real estate development firm, purchased the property where the original park stood under the condition that Elitch Theater and the carousel's shell be preserved; they remain and stand as the centerpiece of the new Highland urban community.

Coors Field, home of the Colorado Rockies baseball team, replaced a property I managed in the 1960s. In 2007 it hosted game three of the World Series. Light rail has made accessing the city's sports and entertainment venues easy and affordable. Residents from across the metro area leave their cars behind to attend baseball games at Coors Field; hockey games, basketball games, and a host of other events at the Pepsi Center; and Bronco football games at Sports Authority Field. Another main stop for the light rail system is the Denver Center for the Performing Arts, where a number of venues offer a wide variety of concerts, plays, comedy shows, and other entertainment. Redevelopment has made downtown Denver more vibrant than ever.

Union Station was the highlight of 2014 for Denver's LoDo neighborhood. Its restoration marks another triumph for historic preservation. The original Union Station, built by the Union Depot and Railroad Company, opened in 1881, eleven years after the first train rolled into Denver. Until then, each of the six railroads that serviced Denver had had its own station. The complex that connected those individual stations was quickly rebuilt following a fire in 1894 that destroyed much of the main building. In 1912 Union Station's owner, the Denver Union Terminal Railway Company, a private partnership created by the independent railroads serving Denver at that time, started a remodel that took two years to complete. The end result was the building that still stands at the end of Seventeenth Street.[1]

In 1958 Stapleton International Airport displaced Union Station in having the greatest volume of arriving and departing passenger traffic. As Americans gravitated to faster airline travel and the major railroads serving Denver abandoned passenger service, Union Station declined. Eventually, Amtrak became the nation's primary passenger railroad. The Denver and Rio Grande Western Railroad (the Rio Grande) continued to operate the California Zephyr as the Rio Grande Zephyr three days a week until daily service was restored when Amtrak took over the route. Other than the occasional resurrection of a passenger excursion, such as the Ski Train from Denver to Winter Park or the *Denver Post* Cheyenne Frontier Days Special Train, the glory days of the railroads are gone forever, having become just a fond memory for those who experienced the heyday of railroading.

With the demise of passenger train service, Union Station might have been demolished, just as many other historic buildings succumbed to the wrecking ball of urban renewal. However, the efforts of Denver's historic preservation community were rewarded when the property was approved for inclusion on the National Register of Historic Places. During the late 1970s the owner, the Union Terminal Railway Company, invested $300,000 to renovate the office spaces surrounding the main waiting room, known as the Great Hall. A few years later the company spent another $100,000 to repaint the Great Hall and re-gild the chandeliers.[2]

Journalist Bill Hemingway characterized Union Station as a "jilted bride" after the Greyhound and Trailways bus companies built a separate bus terminal.[3] The bride stood waiting at the altar hoping the concept of becoming a regional transportation hub that had lingered through various proposals for nearly twenty years would reappear. In 2001 the Regional Transportation District (RTD) purchased Union Station and the following year began work on a master plan. Three years later the plan determined that "Denver Union Station will be a multimodal transportation hub of international significance and a prominent and distinctive gateway to

1   Bill Hemingway, "Rebirth of Lower Downtown," *Empire Magazine of the Denver Post*, July 12, 1981, 15.
2   Ibid.
3   Ibid.

downtown Denver and the region." The plan combined regional bus and rail service.[4]

The intergovernmental agreement that resulted in RTD's purchase of Union Station and its 19.5 acres went beyond the creation of a multimodal transportation hub. It called for a mixed-use redevelopment that would create a twenty-four-hour Activity Center. The agencies involved included RTD, the City and County of Denver, the Denver Regional Council of Governments, and the Colorado Department of Transportation. They selected the Union Station Neighborhood Company as a master developer for the $500 million project. The plan called for 2,000 new apartments, a 400-room hotel, and 850,000 square feet of office and retail space. The project spurred additional investment and excitement in the neighborhood.[5] Today, the Great Hall serves as the hotel's lobby.

The project received a $300 million federal grant from the US Department of Transportation to help fund the development of the regional light rail system and the heavy rail commuter tracks that will eventually provide service to Denver International Airport and other Front Range communities. Additional funding was provided by RTD following voter approval of the Fast Tracks light rail plan in 2004, "one of the largest single mass transit expansion programs in the country."[6]

Preservation, redevelopment, and changing land use have not been limited to Denver or even to urban areas. Land trusts, businesses, foundations, and nonprofits, in partnership with local and state governments, are using various tools of conservation finance to preserve farms and working ranches along with valuable watersheds and wildlife habitats. The Great Outdoors Colorado Trust Fund, financed largely from the proceeds of the state's lottery, has provided $2.5 billion for recreation, parks, wildlife, and open space.

Although this book, part memoir and part history, spans 150 years, we recognize some obvious omissions. We did not discuss the establishment and importance of real estate investment trusts, sovereign wealth funds, and

---

4   Denver Union Station Project Authority, "Union Station Master Plan," accessed March 3, 2015, http://www.denverunionstation.org/index.php?option=com_content&view=article&id=60&Itemid=48.

5   Union Station Neighborhood Company, "The History: Timeline," accessed December, 1, 2015, http://unionstationdenver.com/history/#/timeline.

6   Ibid.

other global investment funds. We only briefly discussed a few of the area's New Town developments while virtually ignoring the Platinum Triangle, Stapleton, and Fitzsimmons redevelopments—multi-billion-dollar infill projects that contributed to the transformation of the region. These are beyond our scope to speak about authoritatively. Perhaps someone else will tell their story. We acknowledged other subjects that deserve considerable attention, but we could not explore them in depth. We apologize if our omissions have left anyone in a lurch.

The amount of public and private capital coming into Colorado projects now exceeds the scope and grandeur of the Rocky Mountains, whose resplendent vista we embrace across the Front Range and from every angle as we travel throughout the state. The continued investment in Colorado results from the hard work of the men and women of the real estate finance industry and matches the stature of Pike's Peak and the other Colorado mountains that soar into the state's endless sky.

Appendix A

FHA Mortgage Insurance Programs

This is a summarization of information taken from the Department of Housing and Urban Development (HUD) website portal.hud.gov. Follow the links to single family, healthcare programs, and multi-family for more complete information about these and other loan programs.

NATIONAL HOUSING ACT OF 1934, AS AMENDED
SINGLE-FAMILY PROGRAMS
TITLE I
HOME AND PROPERTY IMPROVEMENT LOANS

Provides mortgage insurance on loans for alterations and repairs and for site improvements of single-family homes, including manufactured homes. Loans on multi-family structures are limited to building alteration and repairs; they cannot be used for site improvements.

DOI: 10.5876/9781607326236.c016

TITLE II
SECTION 203(B) MORTGAGE INSURANCE
FOR ONE- TO FOUR-FAMILY HOMES

Insures mortgages made by qualified lenders to people purchasing or refinancing a primary residence. Insured mortgages can be used to finance the purchase of new or existing one- to four-family housing, as well as to refinance debt. Down payment can be as little as 3.5 percent. Maximum allowable mortgage amount can vary by location.

POWERSAVER PILOT 203(K) LOANS

Allows eligible home buyers and homeowners access to low-cost financing when they include energy-saving upgrades with their home improvement project. The energy-efficient upgrades must cost at least $3,500 and can include a variety of items, such as an HVAC system, windows, insulation, caulking, and solar or other renewable technologies.

STREAMLINED 203(K) MORTGAGE

Allows home buyers and homeowners to finance the purchase or refinancing of a house and include up to an additional $35,000 in their mortgage to repair, improve, or upgrade the property. Home buyers can make their new home move-in ready by remodeling the kitchen, painting the interior, purchasing new carpet, or making other improvements. Homeowners can make property repairs and improvements or prepare their home for sale.

SECTION 203(K) REHAB MORTGAGE INSURANCE

Enables home buyers and homeowners to finance the purchase or refinancing of a house and the cost of its rehabilitation through a single mortgage or to finance the rehabilitation of their existing homes. The property must be at least one year old, and the cost of the rehabilitation must be at least $5,000. The extent of the rehabilitation may range from relatively minor (though exceeding $5,000 in cost) to virtual reconstruction as long as the existing foundation system remains in place.

SECTION 235 SINGLE-FAMILY PROGRAM

This program provided an interest subsidy for low-income borrowers. The FHA subsidized the amount of interest charged under the rate dictated by the terms of the loan to as low as 1 percent. For example, if the loan was written at 8 percent and the borrower qualified for enough assistance to pay only 1 percent, FHA would pay the balance, in this case 7 percent. Borrowers were required to re-qualify annually. The program was replaced by Section 8 housing vouchers.

SECTION 237 HOME BUYER COUNSELING PROGRAM

This program, designed for first-time home buyers, requires pre-purchase counseling and additional counseling for delinquent or defaulting borrowers. It also requires counseling for borrowers applying for FHA reverse mortgages.

SECTION 8 HOUSING CHOICE VOUCHER PROGRAM

The Section 8 Voucher program assists very-low-income families, the elderly, and the disabled in affording decent, safe, and sanitary housing in the private market. Public housing agencies determine a payment standard that is the amount generally needed to rent a moderately priced dwelling unit in the local housing market and that is used to calculate the amount of housing assistance a family will receive. Eligible families can then find any housing, including the unit they reside in currently, that meets the program standard. However, the payment standard does not limit or affect the amount of rent a landlord may charge or the family may pay. A family that receives a housing voucher can select a unit with rent below or above the payment standard. The housing voucher family must pay 30 percent of its monthly adjusted gross income for rent and utilities; if the unit rent is greater than the payment standard, the family is required to pay the additional amount. By law, whenever a family moves to a new unit where the rent exceeds the payment standard, the family may not pay more than 40 percent of its adjusted monthly income for rent.

Eligible properties: single-family homes, townhouses, and apartments.

SECTION 248 INSURED MORTGAGES ON INDIAN RESERVATIONS AND OTHER RESTRICTED LANDS

The 248 Program provides for FHA-insured loans to low- and moderate-income Native Americans to buy, build, or rehabilitate houses on Indian land. These loans are fundamentally the same as regular Section 203(b) loans except that they are only available to Native Americans on Indian land. Up to 97 percent of the purchase price can be financed.

Although the tribe is not a party to the mortgage, the program cannot operate without the tribe's active participation because there are program requirements that must be satisfied by the tribe before the FHA will insure mortgages on the reservation.

Eligible borrowers: any Native American who wants to live on Indian land and intends to use the mortgage property as the primary residence and who meets the standard FHA credit qualifications.

Eligible properties: any existing single-family home, including FHA-approved manufactured or mobile homes and new construction. The property must meet the property standards required by the FHA, including water, sewer, and electrical systems. If new construction, the plans need to be approved by the FHA.

HOME EQUITY CONVERSION MORTGAGES FOR SENIORS

Also known as reverse mortgages, FHA's Home Equity Conversion Mortgage (HECM) program is designed to supplement seniors' income by converting the equity they have accrued in their home into a lump-sum cash payment or a series of periodic payments.

Borrower eligibility requirements: At least one of the homeowners (if a couple) must be age sixty-two or older, have paid off the mortgage or paid down a considerable amount, and be currently living in the home. The borrower cannot be delinquent on any federal debt and must continue to make timely payment of ongoing property charges, such as property taxes, insurance, and homeowners' association fees. The borrower must also participate in a consumer information session given by a HUD-approved HECM counselor.

Eligible properties: single-family homes, including one- to four-unit properties, units in HUD-approved condominium projects, and FHA-approved manufactured homes.

FHA MULTI-FAMILY HOUSING AND HEALTHCARE
FACILITIES FINANCING PROGRAMS
SECTION 207—MORTGAGE INSURANCE FOR RENTAL HOUSING

Provides mortgage loan insurance to finance the construction or rehabilitation of a broad range of rental housing. Section 207 mortgage insurance, although still authorized, is no longer used for new construction and substantial rehabilitation. It is, however, the primary insurance vehicle for the Section 223(f) refinancing program. Multi-family new construction and substantial rehabilitation projects are currently insured Section 221(d)(4) programs. The intent of the program is to increase the supply of quality, reasonably priced rental housing for middle-income families.

Eligible properties: new construction, substantial rehabilitation, semi-detached walk-up or elevator-type structures with five or more units.

SECTION 207—MORTGAGE INSURANCE FOR
MANUFACTURED HOME PARKS

Provides mortgage loan insurance to facilitate the construction or substantial rehabilitation of multi-family manufactured home parks. The intent of the program is to promote the creation of manufactured home communities by increasing the availability of affordable financing and mortgages.

SECTIONS 207/223(F)—MORTGAGE INSURANCE FOR PURCHASE
OR REFINANCING OF EXISTING MULTI-FAMILY RENTAL HOUSING

Provides mortgage insurance to facilitate the purchase or refinancing of existing multi-family rental housing. Properties requiring substantial rehabilitation are not eligible for mortgage insurance under this program. The program allows for non-critical repairs that must be completed within twelve months of loan closing. The program allows for long-term mortgages (up to thirty-five years) that can be financed with Government National Mortgage Association mortgage-backed securities.

Eligible borrowers: for-profit and nonprofit borrowers.

Eligible properties: must contain at least five residential units with complete kitchens and baths and have been completed or substantially rehabilitated at least three years prior to the date of the application for mortgage insurance.

SECTION 220—MORTGAGE INSURANCE FOR RENTAL HOUSING FOR URBAN RENEWAL AND CONCENTRATED DEVELOPMENT AREAS

Provides mortgage insurance for multi-family housing projects in urban renewal areas, code enforcement areas, and other areas where local governments have undertaken designated revitalization activities. It provides good-quality rental housing in urban areas that have been targeted for overall revitalization. The program has statutory mortgage limits.

Eligible borrowers: private profit-motivated entities, public bodies, and others who meet HUD requirements for mortgagors.

Eligible properties: new construction or rehabilitation of detached, semi-detached, row, walk-up, or elevator-type rental housing or to finance the purchase of properties that have been rehabilitated by a local public agency.

SECTION 221(D)(4)

Provides mortgage insurance to facilitate the new construction or substantial rehabilitation of multi-family rental or cooperative housing for moderate-income families, the elderly, and the handicapped and for multi-family properties consisting of single-room–occupancy (SRO) apartments. It assists private industry in the construction or rehabilitation of rental and cooperative housing for moderate-income and displaced families by making capital more readily available. It also encourages construction or substantial rehabilitation of single-room apartment buildings, thus enabling people with very limited incomes to find clean and safe housing. The program allows for long-term mortgages (up to forty years) that can be financed with Government National Mortgage Association mortgage-backed securities.

Eligible properties: new construction or rehabilitation of detached, semi-detached, row, walk-up, or elevator-type rental or cooperative housing containing five or more units and the new construction or substantial rehabilitation of projects consisting of five or more SRO units, with no more than 10 percent of total gross floor space dedicated to commercial use (20 percent for substantial rehabilitation projects).

Eligible borrowers for multi-family rental properties include public profit-motivated sponsors, limited-distribution entities, nonprofit cooperatives, builders-sellers, investors-sponsors, and general mortgagors. Borrowers for

SROs include nonprofit organizations, builders or sellers teamed with a non-profit purchaser, limited-distribution entities, profit-motivated firms, or public agencies.

SECTION 231

Provides mortgage insurance to facilitate the construction and substantial rehabilitation of multi-family rental housing for elderly persons (sixty-two or older) and persons with disabilities. However, few projects have been insured under Section 231 in recent years; developers have opted to use Section 221(d)(4) instead.

Eligible borrowers: private profit-motivated developers and nonprofit sponsors.

Eligible properties: new construction and substantial rehabilitation of detached, semi-detached, walk-up, or elevator-type rental housing designed specifically for elderly or handicapped individuals consisting of eight or more dwelling units.

SECTION 232

Provides mortgage insurance for residential care facilities to finance the purchase, refinance, new construction, or substantial rehabilitation of such facilities for the frail elderly.

Eligible properties: nursing homes, assisted living facilities, and board and care facilities for the elderly.

SECTION 236 MULTI-FAMILY PROGRAM

As in the Section 235 single-family program, the FHA would subsidize the interest rate down to 1 percent, and the sponsor, typically a local housing authority, would have to re-certify the property annually. The loans had terms up to forty years.

SECTION 242

Provides mortgage insurance for acute-care hospital facilities ranging from large teaching institutions to small rural critical-access hospitals.

SECTION 542(C)

Enables HUD and state and local housing finance agencies (HFAs) to provide new risk-sharing arrangements to help those agencies provide more insurance and credit for multi-family loans. The program provides credit enhancement for mortgages for multi-family housing projects whose loans are underwritten, processed, serviced, and disposed of by HFAs. HUD and HFAs share in the risk of the mortgage. The program also provides full FHA mortgage insurance to enhance HFA bonds to investment grade.

Eligible borrowers: investors, builders, developers, public entities, and private nonprofit corporations or associations.

(HUD- *6 (4-72) PREVIOUS EDITION MAY BE USED

Memorandum

U.S. DEPARTMENT OF
HOUSING AND URBAN DEVELOPMENT

TO   : Dwight G. Moore, Director   DATE: OCT 1 5 1973
                 Program Planning and Evaluation Staff
                                        IN REPLY REFER TO:
                                        8SDP

FROM : Don L. Johnson, Regional Economist
                 Region VIII (Denver), 8SDP

SUBJECT: Review of paper entitled <u>FHA Subsidized Housing: Its Past and Future</u>
         by Edwin Rosser

Edwin Rosser, as noted on the title page, prepared the subject paper
for a class at the Center for Special and Advanced Programs at the
University of Northern Colorado. I have met Edwin Rosser at a class
and he is a market analyst for a local mortgage banking concern. Many
of the views expressed reflect his mortgage banking affiliation.

While quite brief, I think Rosser's paper is quite even handed. He
points out the possitive contributions of the FHA and points out some
negative things too, but quickly shows that many of the negative
complaints are not valid when gauged by the mission assignment given
to the FHA. The new assignments put on the FHA in the sixties were
related to the hard felt housing needs of low income people. This
was a significant departure from their previous assignment. In
carrying out this new assignment, the FHA was handicapped by the grossly
underfunded Section 237 counseling program, a departure from underwriting on the basis of economic soundness in favor of acceptable risk,
and some criminal activity. Despite this, Mr. Rosser presents
statistics showing that the results were not all that bad, given the
social goals which were not always compatible with sound underwriting.

At this point Rosser makes his recommendations for the improvement of
the FHA. He indicates that the FHA should be removed from HUD, and
become a separate independent agency devoid of all subsidized activity.
This proposal has some merit, particularly from the point of view of
the mortgage banker. However, there are just too many advantages
in coordination of housing activities and administration savings to
recommend this approach. A better alternative would be to separate
the unsubsidized programs from the subsidized programs on functional
lines. Have an unsubsidized underwriter and a subsidized underwriter
handling public housing as well as the FHA subsidized programs while
sharing staff support.

Another point that Rosser makes is the desire to have his new Federal
Mortgage Insurance Administration self-supporting and not depend on

2

annual funding from Congress. While again, this may have strong
appeal to mortgage bankers, there would be a danger of the mortgage
bankers controlling this independent agency. Unfortunately, the
history of such independent agencies have not always shown that such
agencies can maintain their independence if they serve one interest
group.

Another point that is raised is a proposal to let the FHA interest
rates float. This is one of the Administrations new proposals and
make sense. While they are about it, I think that the mortgage
insurance rate ought to be lowered on those loans which are less
risky and raised on those which are more risky. The rate of $\frac{1}{2}$ of 1%
is the same if the loan is a 50% loan to a good credit risk or a
95% loan to a poor credit risk. It is a regressive tax on good
creditors. If it is desired to insure poor credit risks the burden
ought to be carried by the general tax payer, not the good credit
risk who seeks a FHA loan.

The paper goes on to say that the subsidized housing should be handled
by HUD. See my comments above. The paper also advocates a fair
share plan for housing in the suburban areas and a housing assistance
allowance. This appears to be the direction that HUD is now turned.

Rating of Mortgagor

1630 (1). To facilitate uniformity of analysis and rating, a risk-rating grid is used for the rating of mortgagor. The making of a rating of mortgagor takes into consideration all elements of risk arising from the mortgage credit aspects of the transaction. The grid provides a medium for tallying the conclusions with respect to the risk as the analysis progresses and provides for conversion of the conclusions into numerical ratings of risk.

1630 (2). The Rating of Mortgagor is an expression of the results of a detailed analysis of the degree of the mortgage credit risk as determined by prescribed standards. It is not a mechanical compilation of facts and figures, a perfunctory analysis, nor an expression of a casual conclusion or judgment.

1631. THE RATING GRID. The rating grid provides a means of rating the mortgage credit risk by grouping its elements into features. Each feature receives independent consideration. Columns to express the quality or condition found are provided opposite each feature, that is, one column for recording a condition which is too poor for acceptability, followed by five columns for rating degrees of acceptable conditions in each feature. These are referred to, respectively, as the *Reject* column, the *1* column, the *2* column, and so on. The column which is determined to be representative of the condition found for each feature analyzed is

RATING OF MORTGAGOR

FEATURES		Reject	1	2	3	4	5	Rating Factors	Totals
Motivation	Credit Characteristics of Mortgagor		4	3	2	1	0	X —	
	Motivating Interest in Ownership of the Property		4	3	2	1	0	X 3 —	
	Importance of Monetary Interest to Mortgagor		4	3	2	1	0	X —	
Ability to Pay	Adequacy of Available Assets for Transaction		4	3	2	1	0	X 2 —	
	Stability of Effective Income		4	3	2	1	0	X —	
	Adequacy of Effective Income for Total Obligations		4	3	2	1	0	X —	
Order of assignment of Rating Factors 6-4-3-2						Total Deductions			
RATING OF MORTGAGOR					Maximum possible rating 100 minus Total Deductions ___				

MORTGAGE CREDIT ANALYSIS   1630 — 1631
899041°—47-89

Appendix B

Colorado Foreclosure Hotline

STATE OF COLORADO

DEPARTMENT OF LOCAL AFFAIRS
DIVISION OF HOUSING
1313 Sherman Street, Suite 518
Denver, Colorado 80203
(303) 866-2033

Kathi Williams, Director

Bill Owens
Governor

Brian Vogt
Executive Director

November 15, 2006

Re: Foreclosure Prevention Efforts in Colorado

Dear Mortgage Lenders and Servicers:

Colorado continues to rank near the highest in the nation for homes entering foreclosure. Public exposure of the increase in foreclosures has been increasing. Local media on foreclosure numbers has consistently increased over recent months and has presented home foreclosures as a serious and alarming challenge for the local economy.

The Colorado Foreclosure Prevention Task Force, made up of Realtors, lenders, public trustees and housing counseling agencies, has been working since 2005 on preparing and putting in place a response to the high numbers of foreclosures in the state. On June 6, members of the task force, including representatives from JP Morgan CHASE, The Colorado Division of Housing, The Federal Reserve Bank of Kansas City, and The Colorado Attorney General's Office, met with several national lenders and servicers to explore ways to mitigate the high numbers of foreclosures in Colorado.

At the June 6 meeting, the Task Force and the Colorado Division of Housing presented its plan to facilitate homeownership counseling with borrowers who are delinquent or in foreclosure. In talking with the servicers present at the meeting, we found that they are certainly making strong and continuing efforts to reach out to delinquent borrowers, but that connecting borrowers and servicers continues to be a challenge. Taking into account the concerns and insights presented by servicers at the meeting, we will move forward in partnership with participating servicers in implementing the statewide foreclosure prevention network.

The plan consists of two pieces. First, using the existing network of foreclosure prevention agencies, a statewide hotline will allow any borrower anywhere in the state to connect easily with a local foreclosure prevention counselor. The hotline will direct calls to the hotline prevention network's local agencies based on the location of origin for the call. The counselors will then work with the borrowers to help the borrower avoid foreclosure, even when this means helping the borrower sell or liquidate his or her home.

The second step is working with servicers. Our counselors must move quickly in order to realize success with delinquent borrowers. Establishing accountability between borrowers and servicers is essential to any loss mitigation efforts, and our number one goal is to inform the borrowers of their options for forbearance, refinancing, or sale of the property as the key to foreclosure avoidance. A critical role of the task force will be to bring servicers on board as partners with counselors to help borrowers with their financial difficulties.

The benefit of avoiding foreclosure, even if it means moving out of the home, is that it is far less costly for the borrower in the long run, and, as you know, it is far less costly for the servicers as well.

We are asking for servicers to meet with us and to help us refine our process so that we can be sure that our network of counselors are using loss mitigation resources to the fullest extent possible. By creating a closer relationship between counselors, lenders and servicers we hope to turn the tide on the growing foreclosure problem that faces our state. We are committed to helping you create a closer relationship with delinquent borrowers to help you preserve the value of your servicing portfolio as well as the value of the housing stock in Colorado.

DOI: 10.5876/9781607326236.c017

In addition, we are asking for a small initial contribution of 5,000 dollars to assist in implementing the foreclosure prevention plan and in ensuring that counseling agencies are fully staffed and ready to serve borrowers as they seek ways to avoid foreclosure. Naturally, we want you to be assured that our counselors and foreclosure prevention partners are accountable for the financial and human resources devoted to this effort, and we will work with you to establish this accountability as part of the foreclosure prevention effort.

We have reviewed and analyzed several foreclosure prevention and homeownership preservation efforts across the country and determined that we have the model that will work best for Colorado. Lenders and servicers will be a key part of this plan, and for this reason we welcome any collaboration that we can work to find which will be mutually beneficial.

The Colorado Division of Housing has put $250,000 into this effort, and has been joined in its support by Freddie Mac which has contributed $50,000, the Colorado Association of Realtors which has contributed $30,000, the Colorado Mortgage Lenders Association which has committed $30,000 and by JP Morgan Chase, which in addition to its substantial in-kind contributions, has contributed $12,500 to the effort. Fannie Mae and a variety of housing counseling agencies continue to contribute resources as well.

Since the Hotline launched last month, the hotline has received over 4,500 calls. As the enclosed press release indicates, this is very high volume compared to other foreclosure prevention hotlines around the country. Partially due to the fact that media coverage of foreclosures in Colorado has been widespread for months, the Hotline has benefited from substantial amounts of coverage of the Hotline with print, radio, and television outlets carrying stories on the Hotline and the local effects of foreclosures. National media has been covering the Hotline as well, with Fox News carrying a piece on the Colorado Hotline on November 13, and other networks expressing continued interest. We plan continued media and marketing efforts to promote the Hotline through 2007. If your organization is able to join our foreclosure prevention effort, we would certainly wish to publicize your important role in helping to address the foreclosure challenges in Colorado.

NEW ADDITIONS FOR FOLLOW-UP Feb 2007

1. ask for 10- 25K from lenders
2. ask for dedicated staff to work with lenders
3. ask for them to publish and send out info on hotline.
4. ask for local trainings and counseling sessions hosted by lender – on the CHASE model

Also – update with
1. new hotline numbers
2. hotline success stats
3. success of press event with governor
4. other new developments

Sincerely,

E. Michael Rosser, CMB
Board Member and Former Chairman

Kathi Williams,
Director, Colorado Division of Housing

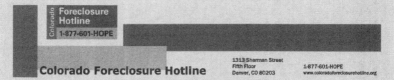

Colorado Foreclosure Hotline

1313 Sherman Street
Fifth Floor
Denver, CO 80203

1-877-601-HOPE
www.coloradoforeclosurehotline.org

May 2, 2008

To our Hotline Partners and Housing Counselors:

The beginning of 2007 has been a quarter of unmatched success for the Colorado Foreclosure Hotline, and it would not have been possible without your dedication to foreclosure prevention and hard work in assisting homeowners across Colorado.

In March, we topped the highest call-volume month, reaching 3,050 calls; and in April we reached nearly 4,000 calls. As more callers contact the Hotline, still you have consistently maintained an 80 percent success rate, assisting four in five homeowners avoid foreclosure. Words could not express our deepest appreciation.

On behalf of the Executive Committee, please accept our sincerest apologies if you have not felt adequately rewarded for your accomplishments. We are aware that you are owed funding and want you to know that the Executive Committee is working to get that to you.

We had been promised certain amounts of funding from various donors for the 2007-2008 year of the Hotline; and unfortunately, receipt of those funds is still pending. Once the money is in our hands, please know that it already has been designated to be distributed to each of our 28 agencies, based on number of clients counseled. It is a payment that is much deserved.

Housing counseling is changing the face of the foreclosure crisis in Colorado. We know that you are dedicated to your work because it is meaningful, not because you receive funding; but we don't want that meaningful work to go unnoticed. You will be compensated for your efforts.

If you have any questions regarding funding cycles, please contact Sarah Kincheloe at sarah@coloradoforeclosurehotline.org. She will ensure that those concerns reach the Executive Committee at a regularly scheduled meeting.

Thank you for your patience, understanding, and again, all that you do for the homeowners of Colorado.

Sincerely,

E. Michael Rosser, CMB
Co-Chair, Colorado Foreclosure Prevention Task Force
Member, State Housing Board

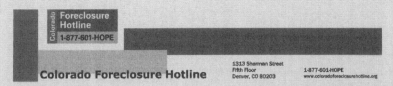

Colorado Foreclosure Hotline

1313 Sherman Street
Fifth Floor
Denver, CO 80203

1-877-601-HOPE
www.coloradoforeclosurehotline.org

October 3, 2008

To Whom It May Concern:

Housing counselors affiliated with the Colorado Foreclosure Hotline have the opportunity to
communicate specific needs and concerns to the entire Colorado Foreclosure Prevention Task
Force. A common message portrayed from many counselors is that of a loss mitigation bottleneck
within the servicing companies. Information clogging in loss mitigation centers is delaying the
delivery of prompt services to the counseling agencies and their clients.

Following conversations with the National Association of Realtors, similar stakeholders, and several
other members of the Colorado Foreclosure Prevention Task Force, I've come to a conclusion
regarding this troublesome issue. It seems that an agreement could be reached that not only aids
our housing counselors, but also alleviates the work stress of the servicers.

In terms of foreclosure mitigation, one remedy that would prove beneficial to the counseling
agencies, servicers, and borrowers would be for major servicers with substantial retail branch
networks to delegate loss mitigation programs to senior underwriters or loan originators. This
would grant servicing departments a first look at a loan application, already partially processed,
and therefore expediting their decision on a foreclosure short-sale or modified payment plan.
Delegating this limited authority of analysis to local branches and regions could substantially ease
the negative effects of the current bottleneck.

Despite encountering these difficulties, Colorado Foreclosure Hotline housing counselors have
assisted more than 9,000 homeowners reach a positive resolution with their mortgage company. I
have enclosed a recent overview of the Hotline's success. However, with assistance in expediting
loss mitigation services, housing counselors could do even more, facilitating positive
homeownership experience across the state of Colorado.

If you would like more information on the Colorado Foreclosure Hotline, or to discuss this issue
further, please contact Sarah Kincheloe at sarah@coloradoforeclosurehotline.org.

Thank you for your time and consideration.
Regards,

E. Michael Rosser, CMB
Co-Chair, Colorado Foreclosure Prevention Task Force

Appendix C

Letter to Aksel Nielsen from President Dwight D. Eisenhower

Appendix D

GSE Affordable Housing Goals, 2000–2003

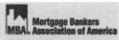

**Mortgage Bankers
MBA. Association of America**

1919 Pennsylvania Avenue, NW
Washington, DC 20006-3438
www.mbaa.org

ISSUE PAPER

Subject: **GSE Affordable Housing Goals**

Issue: The affordable housing goals currently effective for the GSEs were set by the Department of Housing and Urban Development (HUD) in a final regulation published October 31, 2000. That regulation establishes goals for the years 2001 through 2003. HUD is not required to revisit the goals, and if they choose not to do so the current goals will remain in effect in 2004. However, certain "bonus points" and a multiplier for Freddie Mac's multifamily business will expire at the end of 2003 unless expressly extended by HUD.

Background: On October 21, 2000 HUD published in the Federal Register a final rule that established affordable housing goals for the calendar years 2001 through 2003. The new goals were characterized by then HUD Secretary Cuomo as "stretch" goals for the GSEs that would result in "an additional $488.3 billion in mortgages for 7 million more low-and moderate-income families over the next 10 years."

In the final rule, HUD set the goals for 2001 through 2003 at:

Low and moderate income =   50% of the total number of units financed
Special affordable[1] =   20% of the total number of units financed
Geographically targeted =   31% of the total number of units financed

This was based on assumptions of a 39-40% low and moderate income single family market and approximately a 90% low and moderate income multifamily market for a total low/moderate share of 50-55% of the overall market. For special affordable, the single family market was estimated at 14-15% and the multifamily market at 44-50% for a total special affordable share of 23-26% of the overall market.

In its comment letter on the regulation (submitted May 8, 2000), MBA supported HUD's efforts to encourage the GSEs to "lead the industry in making mortgage credit available for low-and moderate-income families" but suggested a number of modifications that we believed should be made in the rule before it was finalized.

Noting that multifamily mortgages comprise a disproportionate share of the number of units counted toward both the low- and moderate-income and the special affordable goals, MBA suggested that the proposed rule could encourage the GSEs to rely primarily on multifamily production to meet their goals. MBA recommended either

---

[1] The special affordable goal is designed to promote housing for very low income families and for low income families in low income areas.

DOI: 10.5876/9781607326236.c019

I.   THE THREE GOALS – WHAT THEY ARE AND HOW HUD SETS THEM

A.   What the Three Goals Are

The three goals are a percentage, or fraction, of a GSE's loan purchase activities that serve certain aspects of the residential mortgage loan market. For each goal, HUD calculates compliance by a fraction:

Numerator: # of units financed by mortgage
                          purchases that meet the goal
                          _____

Denominator: # of units financed by
                          all mortgage purchases

HUD calculates this fraction separately for each of the three goals, for each GSE, annually.

B.   Where HUD Set the Goals

Congress did not set the goal levels (numbers), but left these for HUD to set by regulation. (The goals are based on income levels as discussed in § II below.) Congress authorized HUD to adjust the goals annually.

1.   Low- and Moderate-Income Goal

50% of the number of dwelling units financed by GSE mortgage purchases in a year must be for housing for low- and moderate-income families.

2.   Underserved Areas Goal

31% of the number of dwelling units financed by GSE mortgage purchases in a year must be for central cities, rural areas, and other underserved areas.

(a)   Congress did not define underserved area, but requires that an underserved area be "based on [geographic] location."

(b)   HUD generally defines an underserved area as a census tract with either:

(i)   Median income no more than 90% of the median income of the metropolitan area, or

Glossary of Mortgage and
Real Estate–Related Terms

Most of these definitions were taken from Albert Santi and James Newell's 1997 *Encyclopedia of Mortgage and Real Estate Finance*. Some were updated to fit more current applications. Others were obtained from the Investopedia website.

Abstract of title. A condensed history of the title of real property. An abstract of title should be a chronological history of recorded instruments that affect the title of the subject real property. After a title search, a title attorney issues an opinion that can be used to obtain title insurance. The abstract does not guarantee or assure the validity of the title. The abstract only reveals what is a public record. It does not protect against forgery or fraud, as does title insurance. The person preparing the abstract is called the abstractor.

Adjustable-rate mortgage (ARM). A mortgage in which the interest rate can change and is not fixed. With an adjustable-rate mortgage, the interest rate will increase or decrease over the life of the loan, depending on market conditions. Typically, most adjustable-rate loans have a starting rate or an initial interest rate that is lower than the rate offered on a standard fixed-rate mortgage. A financial index governs the

DOI: 10.5876/9781607326236.c020

changes in interest rate; when the index rises, so does the interest rate. The opposite happens when the index falls. Typically, the interest rate is adjusted at predetermined periods (e.g., annually; every three years). In general, the index is based on the current market for US government treasury securities. Added to the index is a factor called the margin, which represents the compensation paid to the lender over and above the rate on the treasury securities. The index fluctuates over the life of the loan, but the margin is fixed. Example: Assume that the US Treasury rate is 2.5 percent and the margin is 2 percent; then the starting interest rate is 4.5 percent.

Alternative documentation. A marketing tool designed to reduce loan processing time. The term is used in conjunction with so-called low-documentation, low-dock, and stated income loans. The term also applies to the use of utility bills to verify residence and pay stubs to verify amounts or sources of income.

Amortization. Paying off a debt or mortgage on a regularly prescribed schedule. Amortization usually occurs on the monthly payment schedule. Except for interest-only loans and balloon loans, the payment is applied to both reduction of principal and payment of interest.

Annual percentage rate. A uniform method for calculating an interest rate includes the interest rate collected, discount points charge to the purchaser or the seller or both, and certain costs related to the closing and mortgage insurance premiums. An annual percentage rate represents the percentage relationship of the total finance charge to the amount of the loan on an accrual basis.

Appraisal. An opinion of value for a specific purpose on a specifically and well-defined property as of a given date. The appraisal report contains an estimate of the value as of the date of the valuation; the certification signature of the appraiser; the purpose of the appraisal qualifying conditions; and a detailed description of the property, its ownership, and the various approaches to value such as a market data approach, an income approach, or a cost approach. The market approach is used for most residential property; the income approach is used most commonly with multi-family and commercial mortgage loans. The cost approach appears more often in construction lending.

Balloon mortgage. A mortgage loan with periodic payments of principal and interest that do not completely amortize the loan. The balance of this type of mortgage loan is due and payable at a lump sum at a specific time in the future. The borrower pays interest regularly but may or may not make small principal repayments during the loan. This type of loan was typical particularly in farm mortgage banking from its early days until the Great Depression.

Blanket mortgage. A single mortgage used to secure a deed for money loaned on several properties, such as multiple lots owned by a builder/developer for a residential subdivision. Example: The Prudential Insurance Company's loan on Safeway stores across the nation in the 1930s is an example of a blanket mortgage.

Bond. A formal certificate that evidences a debt and outlines the terms of repayment. The repayment schedule of the bond can be secured with or without collateral. A mortgage-backed bond is a pool of mortgages with similar characteristics, such as term, interest rate, type of loan, uniform underwriting standards, and property types.

Certified Mortgage Banker (CMB). A professional designation awarded by the Mortgage Bankers Association of America to those in the industry who prove to have superior knowledge and skills in the field of real estate finance. Qualifications include experience, education, and the successful completion of a written and oral examination. In 2015 the Society of Certified Mortgage Bankers had more than 1,200 members.

Civil Rights Acts (1866–1968). The first act, in 1866, prohibited any type of discrimination based on race. Title VIII of the 1968 act prohibits discrimination in mortgage applications and loans because of race or ethnic background.

Collateralized mortgage obligations. A corporate security in which the collection of principal and interest is passed through to a trusted pool, which, in turn, causes the pool of loans to pay principal and interest to security holders on a class-by-class basis (also known as a tranche), in which one class is completely paid off before any principal is repaid to the next, greater maturity class. This architecture is designed to meet the investment needs of many nontraditional mortgage investors.

Community Reinvestment Act (CRA). A 1977 congressional act that required lenders to meet certain capital needs of their local communities. The act applies to federally insured deposit institutions, such as banks and thrift associations.

Conduit. A secondary marketing term applied to a financial facility that gathers loans from a number of approved lenders using established guidelines. The loans are then resold/remarketed through various securitization processes. Fannie Mae is a government-sponsored conduit. The first privately sponsored conduit was PMI Mortgage Corporation, known as Penny Mae.

Consumer Credit Reporting Act (Fair Credit Reporting Act, 1971). Designed to regulate the consumer credit reporting industry. It placed disclosure obligations on the users of credit reports to assure fair, timely, and accurate reporting of credit information.

Conventional mortgage loan. A loan that is not insured or guaranteed by the Federal Housing Administration (FHA) or the Veterans Administration (VA). Conventional loans are made and purchased by institutional investors, such as banks, savings associations, insurance companies, and Fannie Mae and Freddie Mac. Conventional mortgage-backed securities are made up of mortgages that do not carry a government guarantee but may be insured by a private mortgage insurance company or other bond insurers.

Correspondent. A lender or mortgage banker whose normal practice is to sell some or all of the loans it originates to a particular investor or group of investors.

Covered bond. A bond whose repayment schedule is composed of a pool of mortgage loans in which the collection of principal and interest is passed on to the bondholders. The issuer of the bond retains ownership of the mortgages, and the holder of the bond is entitled to the principal and interest payments less certain fees and charges retained by the issuer.

Debenture. A broad term used for an unsecured long-term debt instrument. Debentures were used commonly in the farm mortgage banking industry. In the past, the Federal Housing Administration used debentures to pay claims on defaulted loans.

Derivative. A market instrument that has underlying security or is created from other securities, such as mortgage-backed securities, in which interest and principal payments called strips are re-securitized to hedge or mitigate interest rate risk.

Discount. The difference between par, or 100 percent, of the face value of a note or obligation and the actual bid price for the obligation. The purpose of the discount is to increase the yield of a mortgage or debt instrument. For example, if a $100,000 thirty-year mortgage sells on the market for $95,000, the discount is 5 percent, or $5,000. If the interest rate on the note is 4 percent, the yield to the purchaser is approximately 4.7 percent, assuming that the loan stays on the books for a twelve-year period.

Equal Credit Opportunity Act (1974). A federal law to prohibit any lender from discriminating against any purchaser because of race, sex, color, religion, national origin, marital status, age, receipt of public assistance, or the exercise of rights under the Consumer Credit Protection Act.

Fair Housing Act (1968). Provides that it is unlawful to discriminate based on race, color, creed, sex, or national origin when selling or leasing residential property.

Federal Agricultural Mortgage Corporation (Farmer Mac). Founded in 1987 by the farm mortgage credit system to provide credit guarantees on mortgage-backed securities composed of loans based on farmlands, farm buildings, or both.

Federal Home Loan Bank System (FHLB). A group of twelve federally chartered regional banks that exist to supply credit to member financial institutions, such as commercial banks, thrift institutions, and insurance companies. The Federal Home Loan Bank Board was originally chartered to oversee the operations of the twelve regional banks, the Federal Savings and Loan Insurance Corporation, and the Federal Home Loan Mortgage Corporation (Freddie Mac). When Freddie Mac became a private corporation, it was removed from the FHLB and reassigned to the Federal Housing Finance Agency.

Federal Home Loan Mortgage Corporation (Freddie Mac). Originally a creature of the Federal Home Loan Bank System and now a private corporation authorized by Congress whose purpose is to provide a secondary market for conventional loans. Freddie Mac's mortgage participation certificates were the first mortgage-backed securities backed by conventional mortgages that were not guaranteed by the US government but did carry the backing of the Federal Home Loan Bank System.

Federal Housing Administration (FHA). Founded under the National Housing Act in 1934 as an insurance arm of the Department of Housing and Urban Development. The purpose of the FHA is to ensure loans that provide rental housing and home-ownership opportunities for first-time buyers, low- and moderate-income families, and other special populations such as seniors with Home Equity Conversion Mortgages. The FHA houses the Mutual Mortgage Insurance Fund, where most of its mortgages are insured. It also maintains a general fund and a high-risk fund designed to meet its social purpose.

Federal Housing Finance Agency. Created under the Federal Housing Finance Regulatory Reform Act of 2008 as the successor to the Federal Housing Finance Board and the Office of Federal Housing Enterprise Oversight in the Department of Housing and Urban Development. This independent agency is the regulator of Fannie Mae and Freddie Mac and was responsible for placing these two government-sponsored enterprises in conservatorship in 2008.

Federal Housing Finance Board. Created in 1989 under the Financial Institutions Reform, Recovery, and Enforcement Act to oversee the Federal Home Loan Bank System. The board banned certain investments by thrift associations, expanded participation in residential mortgages and construction loans, and created a broader basket of consumer loans, such as home equity loans and other second mortgage products. Amendments to the Community Reinvestment Act required expanded standards of disclosures and performance in meeting the needs of underserved communities. For real estate appraisers, new standards of professional performance and standards of conduct, including state regulations, were established.

Federal National Mortgage Association (Fannie Mae). Founded in 1938 as a private, publicly held government-sponsored enterprise that guarantees and holds for its own portfolio residential mortgage loans, both single-family and multi-family loans.

Financial Institutions Reform, Recovery, and Enforcement Act (1989) (FIRREA). One of the most sweeping overhauls of laws governing savings and loan associations since the Great Depression. This act dissolved the Federal Home Loan Bank Board and the Federal Savings and Loan Insurance Fund, which merged into the Federal Depositors Insurance Corporation. The law also created the Office of Thrift Supervision, which is responsible for chartering federal thrift institutions and supervises state-chartered thrift institutions and thrift holding companies. The Office of Thrift Supervision was later abolished under the Dodd-Frank Wall Street Reform and Consumer Protection Act. FIRREA also created the Resolution Funding Corporation, later renamed the Resolution Trust Corporation, which took possession of failed thrift institutions and facilitated the disposition of their assets.

Fixed-rate mortgage (FRM). A real estate loan in which the interest rate is established at closing and lasts through the complete duration of the obligation.

Foreclosure. The legal action allowing a lender to enforce the provisions of a mortgage or deed of trust to sell a property to satisfy the obligations of the borrower when that borrower is defaulting under the terms of the security agreement and efforts to preserve the property for the borrower have failed. There are two types of foreclosure processes: judicial and non-judicial. In a judicial foreclosure the lender cannot foreclose without a court action, and the judge would then order the property to be sold. In a non-judicial foreclosure, available only in certain states, a private trustee, or in the case of Colorado a public trustee, is assigned to the case. The role of the trustee is to determine if the lender can exercise its entitlement to foreclose. If the lender's power of sale is included in the mortgage document, the trustee will approve the foreclosure and sell the property on behalf of the lender.

Government National Mortgage Association (Ginnie Mae). Established by the National Housing Act in 1968. It is a full faith and credit agency of the US government and the Department of Housing and Urban Development. It functions as a guarantor of private issuers of mortgage-backed securities supported by loans insured by the Federal Housing Administration (FHA) and the Veterans Administration (VA). From time to time, Ginnie Mae is called upon to implement various special assistance programs as established by Congress and the administration.

Government-sponsored enterprise (GSE). Consists of privately held corporations with public purposes created by the US Congress to reduce the cost of capital for certain borrowing sectors of the economy. Members of these sectors include students, farmers, and homeowners. GSEs carry the implicit backing, but are not direct obligations, of the US government. For this reason, these securities offer a yield premium over treasuries. Some consider GSEs to be stealth recipients of corporate welfare. Examples of GSEs include the Federal Home Loan Bank, the Federal Home Loan Mortgage Corporation (Freddie Mac), the Federal Farm Credit Bank, and the Resolution Funding Corporation.

Hedge/hedging positions. A technique that has been used for generations, first in agricultural commodities and now in financial instruments, to protect against fluctuations in price and value. Mortgage futures contracts are used to protect the lender from changes in interest rates before mortgages or mortgage-backed securities can be delivered to investors. This is the same technique used by farmers to protect against price fluctuations on the delivery of wheat and corn.

Home equity line of credit/home equity loan/second mortgage/piggyback/ junior lien. Subordinate to and filed behind the senior first mortgage loan. These loans carry a higher risk because in the event of a foreclosure, the second mortgage is eliminated if there are insufficient funds after the first mortgage lender sells the property. These loans were traditionally used for home improvement but are now used as a line of credit, as a substitute for a down payment, or as a device to avoid mortgage insurance on high loan-to-value–ratio loans.

Home Mortgage Disclosure Act (HMDA). Passed in 1975 to provide the public with information on lending patterns and determine whether federally related loans are meeting the housing credit needs of neighborhoods and communities. The lender is required to report a demographic profile of borrowers and to identify the class of investors when they sell their mortgages.

Housing finance agencies. Usually created by state or local governments to facilitate housing policies, such as providing loans to moderate-income borrowers, first-time home buyers, and underserved communities; to fund workforce housing; and to provide financial and credit information and education. Because of their status, these agencies' obligations are free from federal and state income taxes, the benefit of which is passed on to program users.

Interest rate swap. An agreement between two parties to exchange payments that are based on specific interest rates with no transfer of principal. Swaps are cash flow exchanges that allow parties to change their interest rate exposure. Interest rate swaps are used to hedge against the risk of holding long-term fixed interest rate securities.

Investor. Any short- or long-term purchaser or holder of an interest in real estate or real estate mortgages. Investors can be private individuals, trusts, pension funds, insurance companies, investment companies, mutual funds, banks and credit unions, and savings institutions.

Joint-stock bank. A bank that issues stock and requires shareholders to be held liable for the company's debt. In other words, a joint-stock bank combines features of a general partnership, in which owners of a company split profits and liabilities, and a publicly traded company, which issues stock that shareholders are able to buy and sell on an exchange. A joint-stock bank is not owned by a government.

Mortgage-backed bonds/covered bonds. A debt obligation of the issuer in which the revenue stream is pledged to repay the principal and interest to the purchaser of the obligation. The investor relies on the issuer's credit rating but does not "own" the underlying collateral. In the case of mortgage-backed bonds, the issuer is responsible for repayment of the debt, not the pool of underlying mortgages.

Mortgage-backed securities (MBS). Mortgages assembled in pools and sold as pass-through securities. The cash flows from those pools are "passed through" to the investor. In pass-through securities the issuer is obligated to "pass through" the amount due regardless of whether it is collected. Because of this structure, a guarantor is required such as Ginnie Mae or a private conduit with a financial credit rating strong enough to satisfy the security holder's needs.

Mortgage banker. A financial institution that originates, underwrites, sells, and services mortgage loans for institutions and individuals. Over the years the term has been synonymous with mortgage companies, but many institutions such as banks, credit unions, and thrifts have their own departments that serve a mortgage banking function.

Mortgage broker. Typically an individual who originates loans on behalf of mortgage bankers and other institutions. Mortgage brokers do not fund the loans with their own capital; they are funded by the mortgage banker or another lending institution. However, the mortgage broker negotiates the terms and conditions between borrowers and lending institutions.

Planned unit development (PUD). A land-use and zoning technique that became more widely popular in the late 1960s and early 1970s. Depending on local and state laws and ordinances, PUDs can be of mixed use, with some commercial and residential structures along with the ownership and maintenance of common areas. In residential communities this can mean parks, open space, and recreational amenities. PUDs are typically managed by property owners or homeowners' associations under the covenants, conditions, and restrictions established by the developer.

Private conduit. An independently capitalized firm or institution that purchases loans from originators and sells either whole loans or mortgage-backed securities to secondary market investors. In general, conduits prefer larger loans above the Fannie Mae and Freddie Mac guidelines that are insured by private mortgage insurance companies or bond insurers.

Private mortgage insurance (PMI). Industry that insures lenders against losses on high-ratio loans. The PMI or mortgage insurance company can provide first dollar loss coverage on loans that exceed an 80 percent loan-to-value ratio. The first dollar loss can be covered from 10 percent to 40 percent of the outstanding loan amount. Premiums are charged on a risk basis determined by the loan-to-value ratio and other considerations. Preston Martin, former chair of the Federal Home Loan Bank

Board, founded a San Francisco–based company named PMI Mortgage Insurance Company.

Real estate investment trust. Trusts in two forms. First is an equity trust, which purchases and owns real estate, typically income-producing real estate. Second are real estate investment trusts (REIT) that invest in mortgage debt, that is, real estate loans. A REIT provides many income tax advantages and is required to pass through to shareholders a minimum of 95 percent of its income to be exempt from federal taxes.

Real Estate Settlement Procedures Act (1974). A comprehensive law and regulation that sets forth requirements for lenders to provide estimates of closing costs and uniform settlement statements while prohibiting the payment of referral or kickback fees to settlement service providers.

Servicer. The function within a mortgage banking firm charged with collecting payments from the borrower, advancing the principal and interest to the investor, paying property insurance premiums and maintaining adequate coverage, and paying property taxes to the local taxing authority. In addition, a servicer will have a collection and default management area that will contact delinquent borrowers and recommend mitigation strategies or foreclosure.

Soldiers and Sailors Relief Act (1940). Passed by Congress prior to World War II. The act is designed to assist members of the military, called a national service, to enable them to meet their various financial obligations.

Timeshare. A property with a particular form of ownership or use rights. These properties are typically resort condominium units, in which multiple parties hold rights to use the property and each sharer is allotted a period of time (typically one week and almost always the same time every year) in which he or she may use the property. The sharer holds no claim to ownership of the property.

Title insurance. Issued after a search of the title has been made by an abstractor or title agent to protect the lender and the new owner of a property against any defects in the title not discovered by the title search. Typical coverages include protections against encroachments on the property by a neighbor, fraud, misrepresentation, and mental incompetence.

Truth in Lending Act. Popularly known as Regulation Z of the Federal Reserve Board, passed in 1969. It has recently been revised under Dodd-Frank and is now regulated under the Consumer Financial Protection Bureau. Among other items, the act outlines policies, procedures, and information about the obligations of borrowers under their mortgage documentation. It includes the annual percentage rate, allowable fees and charges, and time periods in which disclosures have to be provided to borrowers.

VA or G.I. Guaranteed Loan. A program made available to members of the armed services who have served at least 181 days of active duty and are "entitled" to receive a mortgage up to 100 percent of the value of the home. The veteran is required to produce a certificate of eligibility, which will determine the amount of loan the Veterans Administration is obligated to guarantee. If the veteran borrower defaults and goes into foreclosure, the VA has the option to pay off the lender and take the property, or it can pay the guarantee amount to the lender.

Yield. The annual percentage rate of return a mortgage, mortgage-backed security, or bond will pay. Yield includes the interest rate in addition to discount points that are paid by the seller, borrower, or investor if the loan is sold out of a portfolio.

Bibliography

PRIMARY SOURCES

Biles, Roger. "Public Housing and the Postwar Urban Renaissance." In *From Tenements to the Taylor Homes: In Search of an Urban Policy in Twentieth-Century America*, edited by John F. Bauman, Roger Biles, and Kristin M. Szylvian, 143–62. University Park: Pennsylvania State University Press, 2000.

Bowes, Watson. "Appraisal of the Boston Building: 828 17th Street." AG Bowes and Company Archives, collection reception number 362, client reference number 509, Stephen H. Hart Library, History Colorado, Denver, 1957.

Bowes, Watson. "Appraisal of Lands Covered by the 'Treaty with the Osage, 1865.'" October 15, 1952. A. G. Bowes and Son, MSS01087, File 202, Steven H. Hart Library, History Colorado, Denver.

Editorial Board. "Homeownership and Wealth Creation." *New York Times*, November 29, 2014, SR8.

Eisenhower, Dwight D. "Administrator-Designate Letter to Aksel Nielsen." In *Box 1 of the collection* NIELSEN, AKSEL, *Records, 1956–59, Box 1, folder "Official Correspondence, 1957–1959."* Dwight D. Abilene, KS: Eisenhower Presidential Library, 1958.

Haselbush, W. "'Magic' Changes Montbello Scene." *Denver Post*, October 2, 1966, 73.

DOI: 10.5876/9781607326236.c021

Hemingway, Bill. "Rebirth of Lower Downtown." *Empire Magazine of the Denver Post,* July 12, 1981, 14–18.

Hoover, Herbert. *The Memoirs of Herbert Hoover: The Cabinet and the Presidency, 1920–1933.* New York: Macmillan, 1952.

Jackson, Philip C. "Testimony before the Subcommittee on Housing and Urban Affairs of the Senate Committee on Banking, Housing, and Urban Affairs Relative to Provisions of Senate Bill 1671 Dealing with the Federal Home Loan Mortgage Corporation and Savings and Loan Associations Lending Authority." *Mortgage Banker* (November 1971): 4–9.

Lowe, Warren. "Brooks Towers." *Rocky Mountain News,* June 12, 1966, 1.

"Montbello Industrial Park Success Noted." *Rocky Mountain News,* May 11, 1969, 42.

"Mortgage Bankers Offer Congress Aid." *Chicago Daily Tribune,* October 9, 1914.

O'Neill. *June E. CBO Testimony on Assessing the Public Costs and Benefits of Fannie Mae and Freddie Mac: Statement of June E. O'Neill.* Washington, DC: Congressional Budget Office, 1996.

President's Advisory Committee on Government Housing Policies and Programs: A Report to the President of the United States. Washington, DC: Government Printing Office, December 1953.

Rosser, E. Michael. Letter to Colorado Foreclosure Hotline, 2008.

Rosser, E. Michael. Interview with Charles "Chuck" Froleicher. Denver, CO, 2011.

Rosser, E. Michael. Interview with Al Morrison. Denver, CO, 2012.

Rosser, E. Michael. Interview with James Nelson. Denver, CO, 2012.

Rosser, E. Michael. Interview with Henry K. Burgwyn. Denver, CO, January 13, 2014.

Rosser, E. Michael. Telephone interview with Joe Kelso. Denver, CO, April 16, 2014.

Rosser, E. Michael. Interview with Chuck Perry. Denver, CO, December 30, 2014.

Rosser, E. Michael. Telephone interview with Cheryl Collins. May 8, 2017.

77th Congress of the United States. "Public Law 559: National Housing Act Amendments of 1942, Section 608, 1942." Legisworks. Accessed November 2, 2014. legisworks.org/sal/56/stats/STATUTE-56-Pg.301.pdf.

79th Congress of the United States. "Public Bill 388: Veteran's Emergency Housing Act, 1946." Legisworks. Accessed March 7, 2015. legisworks.org/sal/60/stats/STATUTE-60-Pg.207.pdf.

"Treaty with the Osage, 1861." *Indian Affairs: Law and Treaties,* vol. II: *Treaties,* ed. Charles J. Kappler. Washington, DC: Government Printing Office, 1904. Accessed March 11, 2014. http://digital.library.okstate.edu/kappler/vol2/treaties/osa0878.htm.

Union Pacific Passenger Department. *The Resources and Attractions of Kansas for the Home Seeker, Capitalist and Tourist.* Battle Creek, MI: Wm. G. Gage and Son, 1890.

Union Pacific Railroad Company, Central Branch Land Office. *Farm Homes in Kansas.* Atchison, KS: Union Pacific Railroad Company, 1879.

Union Pacific Railroad Company. *Land Department.* "Cheap Homes: Nebraska Farms Land Guide. Omaha, NE: Union Pacific Railroad Company, 1880.

BOOKS, MONOGRAPHS, AND JOURNAL ARTICLES

Abbott, Carl. "The Federal Presence." In *The Oxford History of the American West*, ed. Clyde A. Milner, II, Carol A. O'Connor, and Martha A. Sandweiss, 469–500. New York: Oxford University Press, 1994.

Acharya, Viral, Matthew Richardson, Stijn Nieuwerburgh, and Lawrence J. White. *Guaranteed to Fail: Fannie Mae, Freddie Mac, and the Debacle of Mortgage Finance.* Princeton, NJ: Princeton University Press, 2011.

American Land Title Association. *Title Insurance: A Comprehensive Overview.* Washington, DC: American Land Title Association, n.d.

Anderson, J. W. "A Brand New City for Maryland: A Big, Bold Dream in the Making." *Mortgage Banking Magazine* (December 1964): 28–32.

Andrews, Thomas G. *Killing for Coal: America's Deadliest Labor War.* Cambridge, MA: Harvard University Press, 2008.

Armitage, Sue, Theresa Banfield, and Sarah Jacobus. "Black Women and Their Communities in Colorado." *Frontiers: A Journal of Women Studies* 2, no. 2 (Summer 1977): 45–51. https://doi.org/10.2307/3346010.

Arps, Louisa W. *Slices of Denver.* Denver: Sage Books, 1959.

Ash, Timothy Garton. *The File: A Personal History.* New York: Random House, 1997.

Athearn, Robert G. *The Coloradans.* Albuquerque: University of New Mexico Press, 1976.

"Athearn, Robert G." In *Search of Canaan: Black Migration to Kansas 1879–80.* Lawrence: Regents Press of Kansas, 1978.

Bailey, James, ed. *New Towns in America: The Design and Development Process.* New York: John Wiley and Sons, 1973.

Bakemeier, Alice M. *Crestmoor Park Heritage: A History and Guide to a Denver Neighborhood.* Denver: Heritage, 2005.

Ballast, David K. *The Denver Chronicle: From a Golden Past to a Mile-High Future.* Houston: Gulf, 1995.

Belcaro Park Homeowners Association. "Covenants: Declaration and Agreement, Article 11." Unpublished document, March 19, 1946.

Bodfish, Morton. "Government and Private Mortgage Loans on Real Estate." *Journal of Land and Public Utility Economics* 11, no. 4 (1935): 402–409. https://doi.org/10.2307/3158524.

Bodfish, Morton. "A Sound System of Mortgage Credits and Its Relation to Banking Policy." *Journal of Land and Public Utility Economics* 11, no. 3 (1935): 217–225. https://doi.org/10.2307/3158150.

Bogue, Allan G. "The Administrative and Policy Problems of the J. B. Watkins Land Mortgage Company, 1873–1894." *Bulletin of the Business Historical Society* 27, no. 1 (1953): 26–59. https://doi.org/10.2307/3110674.

Bogue, Allan G. "The Land Mortgage Company in the Early Plains States." *Agricultural History* 25, no. 1 (1951): 20–33.

Bogue, Allan G. *Money at Interest: The Farm Mortgage on the Middle Border.* Lincoln: University of Nebraska Press, 1955.

Bothwell, James L. *Housing Enterprises: Potential Impacts of Severing Government Sponsorship.* Washington, DC: US General Accounting Office, June 12, 1996.

Cameron, C. C. "A Hard Close Look at Mortgage Banking's Future." *Mortgage Banker* (October 1963): 15–20.

"Certified Mortgage Bankers: The Women at the Top." *Mortgage Banking* (August 1987): 41–46.

Champ, Frederick P. "Reflections by Past Presidents." *Mortgage Banker* (November 1970): 139.

Cole, Albert M. *President's Advisory Committee on Government Housing Programs: A Report to the President of the United States.* Washington, DC: Government Printing Office, 1953.

Colean, Miles L., and the Columbia University Oral History Review. *A Backward Glance–an Oral History: The Growth of Government Housing Policy in the United States 1934–1975.* Washington, DC: Research and Educational Trust Fund, 1975.

Collins, J. Michael, and Collin O'Rourke. *Homeownership Education and Counseling: Do We Know What Works?* Washington, DC: Research Institute for Housing America, 2011.

Colorado Housing and Finance Authority. *CHFA Annual Report, 1999.* Denver: Colorado Housing and Finance Authority, 2000.

Colorado Housing and Finance Authority. *Summary of 1975 Operations, Colorado Housing and Finance Authority 1975 Annual Report.* Denver: Colorado Housing and Financing Authority, 1976.

Colorado Mortgage and Investment Company of London. *Prospectus Statement.* London: Colorado Mortgage and Investment Company of London, ca, 1877.

Colorado Mortgage and Investment Company of London. *Reports of the General Meetings of the Colorado Mortgage and Investment Company of London, Limited; the Denver Mansions Company, Limited; and the Platte Land Company, Limited.* vol. I–II. London: Colorado Mortgage and Investment Company of London, ca, 1877.

Congressional Budget Office. *Assessing the Public Costs and Benefits of Fannie Mae and Freddie Mac.* Washington, DC: Government Printing Office, 1996.

Cronon, William. "Landscapes of Abundance and Scarcity." In *The Oxford History of the American West,* ed. Clyde A. Milner, II, Carol A. O'Connor, and Martha A. Sandweiss, 603–37. New York: Oxford University Press, 1994.

Curry, Timothy, and Lynn Shibut. "The Cost of the Savings and Loan Crisis." *FDIC Banking Review* 13, no. 2 (2000): 26–35.

Department of Housing and Urban Development. "Comment Letter, Office of the General Counsel US Department of Housing and Urban Development, Subject: Proposed Regulation of Fannie Mae and Freddie Mac." Washington, DC: Department of Housing and Urban Development, May 8, 2000.

Dorsett, Lyle W., and Michael McCarthy. *The Queen City: A History of Denver*. 2nd ed. Boulder: Pruett, 1986.

Downs, W.F. *Farms and Homes in Kansas*. Atchison, KS: Central Branch of the Union Pacific Railroad Company Land Office, 1879.

"Downtown Denver: A Report to Downtown Denver, Inc." In *Urban Land Institute panel*. Washington, DC: Urban Land Institute, April 1955.

Elliott, Donald L., ed. *Colorado Land Planning and Development Law*. 9th ed. Denver: Bradford, 2012.

Federal Housing Administration. *FHA Underwriting Manual, Sections 332–334, Revised Underwriting Analysis under Title II, Section 203 of the National Housing Act, National Housing Agency*. Washington, DC: Federal Housing Administration, January 1947.

Fischman, Richard. "'Mortgages for Beginners': An Early Success in Flexible Underwritings." *Federal Home Loan Bank Board Journal* 14, no. 8 (1981): 10–13.

Fishelson-Holstine, Hollis. "The Role of Credit Scoring in Increasing Homeownership for Underserved Populations." BABC 04-12, Joint Center for Housing Studies of Harvard University, Working Papers. Cambridge, MA: John F. Kennedy School of Government, Harvard University, February 12, 2004.

FM Watch. *GSE Mission Creep: The Threat to American Consumers*. Washington, DC: FM Watch, 2001.

Friedman, Gerald L. "Mission Creep: The Threat to American Consumers." *FM Watch* ii–iii (March 2001): 26.

General Accounting Office. *Government Sponsored Enterprises: The Government's Exposure to Risks*. Washington, DC: General Accounting Office, 1990.

Ghent, Andra. *Research Institute for Housing America Special Report: The Historical Origins of America's Mortgage Law*. Washington, DC: Research Institute for Housing America, 2012.

GNMA Mortgage-Backed Securities Dealers Association. *The Ginnie Mae Manual*. Homewood, IL: Dow Jones-Irwin, 1978.

Gray, Robert L. "Good Counseling: The Answer in Successful 235 Housing." *Mortgage Banker* (August 1971): 6–8.

Green, Richard K., and Susan M. Wachter. "The American Mortgage in Historical and International Context." *Journal of Economic Perspectives* 19, no. 4 (2005): 93–114. https://doi.org/10.1257/089533005775196660.

Hagerty, James R. *The Fateful History of Fannie Mae: New Deal Birth to Mortgage Crisis Fall*. Charleston, SC: History Press, 2012.

Hall, Lesley. "The First Century." *Mortgage Banking's Centennial Special Edition* (October 2013): 6–31.

Hamm, Michael. "Report and Recommendations: Certified Mortgage Banker Designation." Internal document submitted to the MBA, February 29, 2000.

Hauk, Paul I. "Chronologies of the Ski Areas on and Adjacent to the White River National Forest." Manuscript Collection #WH1304, Rg 17B, Section 3, Box 2, Denver Public Library, Denver, CO.

Hawley, Ellis W. "Herbert Hoover, the Commerce Secretariat, and the Vision of an 'Associative State,' 1921–1928." *Journal of American History* 61, no. 1 (1974): 116–140. https://doi.org/10.2307/1918256.

Herbert, Christopher E., Donald R. Haurin, Stuart S. Rosenthal, and Mark Duda. *Homeownership Gaps among Low-Income and Minority Borrowers and Neighborhoods. US Department of Housing and Urban Development.* Cambridge, MA: Abt. Associates, Inc, 2005.

Herzog, Thomas, and Alexander Majlaton. "FHA's Costly Experience with Seller Funded Downpayments." *Mortgage Banking* (October 2010): 98–107.

"Highland Neighborhood Plan; General Recommendations." *Denver Planning and Community Development*, April 28, 1990.

Highlands Ranch Historical Society. *Images of America: Highlands Ranch.* Charleston, SC: Arcadia, 2016.

Hoagland, Alison K. "Introducing the Bathroom: Space and Change in Working Class Houses." *Building and Landscapes* 18, no. 2 (2011): 15–42. https://doi.org/10.1353/bdl.2011.0023.

Hosokawa, Bill. *Colorado's Japanese Americans: From 1886 to the Present.* Boulder: University Press of Colorado, 2005.

Housing Policy Finance Center. *Housing Finance at a Glance: A Monthly Chartbook.* Washington, DC: Urban Institute, February 2016.

Howard, Timothy. *The Mortgage Wars: Inside Fannie Mae, Big-Money Politics, and the Collapse of the American Dream.* New York: McGraw-Hill Education, 2014.

Hutchison, Janet. "The Cure for Domestic Neglect: Better Homes in America, 1922–1935." *Perspectives in Vernacular Architecture* 2 (1986): 168–178. https://doi.org/10.2307/3514328.

Issue Paper: GSE Affordable Housing Goals, Department of Housing and Urban Development, Final Regulation. Washington, DC: Mortgage Bankers Association of America, October 31, 2000.

Iversen, Kristen. *Full Body Burden: Growing Up in the Nuclear Shadow of Rocky Flats.* New York: Crown, 2012.

Jackson, Kenneth T. *Crabgrass Frontier: The Suburbanization of the United States.* New York: Oxford University Press, 1985.

Jackson, W. Turrentine. *The Enterprising Scot: Investors in the American West after 1873.* New York: Routledge, 2000.

Jacobs, Jane. *The Economy of Cities.* New York: Random House, 1969.

Jacobs, Jane. *The Life and Death of Great America Cities.* New York: Random House, 1961.

Jensen, F.E. "The Farm Credit System as a Government-Sponsored Enterprise." *Review of Agricultural Economics* 22, no. 2 (2000): 326–335. https://doi.org/10.1111/1058-7195.00025.

Jones, Oliver H. "Easy Credit or Not, 1971 as a Critical Year." *Mortgage Banker* (March 1971): 10–13.

Jones, Oliver H. "An MBA Editorial, What Ails the Mortgage Market." *Mortgage Banker* (July 1970): 4–7.

Jud, G. Donald, and Daniel T. Winkler. "Some Thoughts on Housing Markets Cycles." Paper prepared for and submitted to the MBA, March 4, 2003.

Kerwood, Lewis O. "The Importance of Continuing Education." *Mortgage Banker* (September 1971): 4–6.

Kider, Mitchel, Michael Kieval, and Leslie Sowers. *Consumer Protection and Mortgage Regulation under Dodd Frank.* New York: Thomson Reuters/Westlaw, 2013.

Klaman, Saul B. *The Postwar Residential Mortgage Market.* Princeton, NJ: Princeton University Press, 1961.

Klebaner, Benjamin. *Commercial Banking in the United States: A History.* Hinsdale, IL: Dryden, 1974.

Kozuch, James. "State Housing Finance Agencies: Their Effect on Mortgage Banking." *Mortgage Banker* (October 1972): 12–18.

Lauck, William Jett. *The Causes of the Panic of 1893.* Boston: Houghton, Mifflin, 1907.

Lynd, Robert S., and Helen M. Lynd. *Middletown: A Study in American Culture.* San Diego: Harcourt, Brace, 1957.

Marston, Ed. "Life after Oil Shale." *High Country News* 15, no. 7 (April 15, 1983): 1, 12–13.

Mason, David L. *From Buildings and Loans to Bail-Outs: A History of the American Savings and Loan Industry, 1831–1995.* Cambridge: Cambridge University Press, 2004. https://doi.org/10.1017/CBO9780511511714.

Mattson, Everett. "Certified Mortgage Banker: A Professional Standard for the Mortgage Industry." *Mortgage Banker* (December 1974): 44–47.

McLean, Bethany, and Joe Nocera. *All the Devils Are Here: The Hidden History of the Financial Crisis Portfolio.* New York: Penguin/Portfolio, 2010.

Miles, Barbara. "Government Sponsored Enterprises: The Issue of Expansion into Mission-Related Business." Congressional Research Service Report for Congress, January 19, 1999.

Moore, Mechlin D. "Downtown Denver—a Guide to Central City Development." Technical Bulletin 54. Washington, DC: Urban Land Institute, 1965.

Morgenson, Gretchen, and Joshua Rosner. *Reckless Endangerment: How Outsized Ambition, Greed, and Corruption Led to Economic Armageddon.* New York: Time Books, 2011.

Morman, James B. *Farm Credits in the United States and Canada.* New York: Macmillan, 1924.

Morrison, Andrew, ed. *The City of Denver and State of Colorado.* St. Louis, Geo.: Engelhardt, 1890.

Mortgage Bankers Association of America. "GSE Policy Statement." Unpublished, August 1999.

Mortgage Bankers Association of America. *Handbook of Commercial Real Estate Finance*. Washington, DC: Mortgage Bankers Association of America, 1995.

Moynihan, Betty. *Augusta Tabor: A Pioneering Woman*. Evergreen, CO: Cordillera, 1988.

Muenker, Nancy. *Franklin L. Burns: Master Builder of Denver. Builders Series*. Denver: University of Denver, 1997.

Munnel, Lynn E. Brown, James McEneaney, and Geoffrey M.B. Tootell. *Mortgage Lending in Boston: Interpreting HMDA Data*. Boston: Federal Reserve Bank of Boston, October 1992.

Neal, Larry. "Trust Companies and Financial Innovation, 1897–1914." *Business History Review* 45, no. 1 (1971): 35–51. https://doi.org/10.2307/3113304.

Newman, Oscar. *Defensible Space: Crime Prevention through Urban Design*. New York: Collier Books, 1973.

Noel, Thomas J. *Denver's Larimer Street: Main Street, Skid Row, and Urban Renaissance*. Denver: Historic Denver, Inc, 1981.

Noel, Thomas J. *Denver: Rocky Mountain Gold*. Tulsa, OK: Continental Heritage, 1980.

Norris, Jane E., and Lee G. Norris. *Written in Water: The Life of Benjamin Harrison Eaton*. Athens: Swallow/Ohio University Press, 1990.

Olsen, Joshua. *Better Places, Better Lives: A Biography of James Rouse*. Washington, DC: Urban Land Institute, 2003.

Phillips, Ronnie J. *The Chicago Plan and New Deal Banking Reform*. Armonk, NY: M. E. Sharpe, 1995.

Postel, Charles. *The Populist Vision*. Oxford: Oxford University Press, 2007.

Raabe, Steve. "Denver Dry Revamp to Get Off the Ground —Transformation Should Be Complete by Fall." *Denver Post*, December 14, 1992, 1A.

Reed, L.B. *The First Hundred Years: A History of Federal Savings Bank and Its People since Its Organization on April 25, 1885*. Lakewood, CO: First Federal Savings Bank, 1985.

Rhyne, Margaret. *"Alexis' House at Allis Ranch." Unpublished, available at Allis Ranch Winery*. CO: Sedalia, 2015.

Riegel, Robert E., and Robert G. Athearn. *America Moves West*. 5th ed. New York: Holt, Rinehart and Winston, 1971.

Robins, Kingman Nott. *The Farm Mortgage Handbook: A Book of Facts Regarding the Methods by Which the Farmers of the United States and Canada Are Financed, Especially Intended for Investors Seeking Information Regarding Investments in Farm Mortgages*. Garden City, NY: Doubleday, Page, 1916.

Rosser, E. Michael. "Educating an Industry." *Mortgage Banking* (Centennial Special Edition) (October 2013).

Santi, Albert, and James Newell. *Encyclopedia of Mortgage and Real Estate Finance*. Washington, DC: Real Estate Finance Press, 1997.

Snel, Alan. "Downtown Redo: Historic Has-Beens-Reborn as Chic Housing." *Denver Post*, February 23, 1997.

Snowden, Kenneth A. *Research Institute for Housing America Special Report: Mortgage Banking in the United States, 1870–1940*. Washington, DC: Mortgage Bankers Association, 2013.

Spelman, Everett. "MBA's Testimony on Farm Credit Proposals." *Mortgage Banker* (July 1971): 48–51.

Spelman, Everett. "Meet the New President." *Mortgage Banking* (December 1970): 10.

Spelman, Everett. "MBA's 52nd President." *Mortgage Banking* (December 1970): 10–12.

Spong, Kenneth. *Banking Regulation: Its Purposes, Implementation, and Effects*. 5th ed. Kansas City: Division of Bank Supervision and Structure, Federal Reserve Bank of Kansas City, 2000.

Stone, William G.M. *The Colorado Hand-book: Denver and Its Outings: A Guide for Tourists and Book of General Information, with Some Bits of Early History*. Denver: Barkhausen and Lester, Printers, 1892.

Tabor, Augusta G. "$800,000 Worth of Gold Dust." In *So Much to Be Done: Women Settlers on the Mining and Ranching Frontier*, ed. Ruth Moynihan, Susan Armitage, and Christine Dichamp, 140–46. Lincoln: University of Nebraska Press, 1998.

Thornton, Rosemary. *The Houses That Sears Built*. Norfolk, VA: Gentle Beam, 2004.

Title Guaranty Company. "17 Flags Flew over Colorado" and other segments. Denver: Title Guaranty and Landon Abstract Companies, ca. 1950. Steven H. Hart Library, History Colorado, Denver.

US Department of Housing and Urban Development Office of Policy Development and Research. *Studies on Privatizing Fannie Mae and Freddie Mac*. Washington, DC: US Department of Housing and Urban Development, May 1996.

US General Accounting Office. *Government-Sponsored Enterprises: The Government's Exposure to Risks*. Washington, DC: US General Accounting Office, August 1990.

West, Elliott. "American Frontier." In *The Oxford History of the American West*, ed. Clyde A. Milner, II, Carol A. O'Connor, and Martha A. Sandweiss, 115–49. New York: Oxford University Press, 1994.

West, Elliott. *The Contested Plains: Indians, Goldseekers, and the Rush to Colorado*. Lawrence: University Press of Kansas, 1998.

White, Richard. *It's Your Misfortune and None of My Own: A New History of the American West*. Norman: University of Oklahoma Press, 1991.

White, Richard. *Railroaded: The Transcontinentals and the Making of Modern America*. New York: W. W. Norton, 2011.

Williamson, Harold, and Orange A. Smalley. *Northwestern Mutual Life: A Century of Trusteeship*. Evanston, IL: Northwestern University Press, 1957.

Wilson, Joan H., and Oscar Handlin. *Herbert Hoover, Forgotten Progressive*. Boston: Little, Brown, 1975.

Wilson, Robert H. "Another Tool to Fund Life Insurance Companies' Urban Investment Program." *Mortgage Banker* (May 1971): 98–101.

Yackle, Larry W. "Federal Banks and Federal Jurisdiction in the Progressive Era: A Case Study of *Smith v. K.C. Title & Trust Co.*" *Kansas Law Review* 62 (2013): 255–314.

Zandi, Mark M. *Financial Shock: A 360° Look at the Subprime Mortgage Implosion, and How to Avoid the Next Financial Crisis.* Upper Saddle River, NJ: FT Press, 2009.

ONLINE SOURCES

AARoads Forum. "1960s Denver Freeways: The Columbine and Skyline Freeways." Accessed May 10, 2015. http://www.aaroads.com/forum/index.php?topic=7502.0.

Ahern, Tim. "Millenials May Be Forging Their Own Path to Homeownership." Fannie Mae, August 9, 2016. Accessed May 9, 2017. www.fanniemae.com/portal/media/business/millennials-080916.html.

"August 18, 1894: Carey Act Signed." *This Day in Water History.* Accessed May 21, 2015. https://thisdayinwaterhistory.wordpress.com/2014/08/18/august-18-1894-carey-act-signed/.

Barlow, Kathleen. "Spirits and Scandals on 17th and Stout Streets." Center for Colorado and the West, Auraria Library, Denver. Accessed February 5, 2015. https://coloradowest.auraria.edu/content/equitable-building.

Brunswig, Bob, and George H. Junne, Jr. *The Story of Dearfield, Colorado.* Accessed July 24, 2014. http://www.unco.edu/cce/docs/Dearfield_Talk_CAS_4_2011.pdf.

Buffer, Patricia. *Rocky Flats History.* Self-published, 2003. Published online by Office of Legacy Management, Department of Energy, July 2003. Accessed September 2, 2016. https://www.lm.doe.gov/WorkArea/linkit.aspx?LinkIdentifier=id&ItemID=3026.

Bunch, Joey. "Home on the Ranch." *Denver Post*, February 4, 2006, updated May 8, 2016. Accessed May 12, 2017. http://www.denverpost.com/2006/02/04/home-on-the-ranch-3/.

Bush, George W. "President Bush Signs American Dream Downpayment Act of 2003." White House archives. Accessed May 10, 2017. https://georgewbush-whitehouse.archives.gov/news/releases/2003/12/print/20031216-9.html.

Colorado Business Hall of Fame: David H. Moffat. Junior Achievement–Rocky Mountain Inc. and the Denver Metro Chamber of Commerce. Accessed September 14, 2014. http://www.coloradobusinesshalloffame.org/david-h-moffat.html.

Colorado Department of Regulatory Agencies. "Colorado Real Estate Manual: Rules Regarding Real Estate Brokers." Accessed May 23, 2015. http://www.sos.state.co.us/CCR/GenerateRulePdf.do?ruleVersionId=6098&fileName=4%20CCR%20725-1.

Colorado Health Facilities Authority. "Overview." Accessed July 27, 2015. http://www.cohfa.org/overview.html.

Colorado Housing and Finance Authority. *About CHFA*. Accessed May 2, 2015.
  http://www.chfainfo.com/about.
Colorado Housing and Finance Authority. "Celebrating 40 Years of Financing the
  Places Where Coloradans Live and Work." Colorado Housing and Finance
  Authority. Accessed May 2, 2015. http://www.chfainfo.com/Pages/chfa-40th
  -celebrating-40-years.aspx.
Colorado Housing and Finance Authority. "Foreclosure Prevention." Colorado
  Housing and Finance Authority. Accessed May 3, 2015. http://www.chfainfo.com
  /homeownership/Pages/prevent-foreclosure.aspx.
Committee on Banking and Currency, United States Senate. *Housing Act of 1949:
  Summary of the Provisions of the National Housing Act of 1949*. Washington, DC:
  Government Printing Office, 1949. Accessed May 2, 2015. https://bulk.resource
  .org/gao.gov/81-171/00002FD7.pdf.
CONELRAD. *The Eisenhower Ten, 1999–2008*. Accessed May 20, 2015. http://www
  .conelrad.com/atomicsecrets/secrets.php?secrets=05.
Denver Story Trek. "Moffat Mansion." Accessed February 2, 2015. http://www
  .denverstorytrek.org/sites/12034572aadf8560674292bd78ada7a6fdc2c031.
Denver Union Station Project Authority. "Denver Union Station History and Timeline." Accessed March 3, 2015. http://www.denverunionstation.org/index
  .php?option=com_content&view=article&id=3&Itemid=1.
Denver Union Station Project Authority. "Union Station Master Plan." Accessed
  March 3, 2015. http://www.denverunionstation.org/index.php?option=com_
  content&view=article&id=60&Itemid=48.
Denver Urban Renewal Authority. "The Boston Lofts." Accessed February 9, 2015.
  http://www.renewdenver.org/redevelopment/dura-redevelopment-projects
  /downtown-denver/the-boston-lofts.html.
Department of Justice. "Department of Justice Sues Standard & Poor's," February
  5, 2013. Accessed February 6, 2015. http://www.justice.gov/opa/pr/department
  -justice-sues-standard-poor-s-fraud-rating-mortgage-backed-securities-years-leading.
Elitch Gardens Theme and Water Park. "Park History." Accessed September 19,
  2015. https://www.elitchgardens.com/plan-a-visit/park-history/.
"An Exceptional Heritage among Denver Luxury Hotels." Brown Palace Hotel
  and Spa. Accessed February 8, 2015. http://www.brownpalace.com/
  About-the-Brown/From-the-Archive.
Fishback, Price V., Alphonso Flores-Lagunes, William C. Horrace, Shon Kantor,
  and Jaret Treber. "The Influence of the Home Owners' Loan Corporation on
  Housing Markets during the 1930s." *Oxford Journals*, 2010. Accessed October 25,
  2014. http://frs.oxfordjournals.org/. https://doi.org/10.3386/w15824.
Flaherty, Edward. "National Banking Acts of 1863 and 1864." In *American History:
  From Revolution to Reconstruction and Beyond*. Accessed May 9, 2014. http://www
  .let.rug.nl/usa/essays/general/a-brief-history-of-central-banking/national
  -banking-acts-of-1863-and-1864.php.

Forest City Stapleton, Inc. "Stapleton Sustainability Master Plan 2004." Accessed May 3, 2015. https://www.stapletondenver.com/wp-content/uploads/2014/12/Stapleton_Sustainability_Plan.pdf.

"Highlands Ranch History." Highlands Ranch Metro District. Accessed May 4, 2017. http://highlandsranch.org/community/history/.

Hilzenrath, David. "Fannie Mae Warnings Documented." *Washington Post,* March 13, 2006. Accessed September 8, 2015. http://www.washingtonpost.com/wp-dyn/content/article/2006/03/12/AR2006031200799.html.

"History of St. Joseph Hospital." Exempla St. Joseph Hospital. Accessed March 2, 2015. http://www.exemplasaintjoseph.org/history#.UwJWTWJdWS0.

Hoover, Tim. "GOP Activist Freda Poundstone, 'a Giant' in Colorado Politics, Dies at 84." *Denver Post,* November, 18, 2011. http://www.denverpost.com/2011/11/08/gop-activist-freda-poundstone-a-giant-in-colorado-politics-dies-at-84/.

"Housing Act of 1949/Public Law 171–81st Congress." Government Accounting Office, Washington, DC. Accessed October 10, 2014. https://bulk.resource.org/gao.gov/81-171/00001EE4_595076.pdf.

"Housing Finance: Potential Reforms to Mortgage Markets." Budget Model. Philadelphia: Penn Wharton University of Pennsylvania, November 22, 2016. Accessed May 9, 2017. http://www.budgetmodel.wharton.upenn.edu/issues/2016/11/14/housing-finance-potential-reforms-to-mortgage-markets.

Huspeni, Dennis. "Aging Sakura Square Faces Challenges." *Denver Business Journal,* October 26, 2012. Accessed April 12, 2015. http://www.bizjournals.com/denver/print-edition/2012/10/26/aging-sakura-square-faces-challenges.html.

Investopedia. "Covered Bond." Accessed May 11, 2014. http://www.investopedia.com/terms/c/coveredbond.asp.

Investopedia. "Government-Sponsored Enterprise." Accessed February 24, 2016. http://www.investopedia.com/terms/g/gse.asp.

Investopedia. "Interest Rate Swap." Accessed March 16, 2015. http://www.investopedia.com/terms/i/interestrateswap.asp.

Investopedia. "Office of Federal Housing Enterprise Oversight—OFHEO." Accessed September 23, 2015. www.investopedia.com/terms/o/ofheo.asp.

J. C. Nichols Company Records. State Historical Society of Missouri Research Center–Kansas City, ca. 1886–2007. Accessed April 10, 2015. http://shs.umsystem.edu/kansascity/manuscripts/k0106.pdf.

Jerome B. Chaffee. *Biographical Directory of the United States Congress.* Accessed February 6, 2015. http://bioguide.congress.gov/scripts/biodisplay.pl?index=C000271.

Midyette Architects. "Elephant Corral Redevelopment." Accessed September 26, 2015. http://www.midyettearchitects.com/?page_id=199.

National Association of Realtors. *Realtors® Celebrate 100 Years of Professionalism in Real Estate,* November 7, 2013. Accessed May 5, 2014. http://www.realtor.org

/news-releases/2013/11/realtors-celebrate-100-years-of-professionalism-in-real
-estate.

National Jewish Health. "History of National Jewish Health." Accessed October 10,
2014. http://www.nationaljewish.org/about/whynjh/history/.

PRNewswire. "McGraw Hill Financial and S&P Ratings Reach Settlements with
DOJ," February 3, 2015. Accessed February 6, 2015. http:/www.prnewswire.com
/news-releases/mcgraw-hill-financial-and-sp-reach-settlement.

prweb. "Apartment Community 2020 Lawrence Wins 2013 Mayor's Design Award,"
November 12, 2013. Accessed February 8, 2015. http://www.prweb.com/releases
/2013/11/prweb11322161.htm.

Rhyne, Margaret. "History of Allis Ranch and Allis Ranch House." Allis Ranch
Winery. Accessed September 17, 2015. http://www.allisranchwinery.com/scripts
/historyPg.cfm.

Rietsch, N., T. Miller, and C. Miller. *Portrait and Biographical Record of Denver and
Vicinity, Colorado, 1898*. Mardos Collection, Memorial Library, University of Wisconsin–Madison, 2002. Accessed April 24, 2014. http://www.memoriallibrary
.com/CO/1898DenverPB/pages/pbrd0134.htm.

Roberts, Phil. "Chapter 13: Water and Irrigation." *New History of Wyoming*.
Accessed April 15, 2015. uwyo.edu/robertshistory/new_history_of _wyoming_
chapter_13_water.htm.

Robinson, M., and D. McLaughlin. "S&P Ends Legal Woes Paying $1.5 Billion Fine
to US, States." *Bloomberg Business*, February 3, 2015. Accessed February 6, 2015.
http://www.bloomberg.com/news/articles/2015-02-03/s-p-ends-legal-woes
-with-1-5-billion-fine-to-u-s-states.

Senior Housing Options. "The Barth Hotel Assisted Living: The History of the
Barth Hotel." Accessed February 8, 2015. http://seniorhousingoptions.org
/wordpress/wp-content/uploads/The-Barth-Hotel-History-Sheet2.pdf.

Simmer-Brown, Judith. "Encyclopedia of the Great Plains: Denver Buddhist Temple." University of Nebraska–Lincoln. Accessed February 15, 2015. http://plains
humanities.unl.edu/encyclopedia/doc/egp.asam.009.

Stone, Wilbur Fisk. "David Halliday Moffat." In *History of Colorado*, vol. II. Chicago:
S. J. Clarke, 1918., http://files.usgwarchives.net/co/denver/bios/moffatdh.txt,
Accessed September 23, 2014.

Svaldi, Aldo. "Colorado Tops in '06 Foreclosures." *Denver Post*, January 24, 2007.
Accessed March 15, 2016. http://www.denverpost.com/2007/01/24/colorado
-tops-in-06-foreclosures/.

Union Station Neighborhood Company. "The History: Timeline." Accessed
December, 1, 2015. http://unionstationdenver.com/history/#/timeline.

Urban Land Institute. "Mission and Priorities." Accessed April 20, 2017. https://
americas.uli.org/about-uli/mission-priorities/.

US Fish and Wildlife Service. "Rocky Flats National Wildlife Refuge." Accessed July
7, 2015. http://www.fws.gov/refuge/Rocky_Flats/about.html.

Wachter, Susan M. "GNMA Choice: The Public Policy Issues." Freddie Mac. Accessed October 11, 2014. http://www.freddiemac.com/news/pdf/gnma_0318 .pdf.

Zocalo Community Development. "2020 Lawrence Street Apartments." Accessed August 7, 2015. http://www.zocalodevelopment.com/development.aspx.

Suggested Reading

Barlevy, G., and J.D.M. Fisher. *Mortgage Choices and Housing Speculation*. Chicago: Federal Reserve Bank of Chicago, September 16, 2010.

Bodfish, M. "Toward an Understanding of the Federal Home Loan Bank System." *Journal of Land and Public Utility Economics* 15, no. 4 (1939): 416–437. https://doi .org/10.2307/3158727.

Brueggeman, W.B., and J.D. Fisher. *Real Estate Finance*. 8th ed. Homewood, IL: Irwin, 1989.

Chase, S.B., Jr., and J.J. Mingo. "The Regulation of Bank Holding Companies." *Journal of Finance* 30, no. 2 (1975): 281–292. https://doi.org/10.1111/j.1540-6261.1975. tb01810.x.

Clark, C.E., Jr. *The American Family Home, 1800–1960*. Chapel Hill: University of North Carolina Press, 1986.

Clark, I.G. *Then Came the Railroads: The Century from Steam to Diesel in the Southwest*. Norman: University of Oklahoma Press, 1958.

Council on Ensuring Mortgage Liquidity. *MBA's Recommendation for the Future Government Role in the Core Secondary Mortgage Market*. Washington, DC: Mortgage Bankers Association, 2009.

Davis, L.E. "The Investment Market, 1870–1914: The Evolution of a National Market." *Journal of Economic History* 25, no. 3 (1965): 355–399. https://doi.org/10.1017/S0022050700057363.

Department of Housing and Urban Development (HUD). *FHA Single-Family Mutual Mortgage Insurance Fund Programs: Quarterly Report to Congress*, no. 4. Washington, DC: HUD, 2010.

Downs, A. *Niagara of Capital: How Global Capital Has Transformed Housing and Real Estate Markets*. Washington, DC: Urban Land Institute, 2007.

Edie, L. D. "Why the Dynamic '50s Mean the Dynamic '60s Are Ahead." *Mortgage Banker* (July 1957): 14–18.

Engelhardt, G.V. *The Great Recession and Attitudes toward Home-Buying*. Washington, DC: Mortgage Bankers Association, 2011.

Ervin, M.D. "Give and Take: The FCA Has Foreclosed 40,000 Farms." *Saturday Evening Post*, July 3, 1937, 23, 36, 38, 40.

Federal National Mortgage Association. *The Future of Fannie Mae: Report of the Fannie Mae Advisory Council*. Washington, DC: Federal National Mortgage Association, 1987.

Francis, S. B., II, E. J. Mock, and F. J. McCabe Jr. "From YMAC." *Mortgage Banker* (April 1964): 36–42.

Frederiksen, D.M. "Mortgage Banking in America." *Journal of Political Economy* 2, no. 2 (1894): 203–234. https://doi.org/10.1086/250202.

Gallagher, Jolie Anderson. *A Wild West History of Frontier Colorado: Pioneers, Gunslingers and Cattle Kings of the Eastern Plains*. Charleston, SC: History Press, 2011.

Hammond, B. "Long and Short Term Credit in Early American Banking." *Quarterly Journal of Economics* 49, no. 1 (1934): 79–103. https://doi.org/10.2307/1883877.

Hoch, C., L.C. Dalton, and F.S. So. *The Practice of Local Government Planning*. Published in cooperation with the American Planning Association for the ICMA University by the International City/County Management Association, Washington, DC, 2000.

"Implementation of the Bank Holding Company Act Amendments of 1970: The Scope of Banking Activities." *Michigan Law Review* 71, no. 6 (1973): 1170–1211. https://doi.org/10.2307/1287751.

Keehn, R.H., and G. Smiley. "Mortgage Lending by National Banks." *Business History Review* 51, no. 4 (1977): 474–491. https://doi.org/10.2307/3112881.

"MBA's 52nd President–Everett C. Spelman." *Mortgage Banker* (December 1970): 10–13.

McFarlane, L. "British Investment in Midwestern Farm Mortgages and Land, 1875–1900: A Comparison of Iowa and Kansas." *Agricultural History* 48, no. 1 (1974): 179–98.

Miller, G.H. "The Hawkes Papers: A Case Study of a Kansas Mortgage Brokerage Business, 1871–1888." *Business History Review* 32, no. 3 (1958): 293–310. https://doi.org/10.2307/3111744.

Mortgage Bankers Association. *The Future of the Federal Housing Administration (FHA) and the Government National Mortgage Association (Ginnie Mae)*. Washington, DC: Mortgage Bankers Association, 2010.

Muolo, P., and M. Padilla. *Chain of Blame: How Wall Street Caused the Mortgage and Credit Crisis*. Hoboken, NJ: Wiley, 2008.

Myrick, H. *The Federal Farm Loan System, New Method of Farm Mortgage Finance, under National Supervision*. New York: Orange Judd, 1916.

National Housing Agency. *FHA Underwriting Manual: Underwriting Analysis under Title II, Section 203 of the National Housing Act*. Washington, DC: Federal Housing Administration, 1947.

Painter, N.I. *Exodusters: Black Migration to Kansas after Reconstruction*. New York: Alfred A. Knopf, 1977.

Pease, George S. *Patriarch of the Prairie: The Story of Equitable of Iowa*. New York: Appleton-Century-Crofts, 1967.

Pease, R.H. *Mortgage Banking*. 2nd ed. New York: McGraw-Hill, 1965.

Pease, R.H., and H.V. Cherrington. *Mortgage Banking*. New York: McGraw-Hill, 1953.

Rouse, J. W. "Our Cities Are Obsolete." *Mortgage Banker* (November 1957): 23–25.

Saulnier, R.J. "Urban Mortgage Lending by Life Insurance Companies." National Bureau of Economic Research, n.d. Accessed January 2, 2012. http://www.nber.org/books/saul50-1.

Smith, H.C. "Factors Related to the Regional Placement of Mortgage Funds by Life Insurance Companies and Mutual Savings Banks." *Journal of Risk and Insurance* 31, no. 3 (1964): 429–436. https://doi.org/10.2307/250936.

Snowden, K.A. "The Anatomy of a Residential Mortgage Crisis: A Look Back to the 1930s." Bryan School of Business and Economics, University of North Carolina, Greensboro, June 2009. Prepared for "The Panic of 2008" conference, George Washington University Law School, Washington, DC, April 3–4, 2009. Accessed February 27, 2015. https://sedonaweb.com/attach/schools/NCBEfaculty/attach/chapter-297.pdf.

Stango, J. "Urban Revitalization Looms as a Bright Business Opportunity for Mortgage Bankers." *Mortgage Banker* (May 1979): 20–22.

Todd, T. *The Balance of Power: The Political Fight for an Independent Central Bank, 1790-Present*. Kansas City, MO: Public Affairs Department of the Federal Reserve Bank of Kansas City, 2012.

Zeckendorf, W., and E. McCreary. *The Autobiography of William Zeckendorf*. New York: Holt, Rinehart, and Winston, 1970.

Index

Northern Colorado Irrigation, 47
Northwestern Mutual Insurance Company, 7,
    71–76; in Colorado, 71–76; Palmer, Henry, 74

Office of Comptroller of the Currency, 314
Office of Federal Housing Enterprise
    Oversight (OFHEO), 251
Office of Thrift Supervision (OTS), 307
One-for-One program, 249
O'Neill, June, 252, 254–55

Pacific Railway Act, 5–6, 12, 15, 17, 101
Palmer, Henry, 74
Pillard, Donna, 217
Planned Unit Development (PUD) Act (1972,
    Colorado), 197, 353
PMI Mortgage Insurance Company, 135, 263,
    354
Populists/Populist or People's party, 22, 74,
    101–3
predatory lending, 242
Prudential Life Insurance Company of
    America (Prudential), 64
public housing, 120, 132–34, 141, 250, 329

Raines, Franklin, 222, 257–58, 275, 279
Ramsey, George, 111
real estate valuation/appraisal, 74, 284
redevelopment, 79, 86, 131, 170, 182–83, 189,
    197–200, 202–4, 206–7, 210, 243, 321–22, 324–
    25; Brooks Towers, 207; Elephant Corral,
    82; Elitch Gardens Amusement Park, 203;
    Larimer Square, 78–79, 203; Lowry Air Force
    Base, 204; Market Street Mall, 80–81; Sakura
    Square, 86, 177–78, 180–81, 203
redlining, 162, 274–75; property security maps,
    161
Reliance Funding, 239–40
Rental Acquisition Program, 176, 181
Research Institute for Housing America
    (RIHA), 134, 233, 313
Resolution Trust Corporation (RTC), 176, 219,
    350
Rhyne, Charles, 236–38, 240
risk: credit risk, 143, 154, 169, 253, 257, 278, 286,
    288, 307, 310, 316–17; capital market risk, 154;
    environmental/hazard risk, 35, 38, 154, 261,
    291; predictive models, 154, 297, 307; real
    estate risk, 154; stacking, 155, 159, 291

Rocky Flats Nuclear Weapons Plant, 142–43, 148
Roosevelt, Theodore, 12, 103; Country Life
    Commission, 103
Rouse, James, 170, 187–90; Columbia,
    Maryland, 170, 186–88, 191, 197, 204

Sakura Square, 86, 177–78, 180–81, 203
Saslow, William, 80; Market Street Mall, 80–81
Scottish American Mortgage Company, 25
Sears, Roebuck and Company (Sears), 115–18;
    Book of Modern Homes and Building Plans, 115;
    kit homes, 115–16; mortgage program, 116
Secure and Fair Enforcement for Mortgage
    Licensing Act of 2008 (the SAFE Act), 242
Securities and Exchange Commission, 253, 270,
    314
Service Investment Company (SIC), xxiv,
    88, 92–93, 95–96, 118, 162–63; Denver US
    National Bank, 93; Kirk, Fred E., 44, 92,
    162; renamed United Mortgage Company,
    93; Village East (Aurora), 92; Westlake
    (Jefferson County), 92; Witkin Homes, 92;
    Woodcrest Townhomes, 92
Servicemen's Readjustment Act (1944), 165, 212;
    G.I. loan program, 92, 212, 355
Sherman Antitrust Act, 234
Simon, Robert E., 187, 190–91; New Town
    movement, 187; Reston, Virginia, 187, 190–91
Skyline Urban Renewal District, Denver, 177,
    200
Smith v. Kansas City Title & Trust Company, 113,
    122–23
Snowmass, Colorado, 94, 194–96
Spelman, Everett C., Sr., 124, 134, 235–38
St. Charles Town Company, 81, 83
Standard & Poor's Ratings Services, 282
Starnes, James L., 231
state housing finance agencies, 142, 174
Stevens, David, 244
Still, Debra, 235, 244
strategic default, 38, 129
subsidy benefit distribution, 254

Tabor, Horace, 7–9, 46, 75
Tamai, Yoshitaka (Reverend), 179
tax credit programs, 177, 183; historic preser-
    vation, 183, 209, 210; low income housing,
    183, 210
Tax Reform Act (1986), 218, 296, 311